Contagion and War

John Vasquez explains the processes that cause the spread of interstate war by looking at how contagion worked to bring countries into the First World War. Analyzing all the key states that declared war, the book is comprised of three parts. Part I lays out six models of contagion: alliances, contiguity, territorial rivalry, opportunity, "brute force," and economic dependence. Part II then analyzes in detail the decision-making of every state that entered the war, from Austria-Hungary in 1914 to the U.S. and Greece in 1917. Part III has two chapters – the first considers the neutral countries, and the second concludes the book with an overarching theoretical analysis, including major lessons of the war and new hypotheses about contagion. This book will be of great interest to students and scholars of international relations, conflict studies, and international history, especially those interested in the spread of conflict, or the First World War.

John A. Vasquez is the Thomas B. Mackie Scholar in International Relations at the University of Illinois, Urbana-Champaign. He is author of eight books including *The War Puzzle* (Cambridge, 1993) and *The Power of Power Politics* (Cambridge, 1999), and editor of ten others, including *The Outbreak of the First World War*, with Jack S. Levy (Cambridge, 2014). He is the former President of the International Studies Association and the Peace Science Society (International). In 2017, he received the Lifetime Achievement Award of the Conflict Processes section of APSA.

Contagion and War

Lessons from the First World War

John A. Vasquez
with the assistance of Emily E. Barrett
University of Illinois at Urbana-Champaign

CAMBRIDGE
UNIVERSITY PRESS

University Printing House, Cambridge CB2 8BS, United Kingdom

One Liberty Plaza, 20th Floor, New York, NY 10006, USA

477 Williamstown Road, Port Melbourne, VIC 3207, Australia

314–321, 3rd Floor, Plot 3, Splendor Forum, Jasola District Centre, New Delhi – 110025, India

79 Anson Road, #06-04/06, Singapore 079906

Cambridge University Press is part of the University of Cambridge.

It furthers the University's mission by disseminating knowledge in the pursuit of education, learning, and research at the highest international levels of excellence.

www.cambridge.org
Information on this title: www.cambridge.org/9781108417044
DOI: 10.1017/9781108261166

First published 2018

Printed in the United Kingdom by TJ International Ltd. Padstow Cornwall

A catalogue record for this publication is available from the British Library.

ISBN 978-1-108-41704-4 Hardback
ISBN 978-1-108-40427-3 Paperback

To the Dead

We are the Dead. Short days ago
We lived, felt dawn, saw sunset glow,
 Loved and were loved …

Contents

Plate section can be found between pages 210 and 211

Tables

Preface

Most international relations (IR) scholars become fascinated with the First World War at the start of their careers, and if they write something about it, it is usually early in their careers. I have been fortunate to come to the First World War toward the end of my career. Part of this was occasioned by the approach of the 100th anniversary which provided an opportunity to meet and listen to David Stevenson, Samuel Williamson, and Annika Mombauer. I was able to bring the first two along with Mustafa Aksakal and Frederick Dickinson to Illinois as part of the ConflictSpace project with Paul Diehl, Colin Flint and Jürgen Scheffran. This was followed up by another conference at ISA in San Francisco that I co-organized with Jack Levy related to our 2014 edited book on the war. All of this was part of my growing commitment to study the war extensively and systematically, and I thank each of my colleagues who participated in these conferences for their intellectual stimulation. The First World War remains, as most IR scholars know, the single most fascinating case in the history of our field. I have sought to make a contribution here to one of the less-studied aspects – why the war spread.

To do this I have taken a case-study approach that is informed by relevant data that set the structure and context in which these fascinating decisions were taken. Along the way I have incurred some welcomed debts. The data used in this book were painstakingly collected by many peace scientists, some of them my former students, and their data and contributions are acknowledged in Chapter 2, where the data are described. The actual compilation of these previously collected data was no mean task and was part of a larger project to prepare a Handbook of Interstate Conflict that would have histograms and data boxes on every dyad that had three or more militarized disputes in its history. To accomplish this I was aided over a three-year period by a team of remarkable undergraduate research assistants (RAs): Dannika Andersen, Amelia Berger, Mike Colucci, Haley Coyne, Allison Gerns, Gina Gonnella, Sarah Halko, Hannah Jarman, Dennis Jung, Ada Irem

Karacal, Connor Murray, S. Tyler Muncy, Grace O'Gara, Seung Yeun Oh, Amy Radlinski, Elaine Sine, Marko Sukovic, Ben Sybert, Mina Urbina, Brianna Winkel, Changchang Sophie Wu and Lindsey Zawila. The histograms presented here, out of over 400, were constructed by Emily Barrett, who also supervised many of these RAs and organized their overall work; for this her name has been added to the title page. By the time this book came to fruition, she had long since graduated and joined the work force. Her histograms were prepared for publication expertly by Niti Shah, also an undergraduate RA. During the years 2009–2015 I also taught a study-abroad course in Vienna. The course in 2014 dealt with the First World War, and in each of the other years part of the course was devoted to it. In this course I had four assistants over the years who helped me immensely and kept me on track: Kaily Grabemann, Stephanie Pedretti, Lily Tam, and Victoria Thompson. To each and every one of these students my heartfelt thanks. Your work was invaluable and it was a pleasure working with you.

A number of colleagues were kind enough to read parts of this manuscript and offer very valuable suggestions, some at a 2017 APSA panel: Öner Akgül, Jack Levy, Sean Lynn-Jones, Sara Moller, William Mulligan, Andy Owsaik, Paul Poast, and especially William Mulligan, who caught several errors and ambiguities. My thanks to all of them. None of them is responsible for any remaining errors in the book; that is my responsibility entirely.

Support for this research has been provided by the Thomas B. Mackie bequest to the University of Illinois. This fund has supported much of my research since I came to Illinois, and it was especially useful in the fall of 2017 for providing time to complete the writing of the book.

Cambridge University Press, publisher of several of my books, has as always proved to be the best way to complete the writing process. My thanks particularly to my editor John Haslam, who has been supportive throughout my years with the Press; it has always been a delight to work with him. I would also like to express my gratitude to my copy editor Dr. Steven Holt, who provided informed edits based on a close and thorough reading of the manuscript. Thanks also to Neil Wells for preparing the index, and to Robert Judkins, my production editor, for his excellent stewardship of the manuscript. Lastly, my thanks also to Delinda Swanson, who prepared the references, as she has for most of my books since I came to Illinois.

My wife, Marie T. Henehan, has always been supportive during my research and the writing of the book. She has relatives who live in Alsace and has an interest in the First World War that allowed us to share some of the more remarkable details of this case. Still, what has been important is simply having her at my side, without which it would have been a considerably less pleasant endeavor. Growing old together is the stuff of dreams and songs; it is never easy, but growing old with the love of your life is without comparison. Raising your own family is a great part of this venture. My daughter Elyse, who got married two days short of the 100th anniversary of the Austro-Hungarian declaration of war on Serbia, has reminded me that life goes on. A year later we were proud to have a grandson, Gavin, to keep us focused on the present, and as this book goes to press she and Walter have given us a granddaughter – Avery Jane.

Still, the past is important, and I have dedicated this book to the dead, wherever they are, and not just to the fallen in the "Great" War. Included in these billions upon billions are the dead who haunt my life: Sal Melluzzo, Connie Melluzzo, Terry Melluzzo Voss, John C. Vasquez, Helen J. Vasquez, Aunt Zina Vasquez, Uncle Rene Vasquez, Sebastian "Pa" Cristina, Concetta "Nana" Cristina, J. S. Benvento Vasquez, Sean Henehan Vasquez, Paul Senese, Tracy Jarvis, Tim Henehan, and Virginia Henehan.

Introduction

Overview

There has been much discussion about contagion and diffusion in interstate war, but there has been little discussion of how contagion works. This book seeks to provide a general explanation of the processes that make interstate war spread by looking at how contagion actually worked in the First World War. The logic of the analysis is to begin with some *ex ante* theoretical expectations, refine those on the basis of a general knowledge of the First World War into a set of hypotheses, investigate them empirically, and then infer from the investigation a set of generalizations about how and why wars spread. These generalizations must be seen as a set of untested hypotheses that need to be investigated on other cases before they are accepted.

The book is an exercise in the logic of discovery and not the logic of confirmation (see Scheffler 1967; Freyberg-Inan *et al.* 2016). From a philosophy-of-science point of view it is perfectly fine to derive hypotheses from one case as a way of discovering how processes might work, so long as these hypotheses are tested on a different data sample or set of cases as a way of trying to confirm or falsify them. The discovery of patterns and the formulation of hypotheses may involve a good deal of induction. Confirmation, however, is primarily a deductive exercise with strict rules for testing. The two have different logics, but both are legitimate aspects of the scientific path to knowledge (see Vasquez 1993: 4–5). The logic of discovery simply refers to the process by which hypotheses and theories are constructed. They can have a variety of sources, including derivation from paradigms, reflection on personal experience, hard thinking, counter-factual analysis, and so on and so forth. In fact to call all these sources a "logic" is to stretch the word. There are in fact few criteria that are accepted, although any one source may have criteria. The point is that there are a variety of sources, and Freyberg-Inan *et al.* (2016: 173) call for a social pluralism and inclusiveness of approaches in the realm of discovery, but more exclusiveness with regard to the logic of confirmation. With the latter they argue in favor of some kind of neopositivism. The relevant point here is that the conclusions and inferences of this study, while they may tell us something about why the First World War spread, will only provide some knowledge about war contagion as a general phenomenon once the derived hypotheses have been tested on other cases or data using criteria based on the logic of confirmation.

The cases included in this study are listed in Table I.1. These include all the major dyads that declared war, with the exception of several Latin American and miscellaneous states that had limited involvement and are listed in Table 5.1 in Chapter 5.

Six contagion processes are identified and their underlying logic elucidated. Each of the different kinds of contagion is used to explain how contagion worked to bring in the countries that went to war between 1914 and 1917. The six contagion processes are

1. Alliances
   - Contagion through alliances due to the failure of the coercion game
   - Contagion through alliances as a logical afterthought – valence balancing
2. Contiguity
3. Territorial rivalry
4. Opportunity
   - Opportunity due to changes in a rival's power
   - Opportunity due to the breakdown in the political order
5. Economic dependence
6. Brute force

To study these contagion processes each of the key pairs of states (dyads) that entered the First World War is analyzed in depth. These dyad analyses are presented in chronological order of their declaration of war. The study begins with the Austro-Hungarian–Serbian local war and then discusses how and why Germany–Russia joined that war and so forth until Greece, the last main dyad entry, joined in 1917. These dyad analyses combine both historical case analyses and Correlates of War data on major factors associated with war onset – the number of militarized interstate disputes (MIDs), alliance memberships, territorial claims, rivalry scores, and arms races. Within the dyad analysis, attempts will be made to separate what is unique to the case and what is generalizable. The last part of the book culminates in a set of testable hypotheses on how contagion works.

Table I.1. *Belligerents in the First World War by date*

Date	Country	Country
July 28, 1914	Austria-Hungary	Serbia
August 1, 1914	Germany	Russia
August 3, 1914	Germany	France
August 4, 1914	Germany	Belgium
August 4, 1914	Britain	Germany
August 5, 1914	Montenegro	Austria-Hungary
August 6, 1914	Austria-Hungary	Russia
August 6. 1914	Serbia	Germany
August 8, 1914	Montenegro	Germany
August 12, 1914	France	Austria-Hungary
August 12, 1914	Britain	Austria-Hungary
August 23, 1914	Japan	Germany
August 25, 1914	Japan	Austria-Hungary
August 28, 1914	Austria-Hungary	Belgium
November 2, 1914	Russia	Ottoman Empire
November 2, 1914	Serbia	Ottoman Empire
November 5, 1914	France	Ottoman Empire
November 5, 1914	Britain	Ottoman Empire
May 23, 1915	Italy	Austria-Hungary
August 21, 1915	Italy	Ottoman Empire
October 14, 1915	Bulgaria	Serbia
October 15, 1915	Britain	Bulgaria
October 15, 1915	Montenegro	Bulgaria
October 16, 1915	France	Bulgaria
October 19, 1915	Russia	Bulgaria
October 19, 1915	Italy	Bulgaria
March 9, 1916	Germany	Portugal
March 15, 1916	Austria-Hungary	Portugal
August 27, 1916	Romania	Austria-Hungary
August 28, 1916	Germany	Romania
August 28, 1916	Italy	Germany
August 30, 1916	Ottoman Empire	Romania
September 1, 1916	Bulgaria	Romania
April 6, 1917	United States	Germany
June 27, 1917	Greece	Austria-Hungary
June 27, 1917	Greece	Germany
June 27, 1917	Greece	Bulgaria
June 27, 1917	Greece	Ottoman Empire
July 22, 1917	Siam	Germany
July 22, 1917	Siam	Austria-Hungary
August 14, 1917	China	Germany
August 14, 1917	China	Austria-Hungary
October 26, 1917	Brazil	Germany
December 7, 1917	United States	Austria-Hungary

Organization

The book is divided into three parts. Part I of the book presents the theoretical expectations of the book and its research design. Chapter 1 provides a summary of the theoretical perspective that is taken in the book and lists the hypotheses that will be probed. It reviews the concept of contagion in the international relations (IR) literature, and defines each of the six processes with illustrations from the First World War based on a general knowledge of the war. These were specified *ex ante* before the research in the second part of the book was conducted. Chapter 2 provides a research design for the book. This study is a qualitative analysis, and the chapter outlines how that analysis will be conducted as well as providing an overview of the quantitative data used to supplement each case study. One of the unique features of the book is the utilization of existing Correlates of War data in combination with an historical analysis to write a case study of each pair of states that declared war, with emphasis on those that fought extensively and meet the Correlates of War threshold of being a participant.[1] The data, which have been collected by others over a period of over three decades, are carefully examined using multiple measures for what *ex ante* are regarded as the key factors making for war involvement.

Part II is the main part of the book, with a case study of each dyad that entered the war. In fact, readers interested primarily in the First World War and not so much in models and research design can start the book here and go back to Part I after reading Part III. Part II presents narratives of each of the main cases. The approach is a **dyadic** analysis, which has been found in quantitative IR to be a more fruitful approach than a systems or country-specific approach (see Rummel 1972). A dyadic analysis looks at conflict by examining pairs of states and their interactions with each other. It is assumed that war arises because of what states do to each other. While a dyadic analysis can be misleading in a multiparty event such as the First World War (see Poast 2010), outside parties can be brought into the analysis by examining their impact on the decision-making that takes place between the principal members of the dyad that is being studied. In analyzing

---

[1] To be considered a participant in a war in Correlates of War data a state must have had either 100 battle deaths or a minimum of 1,000 troops in active combat (Sarkees and Wayman 2010: 61). All countries in dyads that met this threshold are included in this analysis; most others that declared war are also included, if they are of historical interest, e.g. Brazil (see Chapter 2).

the war, this will often be done in the dyadic analyses by examining the role of "third parties." Likewise, an emphasis on dyads in the book does not mean that certain structural factors are of little causal import; it is only to say that these structural factors often work through how states behave toward each other. The book centers on a dyadic analysis by examining each and every dyad that legally entered the war, with emphasis on those that did the bulk of the fighting. It also includes a chapter in Part III on those that did not join and why. While dyadic analysis is familiar among political scientists, it is less common among historians. Even among IR scholars the scope of dyadic analysis presented here in terms of case analyses coupled with data is unusual.

Each dyad in the First World War is examined individually, with an emphasis on those that have had intense conflict and subsequent war. Data have been collected on all dyads that have resorted at least once to the threat or use of force during the period 1816–1929. Technically this means that they have had at least one militarized interstate dispute. The analysis of each dyad will include both a quantitative and a qualitative element. A histogram of a dyad's MIDs is presented for all dyads that have had at least three MIDs. Data that are thought to be theoretically relevant for explaining this pattern of conflict and whether a MID escalates to war will also be presented. These include data on rivalry, the dominant issue under contention, the presence of territorial claims, the allies each side has, and whether they have arms races. The heart of each dyad analysis consists of a narrative that explains why war between the two states occurred, if it did.

Part III, the Conclusion, consists of two chapters. The first, Chapter 6, is an analysis of the neutrals. This chapter compares those that entered the war with those that did not. The neutrals serve as a benchmark or comparison group for evaluating the explanation of contagion presented in Parts I and II. If that explanation is correct, then the neutrals should lack most if not all of the contagion factors that brought in the dyads that went to war. Chapter 6 tests whether some of the factors that are thought to have spread the First World War can actually distinguish the states that joined the war from those that remained neutral.

Chapter 7 is the culmination of the qualitative analysis to see how contagion actually worked. It draws upon the individual dyad case studies to present a set of hypotheses on contagion meant to apply to all multiparty wars, past and future. It begins by systematically examining what factors brought each of the main dyads into the war – summarizing the primary, secondary and other contagion processes at work. It reviews what new insights were learned from each case and, where relevant, formulates new supplemental hypotheses on contagion. Next, it provides a set of general conclusions on the role of alliances, why deterrence failed in 1914, and possible causal mechanisms at work that make for contagion, among other topics. The chapter concludes by looking at future research and its relevance to policy and theory.

Part I

Theoretical Expectations

1   Contagion Processes in the First World War

There has been little discussion of how contagion actually works historically and few studies of specific wars in terms of contagion processes (for two exceptions see Haldi 2003; Shirkey 2009). This study seeks to provide a general explanation of war contagion by looking at the spread of the First World War. Six contagion processes are identified *ex ante*. The theoretical expectations underlying these six models are then investigated empirically in Part II to see how contagion worked in this one case. As noted before, but worth emphasizing, the hypotheses in this book are not tested by the First World War case; rather, the case is used to probe some *ex ante* hypotheses and refine them.

The analysis in this chapter begins by discussing the concept of contagion. Next each of the processes will be analyzed and briefly applied to the First World War. Each section will end by deriving a set of general hypotheses about how contagion works. The chapter concludes with some reflections about how contagion worked in the First World War and how it might work generally on the basis of this preliminary review. These questions will then be investigated in Part II of the study.

The Concept of Contagion

Contagion is defined as the spread of war from one set of parties to include new ones. This results in an enlargement and expansion of the war. The etymology of contagion comes from the Latin *contingere*, to have contact with, to pollute (Merriam-Webster). It was first used in Middle English in the fourteenth century. The everyday definition of contagion is based on infection and the catching of a cold or more serious disease through contact. It has a negative connotation, and the word's meaning is expanded to refer to the spread of other undesirable things, like a contagious influence or the spread of a bad idea or theory. There are three causal notions worth highlighting in terms of how the word has been used. The first is the idea of spreading from one person to another. The second is the idea that this spreading is due to contact.

The third is the connotation that what is spread is harmful. In terms of contagious diseases, the underlying biology of infection is now well understood, but this was not the case when the word was first used. In terms of the spread of harmful ideas or practices, the underlying causal factors are still not well understood. Generally, however, a positive or neutral phenomenon is more typically discussed in terms of *diffusion*, with an emphasis on how it spreads.

The concept of diffusion derives more from analogies to the physical world rather than the medical. It refers to the dispersion of particles in a liquid, like dropping sugar crystals into a cup of tea. Diffusion is also used to describe the spread of inventions, like paper or fashion trends. The social sciences use the concept of diffusion to examine how cultural practices, religions, and innovations spread. Recently, social network analysis has been used to map this phenomenon. Geographers use this term in a more objective and neutral fashion without the negative connotations of contagion. For geographers there are two types of diffusion, each of which tries to capture the underlying mechanism at work – contagious diffusion and hierarchical diffusion (Gould 1969). The first refers to something that has spread through contact, or, from the geographers' perspective, things that spread spatially. Here contiguity is a key factor. The second presupposes some underlying structure, which provides a path by which the phenomenon spreads in a non-spatial manner. Fashion trends, for instance, follow a status hierarchy, which means they flow from certain capitals – like Paris and Milan – and then go to New York and so forth down a hierarchy. In IR, alliance structures are seen as a possible diffusion mechanism for the spread of war. Alliances in the First World War are seen as a classic example of hierarchical diffusion.

Studies of interstate war have provided some important distinctions and understandings of why war spreads and the different ways in which diffusion and contagion might occur. Most and Starr (1989) provide an important distinction in terms of the difference between *opportunity* and *willingness*. Opportunity refers to the possibility for conflict. This typically means that if states are contiguous they are more likely to experience diffusion. Opportunity is a pre-requisite for conflict, but it is not sufficient. There must also be a willingness to engage in conflict. In other words, there must be some grievance or reason for conflict. In later work, opportunity has often been seen as related to contiguity and willingness as related to the intensity of issue disagreements between states.

Another important distinction is provided by Davis, Duncan, and Siverson (1978), who distinguish between contagion that results from addiction and contagion that is infectious. Davis *et al.* (1978: 773) find that wars cluster in the international system because of infectious contagion. Bremer (1982) also finds that interstate and civil wars cluster, as do MIDs, which he sees as being a result of contagion. This again would presumably be the result of infectious contagion.

Bremer's (1982) "The contagiousness of coercion" suggests that there is a broader underlying process here, namely, the use of coercion leads others to use coercion. Coercion is contagious in that its use by one actor increases the likelihood that another will resort to it. The concept of a "demonstration effect" may be relevant to describe what is going on here. Contagion is conceived not so much as a result of infection but as the result of learning to copy something that is successful.

Similarly, Levy (1982, 1983: Ch. 7) investigates contagion in broad terms by seeing when war begets war. He identifies various circumstances in which war leads to war. Two in particular are of interest here: when the war of one actor leads it to initiate subsequent wars, as in the series of Napoleonic Wars, and when a victorious war leads to a squabble over the division of spoils, like in the Second Balkan War. Both of these involve contagion, but they seem to involve different kinds of contagion.

It should be emphasized that both Bremer and Levy, when they use the concept of contagion, do not mean to imply that decision-makers have no choice in whether to enter a war. They are not excluding by definition the role of agency in the spread of war. When they refer to contagion they are referring to an outcome of a set of actions; they are not commenting on the role of motivations. The way the concept of contagion is used here, as in most of the political science literature, is to refer to an outcome where a given phenomenon, whether it be smoking bans or war, spreads from one geographical area to another. The extent to which that process is brought about by agents or is more involuntary is left open. In the analysis sometimes demonstration effects are important and decisions are taken that are influenced by what others did. This happens when Romania is influenced by Italy setting the precedent of breaking an alliance and switching sides. At other times demonstration effects are not the key factor; instead, a given structure, like alliance bonds during the playing of the July coercive game, make states act quickly, although not involuntarily. Contagion can have several aspects when one is looking at why it occurs; the concept of contagion as used here, however, is defined in terms of its outcome – the spreading of a phenomenon. Once this has been established, the analysis will then turn to what brings about this spreading. At that point one can talk about the different contagion processes that bring about the spreading, which are more potent, and so forth.

The above analyses and literature, although highly relevant, are not necessarily about world war. World war involves a situation in which an ongoing war expands to the greatest extent possible. It is this situation that Davis *et al.* (1978) are concerned with. They say that the main theoretical question regarding war expansion is what distinguishes the few wars that spread from the many that do not. The question suggests theoretically that there is something about the ongoing war that encourages other states to decide for war. What is that something? This study will answer that question by examining dyadic decisions to join an ongoing war and categorize those decisions by the different underlying processes that are at work.

In this book a world war is defined as "a large-scale severe war among major states that involves the leading states at some point in the war and most other major states in a struggle to resolve the most fundamental issues on the global political agenda" (Vasquez 1993: 63).[1] If one classifies the goals and means used in war in terms of whether they are limited or total, then a world war employs unlimited (total) means and has unlimited goals (Vasquez 1993: 70, 227–228).

The existing empirical findings on big wars, including world wars (Midlarsky 1988, 1990), highlight some possible infectious processes. One set of findings shows that alliances and contiguity are key factors that increase the likelihood of war expansion (see Siverson and King 1979; Most and Starr 1980; Siverson and Starr 1991). Yamamoto and Bremer (1980) provide additional evidence that contagion occurs by finding that as more major powers join an ongoing war it is more difficult for others not to intervene. This conforms to historical analyses (see Stevenson 2011) that show that in the First World War in Europe pressure mounted on states to join as the war dragged on, and in the end few could ward off such pressures.

Reviewing the literature on war expansion, Vasquez (1993, 2009: Ch. 7) posits six mechanisms by which world wars expanded. Initial joining is typically a result of one of three factors: being allied to a belligerent, having a belligerent on one's border, or being a rival of one of the belligerents. When one of these factors brings in the initial joiner, then the war is spread further by one of three additional factors: the breakdown of the prevailing political order, a general bandwagon effect, or the economic dependence of one of the belligerents on a non-belligerent. There is some statistical evidence on the first two factors and the bandwagon effect, but the others are untested hypotheses of the author. Subsequent case studies by him of the Second World War

---

[1] The first part of this definition builds on that of Levy (1985: 365).

in Europe (Vasquez 1996a) and in Asia (Vasquez and Gibler 2001) provide evidence consistent with all six claims, however. More recently Vasquez et al. (2011) used a network analysis of the First World War and found that contiguity, alliances, rivalry, and territorial disputes all played a role in the diffusion of the war.

Yet multiparty wars are fairly rare in history, so the author posits that three necessary conditions be present in the system for world wars to occur: (1) there must be a multipolar system (this is true by definition), (2) alliances must reduce that multipolar system to two hostile blocs, and (3) one bloc must not be preponderant over the other.

In a more recent analysis of all multiparty wars (those involving three or more parties) Vasquez and Rundlett (2016) argue and then empirically show that alliances are a necessary condition of multiparty wars. They also show that for the two world wars over 90% of the participants which committed troops had outside alliances going into the war.

War expansion is also the topic of three recent books. Haldi (2003) tries to explain how wars widen by examining two theories of why neutrals enter wars. The first is that they enter to balance and the second is that they enter for reasons of predation. He then reviews a number of cases to see which theory best predicts which cases. A noteworthy aspect of this study is that it looks at two cases before 1815, namely the Seven Years' War and the French Revolutionary and Napoleonic Wars. Shirkey (2009) considers the spread of war by looking at a number of specific wars, including the First World War, but also conducts a statistical analysis. His focus is to look at why states join an ongoing fray. He examines the role of information and unexpected events in both war joining and war exiting. He finds evidence to support many of his key hypotheses, but some hypotheses had to be reformulated or were rejected (see also Shirkey 2009: 212–213). Weisiger (2013) returns to the idea of big wars and asks what are the factors associated with limited vs. unlimited wars. While the study is not explicitly about the spread of war, unlimited wars include many that have spread, so the book is relevant. He utilizes the bargaining theory of war, and finds that commitment problems are particularly important in long and unlimited wars.

The above conceptual distinctions and empirical findings still leave many questions unanswered about how contagion or diffusion works in actual cases and whether there are different causal processes that bring about contagion. This study delineates the different kinds of contagion at work in the First World War and shows how they are not all the same and often have different underlying logics. It does this by examining how each dyad, for example Germany–France, decided to go to war. Although the study focuses on one multiparty war, the analysis is intended to tell us something in general about how contagion works in international war and how collective violence spreads. Therefore, in the dyadic analysis, attempts will be made to separate what is unique to the case and what is generalizable. The latter can be used to provide a general explanation and testable hypotheses on how contagion works. The First World War is selected as a case because it is the premier modern example of war diffusion. On a philosophical level, it must be noted that generalizations derived on the basis of one case are not conclusions that should be taken as knowledge, but inductions that are presented as hypotheses that must then be tested on other cases.

Nonetheless, although the First World War is used as a basis of empirical investigation and theoretical exploration, this is far from a purely inductive study. Previous theoretical reflection provides a clear *ex ante* stance to the analysis (see Vasquez 1993: Ch. 6). The analysis is less interested in repeating what is already known, for example that alliances played a major role, than in uncovering the specific processes that made contagion work the way it did. For instance, it will be seen that alliances worked in two very different ways to diffuse the war and would presumably work in these two different ways in general. Likewise, where possible, the analysis will try to assess the relative potency of the different contagion processes and which are more important when the two effects are pushing an actor in different directions. The next sections examine each of the six contagion processes in detail. Each section will discuss how the contagion process worked in the First World War and then it will list the dyads that are believed to have been brought into the war by that process.

Contagion Processes

Alliances

Contagion through Alliances Due to the Failure of the Coercion Game Just about everyone knows that alliances brought in the immediate parties in the first week in August. What is not always as clear, but hardly controversial, is that alliances worked in this way because they encouraged the playing of a game of coercion that failed. The dyads brought into the war in this way are listed in Table 1.1. What is also clear historically is that they all had grievances, although some had more than others. Yet these grievances and even the alliance bonds had been in existence for several years. The alliances themselves were meant to be defensive in that they were motivated by aggregating capability to such a degree that it was hoped rivals would think twice

Table 1.1. *Alliance contagion through coercive game*

Aug 1, 1914	Germany	Russia
Aug 3, 1914	Germany	France
Aug 4, 1914	Britain	Germany
Aug 6, 1914	Austria-Hungary	Russia

before they attacked and maybe even be prevented from launching an attack. What led to war, however, was that the alliances were used to play a coercive game (what some would label a chicken game) that failed, resulting in a spread of war to all the players.[2]

The story of the early spread of the war is well known. Most recent interpretations (see McMeekin 2013: 282–284, 309; Clark 2012: 526–527) see Germany entering a period of preparing for war due to Russian mobilization. Then Germany attacked France through Belgium because of the Franco-Russian alliance. This gave Grey the condition he needed to enter the war and live up to the interests he believed that the Anglo-French Entente embodied.

What is less well understood is how alliances were used to make contagion work the way it did. The key decision-makers in each of the major continental states used their alliance commitments to play a coercive game. They tried to use threat and intimidation to make the other side back down. In one sense this was a realist way of avoiding war that also had the advantage of increasing the likelihood of winning if war could not be avoided. In order to win, however, one had to be willing to go to war. The Kaiser and other key German decision-makers believed that the Tsar would not go to war for Serbia and would back down in part because they did not think Russia was yet prepared for war (McMeekin 2013: 105; Clark 2012: 518; Mulligan 2010: 213). The Tsar believed that Germany would be "out of her mind" to attack Russia, France, and England combined.[3] Given these perceptions, both sides were willing to push hard. At the same time, they prepared for war. Mobilization was an attractive policy because it was dual use – it could demonstrate resolve and enhance threat, and, if coercion failed, it

---

[2] I have refrained from calling the July 1914 crisis a chicken game, although it has resemblances to one. This is because it does not meet some of the technical requirements of a chicken game. First, it involves several players and not just two; also it reflects an iterative game among these players going back to at least 1908. Zagare (2011: 115), who relaxes some of these assumptions, also does not call it a chicken game.

[3] Told to the French Ambassador, Maurice Paléologue (Memoirs, July 20, 1914, reprinted in Williamson and Van Wyk 2003: 130).

would give the side which mobilized most effectively an advantage in winning the subsequent war.

Alliances among the major states made war spread because the coercive game failed. Recent work by Bobroff (2014) and by Zagare (2011) discusses how the war came about due to a failure of this game. The logic of the coercive game is that one side will prevent an attack by the other by allying with a state that will give it superior capability. The opponent will recognize this and back down. This strategy had worked in 1908–1909 during the Bosnian crisis, and the Kaiser and others thought it would work now, especially given Germany's relative strength compared with Russia. What the Kaiser and others neglected was that after 1908 the Tsar vowed never to be humiliated again and increased his military accordingly.

The Central Powers believed that the coercive table was set in their favor. The Serbian use of Russia was countered and trumped by the so-called blank check provided by Germany. In the end no one backed down. The chicken game failed. No one swerved and everyone drove straight ahead. The Austro-Hungarians were not intimidated by the Russians, and the Russians were not intimidated by the Germans. Each actor lived up to its commitments – Russia supported Serbia, and Germany supported Austria-Hungary. It was the logic of coercion and the chicken game it promoted that made the war spread through the major-state alliance system the way it did.

Alliances also played a role in the conduct of the coercion game because the re-assertion of firm commitments during the crisis itself made each side play the game to the hilt. Alliances enabled each side to demonstrate its full resolve to go to war if necessary. This is what the blank check did for Austria-Hungary and what Poincaré's and Paléologue's consistent support of the Tsar did for Russia. The alliances on the Eastern Front acted to embolden each side.[4] Lastly, alliances set out who the opponents would be, since one of the ways in which they originally sought ally partners was to force their opponent to fight a two-front war. This resulted in the well-known checkerboard pattern that major alliances often reflect, and the spatial diffusion of the war in the first week of August reflected this checkerboard pattern.

Despite these multiple alliance effects, the failure of the coercion game was essential. While it was the case that the alliance structure made the war spread through hierarchical diffusion, what activated this

---

[4] The Anglo-French Entente did not, however. Grey's public and sometimes private ambiguity led to uncertainty about the British commitment. For an empirical analysis on how alliances enable states, see Kang (2012).

diffusion was the failure of the coercion game. It was not just the presence of alliance ties but using the alliance ties, coupled with the alignment between Russia and Serbia, to try to coerce the other side and win by risking war. The alliance system had been in force for some time and had not produced this kind of war. In fact, one could argue that in 1908–1909 the alliance system had the same sides but the coercion game produced a victor without going to war. It is only when coercion fails to intimidate that alliances produce a contagion process that brings in the major states. Structure alone did not bring about diffusion, but did determine the type and form of that diffusion once the coercion game had failed.

What are some of the lessons that can be derived from this process? First, the alliance system was dominated by major states. Failure of the coercive game partly explains Yamamoto and Bremer's (1980) finding that as each major state enters it becomes more difficult for other major states to stay out. Because of the alliance structure a bandwagon effect occurs among major states.[5] It is not clear that without the playing of the coercion game alliances alone would have made for this bandwagoning effect, at least in the initial stages of war diffusion. Playing the coercion game within the context of the alliance system guaranteed intervention and war joining, and this was likely because the actors were *major* states.

A second lesson has to do with contiguity. A common characteristic of all but one of the allied major states was that they were contiguous with at least one of their opponents.[6] One can see the war as an earthquake with two epicenters. The first was the local war breaking out between Austria-Hungary and Serbia. The second epicenter was on the German–Russian axis, which made all the other major European states (with the exception of Italy) intervene in the local war in a matter of days. In this second epicenter most states were also contiguous.

We are now in a position to derive some generalizations and hypotheses from these lessons. Before doing so, it must be kept in mind what precisely is being explained. Siverson and King (1979) showed some time ago that, since most wars do not expand, being allied to a belligerent does not mean that one will join an ongoing war (see also Siverson and Starr 1991). Indeed, since war joining is rare, no one is likely to intervene. The effect of the alliance is simply to make it more probable

---

[5] Bandwagoning is used here in its initial broad meaning in American politics of jumping on a campaign "bandwagon" going down a street to gain support (see Vasquez 1993: 242–244). Later uses in IR of bandwagoning with the stronger state as opposed to balancing build on this term while narrowing its empirical referent.

[6] Britain is the exception here.

that a state allied to a belligerent will enter the war than a state not allied to the belligerent. Thus the first hypothesis we need to begin with is as follows.

1. Allies of belligerents are more apt to enter wars than non-allies (Siverson and King 1979; Siverson and Starr 1991).

From the analysis in this section two more hypotheses can be derived about the first way alliances spread war.

2. Alliances spread war among major states when they have long-standing grievances and during a multiparty crisis they play a coercive (chicken) game and it fails.

There are three components to this hypothesis. First, the war potential of alliances is activated by a crisis where the alliance system is used to try to intimidate and coerce the other side. Allies come to the defense of their allies. Second, the key actors have grievances with each other. Third, the coercive game fails and the states live up to their commitments and go to war.[7]

3. Coercive games involving allies that are major states and that are contiguous are more likely to spread war than those involving minor states or the non-contiguous.

We turn now to the second way in which alliances spread the war – valence balancing.

Contagion through Alliances as a Logical Afterthought – Valence Balancing As stated above, alliances work in two ways. The less obvious way is how alliance commitments bring about war between states that would never fight each other bilaterally. In other words, these pairs of belligerents do not really have any serious grievances with each other that would make them go to war. They go to war with each other only because they are allied with a state involved in the ongoing war. It can be said, theoretically, that these dyads come to war purely through a contagion process. They go to war because their ally is in a war. Table 1.2 lists the dyads that fall into this category.

Valence balancing embodies the well-known aphorisms that the enemy of my friend is my enemy and that the enemy of my enemy is my friend.[8] The term valence balancing is employed to emphasize that

---

[7] Crises that use coercive games are likely to escalate to war as they repeat. This is known to be the case in general (see Leng 1983) and it was the case prior to 1914 (Midlarsky 1988).

[8] For an empirical analysis including exceptions, see Maoz *et al.* (2007).

Table 1.2. *Alliance contagion through valence balancing*

August 6, 1914	Serbia	Germany
August 12, 1914	France	Austria-Hungary
August 12, 1914	Britain	Austria-Hungary
August 28, 1914	Austria-Hungary	Belgium
November 2, 1914	Serbia	Ottoman Empire
November 5, 1914	France	Ottoman Empire
November 5, 1914	Britain	Ottoman Empire
October 15, 1915	Britain	Bulgaria
October 15, 1915	Montenegro	Bulgaria
October 16, 1915	France	Bulgaria
October 19, 1915	Russia	Bulgaria
October 19, 1915	Italy	Bulgaria
March, 15, 1916	Austria-Hungary	Portugal
August 28, 1916	Italy	Germany
1917–1918	Latin American states, Liberia	Germany
December 7, 1917	United States	Austria-Hungary

this is also a psychological process even though it may satisfy strategic interests. From a psychological perspective humans find it emotionally unsettling to be friends with the enemy of one's friend. It is seen as a kind of betrayal. One's friends and enemies should reflect a consistency. In a war situation the pressure – both psychologically and strategically – becomes more salient because of the threat of conquest. What the dyads in Table 1.2 have in common is that they became belligerents not because of any grievance (and not simply because their alliance commitment to that state was in their immediate material interest) but because of the pressure to avoid ambivalence.

The first three listed dyads – Serbia–Germany, Britain–Austria-Hungary, and France–Austria-Hungary – illustrate this process. Weak Serbia had no grievances with Germany. If it were not for Germany's alliance with Austria-Hungary, Serbian decision-makers would not have dreamed of going to war with Germany. In addition, Germany had no salient grievances with Serbia. Its only objection to Serbia was that it was in deep conflict with its ally, Austria-Hungary. Germany had no ambitions or goals vis-à-vis Serbia that were worth a war. Interestingly, the two had only had one MID with each other – the July crisis. In many ways British foreign policy with regard to Serbia was similar. Grey and other decision-makers made it clear that they would not go to war to protect Serbia. As Clark (2012: 536) notes, "British policy-makers had no particular interest in or sympathy for Serbia."

Britain–Austria-Hungary is another dyad, this involving two major states, that would not normally go to war with each other. They did not share a major grievance. They had only had one militarized dispute prior to 1914, and that was in 1863. Britain went to war with Austria-Hungary not because of the latter's goals in Serbia, but because Germany went to war, and Austria-Hungary was allied to it. Likewise, Austria-Hungary only went to war with Britain because Britain went to war with Germany.

France–Austria-Hungary is also a major state dyad where the states would not have gone to war with each other if left alone. Again their grievances were not so much with each other as with others. France's principal enemy was Germany and Austria-Hungary's was Russia. Indirectly, however, there were tensions. Austria-Hungary was well aware of French financial support of Serbia, and this was an irritation. In addition, France was a steadfast supporter of Russia, Austria-Hungary's immediate opponent in the July crisis. She was contributing militarily to Russian capability in terms of loans for railways and diplomatically to Russian resolve in terms of her support of Russia vis-à-vis Germany. In the end, however, neither expected to face each other on the battlefield.

In each of the above cases, the declaration of war, as with that of Britain–Austria-Hungary, was a way of making the valences (positive and negative attachments) of the alliance system consistent and balanced in order to avoid ambivalence. This was why Serbia declared war against Germany (Austria-Hungary's main ally) and why Britain declared war against Austria-Hungary. This was less true of France and Austria-Hungary, but valence balancing seems to have played a key role, since France's support of Serbia was not such as to bring about a war between the two if no other parties were at play.

The Entente allies that declared war against the Ottoman Empire in November 1914 after Russia did and against Bulgaria after the latter declared war against Serbia in 1915 are also examples of valence balancing. In each case all went to war because their ally declared war or was attacked. Of course, Britain and France had territorial ambitions that led them over the years to encroach on the Ottoman Empire, but valence balancing provided the occasion for a declaration of war.

An example that is theoretically unusual is Italy–Germany. The Italians were reluctant to declare war on Germany. Even though they declared war against Austria-Hungary on May 23, 1915 they did not declare war against Germany until August 28, 1916, over a year later. By that time they were also at war with the Ottoman Empire (August 21, 1915) and Bulgaria (October 19, 1915). Even then they declared war only under direct allied pressure. Why the long delay? One answer is that Italy and Germany had no direct grievance; indeed, Germany had been supportive of Italy's desires for compensation in July 1914. Of equal importance, however, were their prior long-term interactions, which had been friendly. Prussia, after all, was an ally of Italy in 1866, which resulted in Italy gaining Venetia. The Franco-Prussian War of 1870 also provided the context for the Italian acquisition of Rome, although there was no direct alliance. In addition, Italy was still engaged in plenty of trade with Germany, and for Germany this was a valuable overland route. In the end, the Entente objected and the valences had to be balanced. Italy's new allies made it fight against the other major Central Power, even though it had no direct grievances with Germany and it was extremely reluctant to do so. Hence this dyadic war was a product of alliance contagion through valence balancing. The source of valence balancing, however, resided more with Italy's allies (who even threatened to cut off resources) rather than within Italy, which would have preferred to keep its war involvement localized.

The above examples show that even within the alliance ties among the major states in Europe some states went to war not because of a direct threat, but simply because their allies went to war. There was no compelling reason to go to war; alliances were the sole reason. This sort of alliance tie makes countries indirectly enemies. The actual dynamics of the dyad played little to no role in the real decision to join the war. That decision was made on the basis of the relations of some other dyad. The declaration of war by the U.S. on Austria-Hungary is another example of valence balancing. Wilson's grievances were with German submarine warfare; his primary objection to Austria-Hungary was that it was Germany's ally.

A final example of dyads coming to war with each other solely because of their allies is the massive Western Hemisphere declaration of war against Germany after the U.S. declared war. As with the above examples, these states would never have fought a bilateral war with Germany; nor did they have many grievances with Germany, although there were German "imperial" probes before the war. What separates these interventions from the European ones, however, is that they entered the war simply out of loyalty to the U.S. instead of a concern about "the enemy of my friend being my enemy." In part this reflects U.S. hegemony in the region. Except for Brazil, none of these states played an active role in the war.[9] The declarations came in two waves. The first were those that entered the day after the U.S. in 1917, which included those most dependent on the U.S. – Cuba and Panama.

---

[9] Even Brazil, which deployed naval forces, did not satisfy the Correlates of War threshold for war participation (see Sarkees and Wayman 2010: 121).

Then a second wave came with Brazil's declaration in October 1917, followed by several more in the spring and summer of 1918 – Guatemala, Nicaragua, Costa Rica, Honduras, and Haiti. Note that Liberia, which had been founded by free Blacks or former American slaves, declared war on August 4, 1917.[10]

Declarations of war resulting from valence balancing follow naturally almost as a logical afterthought; typically valence balancing is not consciously taken into consideration during the actual deliberation on whether to go to war. This is especially the case because there is no expectation that such dyads would actually fight each other on the battlefield. Nor were there any serious military contingency plans to that effect, which kept the military from raising questions that would shape the initial war deliberations.[11] Other dyads would also come to war purely through a contagion process, but the particular dyads discussed in this section came to war because of the logical extension of their alliance commitments.

Two interesting theoretical points can be derived from the cases in Table 1.2. First, the lack of grievance is uncannily reflected in the chronological order in which each of these dyads declared war. The declarations are later and come *after* the initial conflagration between August 1–4. Germany–Serbia were legally at war on August 6 and Britain–Austria-Hungary on August 12. The declaration of war dates are listed in Table 1.2, and it can be seen that almost all come after those of the states that had grievances.[12] This indicates that the declaration comes about in order to make all enemies of my allies my enemies. This makes the psychological affect (friendship–hostility) consistent; the valences are balanced – the belligerent of my ally is my belligerent (especially if I do not expect to face him on the battlefield). For this reason the contagion process can be labeled "valence balancing."

Another point of theoretical importance is that these states are not contiguous. This in large part explains the limited threat and interests each had with the other. Contiguity poses a threat because land armies can project power quickly and put in jeopardy the actual survival of a

---

[10] Only Panama and Cuba also declared war against Austria-Hungary in December 1917 and Nicaragua on May 8, 1918, after the U.S. had done so on December 7, 1917. These states were more under the "hegemony" of the U.S. than others, like Brazil, which declared war only against Germany.

[11] The exception here is the Ottoman Empire, where Britain and France contemplated military action in late 1914 as Russia and they declared war.

[12] The case that comes close to an exception is Austria-Hungary–Russia, which did not go to war until August 6, 1914, five days after Germany and Russia and the same day as the valence balancing of Germany–Serbia. In part the delay may reflect the contingencies of mobilization and battlefield conditions.

state (Colaresi, Rasler, and Thompson 2007: 246ff). Germany had no way of attacking Serbia before the war started. Later, as the war progressed, its alliance with Austria-Hungary permitted that, but in the initial stages this was not an immediate threat. Contiguity, however, is mostly a problem not because of proximity but because neighbors have unresolved territorial issues. As Vasquez (1995) argues, neighbors typically fight not because they are contiguous, but because they have territorial disputes with each other. Once these have been settled, the probability of war can go way down. Serbia–Germany and Britain–Austria-Hungary had no territorial disputes with each other. This in turn is because they shared no border.

These patterns persist through the remainder of the list. The declaration of war by Austria-Hungary on Belgium reflected these patterns nicely. Austria-Hungary had no military plans to attack France and therefore no need to go through Belgium. It declared war because Germany had those plans. Likewise, the 1916 declaration of war by Austria-Hungary against Portugal was a function of Portugal seizing German ships in its ports (Goldstein 1992: 214 n1) at British instigation. Austria-Hungary followed Germany, and did so because Portugal also seized Austria-Hungary's ships since it had decided to seize Germany's.

What lessons and generalizations about contagion can be derived from the analysis on valence balancing? A key lesson is that alliances are an important mechanism for spreading war because they bring in states that do not have grievances with one another. From this analysis we can derive the following general hypothesis.

4. Alliances increase the likelihood that states that do not have grievances with a belligerent will join an ongoing war (compared with non-allied neutrals) through a process of valence balancing. Such states consider the enemy of their ally to be their enemy because of an underlying psychological pressure to keep positive (and negative) affect consistent.

We turn now to how contiguity made contagion work the way it did.

Contiguity and Contagion: The Different Aspects

Contiguity made the First World War spread in three different ways. The first and most potent role contiguity played in spreading the First World War and most likely plays in generally spreading war is that some states are attacked solely because they are "in the way." If they were not geographically placed where they are, they would not be attacked. This is because the dyad involved is absent of any salient grievance or disputes. The best example of this is Belgium. It is attacked simply because it provides a less defended path to Paris. Interestingly, Joffre and the French military saw Belgium in a similar way. In addition to attacking Germany directly at Lorraine, they wanted to attack Germany by going through Belgium, but Poincaré would not permit them to do so for diplomatic reasons involving Grey and Britain (Williamson and Van Wyk 2003: 206–210). Yet, having said all of this about Belgium being in the way, it must be pointed out that it is "in the way" because the alliance structure made it in the way.

Another example where contiguity plays this role is Japan–Austria-Hungary. Japan and Austria-Hungary had no grievances with each other, but they came to war because Austria-Hungary had a cruiser connected to the German fleet in the area that Japan was going to attack. Contiguity played a role here in that Austria-Hungary's naval forces were "in the way." As with the case of Belgium, alliances again played a role, but not as strong a role as with Belgium, in that the Austro-Hungarian ship was in the area because Austria-Hungary was an ally of Germany that shared some of its interests in the vicinity. Being in the way is an example of how contagion brings to war dyads that would normally not fight. For a list of the dyads that were brought to war in the First World War because of contiguity see Table 1.3.

A second aspect relevant for contiguity has to do with how alliances make contiguity a dangerous condition that promotes contagion. Contiguity needs to be seen as a constant that can become more or less dangerous depending on how actors treat it. The natural geography can be re-constructed to make it more dangerous. This is precisely what the alliance system did prior to 1914. Alliances were constructed not only to enhance power, but also to weaken the other side. One of the best ways to do that was to force an opponent to fight a two-front war and thereby split its army.

The third, and more subtle way, in which contiguity spreads war is that proximity creates a time pressure that promotes military action. As noted above, all the major states, with the exception of Britain and

Table 1.3. *Contiguity: States in the way*

August 4, 1914	Germany	Belgium
August 25, 1914	Japan	Austria-Hungary

Germany, that went to war in the first week were contiguous.[13] This contiguity made their land armies very threatening because they had hardly any loss-of-strength gradient and thus they could in theory bring about a rapid conquest. This threat and the attempts to counter it by various military doctrines (see Snyder 1984) meant that contiguity added a tremendous time pressure on each of the belligerents, but especially Germany and Russia. This was what most agitated the military leaders. It was their responsibility to defend the nation and to do that adequately they needed to mobilize to gain an advantage. Equally important was that they needed to prevent their opponents from gaining an advantage by mobilizing early. This role not only gave military leaders a different perspective from civilian decision-makers, but created a split within the elite as the crisis came closer to war, resulting in different proposals and time horizons. Both Williamson and Van Wyk (2003) and Mombauer (2013b: 28) point out this split. The time pressure contiguity creates helps explain that split. Again a dyadic perspective helps elucidate this process.

Time pressure is also important theoretically because it makes contiguity a variable. This in turn is a function of alliances. The danger of conquest posed by contiguity and the time pressure it exerts are not constant, but constructed by the alliance system that is made. In the last weekend it was really all about pre-emptive war and not so much preventive war, as has often been discussed.[14] All this time pressure happened because of the contiguity between Germany and Russia and to a lesser extent Russia and Austria-Hungary.

At a different level, the same kind of time pressure and threat of conquest was posed by the contiguity between Austria-Hungary and Serbia. The prospect of being overrun gave military leaders and hardliners and their recommendations more attention and influence. Civilian leaders like Bethmann-Hollweg, the Kaiser, and the Tsar were on a different time horizon and were trying to give peace options, like the Halt-in-Belgrade plan, a chance to work. Military leaders, like Moltke and Sukhomlinov, wanted mobilization to insure defensive advantages and lower the probability of defeat. As pre-mobilization plans were implemented and mobilization ordered in Russia, peace plans were shunted aside. Mobilization, which was aimed at avoiding pre-emption, also pre-empted the best peace plan available for avoiding war (Vasquez 2014a: 633–634).

[13] Although the two states were not contiguous, the naval proximity of Britain and Germany made the latter fear a surprise attack on its fledging navy even before the war, as reflected in the so-called Copenhagen complex (see Steinberg 1966).

[14] See Copeland (2014b) and Vasquez (2014b); see also Levy (2014).

A theoretical problem is how potent contiguity is in terms of its causal impact compared with other factors, specifically, the failure of coercion. One way to address this is that the failure of the coercive game is a variable and contiguity is a constant. In principle this means that the coercive game and the logic it embodies for making states intervene in the way they do is more theoretically significant. Contiguity had always been present since the Franco-Russian alliance and the Triple Alliance were formed in the late nineteenth century. The threat of conquest was there; it was only with the failure of the coercive game and with Russia's early mobilization that contiguity was activated as a factor making war spread. In this sense, it can be said that the failure of the coercive game made contiguity a significant factor. So, too, did alliances, because they brought the threat to the border.

Lastly, it should be pointed out that contiguity is important because it makes spatial diffusion possible. As has been shown elsewhere (Vasquez *et al.* 2011: 157), the First World War spread from adjacent country to adjacent country. Very few states went to war without having a warring neighbor, the U.S. being the major exception. The reason for this is that contiguity provides physical access to land armies. Spatial diffusion occurs in this way as in a glass of water spilling. States getting in the way, checkerboard alliances, and time pressure all occur because states are adjacent.

What hypotheses can be derived about contiguity?

5. Wars are apt to spread through a process of spatial diffusion. Contiguity makes wars spread in two ways. First, some states are in the way and are attacked to get at an enemy and not so much because the attacker has serious grievances with the state being attacked. Second, contiguity poses the prospect of a rapid conquest and thus imposes time pressure to act. This makes military leaders put pressure on civilian decision-makers to take actions that pose a threat to the other side.

6. Alliances that are made in a checkerboard pattern make contiguity, which is a constant, into a variable that increases threat. In the presence of a multiparty crisis where a coercive game fails, this checkerboard pattern of alliances will make war diffuse spatially and rapidly.[15]

Up to this point, while grievances have been mentioned as a source of the coercive game that was played, the substantive nature of the

---

[15] This hypothesis is one of the ways in which the First World War is an analogy that is appropriate for the future.

grievances that gave rise to the war and made it spread has not been discussed in detail. Most wars occur because states have serious grievances that they see as being able to be resolved only through the use of force. The modal war in the modern global system is a two-party war fought between neighbors over territory (see Vasquez and Valeriano 2010: 300). In fact, the First World War began with such a war, with Austria-Hungary trying to defend itself from what it saw as Serbian nationalist territorial ambitions. Serbia and other Balkan states had just fought such a territorial war with the Ottoman Empire. Eastern Europe was rife with such potential wars. These territorial wars are often fought bilaterally, but they need not be in certain historical circumstances. The next section tries to dissect just what role territorial rivalries play in contagion and how they relate and interact with the other diffusion mechanisms. Special attention will be paid to the relative causal impact of territorial rivalries.

Territorial Rivalry

Territorial rivalry can be defined as the situation when states are focused primarily on territorial claims and disputes. Not all of their MIDs have to be territorial disputes, but those should constitute a high percentage. It is assumed that territorial struggles are so salient that they will affect contention on other issues. Rivalry can be defined as "a relationship characterized by extreme competition, and usually psychological hostility, in which the issue positions of contenders are generated primarily by their attitude toward each other rather than by the stakes at hand" (Vasquez 1996b: 532; see also Vasquez 1993: 82). This is true even though territorial stakes may produce the sense of rivalry in the first place. This conception emphasizes competition and psychological hostility between relative equals. The hostility implies that states will at times deviate from strict cost–benefit analysis by taking actions fundamentally in order to hurt the other side. Such underlying factors are difficult to observe directly, so the concept of rivalry is often defined operationally on the basis of repeated MIDs (Diehl and Goertz 2000: 44), but one could also use the approach of Thompson (2001), who relies on historians' assessments to determine which states are likely to have repeated MIDs.

The territorial rivalry that started the First World War was Serbia–Austria-Hungary. Serbian nationalists assassinated Franz Ferdinand in order to promote their territorial and nationalist agenda. Austro-Hungarian leaders, like Berchtold and even Franz Josef, wanted to end the territorial threat posed by Serbia by crushing it in a war.

After the territorial rivalry between Austria-Hungary and Serbia, the main territorial rivalry in the First World War was Italy–Austria-Hungary. This is an interesting case theoretically because one factor (alliance) was pushing Italy to join one side and territorial rivalry made it contemplate switching sides. These contradictory factors can be thought of as two different vectors pushing the actor in two different directions. Depending on which way the actor goes and the relative potency of each vector within the decision-making elite, we are provided with evidence from which tentative causal inferences can be made. However, because Italy could have gone to either side, this means that it was brought into the war not just by its territorial rivalry but by another contagion factor, namely, which side it thought was likely to win, a factor that will be discussed in the next section. Suffice it to say for now that territorial rivalry rather than alliance provided a key motive for war joining.

There are other European dyads that went to war in a similar fashion, although the logic of their joining may not be as widely known. These are listed in Table 1.4 and include Bulgaria–Serbia – that had strong territorial disagreements resulting from the Second Balkan War, Romania–Austria/Hungary – where Romania had long-held desires for Transylvania, and Russia–Ottoman Empire – where, beginning with Peter the Great, Russia had encroached on Turkey. These three examples suggest that territorial rivalry was an important factor in determining the spread of war. At the same time, however, it seems that the ongoing war was an important factor that provided an opportunity for pushing each of these territorial rivals into war. This point is best illustrated by Japan–Germany, which entered the First World War within three weeks of its start. Japan wanted to increase its imperial empire in China and the Pacific, and this was an opportunity to do so.

Table 1.4. *Territorial rivals*

July 28, 1914	Serbia	Austria-Hungary
August 3, 1914	Germany	France
August 23, 1914	Japan	Germany
November 2, 1914	Russia	Ottoman Empire
May 23, 1915	Italy	Austria-Hungary
August 21, 1915	Italy	Ottoman Empire
October 14, 1915	Bulgaria	Serbia
August 27, 1916	Romania	Austria-Hungary
September 1, 1916	Bulgaria	Romania
June 27, 1917	Greece	Bulgaria
June 27, 1917	Greece	Ottoman Empire

Its 1902 alliance with Britain provided a nice legal rationale, but its territorial goals supplied the real motive. Nonetheless, the main factor making Japan enter was the *opportunity* the ongoing war provided (see below).

In each of the above dyads territorial rivalry helps explain how contagion worked. These dyads entered the war because they had a history of territorial disputes. At the same time, these dyads were not in a position to fight a territorial war on their own. For them the existing war made the time ripe to pursue these goals. What the First World War provided was an opportunity to fight for them *now*. The interventions after August 6, 1914 of these dyads were the product of the opportunity the war provided for these countries to fight their own private or parallel wars.[16] These were wars where at least one of the parties would have liked to have fought bilaterally but could not because of the existing political structure. The ongoing war changed that structure and thereby removed obstacles that had prevented these dyads from going to war. There are two structures that act in this way – the existing structure of power and the existing structure of the political order. Examining how changes in the two structures affected contagion provides a way of dissecting the idea of opportunity. Each of the structures and the dyads affected by them will be examined in turn.

Before doing so, a few words can be said about what these cases suggest about the causal role of territorial rivalry. First, when territorial concerns push actors in one direction and alliance ties push them in another, the territorial concerns usually win out. This was the case with Italy and with Romania. When territorial concerns and alliance ties are consistent, it also seems that territorial concerns are more of a motivation and ally ties more of a rationale. This was the case with Japan. Territorial rivalry, while underlying and fundamental, did not make for the entry of these dyads into the war; rather it was the opportunity provided by the ongoing war that did that. In this sense, the entry of these dyads into the war was a product of the ongoing war. Without the ongoing war these dyads would not have gone to war at this time, although their territorial concerns may have made them go to war at another time. The ongoing war provides an opportunity, and part of that opportunity is built-in allies who will help them achieve their territorial goals. From this analysis the following general hypothesis can be derived.

---

[16] On this concept, see Stevenson (2011: 173) and Vasquez (1993: 244–245).

7. States that have a prior territorial rivalry are more apt to join an ongoing war than are those which do not. If a state has an alliance that pulls it to join one side and a territorial rivalry that pulls it toward the other, the territorial factor will be paramount, but this will be discounted by an assessment of which side is likely to win.

Opportunity

The idea that an ongoing war provides an opportunity for some action is frequently mentioned in analyses but rarely treated in depth. The major exception is, of course, Most and Starr's (1989: Ch 2) dual concepts of opportunity and willingness. For them spatial and geographical factors can limit interactions and hence the opportunity for conflict. It is this rationale that leads them to emphasize the importance of proximity for permitting conflict in the first place and for borders in spreading it. Thus, actors that are far apart and not major states often cannot have conflict because they have no possibility for it. One of the key notions here is that without this opportunity an action cannot occur. This implies some obstacle that has been removed. Most and Starr look at technology in this way.

It is possible to move beyond their analysis by looking at how ongoing events remove obstacles. What are the main obstacles? There are two. The first obstacle is that the prospect of winning a war is not high (which can be defined as 50% or less, depending on risk propensity). Given this assumption, an opportunity can be said to arise from a significant change (i.e. reduction) in the capability of an opponent. The second obstacle is that the prevailing global political order might prevent the use of war in this particular case.

An ongoing war can remove both these obstacles. The most obvious way is that an ongoing war can reduce the capability of an opponent because it has its hands full and the opening of a new front will split its army. The Italian war against the Ottoman Empire for Tripolitania and Cyrenaica provided such an opportunity for the Balkan League and led them to attack on a different front in the First Balkan War. Nonetheless it must be kept in mind that such ongoing wars are not that common and even when they remove an obstacle and provide an opportunity not all actors seize that opportunity in the short run.

A less obvious way is that an ongoing war can change the prevailing political order by weakening its norms that restrain the use of war as an instrument of change; in fact, the ongoing war may encourage minor states to join the war to seek goals that in the past the political order may have frowned upon. On the basis of the above analysis, the concept of opportunity as a contagion mechanism can be defined as the lifting of two obstacles that previously prevented the use of war: (a) the existing distribution of capability and (b) the norms of the prevailing political order that limit the use of violence to bring about fundamental change. Dyads that have ongoing territorial rivalries are most apt to take advantage of the removal of both obstacles.

Opportunity Due to Changes in a Rival's Power   If your rival has considerably more capability than you then this is an obstacle to pursuing territorial change through the use of force. An ongoing war that involves your rival can produce changes in power that make for a new and often unexpected such opportunity. The First World War once it had started after August 6 was rife with such opportunities. Table 1.5 lists the dyads that that joined the war through this process of contagion due to a change in capability. Japan was the first to take advantage of this sort of opportunity. With a major war going on in Europe, and Germany already faced with two fronts, there was little chance that Germany would be able to deal with Japan's overwhelming local advantage, especially since Germany's naval power was going to be blocked by Japan's British ally.

A second dyad of this ilk was Russia–Ottoman Empire. Given its long-term power disadvantage, Enver Pasha, the Ottoman minister of war, along with other members of the Committee of Union and Progress ruling regime, was looking for a way of improving the Ottoman Empire's long-term prospects. The ongoing war provided more than one, and ultimately he decided that Germany provided the best chance for changing the situation (see Trumpener 2003). A war alliance with Germany would weaken Russia. In addition, the British and French encroachments on the Middle East empire of the Ottomans posed a serious threat. Unlike Japan, however, the decision of which side to join was not obvious, so two considerations entered the Ottoman calculations. The first was to assess the prospect that Germany and the Central Powers would win, and the second was the possibility of conducting an auction and bargaining for the best deal. Bargaining, while important for this dyad, was not as central as the

Table 1.5. *Opportunity through changes in power*

August 23, 1914	Japan	Germany
November 2, 1914	Russia	Ottoman Empire
September 1, 1916	Bulgaria	Romania

reduction of Russian capability due to Russia's fighting both Germany and Austria-Hungary. For this reason the Ottoman dyad is placed in this category rather than the second (below).

Lastly, and more clearly, Bulgaria took advantage of Romania entering the war on the side of the Entente to attack it in its rear to regain Dobrudja. All these examples imply the following hypothesis.

8. When an ongoing war splits a state's army, a rival is more apt to attack if its war will be on a second front. This change in capability, which is a function of the geographical nature of the fighting, lifts an obstacle that had prevented war in the past. The ongoing war provides an opportunity for the new war joiner to fight its own war.

Opportunity Due to the Breakdown in the Political Order   The second obstacle that is removed to make for opportunity is the change in the existing political structure. The Concert of Europe's normative structure made the major states biased against the use of war by minor and at times major states. Even when such wars were conducted and successful, the major states could come together to undo an overwhelming victory, as in the Congress of Berlin in 1878 and in the Sino-Japanese War of 1895. It is hypothesized that in a world war this political order breaks down and the bias switches in the other direction. Major states, instead of restraining minor states and imposing an obstacle to war, now actively recruit minor states to enter the war. This provides a chance (and in some cases an opportunity of a lifetime) for minor states to bring about fundamental territorial change. Contagion occurs because these states are permitted to do what the prevailing normative political order forbade them to do before. The world war becomes a kind of umbrella war that encompasses a number of private or parallel wars.

These minor states are in the most advantageous position when both sides seek their allegiance. However, they do not necessarily go with the best offer, but discount that with the probability of that side winning. A number of decisions to join the ongoing war can be explained by this contagion process. These dyadic war entries are listed in Table 1.6.

Table 1.6. *Opportunity through breakdown of political order*

May 23, 1915	Italy	Austria-Hungary
Oct 14, 1915	Bulgaria	Serbia
Aug 27, 1916	Romania	Austria-Hungary

The Italy–Austria-Hungary dyad provides an excellent example of how bargaining can work in the context of a breakdown of the political order. The decision of what to do was initially pretty much in the hands of San Giuliano, the Italian foreign minister. San Giuliano made the important decision that Italy would be neutral. After his death the main decisions were in the hands of Salandra, the Prime Minister, who was assisted by Sonnino, the new foreign minister (see Hamilton and Herwig, 2003: 376, 382–383).

After San Giuliano had died, Salandra proceeded to look at options and possible bargains for Italy joining the war. From the Triple Alliance he sought compensation on the principle that Austria-Hungary would gain territory from Serbia. Salandra's demands were tough. He wanted not only areas with substantial Italian-speaking populations like Trentino and Alto Adige (Südtirol), but also the strategic naval base of Trieste and then the rest of the Dalmatian coast – demands that also touched upon Serbian interests. Bethmann-Hollweg urged Berchtold to compensate not only because of the importance of Italy on the French front, but also to prevent Austria from having to fight a three-front war. Perhaps victory by the Central Powers would also permit Italy to gain some territory at the expense of France – some colonial territory and perhaps even Corsica, Nice, and Savoy (all of which were part of Italy's ambitions). From the Triple Entente, especially France and Britain, Italy could expect a much greater willingness to bargain away Austro-Hungarian territory, and indeed their offers were much more extensive and came more quickly. The only hesitancy came from Sazonov and the Russians, who were concerned about Serbia's interests.

Italy's bargaining made it clear that which side gave the best offer was not the only consideration in deciding which side to join. Salandra also placed a great deal of emphasis on the proper timing for Italian intervention. He wanted to enter at a time when the Italians were needed the most so they would be able to exact the best bargain, but at the same time they had to avoid entering too late because then they might get nothing. Above all, they had to avoid choosing the side that would lose. Similar problems faced the Ottomans and the other dyads in Tables 1.5 and 1.6. Battlefield outcomes became paramount for this reason. In the end the Italians rushed to enter because they feared that the British–French landing in the Dardanelles would lead Balkan states to join the Allies and then they would be less needed. Russia's losses at this time in 1915 also made the Russians more willing to see Italy enter.[17]

---

[17] On the impact of these battlefield considerations, see Stevenson (2011: 172).

Direct attacks on Italy itself were also a concern. At one point the Germans threatened to attack if Italy left the Triple Alliance (Hamilton and Herwig 2003: 382). More important, however, was the fear of what the British Navy would do to Italy's long coastline, a factor that has been underestimated by analysts. Clearly, the probability of winning, not only for Italy, but for the coalition it would join, was an important part of this contagion process. Italy's entry of course affected the probability of who would win and in this way affected the calculus of the remaining neutral states in the area. Unlike Italy, however, three states – Bulgaria, Romania, and Greece – had severe domestic splits that made their decision difficult. Bulgaria and Romania will be treated in this section and Greece in the next, since it was brought in by a different contagion process.

Bulgaria's rival was primarily Serbia and to a lesser extent Greece and Romania, which had entered the Second Balkan War to take advantage of the pile-on that took place against Bulgaria. Domestic factors were important as the government was split, with the Prime Minister favoring Germany and Austria-Hungary, but with the Tsar less pro-German and other elements pro-Russian. The immediate end result was neutrality, with the leadership bargaining with both sides. A key element in this, as Hall (2003: 397) points out, was what was happening on the battlefield and the probability of who would ultimately win. The Central Powers' greater ability to fully meet Bulgaria's territorial demands pushed the leadership, which was pro-German and Austrian to begin with, toward a decision to side with them. The main theoretical point to keep in mind, however, is that the major states on each side were courting Bulgaria and encouraging it to use violence to gain territory. Contagion occurred because the existing ongoing war produced a breakdown in the political order that removed the normative bias against minor states fighting wars, thereby making an opportunity for Bulgaria to fight its own war within the larger war.

Romania was in a similar situation. The ongoing war was really its only chance of gaining Transylvania, a key part of Hungary. However, Romania had been an ally of Austria-Hungary and Germany for some time. In addition to these alliance obligations, Romania from a power point of view could not take on Austria-Hungary alone. Also, as with Bulgaria, the domestic environment in Romania was split. King Carol was a Hohenzollern. Prime Minister Brătianu, on the other hand, was pro-French, and the ruling National Liberal Party was mostly pro-Entente (Hall 2003). The death of the King in the fall of 1914 left Brătianu and the preferences of the National Liberal Party in control. He began to talk with the Entente, but it would take over a full year until August 1916 before Romania entered on the side of France, Britain, and Russia. The Italian intervention had an impact on the Romanians because they had broken the taboo related to alliance fealty by switching sides in May 1915. Bulgaria also entered the war on the side of the Central Powers in October 1915, which posed a threat to Romania and encouraged her to go toward the Entente.

In early 1916 the Germans tried to break the stalemate on the Western Front by launching a major offensive at Verdun. By June the Entente had threatened not to give Transylvania to Romania, unless she entered immediately, and she did so by August. In the end, things did not go well for Romania. The Central Powers counter-attacked, and with Bulgaria overran Romania and occupied its capital in December 1916.[18] She had chosen the wrong side, but was later able to recoup by returning to the war just before the Armistice.

There are certain common patterns in these three cases. First, all were motivated by territorial rivalries, but these were not easily pursued for one reason or another. For Italy and Romania, their territorial disputes were with a current and important ally which was part of the larger Triple Alliance. In addition, for each of these three states entering the war involved fighting a rival which was more powerful than it in any dyadic contest. Most importantly, however, without the ongoing war the major states would have looked askance at any unilateral territorial grab on their part.

A war of the magnitude of the First World War changed each of these factors. First, the major states wooed each of these other states to join them in return for getting what they wanted. The breakdown of the political order provided a new normative context that would not only allow these states to pursue their territorial ambitions, but also help them to do so by gaining new powerful military allies. In some cases, as with Bulgaria, this meant a joint invasion of a rival. In each of the cases – for Italy, Romania, and even Bulgaria – there was a switching of sides. Second, the wooing of these neutral states permitted them to in effect conduct an auction for their allegiance. Third, and lastly, a vital factor along with promises of territorial gains was an assessment of the probability that the side they joined would actually win. All in all, these factors made the contagion process that brought these dyads to the war different from the other processes that made the war spread. This gives rise to the following lessons and hypothesis.

For minor states an ongoing war among the major states lifts a key obstacle preventing them from going to war with their neighbors with

---

[18] For more details on these events see Hall (2003: 405).

which they have territorial disputes – the bias of the major-states' political order against war. The breakdown of the prevailing political order encouraged war to spread to minor states by each side offering them territorial incentives, which in turn permitted them to conduct an auction for their entry. For many of these nationalist leaders this was an opportunity of a lifetime that was unlikely to come again soon.

9. Ongoing war among the major states increases the probability that minor states will join the war because it leads to a breakdown of the political order and a lifting of the prohibition on the use of war to bring about large-scale territorial change among minor states.

Contagion through Economic Dependence

Economic factors always play a role in decisions about going to war.[19] The focus here is not so much on the role of economic factors in bringing about war or their effect on foreign policy decisions generally, but upon the role economic dependence plays in the spread of war specifically. What is of theoretical interest is those cases where a country enters the war after it has started because of some economic activity *associated with the ongoing war.* This is what is meant by contagion.

Trade with one or more belligerents is seen as the most important economic factor associated with war bringing in a new party. Trade is important causally because it can affect the outcome of the war, by giving one side a relative advantage. Political science research has shown that a significant predictor of victory is state revenue (Rosen 1972) and access to credit (Rasler and Thompson 1983). In other words, the side that has more money at its disposal tends to win. Trade on credit can become an important advantage and have a large impact on the outcome of the war. Belligerents realize this, and try to weaken their opponents by reducing their ability to gain war material or feed their population.

When trade begins to make a difference, two factors come into play that can make for contagion. The first is that the opponent of the side that is benefiting from the trade begins to think that it might win the war if it can stop or interrupt the trade so as to "starve" out the other. In this sense the benefiting side is seen as economically dependent on the trade, and the opponent directly attacks or blockades the trading partner. Such a decision must also involve a calculation of whether stopping the trade is worth adding a new belligerent. The second factor

---

[19] On the role of economics in war onset, including the First World War, see Copeland (2014a).

is that the trading state may become so economically invested in trading with a given belligerent that it cannot afford it to lose, and hence may intervene without being attacked to help save the day. This situation is particularly likely when trade is based on extensive credit.

The term "economic dependence" is used to cover both these situations in which one or both sides are economically dependent on the trade either positively, as in the provider, or negatively, as in the belligerent which is hurt by it. Belligerents that benefit from the trade are also dependent on the trade. It is this set of economic relations during the ongoing war that draws in the neutral trading state.[20]

Within the First World War evidence for both these logics can be seen as being played out, but mostly with just the U.S.–Germany dyad. These general factors related to relative gains were also mixed with the specific normative concerns of Wilson and the military contingencies of the exhaustion produced by the stalemated Western Front.

The normative concerns had to do with the American insistence, led by Woodrow Wilson and widely supported in Congress and among the public, on the rights of neutrals under international law to trade with belligerents. While the U.S. insisted on the rights of its companies to trade with any country, trade with Britain was more extensive. Germany hoped to limit that trade by the use of U-boats. Such a technique was condemned as morally outrageous; it was, however, an effective tool. The sinking of the Lusitania in 1915 and then the Sussex about ten months later brought the issue to a head. Germany relented, and agreed in 1916 to halt such attacks.

American trade began to make a difference as France and then Britain ran short of funds and extensive credits were used to pay for U.S. goods. The German Imperial War Council in 1917 felt that, if they could cripple the flow of supplies, Germany would be able to turn the tide. They took a calculated risk that they could do this before the U.S. could intervene with troops. This turned out to be a mistake.

Theoretically, U.S. intervention can be explained as resulting from contagion by economic dependence. Extensive trade with the U.S. was an important lifeline to the Entente, and Germany attacked to sever it. This material link was coupled with the moral outrage Wilson felt and could use regarding unrestricted submarine warfare. This outrage was accentuated because the 1917 actions meant a breaking of the earlier

---

[20] I use this concept mostly to dissect the economic relations between the U.S. and the belligerents, examining both U.S. trade with the Entente and the reaction of Germany to it. Later in the study I look at economic dependence slightly more broadly in the case of Brazil and in the case of British economic warfare toward Germany involving the neutrals in 1916–1917.

1916 agreement after the sinking of the Lusitania and the Sussex. Counterfactual reasoning suggests that the direct German attack brought about the war entry, since, even if there had been no normative taboos about the submarine warfare, the U.S. would have responded.

The physical attacks were the main factor and not so much that the U.S. had a vested interest in the Allies not losing since it had extended so much credit. Once they had been attacked, this was no longer a factor. Wilson was aware of the vested interest, but it did not motivate him to enter on the side of the Entente; if anything, he thought of using it to get the Entente to accept his mediation. What does seem to have been an additional factor for Wilson was that he wanted to intervene to get a seat at the Peace table. Stevenson (2011: 175) mentions this as does Cooper (2003: 439) indirectly. The main thing to remember, however, is that it was the German decision to attack that brought about U.S. entry and not any initiative on Wilson's part (Table 1.7).

Several things can be concluded about the role of economic dependence. First, being attacked by a belligerent which is being hurt by trade is a more likely path to war joining than the trading state entering the war to protect its economic investment. Certainly, the latter would be more difficult to justify domestically. Second, economic dependence makes war spread because an economic relationship, typically trade (and especially trade based on credit), gives one side an advantage in fighting the war. The disadvantaged side tries to end that by attacking. Third, the decision by one side to spread the war is associated with a strategic calculation about whether changing the dominant economic relationship is worth bringing another adversary into the fighting. Lastly, economic dependence brings in countries that do not have sufficient grievances to bring them in at the beginning. The main hypothesis on economic dependence is as follows.

10. Unbalanced trade that is affecting the war increases the probability that the belligerent being hurt by that trade will attack the neutral and thereby expand the war, *ceteris paribus*.[21]

Table 1.7. *Contagion through economic dependence*

April 6, 1917	United States	Germany

---

[21] This assumes the strategic calculation that cutting the trade will offset the disadvantage of adding a new enemy.

Table 1.8. *Contagion through brute force*

June 27, 1917	Greece	Austria-Hungary, Germany, Bulgaria

Contagion through Brute Force

What is remarkable about all the dyads discussed to this point is that, while threat was used to keep states neutral and incentives were used to get them to come in, what was not used in most states was outright brute force to make them join. Most states were not all, however. The last European case – Greece – reflected the use of outright brute force to bring a state into the war (Table 1.8).

Greece had clear territorial ambitions, but was severely divided in its loyalties. Of paramount importance was that it had just fought two wars and had not fully recovered. King Constantine was the brother-in-law of Kaiser Wilhelm. Prime Minister Venizelos, like many in Greece, was pro-English. Unlike in the cases of Italy, Romania, and Bulgaria, the domestic split prevented Greece from engaging in any serious cross-bloc bargaining because no one was fully in control to commit the state. This resulted in neutrality until late in the war. When Serbia was over-run, Bulgaria was left in control of some of the territory Greece had wanted, and its Northern border was exposed. This resulted in Greece giving permission to an Entente landing at Salonika. This military situation led in August 1916 to a coup by those in the army favoring the Entente, and parts of the Greek army took over Salonika. Venizelos knew about the coup and set up a government there, which was opposed by the legitimate government headed by King Constantine in Athens. In December 1916 the British and French landed troops in Athens to topple the legitimate government, but withdrew taking losses. In June 1917 they issued an ultimatum for the King to abdicate, and, faced with a tremendous force, he did so. On June 17, 1917, Greece entered the war against the Central Powers. The Entente had coerced the last key European state to join the war as the interstate war brought civil war to Greece.

The Greek case illustrates three points about contagion. The first is that when the Entente Powers were pushed to the wall – with the defeat of Serbia and the stalemate on the Western Front – they were more prepared to use outright brute force against the remaining neutrals. Second, the war itself encouraged civil war. The tensions of the external war helped aggravate the divisions within the society. In turn, however, the severe split in the domestic society encouraged external intervention. Without the partial coup d'état and the inability of Venizelos or the King to control the entire country geographically, it was unlikely that the Entente would have resorted to armed intervention. Third, both the external use of force and the onset of civil war reflected a further breakdown of the political order. The coup was spurred on by the presence of foreign troops in the state and then they intervened to bring the civil war to a head. Normatively, the political order looks askance at such blatant interference in the domestic affairs of a sovereign state. The pressures of fighting the war overrode this normative prohibition.[22]

Generally, it can be inferred that contagion through brute force is associated with pressing nearby battlefield contingencies, severe internal conflict leading to civil war, and the inability of one side to domestically control the entire country. The battlefield conditions in Serbia were important motivations for the Entente's interventions in Greece, and the interstate war affected the stability of Greece. Since war entry through brute force affected only two dyads in the First World War (if one includes Russia), it should be expected to affect only a few in other situations. More typically, dyads join an ongoing war through the other processes delineated and through their own free will. Nonetheless the following hypothesis is warranted.

11. Ongoing world war increases the probability of civil war and can result in intervention by major states to compel a state to enter on their side if there are nearby pressing battlefield conditions and the domestic polity is split.

Reflections on Contagion

We are now in a position to describe and explain how contagion worked in the First World War after a preliminary review. There are six processes, each of which is distinctly different and brings in a different set of dyads. These processes have not been clearly identified before, and delineating them provides more detail about how and why the war spread, and in turn how contagion works generally to spread war.

As has long been known, alliances are a crucial diffusion mechanism. They made the war diffuse rapidly and hierarchically. What has not been understood is that there are two different contagion processes underlying the way alliances spread the war. The first way is that they provided an underlying structure of commitment that shaped the playing of a coercive game, and when that game failed almost all of the allies

[22] The 1917 Allied intervention in Russia is similar to the Greek case.

lived up to their commitments and went to war. This contagion process brought in the major states that made threats that they would go to war if the other side persisted in its demands. These dyads are listed in Table 1.1. A theoretical implication of this analysis is that it is not the alliance structure itself that directly brings about contagion, but the failure of the coercive game. Alliances play an indirect but essential role.

They played an essential role in that without the alliance ties the war would not have diffused the way it did.[23] The alliance system provided an underlying structure that made for hierarchical diffusion. In fact, the First World War represents hierarchical diffusion *par excellence*. In addition, once the alliances had tightened, in that each side confirmed its commitment in the July crisis, the alliances seemed to have made each side more resolved and less willing to back down, which in turn led to the failure of the coercion game. Alliances also provided an important causal role in that they identified which states were on which side. This in turn had an impact on how contiguity made the war spread, especially by determining which states were "in the way."

While alliances brought about the spread of the local war to the initial major-state belligerents, at the same time alliances brought about a further spread of the war through a second contagion process. This process affected the dyads that mostly joined the war later in August. They are listed in Table 1.2 and consisted of dyads that had no real grievance with each other and were not rivals. They came to the war almost entirely because their allies had gone to war. The enemy of their ally became their enemy. For this reason alliances are seen as following a contagion process brought about by "valence balancing." Valence balancing occurred only after the war had started because others had grievances that led to the war in the first place. This implies that grievances are more important than alliances.

A second set of contagion processes is associated with contiguity. The most basic manner in which contiguity makes war contagious is that some state is "in the way." Belgium was the classic example. Neighbors, especially small neutral neighbors between major states, are often attacked so one major state can get at the other.

However, alliances play a role in identifying which contiguous states are "in the way." Belgium was attacked only because France was allied to Russia. The tendency of states to make alliance commitments in a checkerboard pattern so that their opponents will be more likely to back

---

[23] Levy (2007) labels something that is a pre-requisite for a war to occur a "necessary condition" for the particular case. The system of alliances in 1914 would be such a necessary condition.

down in a coercive game shows how alliances affect how contiguity makes war contagious. In this role alliances are more important causally than mere contiguity. Checkerboard patterns also pinpoint when contiguity is more dangerous. Put another way, the presence of checkerboard alliances shifts contiguity from being a constant to becoming a variable, thereby giving it more of an impact.

Lastly, a way in which contiguity plays a role in bringing about war in its own right is that the proximity of a powerful land army leads to a time pressure to attack first or pre-empt. This activates military leaders, and can increase their influence in decision-making. This sort of time pressure can also prematurely foreclose peace proposals, which it did in the last week of July 1914.

A third contagion process is the presence of territorial rivalries between states. These states are brought into the war because of their long-standing territorial disputes. Grievances are always a key reason for resorting to war. States with territorial rivalries are primed for war, but for one reason or another may not be ready for a dyadic war. The ongoing war removes an obstacle that has prevented these states from going to war up to this point. One of the theoretically interesting things about world wars is that they serve as umbrella wars that permit other states to fight their own or parallel wars. World war thereby provides an opportunity for war, which is the fourth contagion process.

Opportunity occurs by definition when an obstacle has been lifted. The two main obstacles that are lifted for non-belligerents in an ongoing war are the existing distribution of power and the major states' normative prohibition on the use of violence, especially by minor states, to change fundamentally the status quo. An ongoing war makes a state vulnerable to attack on another front, so this encourages third-party intervention, particularly by those with territorial rivalries. Likewise, minor states that in the past might have avoided a resort to war may find the ongoing war a once-in-a-lifetime opportunity to gain major-state support, indeed encouragement and aid. In the First World War this was an essential path to war for East European states. War that spreads because of the opportunity provided by the ongoing war often permits smaller states to auction off their support. In doing so, an assessment of who is likely to win, as well as what each side will give, is an important part of the calculus.

There has been much reference to opportunity in the historical and political science literature. Commentators often refer to the opportunity provided to one state or another.[24] However, little attention is given to

---

[24] See for example Hall (2003: 399, 404).

how opportunities might differ and what precisely makes something an opportunity causally. This analysis spells out the differences and shows how opportunity is connected causally with territorial rivalry to promote contagion.

Economic dependence is also a key contagion process. This mostly occurs when the trade of a neutral state begins to make a difference in the ongoing war. The economic dependence of a belligerent on the resources supplied by the neutral trading state poses a danger that the neutral might be drawn into the war. This most likely occurs when the belligerent hurt by that trade tries to end it, either through a blockade or by a direct attack on shipping. There is also a possibility that the neutral might intervene to protect its sunk costs with its trading state. This is less likely, but not impossible. German decision-makers decided on unrestricted submarine warfare against the U.S. in January 1917 knowing it would probably produce American intervention, but thought ceasing the cross-Atlantic trade would bring Britain to its knees before the U.S. could make a difference. Dyads brought to war because of economic dependence are not likely to have fought a war with each other, but come to war because of the ongoing war itself. Because belligerents and neutrals are risk-averse, economic dependence does not produce war joining until the war has dragged on.

All of the above contagion processes involve states joining an ongoing war through their own decisions. Some states, however, join because of armed intervention and brute force. These states have been unable to decide whether to enter and on which side, typically because of severe domestic splits. These states tend to have weak governments in that they are unstable and no one faction is able to make a definitive decision for the entire polity. There is then not only a breakdown in the external political order that removes normative obstacles against external armed intervention, but also a breakdown of the internal political order that results in civil war. The use of brute force to make states join the war is comparatively rare, although it does occur, and it tends to come late, as sides become desperate for additional allies.

The six processes identified in this study provide a deeper and more precise understanding of how the First World War spread. These insights have been systematized at the end of each section into a set of hypotheses that can be explored in more detail for each dyad that entered the war as well as in other cases in the past and the future. In Part II we will turn to a detailed empirical examination of each of the key dyads that entered the war to see what further insights can be learned about war contagion and how these six contagion processes worked in specific historical cases and why. These additional lessons will be used at the end of the study to further assess the six models presented here. Before doing so, Chapter 2 presents the research design of the book, including a review of how the data presented in Part II were collected

2   Research Design

Basic Question

This book is somewhat unusual in that, while it is informed by a mostly positivist philosophy of science and it will use data to inform its inferences, it does not test hypotheses per se. Instead, it is a qualitative study that tries to derive new hypotheses from an exemplar case. Eckstein (1975) justifies the study of a single case if it is a *crucial* case. This is similar in that the First World War can be seen as the exemplary case of contagion. The study thus works within the realm of the logic of discovery rather than the logic of confirmation, as noted in the Introduction. This makes the research design different from those where the main purpose is hypothesis testing. The chapter will begin by looking at the logic of discovery and outlining what kind of research design should guide its inquiry and how this kind of research design is justified – dealing with issues of case selection, how the research will be conducted, and so forth. It will then turn to why a case-study approach was used rather than an aggregate large-N study. Next the unit of analysis of the study – the dyad – will be explained and justified. The chapter will conclude with a review of what data have been compiled, what measures are used, and how to read the histograms that appear in the middle of the book. The appendix lists the questions that will guide the case research.

A Research Design for the Logic of Discovery

The field of IR has been generally loose about where theory comes from. There has been a certain *deus ex machina* to it, saying that it comes from genius or "hard thinking." Generally, what this means is that there are few rules or guides to discovering relationships and patterns. Traditionalists, of course, always wrote books trying to "discover" patterns, even laws, but they have often been set aside as having no method at all. Can a method be established for creating theory and a

45

body of hypotheses about a subject where little is known, even though there may be many opinions about it? The conventional answer to this question in philosophy of science is induction.

J. David Singer (1969) was a great advocate of induction as a solution to a field dominated by theory uninformed by empirical investigation. Induction as a strategy has received a great deal of attention within philosophy of science, and it has generally been thought that a logical basis for it leading to knowledge cannot be established (see Carnap 1962). Nonetheless, that does not mean that the investigation of "facts" cannot be informative and that observation is not vital to understanding and theory construction. Indeed, we can think of a research design for the logic of discovery as really a set of guidelines for theory construction, and that is what this book is all about.

In a previous study (Vasquez, 1993) I tried to make sense of the disparate and sometimes contradictory findings of the Correlates of War project and related quantitative studies by carefully sifting through them and coming up with a set of propositions to produce a coherent explanation of the onset of war. This was primarily an exercise in the logic of discovery rather than a meta-analysis. What was being observed were statistical studies over a thirty-year-plus period and what was being derived was a set of testable propositions, many of which had to be further tested before they could be accepted or be said to have been "confirmed" (or more technically failed to be falsified – see Popper 1959). In my next major book (Senese and Vasquez 2008) these propositions and the steps-to-war explanation were tested on the basis of the logic of confirmation.

This book is similar except that, instead of reviewing a large number of statistical studies, I am examining a specific case in depth to see how contagion worked. Two questions arise from such a choice – how should one pick the case and can anything be generalized from a single case? These are classic questions, and they have been addressed by many scholars, especially within comparative politics, and before that within experimental research (see Eckstein 1975; George 1979; Geddes 1990; Campbell and Stanley 1963). Each question will be treated in the next section. Before doing so, some other questions about induction need to be addressed.

One common criticism of induction is that it cannot be done without some pre-existing theory. More harshly, post-modernists sometimes argue that there is no reality and therefore nothing to be "discovered" – all reality is a construction. Some go so far as to say things cannot be tested because "what is taken to be the 'world'" is actually constructed by theory and therefore not independent evidence (Hawkesworth 1992: 16–17). I have dealt with these issues systematically elsewhere, so I will not repeat my responses here. Suffice it to say that many who do empirical work do not accept this stance. They assume that there is something separate from their own theory and beliefs that can be observed to evaluate the former. This is not to deny that concepts play a role in permitting us to see things. After Freud we saw things we did not see before. Still, the world is not so fungible that we cannot assess theories and explanations through observation of the world.

Having said that does not mean that it is either possible or desirable to create an explanation or a theory without some pre-theoretical hunches as Rosenau (1966) used to say. These have already been outlined in Chapter 1. The logic here is to take those pre-theoretical hunches, namely the six models of contagion, and use them to study a case of contagion to see what can be learned about the models. I engage in what George and Bennett (2005: xi) call analytic induction as opposed to raw empiricism. To do that, though, one must pick a good case.

Case Selection

What are the requirements of a good case on which to build knowledge or "discover" patterns? First, the case should clearly represent the phenomenon under study. Since this book is about war contagion, we want a case that is likely to embody it in its classic form – i.e. one that would be typical of other instances of war contagion. The purpose of studying the case is to learn how contagion actually worked in this instance so that generalizations to other instances can be made. The First World War fits this criterion in that it is one of the premier cases of a war that spread first within Europe and then across the globe, and one that eventually encompassed all the major states in existence. If one wants to learn about contagion in war, then studying in depth what in effect is an exemplar of war contagion is an obvious choice.

Will it be representative of other cases, though? This is not known. One way to insure that is to identify the population wherein war contagion takes place and take a random sample. By definition war contagion is the spreading of war, so the population would be all multiparty wars. The process by which wars spread, however, could in principle differ depending on the size of the war. This is most likely with smaller wars, those with fewer than four parties, since we know that those are more frequent than those with four or more (see Richardson 1960: 248–249 and Vasquez and Valeriano 2010: 296). It could also be true that the wars that spread the most – the world wars – have the most contagion processes at work or unique ones. These questions cannot be known before the fact, but analyzing a random sample of the population would be a way to solve the problem. Still, there is a difference between a population of all multiparty wars and just world wars. In this study I have opted to look at war contagion in the most extensive cases – the world wars – in the belief that these will contain the most varied and full set of contagion processes and that at least a good portion of these will be represented in wars that spread to a lesser extent. Put another way, the assumption is that smaller multiparty wars will not have contagion processes that are not present in a world war, but one cannot know that *ex ante*. Nonetheless, a single study cannot do everything and, if a choice has to be made, then the world war is likely to be more informative. Of course, science is a collective enterprise, and what is not done here can be supplemented in other studies.

Levy (1983: 75, Table 3.2) has listed what most consider the population of world wars, or general wars as he calls them, from 1648 on.[1] These are the Thirty Years' War, the Dutch War of Louis XIV, the War of the League of Augsburg, the War of the Spanish Succession, the War of the Austrian Succession, the Seven Years' War, the French Revolutionary and Napoleonic Wars, the First World War, and the Second World War. Levy (1983: 27) defines general war "as [that] involving nearly all the great powers and resulting in high levels of destruction." Since all I add is that such wars include "major states in a struggle to resolve the most fundamental issues on the global agenda," his list is suitable for me.

The list, however, has limits in terms of drawing a random sample. The main one is that, since I want to include a number of quantitative indicators about the states that might join an ongoing war, only two wars meet this criterion, since the Correlates of War data go back only to 1816. This obviates the possibility of any truly random sample.

The reason why I selected the First World War over the Second was somewhat idiographic, but the former has advantages over the latter. The First World War is of idiographic interest at this time because it is the hundredth anniversary of the war. Elsewhere, I have done theoretical case studies of the Second World War to probe the adequacy of the steps-to-war explanation of world war onset (see Vasquez 1996a, Vasquez and Gibler 2001). These were more in the realm of the logic of confirmation rather than the logic of discovery. The First World War is a better case for study because it has a much richer literature and,

---

[1] We have no systematic data before 1648.

with a hundred years having elapsed, it is just emerging from the more normative concerns and playing of the "blame game" (Clark 2012: 560) that still plague the scholarship on the Second World War. It is just easier to be more objective about the First World War than the Second, in part because we still live in the shadow of the latter. Lastly, from an analytical point of view the First World War is a more complicated case theoretically. It has spurred more debate and its document collection, which continues to grow (see Lieven 2015: 3–4), has been more carefully sifted and analyzed. All of these were reasons for which I selected this case rather than one of the others. The end result, however, is that we have no *ex ante* assurances that the patterns observed from this war and the hypotheses derived from them are generalizable to other cases of war. That is a topic for the logic of confirmation; all I can say is that I think the assumption that it is generalizable is reasonable. Even if it turns out that it is not, a study of why the First World War spread is of intrinsic interest, especially at this time.

Why the First World War was selected is the main issue that needed to be addressed in this chapter, but an important secondary issue is how to select the dyads that made up the First World War. There are two different criteria that could be used – those states which entered the war legally through a **declaration of war** or those that fought at a certain level that met a pre-determined **threshold** for participation. Data are available on both. The declaration-of-war criterion will be the primary one used because it is highly reliable and casts a wider net. At the time the norm of declaring wars was accepted and major and minor states respected that. Two sources will be used – Goldstein (1992: Appendix A) and Stearns and Langer (2001: 650). Both list declarations dyadically. Nonetheless, many of the declarations were nominal and did not result in a heavy involvement. For this reason the second criterion is also employed. The Correlates of War project has clear operational rules that establish *ex post facto* a threshold for participation in multiparty wars. To be a war in the first place there must be 1,000 battle deaths between the main belligerents. The category of battle deaths is confined to uniformed military personnel. To be a participant in a multiparty war, an actor must have either 100 battle deaths or at least 1,000 armed personnel engaged in active combat (Sarkees and Wayman 2010: 53).

The Correlates of War threshold will be used in deciding what dyads will be given more attention in the narratives. In addition, dyads that have narratives where one party does not meet the threshold will have that noted. These are few in number, but are included for theoretical and historical reasons for possible insights they provide and also to indicate the global reach of the war. Such countries include China and Siam, which did not see combat with Germany and Austria-Hungary, though they declared war. Brazil is also briefly discussed – it engaged Germany in naval actions, but does not meet the threshold. Most of the dyads that do not meet the threshold are the Latin American states and Liberia that entered in 1917–18 after the U.S. Also, as would be expected, some of the cases of valence balancing do not make the threshold either.

Table I.1 in the Introduction lists the case studies in this book. These include all main states that declared war. The dyads that declared war, but do not have a case study devoted to them, are considered miscellaneous cases and are listed in Chapter 5 in Table 5.1. Since the latter do not have narratives or histograms with their MIDs, their MIDs are listed in the table to give the reader some idea of their conflict with the other side.

Table 2.1 lists the participants and the side on which they fought according to the Correlates of War project. One problem with this list is that a dyadic configuration of the participants would result in some pairs that never actually fought each other or even declared war on one another, such as Japan–Bulgaria and Belgium–Bulgaria. Such pairs are not included in this study. In many data analyses that look at escalation of dyadic MIDs to war such pairs are dropped according to Maoz's dyadic MID dataset (http://vanity.dss.ucdavis.edu/~maoz/dyadmid.html) (see for instance Senese and Vasquez 2008: 61–62).

Conducting the Case Studies: The Narratives

The development of qualitative methods as a subfield has prompted much discussion on how to make case studies more rigorous, particularly in the selection of cases. Since these are rarely selected randomly, attention has been paid to how generalizations can be made by taking pains to make sure the sample is at least representative. Thus, from Alexander George (1979) on to George and Bennett (2005), Gerring (2007), and Bennett and Checkel (2015), there has been an emphasis on structured focused comparative case studies and selection of cases in terms

Table 2.1. *States making the Correlates of War threshold for the First World War*

Participants: Russia, Greece, United States, United Kingdom, Belgium, France, Portugal, Serbia, Romania, Japan, Italy vs.
Germany, Austria-Hungary, Bulgaria, Ottoman Empire

Source: Sarkees and Wayman (2010: 121)

of John Stuart Mill's (1843) *A System of Logic* method of agreement and method of difference (George and Bennett 2005: 153) or most similar and most different designs. These often reflect concerns that have some conformity with the logic of confirmation, even though the contribution is often at the level of the logic of discovery and hypothesis generating rather than hypothesis testing. Many of these criteria are not applicable here because this is a single-case study and not one that compares several cases. Still, the many dyads that make up the study can be compared in terms of similarities and differences in light of some of the criteria outlined by George and Bennett (2005: Ch. 3). However, since these dyadic cases were not pre-selected on this rationale, a better example of what is being done is the earlier study of George and Smoke (1974) (see also George and Bennett 2005: 321–325).

What I have found most useful is the advice on how to conduct process tracing within a case (see Bennett and Checkel 2015: 5–6). George and Bennett (2005: 7, 209) explicitly mention this as a strategy to generate hypotheses through induction. Process tracing involves making inferences about what events or factors brought about a particular outcome in a given instance (in the manner that was hypothesized). Specifically, in the cases I look at each of the major decisions leaders took, what led them to make those decisions, and the impact of those decisions on future decisions. In each case I re-trace the decisions and interactions that may have led to the outcome (George and Bennett 2005: 207), often with the steps-to-war explanation as a guide.

Process tracing can be used either for the development of general explanations or to provide an historical explanation of a particular case. George and Bennett (2005: Ch.7) give some specific rules for this with regard to historical explanation. In my study I am interested in seeing how and why a given dyad entered the First World War. As with others using this technique to develop general explanations, I look to see whether particular causal processes are present or not (Goertz 2017: 194). I note these in the narratives and later formally mark them in a table (see Tables 7.1 and 7.2 in the concluding chapter).

I also use the advances in qualitative methods (see Goertz 2017 most recently) to provide me with some guidance on how case studies that use narratives can be made more rigorous. The most obvious approach is to lay out a set of questions that will be investigated beforehand and rules for addressing them. The two most fundamental questions that I ask for each dyad are why it went to war and what contagion process played a role in bringing it to war. A decision-making approach is used in that the answers to the above questions are sought in terms of how and why actors made the decision to enter the war and how the decisions of other actors affected this deliberation, as well as the impact of domestic politics. This is accomplished by attempting to reconstruct the events by an examination of the historical record. This tack is taken rather than looking primarily at structural factors.[2]

To construct these narratives I rely on historians' accounts, which are extensive and have been part of a continual discussion and debate (see Trachtenberg 2017 in the recent H-Diplo symposium). This study, then, is not a product of original archival work, but based on the rich secondary sources that have used archives. The narratives do not seek to provide new "facts" about the cases, but build on a consensus about what happened to address certain theoretical questions. The latter makes this a work of political science rather than history. The contribution is not in elaborating the historical record, but in the application of new concepts and a theoretical framework for explaining aspects of that record. It is also not a contribution to the field of history proper, because I am seeking to derive hypotheses that will be applicable to other instances of contagion. I examine each dyad with an eye on separating what is generalizable and what is unique to the case. In each case I focus on (and limit myself to) what brought about contagion or the spread of the war, rather than trying to reconstruct the historical record and analyze all the factors that produced that record.

The theoretical questions that are asked come from the six models that were presented in the previous chapter. These are pre-theoretical expectations I had on the basis of my general knowledge of the First World War, but before the systemic study of each dyad. These models provide a guide for examining each case in that they tell me to look for certain things and report whether and how they occur. Thus, I looked for alliances – why they were made and whether and how they affected decisions. I looked to see whether the ongoing war provided an opportunity and what that meant in terms of changes in capability and the breakdown of the political order. I examined how third parties affected dyadic relations. Likewise, I looked at grievances that states had and whether their current decision-makers pursued them in this instance, and so on and so forth. A complete list of the questions that I asked systematically is given in the appendix to this chapter.

---

[2] For an historical analysis of structural factors in the First World War, see Joll (1984). The earliest data-based political science analysis on the First World War was the 1914 project or "Stanford Studies" directed by Robert C. North. For the project's statistical analysis of structural factors in the First World War, see Choucri and North (1975). For the project's analysis of the role of perceptions in decision-making see Holsti (1972).

Theory (broadly defined) guided my inquiry, but I made sure not to see just what I was looking for, and I took pains not to be Procrustean. The latter actually turned out not to be much of a problem, somewhat to my surprise. In the end, I found with some ease that certain factors like alliances were important in certain dyads and not in others. An unexpected finding was that there was a temporal sequence to these factors or contagion processes.

In writing the narratives a number of new factors came to light that seemed to repeat themselves. I found that certain states entered the war because of a strong leader. I found that others were plagued by divided government. Battlefield conditions played a more important role than I expected. As these factors came to light I added them to my list of questions and went back to investigate them. The organization of the narratives varies depending on whether these factors were present; however, all the narratives had certain common sections for the sake of comparative analysis. For instance, all the narratives had a section on why and how the leaders decided to go to war, and I ended each narrative with a theoretical analysis highlighting why contagion occurred in this instance. Lastly, some cases had instances that represented anomalies for IR theory in general, and in two of the cases this was so significant I included a discussion of it. These were the implications for the bargaining theory of war of Belgian resistance to Germany and the implications for the concept of the national interest posed by the split in the British Cabinet in 1914.

The main point of the narratives is to derive a set of generalizations from that particular case. The cross-case generalizations are reserved for the concluding chapter. Here I use the results of the dyadic process tracing to reach some conclusions about the key contagion processes and how they interact. I also look at what the dyadic case studies might tell us about causal mechanisms. Goertz (2017: 49) argues that one of the central purposes of process tracing is to investigate causal mechanisms. In the concluding chapter I reflect on the dyadic case studies in terms of what they imply about the underlying causal mechanisms that produced the patterns uncovered in the study. Such a procedure is the hallmark of the inductive method – going from the particular to the general. From a research design perspective the case studies are completed only in the concluding chapter when they are used to make cross-case inferences. That it is the culmination of induction is indicated by the chapter title: How Contagion Actually Worked. All of this was part of the initial research design plan.

In order to avoid being trapped by too much of a focus on what people said and did, I always examined the data that I have compiled to see where the data reinforced or undercut certain inferences. The way in which I tried to use the data can be seen from a set of questions I laid out before the research was conducted (see the appendix to this chapter). These data are often interpreted as background or contextual factors providing a structure within which decisions are made and policy is formulated. From certain theoretical perspectives they may be seen as the real causal factors that brought about the war. Here, however, I just wanted to include them in the case study to see what they would tell us. The data and why they are utilized will be discussed below, but suffice it to say for now that they are derived from the steps-to-war explanation as to what is important in bringing about decisions to go to war in general (see Senese and Vasquez 2008).

Data are provided to see what pattern of MIDs the dyad had both before and after the war. These are presented in the colored histograms in the middle of the book. These histograms provide a snapshot of the conflictive interactions of the two parties – in reality an overview of their relationship and the level of hostility it exhibited over time. Data on territorial claims are also reported because the steps-to-war explanation posits that territorial grievances are a key variable in bringing about war. The alliances of each side are examined to see who their allies are. Data on whether they are rivals is provided in terms of three measures – Diehl and Goertz (2000), Thompson (2001), and Senese and Vasquez (2008). The dominant issue as well as whether they have at least 25% of their disputes with each other is listed. Finally, whether the dyad was engaged in an arms race during a MID that escalated to war is listed in the histogram, with others in a text box.

The data are provided in text boxes within the narrative for easy reference, but they are also integrated into the narrative to see how they might reinforce (or undercut) certain interpretations. From a research design perspective the data present variables that have been found to play a statistically significant role in war onset. Their inclusion here is a way of seeing whether that holds for war contagion as well.

What needs to be kept in mind is that these data are of the highest caliber. They are well-known data of the Correlates of War project that meet the most rigorous standards of replicability and transparency. The data not directly associated with the Correlates of War project have been inspired by it, like the data of the ICOW, Susan Sample's arms race data, and the rivalry data of Diehl and Goertz and of Thompson (see the section below on data sources). The incorporation of such scientific data in a case study of the First World War is fairly unique.

A Study of Variance

Any quantitative study can be of two sorts – one that seeks to account for most of the variance of the dependent variable, Y, or one that tests a theoretical explanation that specifies that in the presence of one or more independent variables, X, the probability of Y will go up. The former wants to understand all the factors associated with a given phenomenon, while the latter wants to test whether particular variables are a sufficient condition for the phenomenon. This study is of the former type. It wants to understand why and how contagion works. By their very nature, studies that seek to maximize the amount of variance for which they can account have multiple variables or even models that they examine. That is the case here. Six models were adduced before systematic research was undertaken and then a seventh – Imperialism/ Hegemony – was added as a result of the empirical examination.

Having multiple independent variables is not a problem so long as there is a reasonable limit and the number does not result in a kitchen-sink theory (see also Achen 2002 and Ray 2003). The number of variables here is limited to seven. The complexity of the subject as well as its rarity makes this a reasonable number. Also, as will be seen, the applicability of the variables and models varies with the time period in which dyads enter – first, second, or third wave – which strongly suggests a temporal sequence. Focusing on trying to account for the factors that increase the probability of the dependent variable also permits an examination of the role of necessary conditions (see Goertz 2017: 115–116). Opportunity is an important necessary condition in this analysis. Examining the dependent variable and trying to identify all the major factors that produce it is a way of dealing with the problem of equifinality that George and Bennett (2005: 161–162) point out. The models here in many ways can be seen as various paths to contagion. The extent to which they may actually build upon one another is discussed in the concluding chapter.

Why Not a Large-N Study?

A natural question is whether a large-N study would not have been better to get at the question of contagion. In particular, it might have been better to conceptualize the contagion process in terms of network analyses and describe its characteristics using that method. My response to that question is to do both, but not in the same book per se. Elsewhere, I am involved in a team project – the ConflictSpace project (Flint *et al.* 2009) – that has been conducting a series of statistical studies on the spread of the First World War using network analysis. Vasquez *et al.* (2011)

used network analysis to predict whether countries would enter the First World War on the basis of the changing network density from 1900 on in alliances, rivalries, and territorial disputes. A network analysis of alliances with specified targets helped elucidate how alliances spread the war. Chi *et al.* (2014) went beyond this study and successfully predicted not only which states would enter the war, but when (see also Radil *et al.* 2013). These studies do not necessarily contradict this one, and at times I interpret or explain some of the patterns identified here in terms of a network. Network analysis has two limitations that make a study like this desirable. The first and more important one is that it cannot get at the decision-making involved, let alone the nuances of those decisions. It is by its very nature an analysis of structure, albeit, as we have said, a structure produced by decisions. This book adds some flesh and bones to the networks. It looks in depth at the decisions that were made to go to war and how leaders interacted with each other in such a way as to result in war. While the focus is on decision-making, structural factors, like the system of alliances and global governance, as well as other factors, like rivalry, territorial grievances, and contiguity, are given their due worth. It was decided the best way to do this was to look at dyads.

The Dyad

Dyadic analysis began to supplant systemic analyses in quantitative studies of peace and war with the publication of Bremer (1992), which was contemporaneous with the release of the MID data. Prior to that, early studies in comparative foreign policy (namely Rummel 1972) began to obtain more robust findings if they studied patterns not in terms of the behavior of a single country – as had been done for years in the study of American foreign policy or Soviet foreign policy, but in terms of how two countries interacted with each other. Rummel's (1972) big "discovery" was that there was no single American foreign policy, but a set of policies that varied by target and issue area, for example Anglo-American cooperation, deterrence, foreign aid, Cold War. Taking a dyadic approach led to an increase in statistically significant findings. Theoretically, the reason for this was simple; namely, that the key to understanding foreign policy behavior was to understand that it was a function of the *relationship* between two countries. That insight remains true today and is the primary theoretical reason why a dyadic analysis was chosen as a way of conducting the analysis.[3]

---

[3] For a recent defense of the use of dyads see Diehl and Wright (2016).

The case studies in this book are all dyadic case studies. It is assumed that the question of why two states go to war is best approached by understanding the underlying relationship between the two that shaped their prior behavior, their level of affinity (friendship–hostility), and their current interactions (see Mansbach and Vasquez 1981: Chs. 6 and 7). This does not mean that third parties do not affect these inter-actions. When they play a large role, as in the July coercive game, these factors can be brought in. A dyadic approach is useful even when third parties are examined because it permits one to see whether certain dyads are driving the decision to war more than others and/or playing different roles along the road to war. For instance, as will be seen, the interactions of the Kaiser and the Tsar were critical in bringing the entire system of major European states to the brink of war with their mobilization. France–Germany and Austria-Hungary–Russia played important roles in this coercive game, but notably different roles in bringing about an escalation to war.

A dyadic approach is also justified because, in the end, states go to war with specific other states. Even when they decide to go to war primarily with one state, they consider the strategic implications of this decision for whether they will go to war with its allies. That decision is often made separately, albeit influenced by the former. Some states, like Italy, deliberately tried to avoid going to war with the ally of an enemy, as it did with regard to Germany, against which it did not declare war until a year later. Other states, like the U.S. with Wilson at the helm, just assumed that they will go to war with both countries in an alliance and then decided, because of peculiar circumstances, not to do that, but to treat the two differently. Thus, in the hope that Austria-Hungary might be willing to engage in peace efforts, Wilson delayed a decision to declare war on it. The bias in foreign policy decision-making to deliberate about whether to go war, state by state, was reinforced by the legal system of the time that required a declaration of war on each state. All of this warrants a dyadic approach.

Lastly, it should be noted that there are few triangular relationships in international relations, although they exist. The U.S.–Soviet Union–China triangle is an important example (see Goldstein and Freeman 1990). Triangles have a different dynamic, but even here insights can be gleaned by looking at each pair dyadically. The real problem is when we move beyond the triangle to multiple actors engaged in a crisis, like July 1914. Poast (2010) makes an important set of points about this problem when he argues in favor of examining all the actors in a crisis or interaction together in a "k-adic" format rather than two by two (see also his application in Poast 2012).

One way to address his position is to ask the following question: what would a dyadic approach obscure? The main factor that could be obscured (or at least underestimated) in this analysis is when third-party allies take actions that have a major impact on the dyadic relations being analyzed. This happens in several instances in the First World War. The most obvious is the July 1914 coercive game, but the spread of the war has no dearth of third parties playing crucial roles, even when they do not say anything, as in the case of Bulgaria in Romania's 1916 decision to attack Austria-Hungary. Nonetheless, this becomes a severe problem only if one is so fixated on a dyadic approach that these third and nth-parties are not brought into the narrative. This is easily done, as will be seen in Part II of the book. The thrust is still a dyadic analysis in that the behavior of those outside the dyad is examined in terms of how it affects the decision to go to war within the dyad, but I make efforts to be flexible in looking at multiple parties.

Still, there are situations where the decision to go to war in a given dyad is really a consequence of what some third party has done rather than the relationship within the dyad proper. This in itself is an important observation. This phenomenon is most common in valence balancing, and the very logic of it – the enemy of my friend is my enemy – is elucidated by a dyadic framing. Thus, while the dyadic approach has limitations, these are much more easily corrected in narratives than in data analyses.

A final reason for using the dyad is that the data that will be employed in the study are typically in dyadic form. The MID data constitute the best-known example. Also, the rivalry measures of Diehl and Goertz (2000), Thompson (2001), and Thompson and Dreyer (2012) are all in dyadic form. So too are the data on territorial claims from the ICOW data that will be listed (see Hensel et al. 2008). Lastly, the data on arms races collected by Sample (1997, 2002) are dyadic. These data and how they will be used in this study are discussed in more detail below.

Let me conclude by noting two caveats about using the dyadic approach. First, it must be kept in mind that the two members of a dyad might have different reasons for war. Sometimes this difference can be so extreme that one side is willing to go to war and the other wants to avoid it at all costs. This is certainly the case with Grey in Britain, who is prepared, even determined, to go to war if France is attacked, while the Kaiser and Bethmann-Hollweg want to keep Britain out at all costs. The analysis makes clear the role of each member of the dyad by treating them separately. Likewise, in every dyad there is an initiator and a target. Which these are is discussed in each case, especially when those which formally declare war first, like Russia on the

Ottoman Empire, are not the real initiator but manipulated into it by the alleged target.

Second, the inclusion of all the most important dyads in the First World War does not mean that they are all equally important. The analysis looks at how the cases are related to each other and there is much cross-case comparison. In doing so, the role that one may play for others is dissected. An assessment is made of which dyads were empirically responsible for expanding the local war into a general war and what role they played in that expansion, without engaging in the "blame game." Likewise, the key dyads, the engines of contagion, if you will, are identified.

Data Sources and Measures: How to Read the Histograms and Text Boxes

Quantitative data will be provided on every major pair of states that entered the First World War. These will be provided in a histogram and text boxes for specific indicators. The histograms provide a quick overview of the relations of a dyad depicting some of its most theoretically important characteristics. The narratives will use the histogram and text boxes to capture the essence of the relationship between the two states from the beginning of their interactions to the present. Thus one can visually see what MIDs preceded the war and which followed. Each of the major MIDs and wars prior to 1914 will be reviewed. Readers will have an instant understanding of the core issue(s) driving the relationship, how it evolved over time, and some sense, based on the steps-to-war theory, of the underlying factors shaping conflict. This review of the data will then be used to explain why conflict escalated to war.

The core of this picture is provided in a histogram of the main dyads that entered the war. Each histogram provides a pictorial history of a dyad's conflict as captured by major Correlates of War and related data sets. These histograms depict the year of each MID by level of hostility. The MID data record every instance of the use or threat of military force between legally recognized states and measure the highest level of hostile force employed (see Jones, Bremer, and Singer 1996; Ghosn et al. 2004). There are approximately 3,500 dyadic MIDs in the data for the entire world from the years 1816–2001, which is the period used here. Each MID will be color-coded to indicate the issue over which it occurred: territory, general foreign policy disagreements, disputes over the regime of a state or its type of government, or "other." In addition, whether the two states had allies (and how many) or were engaged in an arms race during the MID is portrayed. Although histograms will be drawn only for all states that have at least three MIDs for reason of space, some dyads with fewer MIDs (for instance Japan–Germany and Romania–Austria-Hungary) will have a histogram included because of their historical importance.

How to Read the Histograms

Hostility Level   The data record only the highest level of hostility that a MID reaches. Hence there are few MIDs with only a threat since most escalate beyond that.

1. No militarized action
2. Threat to use force
3. Display of force
4. Use of force
5. War

> *Issue*
> Territory = Red
> Regime = Blue
> Policy = Green
> Other = Gray
> Not Available = White (i.e. there is no issue code in the data)

Alliances   The histogram displays different forms of alliances for each MID. Each kind of alliance is depicted in the following manner:

No alliances: No lines surrounding bars (PR 0)[4]

Allied to each other: Double thick line around bars (PR 1)

One outside alliance: Dashed lines around bars (PR 2)

Both sides have one outside alliance: Patched pattern within bars (color of patch dependent on issue type) ▨[5] (PR 3)

Allied to each other, but one side has an outside alliance of which the other is not a member: Dots (PR 4)

It should be noted that the histograms follow the Correlates of War rule that alliances made three months before a war are dropped from

---

[4] (PR = Politically Relevant Alliance variable label in the data, see Senese and Vasquez 2008: 68 for more detailed codes).

[5] When the issue type is other and both sides have one outside alliance, there will be dark gray patched columns ▨.
   When the issue type is not available and both sides have one outside alliance, there will be light gray patched columns ▨ .

the data analysis. This affects only the Ottoman Empire's alliance with Germany and Bulgaria (3015, 3016), which was made in August 1914. As a result, MIDs involving the Ottoman Empire in 1914 have dashed lines around the bars indicating that only one side had an outside alliance. The text boxes, however, report this alliance and its dates – this pertains to Text Boxes 11.3, 12.3, 13.3, 15.3, 16.3, and 26.3.

Arms Race   If the disputants are engaged in an arms race during a MID, a blue line follows the two bars (with the label of "arms race" next to it).

Sources and Measures

MID Data   The MID data consist of every instance of the threat or use of armed forced by one legally recognized sovereign state in the international system toward another. These data are available at the Correlates of War website (www.correlatesofwar.org/data-sets) and described in detail with some descriptive statistics by the collectors of the MID.2 and MID.3 data sets. Our interest here is primarily in whether and when a dyad has had a militarized dispute. The issue variable is derived from the revision type code, which classifies the revision an actor is trying to bring about.

Alliances   The Correlates of War alliance data are used in the histogram, but this usage is confined to politically relevant alliances for the dyad. An alliance is defined as relevant if it is with a major state or with a minor state that is in the same region as the target of the dispute or contiguous to either party (Senese and Vasquez 2008: 67–68).

In contrast, the alliance data in the text boxes do not distinguish whether an alliance is relevant. For reasons of space only the alliances in force in 1914–1918 are systematically listed; other alliances that do not meet this criterion are listed if they are seen by historians as relevant to the onset of the war, and these are discussed in the case analyses. Examples of this would be the League of Three Emperors between Germany, Russia, and Austria-Hungary, 1881–1887 and the Reinsurance Treaty between Germany and Russia, 1887–1890.[6]

The alliance text boxes include the start and termination dates for each alliance. The Correlates of War alliance number is included, so

---

[6] Data that included all the alliances that members of the dyad had that were in force from their first MID to the last, i.e. during the period 1816–2001, were, however, gathered as part of a larger project on interstate conflict. For the relevance of the League of Three Emperors and the Reinsurance Treaty see Weitsman (2004: 39–64, 101–104).

the items can be checked with the original data. The alliance data are from Gibler and Sarkees (2004), which is a revision and update of the original Correlates of War alliance data collected by Singer and Small (1966) and Small and Singer (1969). Gibler (2009) has also provided a handbook of the formal treaty texts of these alliances that were used to create the data.

These data are sometimes different from the data in the Alliance Treaty Obligations Project (ATOP) by Leeds *et al.* (2002). Initially the difference was going to be reported in the alliance text boxes, but this proved too cumbersome. In terms of the First World War there are no differences of any import; most discrepancies are in the post-Cold War period and deal with the many treaties of friendship with former colonies. Substantively, ATOP is distinguished from the Correlates of War alliance data in that it classifies alliances as defensive, offensive and so forth on the basis of their legal commitments that are written down. These data also list whether a target is mentioned in the treaty.

Territorial Claims   To get at territorial grievances, text boxes are included for the territorial claims one member of the dyad has made on the other, including the date of the claim (both start and end dates), which state was the challenger, and whether any third parties also claimed the territory. For purposes of reference, the Claim Dyad number is included. These are taken from the Issue Correlates of War data collected by Paul Hensel and Sara McLaughlin Mitchell (www.paul-hensel.org/icow.html).

Rivalry   Four different measures of rivalry – Klein *et al.* (2006: 105–108); Diehl and Goertz (2000: 145–146); Thompson (1995, 2001), see also Thompson and Dreyer (2012); and Senese and Vasquez (2008) – are used to indicate whether the two sides were ever rivals and when.[7] The main differences are between the Thompson measure and the other three. Thompson (1995, 2001) uses perceptions derived from historians as to whether the two sides regard each other as rivals. He starts with whether they regard each other as principal enemies, but then adds other countries as rivals even if they are not principal enemies if they consider each other as rivals. The main criticism of these data

---

[7] The actual data used in the text boxes are drawn from the published print lists of Klein *et al.* (2006) and Diehl and Goertz (2000). The Thompson data are drawn from an electronic data set given to the author by Thompson, for which the author is grateful. The Senese and Vasquez information is drawn from the histograms in this book. Multiple MIDs in the same year are counted (see the histograms).

is that they are based on historians' perceptions, and these could be influenced by whether the states go to war, which is problematic if one wants to use the data as a predictor of war onset. The Diehl and Goertz measure is strictly behavioral. It examines whether the two sides have had six or more MIDs within a roughly twenty-year period (see Diehl and Goertz 2000: 41, 45). It then goes back to the first MID to date the start of the rivalry. A rivalry is coded as ended if there has not been a MID in ten years. The Klein *et al.* measure eases the last restriction and identifies the rivalry as continuing after a hiatus of ten years if additional MIDs occur over the same issue. The Senese and Vasquez (2008: 189) measure builds on the latter, and looks at when a sixth MID occurs regardless of the number of years that have passed. All these measures have been found to be statistically significant in predicting war onset.

Issue   The dominant issue underlying the rivalry is taken from two sources – Vasquez and Leskiw's (2001; 311–312) Issue Dom measure derived from the MID3.1 data is the first. This is derived from the MID data in terms of the modal revisionist type. Unless there is a combination of more than one revision type, the code can be discerned from the histogram. In addition to the dominant issue, the issue box records whether 25% of the MIDs are over territory. This too is from Vasquez and Leskiw, but it can also be derived from the histogram. It is included because this threshold is a predictor of escalation from MID to war. Thompson's data also identify whether a rivalry is spatial (i.e. over territory) or positional (i.e. a struggle over status, including global or regional leadership).

Arms Races   The arms race data are from Sample *et al.* (2013), which is an update of her earlier analyses (Sample 1997, 2002). The measure is based on Horn (1987), but she calculates this using her own military expenditure data. Arms races that occur during a MID are reported on the histogram. The text box reports all arms races, including those in years with a MID and those where there is no ongoing MID.

Sample (1997, 2002) finds that the Horn measure better captures the likelihood that a MID will escalate to war within five years than the Diehl (1983) measure that looks simply at an 8% increase in military spending between the two sides. She has also calculated the Diehl measure for each dyad year, but these values are not reported here. She uses the Horn measure to see whether the military expenditures match in such a way as to indicate an arms race in any year irrespective of whether there is a MID or not. In her earlier data she calculated this measure for years within which a war starts, and these values are used in this analysis and reported in the histogram as a blue line to the right of the MID bar. These measures in the war years were dropped in her later data, but they are still reported here, albeit only in the histogram. Her current data are reported in the text boxes. The arms race data are reported only for the years between the first and last MID that the dyad has. These include years in which there may not have been a MID, but, where there is a MID, this is also reported in the histogram.

Overall Design

Part I lays out the pre-theoretical expectations and a list of hypotheses that guide the cases. Part II, which is the heart of the book, presents case studies of each dyad that entered the war through a declaration of war and elucidates the contagion processes and related factors that made the First World War spread. There are chapters for each wave of contagion corresponding to specific years – 1914, 1915–1916, and 1917. Part III draws some lessons from the First World War to reach some theoretical conclusions. If the factors that have been inferred as bringing about contagion have some significance, then their absence should be associated with neutrality or non-joining. Chapter 6 looks at the neutrals to see whether this is the case as well as trying to discern why these countries did not join the war. Each country is examined in terms of what contagion factors were absent and which were present. Because the First World War spread so extensively, the number of neutrals, especially in Europe, was small, so we must be cautious in the confidence we place in our inferences. Nonetheless, these inferences can be tested in other multiparty wars to see whether they account for neutrals in those wars. Finally, the concluding Chapter 7 makes a set of cross-case comparisons to see how contagion actually worked in 1914–1918. This includes a set of new supplemental hypotheses of insights about contagion that was gleaned from the study and that was not known before. Each of the three parts builds on each other part, and the parts are logically tied together. We now turn to the narratives themselves.

Appendix: Questions Guiding Case Studies

I. Questions based on pre-theoretical expectations
   *1. Are alliances present in the dyad? With which states and how tight? If there are no alliances, are there tight alignments?
   *2. What role do alliances play in the case to bring about an escalation to war, a spreading of the war?

3. What role do alliances play in any games of coercion that occur?

4. Do alliances interact with any of the other factors, e.g. contiguity?

5. Do allies switch sides? Why?

*6. What is the role of previous MIDs, if any, in the decision to go to war? Is there learning?

7. Were there attempts to avoid war? Why did these fail?

8. Do contagion factors push actors in different directions?

9. Do any norms, such as compensation, play a role in the deliberations about entering war?

10. What factors push a country toward neutrality, if only in the short term?

11. Do alliance ties make for valence balancing? How can one tell whether it is valence balancing and not something else related to alliances? Look at whether there are grievances. Use counter-factual analysis to see whether they would have declared war in the absence of an alliance. Do they expect at this time to actually engage in combat with the foe?

*12. Are the members of the dyad contiguous by land? Are they proximate to the battlefield and subject to a spillover? Note when a state is brought into the war because the battlefield "spills" over to it. When this does not happen, what role is contiguity playing in the spatial diffusion of the war?

13. Does contiguity increase the time pressure for decision-making? Does this make the military more anxious and give the military more of a role?

*14. What is the balance of hardliners and accommodationists before the crisis and how does that change as time goes on?

15. Does the ongoing war provide any clear and specific opportunities for non-belligerents? Does this opportunity change the existing distribution of capability and/or lead to a breakdown in the prevailing political order?

*16. Are there territorial rivalries that precede the war and are these consciously seen as a reason to enter the war by decision-makers and other relevant actors?

*17. Is there excessive trade dependence among the states that is advantaging one side over the other?

18. Do belligerents, in particular major states, use brute force to make a state enter the war? What are the characteristics associated with this? Why does it not occur in other situations?

19. Do neutrals lack one or more of the main factors making for contagion: alliances with a belligerent, a warring neighbor on the border, territorial rivalry or grievances that could provide a motive for entering, excessive trade with one side? In general are they on the periphery?

20. What was the outcome of the war and long-term consequences?

II. New questions that arose during the research

21. Is there a strong leader who brings about the entry into the war?

22. Is the government split or divided about which side to support? What is the basis of this division – affinity, direct ties, political differences?

23. Do belligerents and non-belligerents engage in an auction to see whether they will enter the war and on which side or remain neutral?

24. What role do battlefield conditions play in the decision to enter the war, including on which side to enter?

25. Is there colonial competition that affects the decision to go to war? Do colonies supply resources or troops? Is there fighting in colonies?

III. Questions for data sources

26. What territorial claims do actors have against each other? When were these made? Who is the challenger and target? Are there third-party claims? How long do they last?

27. What are the MIDs that occur between the two sides during the life of their relationship? How hostile are these and over what issues?

28. Who are the allies for each side during the period in which they have MIDs? When was the alliance made and terminated? During any given MID do both sides have politically relevant allies or does only one side have an ally? Are they allied with each other and, if so, do they also have an outside alliance with another party?

29. Are the two actors rivals and by what measures? What are the dates of the rivalry?

30. What is the dominant issue of the rivalry? Are at least 25% of the MIDs over territory?

31. Does the dyad have arms races at any time during the time they have MIDs?

IV. Questions for cross-case inferences
  32. What are the primary and secondary contagion processes at work in the case? Are these easily determined? When in doubt, list them under the same category. What other factors play a major role in the case? What new insights does the case provide? Are these generalizable enough to be used to formulate a new hypothesis?

Items marked with an asterisk (*) are derived from Vasquez (1993: Chs. 5 and 7).

Part II

Dyadic Case Analyses: History and Data

3 1914: The Local War and the First Wave

Austria-Hungary–Serbia, July 28, 1914

Overview

The First World War began as a local war between neighbors over territory. Such local wars are the typical type of war in the international system in the post-Napoleonic era (Vasquez and Valeriano 2010: 300). They are not overly complicated. They involve two neighboring states disputing the border between them or, as in this case, one or the other claiming large areas between them. Two things complicated this local war, making it atypical. The first was that it expanded to become a world war. The second was that a non-state actor played a crucial role in triggering the war and before that shifting the relations between the two main states to a hostile rivalry.

Background

Serbia was part of the Ottoman Empire, having been defeated at the battle of Kosovo on June 28, 1389 (here dated using the Gregorian calendar), a day that still lives in the hearts of Serbs. It took until 1521 for the Ottomans to take Belgrade, however. This powerful empire, which twice reached the gates of Vienna (in 1529 and 1683) and conquered the Balkans and Hungary, was a key player in world politics during the period from the fourteenth to the nineteenth century. By the nineteenth century it had grown weaker, and many of the Balkan states began to rebel and received the support of the West, especially Russia, which saw itself as the protector of Christians. By 1821 Greece was on its way to independence, although it took the Battle of Navarino Bay and the subsequent Russo-Turkish War of 1828–1829 to confirm it. After several revolts going back to 1804, Serbia became an autonomous kingdom in 1817, and was recognized as an independent state by the Congress of Berlin in 1878.

Until 1903 Austro-Hungarian–Serbian relations were cordial. Austria-Hungary as a major state dominated the relationship with Serbia. Austria-Hungary was the major trading partner of Serbia, and King Milan I even signed a secret treaty giving it control over whether Serbia could enter "any kind of treaty" with another foreign state (Clark 2012: 28).[1] On June 11, 1903 all this changed with a coup d'état and the assassination of King Alexander of the Obrenović dynasty and his wife Queen Draga by Serbian members of the Army. These assassins, one of whom was Apis (Dragutin Dimitrijević) installed a new king – King Peter from the competing Karađorđević family line. At the time, relations did not change, and the Austro-Hungarians and their Habsburg rulers did not realize the implications of the domestic shift; they remained open to the new regime. Soon it became clear, however, that the Karađorđević regime would end its client status.[2] Eventually, they would turn to a new patron – Russia, a rival of Austria-Hungary in the Balkans. More importantly, the Serb military officers and fellow nationalists who had put King Alexander in power influenced Serbian foreign policy in a nationalist direction of uniting Serbs toward a Greater Serbia. This would prove to be a threat to Austria-Hungary, which in 1903 already had a number of Slavs within its borders and would get more as the Ottoman Empire lost control of its European provinces.

A key turning point came in 1905–1906 with a trade disagreement that led Serbia to switch to others for its armament orders. This, coupled with increasing hostility, resulted in the so-called Pig War, where Austria-Hungary cut trade and refused to import Serbian pork. Even though most of Serbian pork exports were to Austria-Hungary, Serbia was able to survive the "war" by getting new markets in France, Belgium and even Germany. However, it was the French loan of 1906 that was pivotal in permitting Serbia to endure in the face of the economic might of its powerful neighbor. The Pig War lasted until 1909, with the end result that hostility grew between the two countries.

The key to the relationship, however, was the underlying nationalism that motivated not only Crna Ruka (the Black Hand) but also the state and most of its leaders. Nikola Pašić, the Prime Minister for three periods during the years 1904–1905, 1906–1908, and 1909–1911, had been an advocate of gaining Bosnia and Hercegovina from the Ottoman Empire long before he was in power, and after 1908 held this position

---

[1] They had a formal alliance during the years 1881–1895.
[2] For a detailed account of Serbian–Austro-Hungarian relations in the early years, see Clark (2012: 3–38).

even if it meant defeat at the hands of Austria-Hungary (MacKenzie 1994: 77). It was this nationalist drive and the fear it caused within Austria-Hungary that brought about the war between the two. The Serbian nationalists were bold, even calling their paper *Pijemont* (Williamson and Van Wyk 2003: 31) in reference to the Italian state that wrested Italian speakers from the Austrian Empire. The loss of Italian lands was still a sensitive point in Vienna. Hardliners, like Conrad, the Chief of Staff, wanted a war of revanche to re-capture the lost lands. He persisted at every opportunity where he saw Italy weaker, the most recent being the 1911–1912 Italo-Turkish war. The latter instance resulted in his dismissal by Franz Josef.

Serbian nationalist agitation focused on both the Ottoman Empire and Austria-Hungary. In 1878 when Austria-Hungary was given the right to occupy and administer Bosnia and Hercegovina at the Congress of Berlin, nationalists protested. Then a major political crisis came when Austria-Hungary formally annexed Bosnia and Hercegovina in 1908. They did this with the agreement of the Russian foreign minister, Izvolsky, who thought he had secured a *quid pro quo* from the Austrian foreign minister, Aehrenthal, in which he would give his support for annexation in return for Austro-Hungarian support for Russian free passage through the Turkish Straits. Serbia protested the annexation vehemently. Political leaders of the various parties all united in calling for war. Steps were taken to mobilize the army, and in response Conrad increased troops on the Serbian border and prepared to mobilize the army in Galicia near Russia.[3] As the deal with Aehrenthal fell apart, Russia was more open to support the Serbian position. In the end, Germany stood by Austria-Hungary and in effect gave Russia an ultimatum when they said they would "let events take their course" if Russia did not accept the annexation.[4] Russia was still recovering from its defeat in the 1904–1905 Russo-Japanese War, including the sinking of two of its fleets, and it had to back down – with this, so did Serbia.

Serbian nationalists felt the Bosnians were really Serbs, as they believed were the Croats within Austria-Hungary proper. The settlement that ended the 1908 crisis made Serbia formally recant these ambitions, as can be seen in the text box on territorial claims (see below), but this did not last; nor was it taken seriously by non-state actors. What did happen was that the Serbian state focused its nationalist foreign policy

[3] MacMillan (2013: 430); see also Stevenson (1996: 125–126), cited in MacMillan (2013: 676 n74).
[4] MacMillan (2013: 433).

on its other rival – the Ottoman Empire – which in 1912 resulted in the First Balkan War in league with Bulgaria, Montenegro, and Greece.[5] Shortly afterward Bulgaria, in a disagreement over the spoils of war, attacked Serbian forces in the disputed Macedonia, which resulted in the Second Balkan war in 1913. This produced a "gang up" on Bulgaria with Greece, Romania and even the Ottoman Empire intervening and handily defeating Bulgaria. The end result was that Serbia just about doubled its population to 4.4 million and territory to 34,000 square miles (Williamson and Van Wyk 2003: 15; see also Clark 2012: 43). This in turn alarmed Austrian leaders even more. It was in this context that the assassination occurred.

Assassination

Archduke Franz Ferdinand, the heir to the Austro-Hungarian throne paid a state visit to Bosnia, the disputed territory of 1908, and was assassinated on June 28, 1914 by a young Serbian, Gavrilo Princip. The Archduke visited on Vidov Dan, St. Vitus Day, one of the holiest nationalist days in Serbian history when they were defeated by the Turks in 1389 at Kosovo Polje. While the date inflamed feelings, the actual assassination was planned before without regard for the day.

There is some debate as to whether the plot was a bottom-up affair with the young students initiating it or a top-down plan with Apis as the central figure. There is much to indicate that the plan started with a coterie of young nationalists who were looking to do something to advance the nationalist cause. At the center were Trifun "Trifko" Grabež, Nedeljko Čabrinović, and Gavrilo Princip. Initially Čabrinović sought to target Oskar Potiorek, the military governor of Bosnia and Hercegovina, but was talked out of it by Princip (McMeekin 2013: 6–7). They read that Archduke Ferdinand was coming, and Princip was able to substitute this more visible figure. They traveled to Belgrade, where they received arms from Crna Ruka, and Apis played a key role in shaping the plot. How much of a role he played and whether he was the mastermind is open to interpretation, but it seems to have been more like a bottom-up scheme, or at least we have more evidence on the activities of the youths than we have on Apis. Crna Ruka and Apis were crucial in supplying arms, but other related organizations like Mlada Bosna (Young Bosnia) and Narodna Odbrana (People's Defense)

---

[5] The Balkan League was based on a formal alliance between Serbia and Bulgaria and a separate formal alliance between Bulgaria and Greece; see the alliance text box. The later alliance between Serbia and Greece occurred after the first Balkan War and was directed at Bulgaria.

were also key nationalist groups.[6] Beyond Apis, the government and Pašić, the Serbian Prime Minister, were not directly involved, but Pašić may have known that something was up without knowing the details. Some analysts even argue that he thought of warning the Austrian government (Williamson and Van Wyk 2003: 26–27).

The actual assassination had a random quality to it. Only two of several assassins actually made attempts; the others lost their courage at the last moment. The open-air car that the Archduke was traveling in with his wife, Sophie, was initially attacked by a bomb thrown by Nedeljko Čabrinović, which bounced off the car and exploded under the car behind (Clark 2012: 370–371). The Archduke then proceeded to the City Hall, where he gave his speech. Potiorek, the military Governor, made a change in the planned route, but the driver took the original turn where Princip was stationed. As the car tried to get onto the correct route, he emerged from the tavern and fired, hitting the Archduke critically and then Sophie (who apparently was not his intended target). The Archduke's last words were "Sophie, Sophie, don't die, stay alive for our children" (Clark 2012: 375).[7]

The assassination had two immediate effects.[8] Domestically it eliminated the main accommodationist and increased the number of hardliners. Internationally, it created sympathy for Austria-Hungary and an opportunity for it to carry out armed retaliation. Domestically, Archduke Franz Ferdinand knew that nationalism and the attempt to create a greater Serbia by absorbing parts of the Empire's territory was one of the main issues facing the Empire. He had a plan – trialism – to solve it by creating a South Slavic option that would be equal to the Hungarians in both autonomy and status. This plan was opposed by the Hungarians. With his assassination one of the main non-violent options was gone. The young assassins and Crna Ruka played into the hands of the Austrian hardliners.

Berchtold, the foreign minister, who ran the government after Franz Ferdinand's death, switched to the hardline position. Together with Conrad, he felt the assassination required a dramatic response if Austria-Hungary were to maintain its great-power status. At the same time, internationally, this was also an opportunity for action, since all

---

[6] Indeed, each of the three major young assassins had contact with these groups (McMeekin 2013: 6–8).
[7] These and other details of the assassination can be found in Clark (2012: 370–375).
[8] For an interesting counter-factual analysis of what might have happened if the assassination had not occurred see Lebow (2010).

the major states were sympathetic and regarded the assassination as a heinous crime. The Kaiser, Bethmann-Hollweg, the Chancellor, and the rest of the German entourage encouraged Austria-Hungary to engage in a quick war to seize the moment.

The Ultimatum and the Decision for War

Within Austria-Hungary, Berchtold and Conrad felt this was the moment to crush Serbia once and for all. Franz Josef had similar if not as extreme sentiments, but would not go along with this unless they had a guarantee of German support.[9] He felt that they could not take on Russia alone, and that German support had been wanting in the Balkan Wars (Willliamson and Van Wyk 2003: 99; McMeekin 2013: 84–85). Count Alexander von Hoyos, a young hardliner, was dispatched to Berlin. He met with the Kaiser, who agreed to support Austria-Hungary pending the agreement of Chancellor Bethmann-Hollweg (Williamson and Van Wyk 2003: 97). This was the so-called "blank check" that gave Austria-Hungary complete support.[10]

With that, Emperor Franz Josef, who was eighty-four, was on board and receded to let Berchtold to work out the details. The government was split, however, because Count Tisza, the Hungarian Prime Minister, opposed a war, fearing it would lead to the absorption of Serbia and a great increase in the number of Slavs within the Empire. Under the Dual Monarchy the Prime Minister had a special role in matters of war and peace and could exert a great deal of influence on such a decision. He demanded that if war came there would be no conquest of Serbian territory, a demand to which Berchtold acceded, with a caveat that Serbia might be dismembered or at least greatly reduced in size by distributing her territory to others and that Austria-Hungary would just take some small areas for strategic purposes. Conrad asserted that he would see what happened when the time came, but said nothing formally.[11] Still, Tisza had to be convinced to go along; he only relented on being threatened that Serbia might form an alliance with Romania to wrest Transylvania from Hungary and that war was necessary to prevent this.

[9] On Franz Josef's tendency to oppose war generally, see Keegan (1998: 53). This view of the Emperor was common among major-state leaders. Documents (in this case French) that the Emperor was an accommodationist are reflected in Mombauer (2013b: 177, doc 113).

[10] See the document in Williamson and Van Wyk (2003: 99–100).

[11] Later he would raise the question to no avail when he and Berchtold met with the Emperor on July 30 to secure Franz Josef's agreement to general mobilization (Otte 2014: 434).

The Austro-Hungarian decision to go to war was a direct response to the nationalist territorial threat to the integrity of the Empire posed both by the various non-state actors, led by Crna Ruka, and by the Serbian state. It was this territorial issue that brought about the local war between Austria-Hungary and Serbia. Of this there can be little doubt. As Williamson (1991: 59, 62) states,

> Yet it was precisely Pan-Slavism's relentless claim to … the kinship of all Slavs, wherever in the Habsburg monarchy and in the Balkans, that challenged the Habsburg monarchy's very existence.

> Serbian speeches about uniting Bosnia and Herzegovina with Belgrade at some future point were not comforting. Indeed, preventing the very possibility of a Serbian grab of the two provinces had long preoccupied the Habsburg military.

The official minutes of the Joint Council of Ministers on July 7, 1914 recorded even Tisza, the only accommodationist, as saying (with regard to the assassination) that the Monarchy's "Slav provinces he considered lost if nothing happened" (Mombauer 2013b: 214, doc 134).[12]

With a rough consensus within the decision-making elite, it was decided to compose an ultimatum (technically called a "note with a time limit") that would be written so as to be rejected. The ultimatum was not sent immediately but delayed because Poincaré, the President of France, and Viviani, the Premier, were on a state visit to St. Petersburg, and Berchtold did not want to give them the opportunity to react jointly with the Russians to the ultimatum. Thus, the idea of a quick war went by the board.

The ultimatum was delivered on July 23, and Serbia was given 48 hours to respond. At the time of delivery Pašić was out of town campaigning for re-election. At first he and others in the decision-making elite were at a loss regarding what to do because they did not have clear support from Russia in the 48 hours immediately after the ultimatum (Williamson and Van Wyk 2003: 37, 40). The Serbian Prince-Regent telegrammed that they would fully comply if that was what the Tsar advised (McMeekin 2013: 185). Despite the short delay, Sazonov was completely supportive, even saying that they had to reject two articles, especially the demand that Austria-Hungary would conduct its own investigation on Serbian soil of the assassination, a clear violation of

---

[12] On the territorial motive being the key factor in the decision of the Austro-Hungarian leaders to crush Serbia, also see the French military intelligence report (Mombauer 2013b: 267, 291, docs 169, 180). For a detailed discussion of the "Serbia first" objective see Fried (2014: 34).

their sovereignty. Ultimately, Pašić rejected only this last clause. Edward Grey, the Foreign Secretary of Britain, referred to the ultimatum as "the most formidable document I had ever seen addressed by one State to another that was independent" (McMeekin 2013: 204).

As Williamson and Van Wyk (2003: 40–41) point out in an astute analysis, the ultimatum posed a difficult dilemma for Pašić. If he rejected the ultimatum his country would likely be overrun and tens of thousands killed. If he accepted it, he would be seen as a traitor, and Apis and the Crna Ruka would likely kill him. He had to decide between humiliation and possible assassination or heroic resistance that would lead to defeat. He chose the latter. Although he was far from a hardliner and not someone who thought war with Austria-Hungary should be a strategy for gaining Bosnia and Hercegovina, Pašić was brought to the hardline position of going to war.

Gavrilo Princip and the Young Bosnians did not have a clear strategy in terms of what they thought the assassination would accomplish, but what in fact this non-state actor accomplished was to force Pašić and the government of Serbia to do more about Serbs within Austria-Hungary and specifically Bosnia. This was at a time when the government was still absorbing the major nationalist gains it had made against the Ottoman Empire and its Bulgarian Balkan competitor. The non-state actor provided the **trigger** for the war and provided **the issue** for the local war that expanded into the greater European war.

Non-state actors excel at placing things on the agenda, and the students and the more organized Crna Ruka did that. At the same time they played into the hands of the hardliners in Vienna. They provided an opportunity – a situation like no other – that gave Austria-Hungary a legitimate reason for going to war with the sympathy of the old major states of the Concert of Europe. The assassination provided an immediate issue that permitted the more long-term and salient nationalist–territorial issue to be re-framed so that the major states would permit Austria-Hungary to do something that they would not permit before – namely, punish Serbia. Certain new issues have this effect in politics in that they permit actors to get their position implemented by re-framing it in a new guise that is acceptable to some of those who had hitherto stood in opposition;[13] the opportunity is created by removing some of the obstacles to favorably resolving the old issue – in this case by reducing the opposition of major states which stood against the Austro-Hungarian

---

[13] For some theoretical insights on how agendas are changed see Kingdom (1995).

punishment of Serbia. There was even a belief, held by some prominent figures, including Kaiser Wilhelm II, that Tsar Nicholas might stand aside because this was a question of regicide (see Mombauer 2013b: 197, doc 125; see also Röhl 2014: 153). This was always more a hope than a realistic expectation, but the failure to act quickly and produce a *fait accompli* put an end to it.

On Saturday July 25, Pašić gave Serbia's reply in person to Giesl, the Austro-Hungarian ambassador to Belgrade, accepting all but one of the clauses. Giesl, following orders that only an unconditional acceptance was permitted, broke relations and left immediately for Vienna. Berchtold declared war on July 28, one month after the assassination. Normally, a declaration is followed by military action. Conrad indicated that the army would not be ready until August 12; so, ironically, he advised against an immediate declaration. Berchtold went ahead anyway, since he worried that Germany might be weakening in its support, and he had Belgrade bombarded on July 29. The local war had begun and a frantic race now began by the Kaiser and Grey to limit it.

The Impact of Previous MIDs

The assassination produced the fourth militarized dispute between Austria-Hungary and Serbia, as can be seen in Histogram 1 (see the colored plates in the middle of the book). Contemporary theory believes that as crises repeat the probability of war increases, because actions become more hostile over time and this in turn increases the number and influence of hardliners on each side (Leng 1983; Vasquez 1993: 213–214, 223–224). The sheer number of crises makes it more difficult to handle and manage them in such a way that war is avoided (Midlarsky 1988). This position has also been part of the conventional wisdom of why the First World War came about (see, for example, MacMillan 2013). Recently, however, it has been pointed out that the fact that other crises had been resolved encouraged decision-makers in 1914 to think that this one would also (Afflerbach and Stevenson 2007; Stein 2015). The length of time that passed since the assassination added to this impression. The dyadic case analyses presented in this study permit an empirical examination of just what impact each MID had on overall relations.

Certain elements of the four MIDs between Austria-Hungary and Serbia are consonant with the general overall claim that repetition of crises makes for more hostility. The most important finding that can be derived from the four MIDs is that Austrian decision-makers became fed up with Serbia primarily because of its claims to Bosnia and Hercegovina and the larger claims to Croatian areas, especially along the Dalmatian coast (Mombauer 2013b: 200, doc 126). It is the territorial claims rather than nationalism per se that are crucial. Despite what the Austrians thought was an agreement to cease these claims to Bosnia and Hercegovina (see the territorial claims in Text Box 1.1) and an agreement to end agitation at the end of the 1908 crisis, this did not happen, especially at the non-state level.

The territorial explanation places more causal importance on the territorial claims than on the nationalist concerns, since it is the linking of nationalism with territorial claims that increases the probability of war; nationalism without territorial claims is not as apt to result in war. This can be seen in the fact that nationalism is fairly recent, but wars over territory are ancient. A purely nationalist explanation cannot explain earlier wars over dynastic succession, but the territorial explanation can (Vasquez 2009: 367).

The Balkan wars, portrayed in the second and third MIDs, provided further threats by accentuating Serbian success and subsequent increases

---

Text Box 1.1. Austria-Hungary–Serbia territorial claims

1878–1881: Bosnia-Hercegovina and Novi Pazar
(Claim Dyad 35402)
SER–AUH
1904–1908: Novi Pazar (Claim Dyad 35601)
SER–AUH
1908–1909: Bosnia-Hercegovina (Claim Dyad 35403)
SER–AUH
1914–1918: Dalmatia (Claim Dyad 33402)
SER–AUH
Third Party: ITA
1917–1918: Carinthia (Claim Dyad 31801)
SER–AUH
1915–1918: Banat–Bačka–Baranja (Claim Dyad 32203)
SER–AUH
1915–1918: Bosnia-Hercegovina (Claim Dyad 35404)
SER–AUH
1917–1918: Prekmurje and Medimurje (Claim Dyad 32401)
SER–AUH

in capability. The First Balkan War started in October 1912 and led by November to the Winter Crisis of 1912–1913, in which Austria-Hungary and Russia mobilized against each other, which resulted in a Europe-wide fear that war might break out. By March this was defused, with troop reductions on both sides of Galicia.[14]

The fight over the creation of Albania to prevent Serbian access to the Adriatic along with Montenegro's intransigence over withdrawing from Scutari (Shkodër) led to an intense set of confrontations. Only in May 1913, just before the Second Balkan War started, did King Nikola I agree to abide by the decision of the major states and withdraw from Scutari. During the Second Balkan War the belief that Serbia would not withdraw from Albania culminated in Austria-Hungary issuing on October 17 an ultimatum that it would use military force to get Serbia to leave. In both instances Russia withdrew support. These confrontations not only increased Austro-Hungarian hostility, but also reinforced the lesson that resolve coupled with an ultimatum would lead Serbia to comply and Russia to back down.

The assassination that resulted in the 1914 MID pushed all the Austrian leaders, but not Tisza, to the sentiment that something had to be done to end the larger territorial threat or the Empire would end up having another Italy (Williamson 1991: 8–9, 61, 75). They also believed that a diplomatic humiliation was insufficient and that Serbia needed to be defeated militarily.[15]

Three results were produced by the series of MIDs. The first was that hostility increased to the point that by July 1914 there was a consensus that included the Emperor that only force would solve the problem and that a crushing war should be initiated to end the threat once and for all. The second was that in light of Russia backing down in 1908 in the face of a German threat and then again failing to continue to support Serbia's actions in the Balkan wars there was a belief that Russia might not go to war in 1914, if Austria-Hungary had clear German support. This was also the Kaiser's opinion and that of several German decision-makers.[16]

---

[14] It was in December 1912 at the height of the crisis that the famous war council held by Kaiser Wilhelm occurred. Fischer (1967) and subsequently Copeland (2014b: 174–176) emphasized the council as evidence that Germany was planning a preventive war long before 1914. Clark (2012: 330), however, says that Bethmann-Hollweg, who was not at the meeting, subsequently "'put the Kaiser in his place' and 'nullified' the decisions taken at the conference."

[15] See the minutes of the Joint Council of Ministers, July 7, 1914 (Mombauer 2013b: 215, 217, doc 134).

[16] See for example Mombauer (2013b: 193, 208, docs 120, 131).

The third was that the two Balkan Wars increased not only hostility but also threat perception within Austria-Hungary.[17]

The histogram underestimates the role of territory because of the overly technical nature of the coding. Only the 1908 MID is coded as territorial. The 1914 dispute that gave rise to war was initiated by Austria-Hungary and was aimed at ending the Serbian threat to the territorial integrity of the Empire. On both sides the territorial nature of the issue was clearly understood, although it was only the non-state actor that pushed the issue on the Serbian side. The coding, however, focuses on the ultimatum, which is seen as a "policy" that Austria-Hungary demanded that Serbia accept. This policy, however, embodied a set of measures, including changes in the educational system and control of the press, to limit the expression of nationalist territorial agitation. Likewise, the two Balkan Wars-related MIDs are coded as policy because of Austria-Hungary using force to implement demands related to the wars. The most intense demands in the Second Balkan War again were associated with Serbian expansion into territory near modern-day Albania and the attempt it made to gain access to the Adriatic. Nonetheless, despite these coding issues, the 25% territory indicator, which is statistically related to an increase in the probability of escalating to war, is satisfied (see the issues in Text Box 1.2).

Text Box 1.2.   Austria-Hungary–Serbia/Yugoslavia rivalry

Enduring Rivalry	Issue
THOMPSON: 1903–1920	Dominant MID Issue: Policy 25% (+) Territory THOMPSON: Positional and Spatial
ARMS RACE HORN: 1912	

---

[17] It should be noted that the middle two MIDs (1912 and 1913) are Austrian diplomatic interventions into the First and Second Balkan Wars and differ from the 1908 and 1914 MIDs in that they were not direct confrontations from the very beginning of the crisis, but occurred in the context of battlefield fighting. These details do not make the four MIDs a clear pattern of hostility increasing in a spiral-like fashion until war breaks out, like a barroom fight. Instead we see Austria-Hungary getting embroiled in the two Balkan Wars because its interests were affected and Serbia tried to get access to the sea, which posed an additional threat.

With regard to the histogram, the criterion of territorial claims better captures the underlying issue, as does Thompson's measure of rivalry. The territorial claims (see Text Box 1.1) to Bosnia and Hercegovina as well as the Sanjak of Novi Pazar go back to 1878 and reflect the Austro-Hungarian and Serbian rivalry over the territories of the declining Ottoman Empire.

This conflict continued for three decades, reaching a height in 1908 when the Serbs mobilized and various non-state groups intensified their actions, culminating in the assassination. All of this resulted in Austria-Hungary attempting to end the growing threat by composing an ultimatum meant to produce war. Once the war had started, more claims to Slavic areas were formally made by Serbia. At the end of the war the nationalist dreams were fulfilled by the creation of a Kingdom of Serbs, Croats and Slovenes – a Yugo(South)Slavia.

Thompson's measure of rivalry, because it relies on historical judgments, validly captures the nature of the relationship. He marks the start date as 1903, with the assassination of King Peter by Apis and his compatriots, and imposes an ending in 1920 after Austria-Hungary was dismembered. He sees the rivalry as "spatial," i.e. territorial, and positional (see the issue box), namely, a struggle over dominance in the Balkans in terms of gaining Ottoman territory.

Third Parties and the Origin of the Coercive Game

Third parties played an important role in bringing this dyad to war, but Austria-Hungary–Serbia was the pivotal dyad that brought them to war. It was their local war and their rivalry that brought the other dyads to a world war. The First World War can be viewed as having two epicenters, with the first axis being Austria-Hungary–Serbia that brought about a local war and the second axis being Germany–Russia that brought about an expansion of the local war to a world war (Vasquez 2014a: 629–631).

For Austria-Hungary the crucial third party was Germany. Without German support in terms of the Kaiser's and Bethmann-Hollweg's blank check, Franz Josef would not have supported a war against Serbia and none would have occurred. For Serbia, without Russian support Pašić would not have rejected the ultimatum.

The logic of each side was to get these third parties to play a coercive game (a kind of chicken game) to get the other to back down and avoid war. Each side used its third-party support to threaten a war that would make the other side back down because they did not think they could win the expanded war. For Franz Josef, German support in terms of protecting Austria-Hungary from a Russian attack was meant to give it a free hand vis-à-vis Serbia. The goal was not to get Serbia to back down, but to prevent Russia from intervening in the local war to crush Serbia. For Serbia, Russian support was meant to prevent that war by threatening a wider war that Austria-Hungary could not win. It was anticipating this that made Franz Josef secure German support. Beyond this standoff, Tsar Nicholas knew he could count on France, and Sazonov tried to get British support from Buchanan, the British ambassador (see the Germany–Russia dyad).

While German support made it possible for Berchtold to convince Franz Josef that a war could be risked, this dependence also meant that Germany could restrain Berchtold as the crisis unfolded. This happened as war became more likely with the Serbian reply to the ultimatum. Kaiser Wilhelm did not read the reply until the morning of July 28. His immediate reaction, which he wrote to Jagow, was that "every cause for war has gone" (Mombauer 2013b: 408, doc 277; cf. McMeekin 2013: 242). He thought the final rejected clause could be negotiated. It was in this context that he came up with his Halt-in-Belgrade plan to avoid war. The plan would permit Austria-Hungary to occupy Belgrade and conduct its investigation under force of arms. What he did not fully realize was that Berchtold was not interested in the substance of the rejected clause, but wanted it as an excuse for war. Before the Kaiser could act, Austria-Hungary had already declared war. As Berchtold became aware of some of the German second thoughts, he rushed to bombard Belgrade on the 29th. Both of these actions, but especially the declaration, were meant to avoid mediation efforts by Grey in Britain. Very late in the night (3am on the 30th) Bethmann-Hollweg finally acted on the Kaiser's Halt-in-Belgrade plan and told Austria to accept talks, warning that Germany "must decline to let ourselves to be dragged by Vienna, wantonly and without regard to our advice, into a world conflagration ..." (McMeekin 2013: 281–282). This amounted to a threatened withdrawal of the blank check.[18] Subsequent events, in particular Russian mobilization, made this moot.

Nonetheless, Berchtold saw this third-party diplomatic intervention coupled with Grey's plan to avoid the war as undercutting his aim for war. So did Moltke, who became anxious that talks would delay German mobilization; he undercut Bethmann-Hollweg by telegraming Conrad on July 30 that Austria should mobilize immediately against

---

[18] For a detailed analysis of the Halt-in-Belgrade plan and the diplomatic traffic it generated, including attempts to "reverse" the blank check, see Otte (2014: 346–354, 407–414, 417, 426, 435–436, 439–440, 452).

Russia (see Mombauer 2013b: 451, doc 318). Berchtold quipped "who runs the government: Moltke or Bethmann?" (Albertini 1952, Vol. 2: 674), and followed the advice of the former, who agreed with his plans. These examples show that third parties often play the role that the main belligerents want them to play, because the impact of their interventions can be shaped by the intended targets. It also underlines the point that bureaucratic actors can undercut their leaders and that it is necessary to open the black box and not treat countries as unitary actors. In July 1914 there is really no "Germany," but only the Kaiser, Bethmann-Hollweg, and Moltke, each struggling to control policy.

The Role of Alliances and Arms Races

The main role of alliances was to make each side play the coercive game to the hilt (Text Box 1.3). For Austria-Hungary, the key alliance was with Germany, which went back to 1879 and became the Triple Alliance with Italy in 1882. Romania was added a year later. Serbia, as can be seen from the alliances boxes,[19] did not have a formal alliance with Russia. Instead, this was a firm and long-term alignment reflecting a

---

Text Box 1.3. Austria-Hungary–Serbia alliances

Austria-Hungary Alliances	Serbia Alliances
1879–1918: GMY 2065	1912–1913: BUL 3011
1881–1895: SER 2066	1913–1918: GRC 3014
1881–1887: GMY, RUS 2067	
1882–1918: GMY, ITA 2068	
1883–1918: GMY, ITA, ROM 2069	
1904–1908: RUS 3003	
1914–1918: BUL 3017	
1915–1918: BUL, GMY 3030	

---

[19] With few exceptions, the alliance boxes only report alliances in existence during the years 1914–1918. The alliances Serbia had reflected the dynamics of the two Balkan Wars, with an alliance with Bulgaria against the Ottoman Empire and then with Greece against Bulgaria in the Second Balkan War. The alliance with Greece played no role in the onset of the 1914 local or expanded war because, although Greece stood with Serbia by maintaining a "benevolent neutrality," it made it clear that it would not enter the war (Hall 2003: 407).

patron–client relationship. The Second Balkan War and Russia failing to support Bulgaria in its dispute with Serbia made this relationship closer. However, it was not clear in 1914 that Serbia could automatically count on Russia without an explicit commitment, since in 1908 Izvolsky, the Russian Foreign Minister, had been willing to strike a deal with Aehrenthal of Austria-Hungary at Serbia's expense. Still, with all the commitments in place in 1914, the alliance and alignment system meant that the coercive game could be played without restraint and it was.

From a realist perspective, one side should have backed down in the face of this aggregation of capability and resolve. From a game-theoretic perspective both sides should have backed down if this was a chicken game.[20] Neither of these deductive outcomes occurred. Instead, the steps-to-war perspective (Senese and Vasquez 2008: Chs. 5 and 6), which maintains that alliances increase the likelihood of war, is supported. What the First World War case tells us is that alliances bring about war by firming up resolve in the playing of a coercive game, which in turn overrides the rational-choice logic of chicken games. This may be due to the psychological bolstering of not standing alone, and/or the result of a miscalculation of power and predicted war outcomes, and/or wishful thinking (see the Germany–Russia dyad). In the end, alliances were an indirect cause of war in this case because they helped produce the failure of the coercive game; still, without them it is unclear that the coercive game would have failed.

There were two arms races between the two countries – in 1912 and 1914 (for the latter see the histogram). The 1912 arms race was a mutual ongoing military buildup reflected in the Balkan Wars. From Serbia's perspective these buildups were aimed at the Ottoman Empire and later Bulgaria. For Austria-Hungary, Serbia's buildup posed a threat because there was an increase in capability that, coupled with its success in the two Balkan Wars, led Austria-Hungary to respond, despite the general non-support of defense bills by the Hungarian legislature (Stevenson 1996: 283). By 1914 both were preparing for hostilities with each other. Nevertheless, it must be remembered that military

---

[20] A chicken game is illustrated by the teenage game where two cars drive toward each other head on and the first one to swerve is a chicken. To win a chicken game, one must show resolve or alternatively, as Schelling (1960) notes, an inability to swerve. In principle, because the costs of a head-on collision are so great, both sides should swerve. From a game-theoretic perspective this makes chicken a cooperative game. For a more technical description of the dynamics of what I am referring to as a chicken game see Zagare (2011); see also the earlier and still useful Snyder and Diesing (1977). Zagare (2011: 110–129) analyzes the July 1914 crisis as an asymmetric escalation game, and contrasts it with the general mutual deterrence game and the unilateral deterrence game (Zagare 2011: 44–48).

buildups are fungible and can be used against multiple targets. Whether the arms races actually increase hostility and thereby the probability of war is always difficult to discern. It does seem that the Serbian buildups did increase threat perception within Austria-Hungary, especially given Serbia's success in the Balkan Wars. Once the accommodationist Franz Ferdinand had been removed, this made the elite want to move toward war. The Serbian buildup then did not restrain Austria-Hungary, and any buildup provided Conrad with more evidence to support more urgent "now better than later" calls for war. From Serbia's perspective, the buildup was done more as an offensive measure in preparation for war against the Ottoman Empire and, later, Bulgaria. Any buildup Serbia could fund was no match or defense against Austria-Hungary.

Outcome

Austria-Hungary had two military successes in the war, and it was not until the end that the prospect that it could lose was evident. Conrad's main intention was always to crush Serbia, but Moltke counted on him to move his army to the East by Galicia to hold the Russians while he went to the West. At the beginning of the war, Conrad thought that Russia might not attack, so he moved more troops to the South and Serbia. This proved to be a bit of wishful thinking, and he had to move the bulk of the army to the Russian front, as a result of which the Serbian invasion failed.[21] It was not until October 1915 when Austria-Hungary and Germany made a deal with Bulgaria and attacked on multiple sides that Serbia was overrun. Two years later, in October 1917, Austro-Hungarian troops, supplemented by German divisions, broke through the Italian line by Caporetto in a major victory.

These victories marked the two highpoints for Austria-Hungary on the battlefield. A year after Caporetto, on October 24, 1918 the Battle of Vittorio Veneto saw Austria-Hungary defeated on the battlefield by the Italians aided by their allies. At the same time the Empire started to dissolve – the Czechs declared their independence, and Hungary moved to leave the Dual Monarchy. In addition, a south Slav state that would become Yugoslavia was proclaimed, as Poles within the Empire and other nationalities, such as Romanians, began to coalesce and leave (Keegan 1998: 416). By late October, German war efforts were also under severe pressure, and Austria-Hungary left the war shortly before the November 11 Armistice on the Western Front, as Karl Renner, leader of the Social Democrats, took over in Vienna.

[21] For the details on these war plans and movements see Keegan (1998: 152).

At Versailles, Austria received much harsher treatment than Germany, in part because of its internal dissolution and the nationalist sentiment of the victors, especially Wilson. Czechoslovakia was recognized as an independent state, as was Hungary and a new Kingdom of Serbs, Croats, and Slovenes, which in 1929 became Yugoslavia. Italy gained large areas. What was left was a small German-speaking portion that represents the Austria we know today. The population of 48.5 million in 1914 was reduced to 6 million, and the bulk of its territory was lost. A democratic form of government was established, and the Habsburg monarchy, going back to the end of the thirteenth century, was ended by force. No one in Austria-Hungary, let alone in Serbia, could have imagined the catastrophic outcome for the Habsburgs and Austria itself.

The Role of Alliances: The Failure of the Coercive Game

Germany–Russia, August 1, 1914

The local war between Austria-Hungary and Serbia was a typical two-party war in the system. The main theoretical question is why, of all the dyadic wars between neighbors over territory, did this one spread to become a world war. A good part of the answer to that question can be found in the German–Russian dyad, which is the key dyad that spread the war. Germany and Russia were the first to join the war. They were the ones that made the local war **expand** to become a European war that would eventually engulf most of the world. It is with this dyad that the First World War began. What is ironic is that this dyad was ruled by comparatively absolute monarchs, neither of whom wanted war, but the war started anyway. Dissecting why they joined the war tells us something about the dynamics of contagion and the underlying theoretical complexities of the war's origins and causes.

The essential factor that led each of the monarchs to decide for war was that they got caught up in a game of coercion in which they sought to support an ally by making the other side back down. They hoped to win without going to war. This game of power politics and coercion had been played by them before in 1908–1909 in Bosnia and other major states, including them, had played it most recently during the Balkan Wars. The game has a script, and both actors followed it: intimidate and show resolve and the other side will relent instead of going to war.[22] For a variety of reasons, neither side was able to do that.

---

[22] Zagare (2011), a game theorist, and Bobroff (2014), a historian, are the most recent to emphasize the failure of the coercive game as a key cause of the First World War.

The monarchs lost control to their military and hardliners, and the game escalated to war. Their joint intervention then set off a concatenation of events that made for additional interventions into the war.

Because of Slavic affinity, Russia saw itself as a patron of Serbia, and was prepared to defend it against being bullied by the larger Austria-Hungary. Alone, Serbia could not have stood up to Austria-Hungary, especially with the need to recover after the two Balkan Wars. Pašić, the Serbian Prime Minister, asked for Russia's advice soon after receiving the ultimatum. Sazonov, the Russian foreign minister, was actually more intransient than Pašić, and supported a rejection of more than the one point that Serbia ended up rejecting on July 25 in its reply. So Russia's alignment with Serbia was necessary for blocking Austria-Hungary's desire to overrun Serbia.

Berchtold, the foreign minister of Austria-Hungary, knew that, if Russia supported Serbia, the tables would be reversed and he would be faced with a stronger power if he persisted. Therefore, intimidation by Russia would have protected Serbia, and Austria-Hungary would have backed down because it was apt to lose a war with Russia. Berchtold and Emperor Franz Josef anticipated this and turned to their own ally – Germany, which gave them the unequivocal support they sought in the so-called blank check.

For the Kaiser and Chancellor Bethmann-Hollweg of Germany, as well as Berchtold and Franz Josef, this should have ended the matter, since Germany was more powerful than Russia. Russia should have backed down, and Austria-Hungary would have been free to attack Serbia. The Kaiser and other key German decision-makers right up to the end did in fact believe that Russia would back down (McMeekin 2013: 105; Clark 2012: 518; Mulligan 2010: 213).[23] The Tsar did not see it that way. He thought Germany would be out of her mind to face the combined might of Russia, France, and Britain. He said to the French ambassador, Paléologue, "Unless she has gone out of her mind altogether Germany will never attack Russia, France, and England combined" (Williamson and Van Wyk 2003: 130). So the Tsar matched Austria-Hungary's Triple Alliance with his own Triple Entente. He too thought his opponent would back down in the face of an overwhelming threat. Normally, in a chicken game of this sort both sides should swerve to avoid a catastrophe. Neither did, however.

---

[23] See for instance, Mombauer (2013b: 275, doc 171), Schoen to Hertling, which is not atypical.

Text Box 2.1.   Germany–Russia alliances

Germany Alliances	Russia Alliances
1879–1918: AUH 2065	1881–1887: AUH, GMY 2067
1881–1887: AUH, RUS 2067	1887–1890: GMY 2072
1882–1918: AUH, ITA 2068	1893–1917: FRN 2074
1883–1918: ITA (–1915), ROM	1909–1917: ITA 3009
(–1916), AUH 2069	1910–1916: JPN 3010
1887–1890: RUS 2072	1914–1916: ROM 3018
1914–1918: OTM 3015	1915–1917: FRN, ITA, UKG 3019
1915–1918: AUH, BUL 3020	1916–1917: JPN 3021
	1916–1917: FRN (–1918), ITA (–1918), ROM
	(–1918), UKG (–1918) 3022

The Role of Alliances   While the coercive game was essential for bringing about a sequence of actions that led to war, the playing of this game was accentuated by pre-existing alignments and alliances. The formal alliances are listed in Text Box 2.1. The logic of the coercive game that the alliance structure produced was clearly understood by all the principal players, and cartoons of it were printed afterwards.[24]

Of the alliances listed, the two most important sets were the alliances formed between Austria-Hungary and Germany and between France and Russia. The alliance between Austria-Hungary and Germany went back to 1879. A few years later in 1882 Italy joined (because of its colonial disagreements with France) to make it the Triple Alliance. Romania was tacked on in 1883. The initial alliance was meant to protect Austria-Hungary from attack by Russia. Such an alliance, however, could be seen as a threat to Russia, and for this reason Bismarck formed in 1881–1887 the Three Emperors' Alliance among Germany, Austria-Hungary, and Russia and, as that became strained, the Reinsurance Treaty between Germany and Russia in 1887. The Reinsurance Treaty said that neither would join a third party in the event of a war involving either unless that war was an attack by Germany on France, or by Russia on Austria-Hungary. Bismarck's intention here was to keep France from allying. When Kaiser Wilhelm II pushed Bismarck out in 1890, the Reinsurance Treaty was allowed to lapse (see Röhl 2014: 53–54 for details).[25]

---

[24] See, for an example, the cover of Zagare's (2011) book.
[25] On this configuration of alliances see Clark (2012: 121, 124–129) and Snyder (1997: 101–106, 215–217). On the 1904 Entente see Williamson (1969).

Shortly thereafter, the Franco-Russian alliance was formed in 1893. It was meant to avoid war and enhance the power of France and Russia by posing Germany with a two-front war. The Franco-Russian alliance was the only formal alliance at the time that specified a *casus belli* and even mobilization plans (Clark 2012: 131). It ended the isolation of France that Bismarck had diplomatically imposed after the Franco-Prussian war of 1870–1871 and thereby gave it an ally in any future war with Germany.

In 1904 Britain entered an entente with France that eventually became more of an informal alliance against Germany. This made for an aggregation of power, and the 1907 Entente with Russia completed the two blocs.[26] The 1904 Entente Cordiale between France and Britain was initially a colonial understanding, and after the First and Second Moroccan crises of 1905–1906 and 1911 became more of a military understanding. Negotiations to this end were led by Grey, the British Foreign Secretary, and involved military talks between the two sides without the full cabinet, let alone Parliament, being apprised thereof.

Still in 1914, Grey was personally committed to go to war if France were attacked. Lastly, the 1907 Entente between Britain and Russia, which France pushed, involved the lowest level of commitment to go to war. This was an attempt to moderate a fairly intense rivalry based on colonial competition. Grey was not willing to go to war to support Russia and did not feel supporting Serbia by threatening war was in Britain's interests. Grey's main concern was to support France if she were attacked by Germany, but even here he knew the cabinet was not in agreement with him. These doubts meant he could not publically support France in the coercive game, which gave Bethmann-Hollweg and the Kaiser hope, a false hope really, that Britain might stand aside. They did not want a war with Britain. The Kaiser wanted to avoid war with Britain at all costs. Tirpitz, the head of the navy, knew they were not ready. Bethmann-Hollweg was an Anglophile, and much of his diplomacy was based on keeping Britain neutral.

The other key players in the coercive game that were not buttressed by written alliances were Russia and Serbia. Russia's support of Serbia was completely unwritten and just the support of a patron of a client – support which dissipated in the Bosnian crisis, leaving Serbia in the lurch, but which in 1914 was firm. This arrangement and the ententes showed that a formal alliance was not necessary to produce war.

---

[26] However, neither entente was a formal alliance, and so neither is listed in the Correlates of War alliance data.

All in all, the alliances and alignments had two causal effects. First, as with the Austria-Hungary–Serbia dyad, they made countries play the coercive game to the hilt. In the Germany–Russia dyad, however, they had a second additional effect – they made the war expand. Because France was a committed ally of Russia, Germany had to attack France. France, because it was so committed to its alliance with Russia, was seen by Moltke, Bethmann-Hollweg, and the Kaiser as inevitably intervening, so much so that they attacked first. This activated Grey's personal *casus belli*, albeit not those of the cabinet.

The Franco-Russian alliance turned out to be in fact a "fateful alliance" (Kennan 1984).[27] It guaranteed that Germany would attack France if war erupted between Germany and Russia. Because Grey was committed to defending France, this would bring in Britain. This meant that no matter how much the Kaiser and Bethmann-Hollweg wanted to avoid war with Britain they faced a powerful alliance structure that worked against them. The Franco-Russian alliance insured that both a continental and a world war would occur.[28] It is for these reasons that Christensen and Snyder (1990) see the alliance system in 1914 as leading to "chain ganging" and the rapid expansion of the local war.

Third Parties   There were three third parties that affected this dyad – Serbia, Austria-Hungary, and France. Of these the most crucial was France, as hinted in the discussion on alliances. France was important in bringing about war between Germany and Russia, both for what it did and for what it did not do. What it did was support Russia unequivocally. Poincaré, the President of France, and his ambassador in Russia, Paléologue, supported hardline Russian action throughout the crisis and repeated their commitment to support their ally. They consciously hoped to stiffen the Tsar, whom they regarded as indecisive and/or weak (McMeekin 2013: 146–147). In this way they buttressed the hardliners in Russia and provided little support for the Tsar's inclinations to avoid war.

The latter is what they did not do. Poincaré and Paléologue did not encourage the Tsar to support the Halt-in-Belgrade plan or even the Tsar's own idea of taking the dispute to the Hague. In addition, they provided no warnings of the dangers of mobilizations: all of this made the advice given to the Tsar, both domestically and internationally,

---

[27] On this alliance see also Langer (1967).

[28] A continental war has been defined as a war without Britain and a world war has been defined as one in which Britain entered (see Levy 1990/1991).

singularly in the hardline direction. If an accommodationist role was to be played it had to come from Viviani, but this did not seem to be in the cards, and he was overshadowed by Poincaré.

Serbia was the other key third party for Russia, since without it there would be no coercive game in the first place. It, however, was willing to follow Sazonov's lead throughout, even to the point of accepting the ultimatum. However, Serbia was cautious because Russia had backed down in 1908 and had failed to support some of Serbia's more belligerent actions in the two Balkan Wars. Thus, it was Russia that made Serbia a key third party rather than Serbia itself; of course, the Serbian non-state nationalists were a pressure.

On Germany's side, Austria-Hungary was the main third party. Berchtold together with Franz Josef got the Kaiser committed to supporting them, which was a major difference between 1914 and the recent Balkan Wars. This was, in part, due to the Kaiser's personal relationship with Franz Ferdinand and the emotional impact the assassination had on him. Nonetheless, as the Kaiser had second thoughts, Berchtold pre-empted by bombarding Belgrade and then undercut his peace plan by ignoring it. This was done with the help of Moltke, who encouraged Conrad to mobilize even after Bethmann-Hollweg's telegram demanding that Austria-Hungary accept talks.

The only other third party of note was Grey, who offered his own mediation efforts and eventually supported a plan very similar to the Kaiser's. With the strongest members of the Triple Alliance and the Triple Entente pushing similar plans, one would have thought that something like the Halt-in-Belgrade plan could have been adopted. To do this the Kaiser had to deliver Austria-Hungary, which he failed to do, in part because of insufficient and too tardy pressure by Bethmann-Hollweg, and Grey had to deliver the Tsar, presumably through Poincaré, who failed to play any role like this. In the end, the three main third parties were vectors that pushed Germany and Russia toward war.

Decision-Making and the Failure to Avoid War The Kaiser did not read the Serbian reply to the ultimatum until the morning of July 28. When he did, he thought all reason for war had gone. But before noon Berchtold, sensing Germany's unease, declared war. Meanwhile, the Kaiser thought war could be averted by negotiating the remaining points, and that Austria-Hungary could have some victory by attacking Belgrade and occupying the capital until its demands were met. This "Halt-in-Belgrade" plan became the basis of a peace plan to avoid war between Austria-Hungary and Serbia as well as between Germany and Russia.

It did not contradict Grey's proposal for four-power talks among the major states. Together the two proposals, and a later plan for just direct talks, formed a competing script in the last weekend before the war. This script embodied the use of diplomacy and the legacy of the Concert of Europe to avoid war and reach a resolution, in contrast to the traditional realist script of power politics that sought to avoid a war through coercion.

The nature of the military plans for fighting a two-front war, however, led the militaries in both Germany and Russia to pressure for mobilization. Moltke, who all along was in favor of a preventive war, needed to attack France before Russia began mobilization. As it became clearer that Russia was mobilizing, this put more pressure on Germany to enter a period of imminent danger of war, *Kriegsgefahrzustand*, and Moltke became more frantic and insisting. The Tsar was convinced by Sazonov to order what both thought was a partial mobilization, i.e. a mobilization against Austria-Hungary and not Germany, on July 29. When he received another telegram from the Kaiser he rescinded the order on the same day.

Both he and the Kaiser had taken matters into their own hands by exchanging a series of telegrams beginning July 28 to avoid war – the so-called Willy–Nicky telegrams.[29] The Kaiser pressed Bethmann-Hollweg to get Berchtold to accept the Halt-in-Belgrade plan, with the most important instruction from Bethmann to Austria-Hungary being that on July 30 around 3am.

However, in the July 30 telegram the Tsar inadvertently revealed that military preparations had begun five days earlier. This astounded the Kaiser, who wrote "So that is almost a week ahead of us … the tsar has been secretly mobilizing behind my back" (McMeekin 2013: 285). Pressure for German mobilization reached a fever pitch. At the same time the August 1 misunderstanding with Grey occurred in which he gave the impression that Britain and even France would stand aside if Germany attacked only Russia. The Kaiser immediately called in Moltke and demanded that he switch his plans, which he refused to do, saying it was impossible. The Kaiser said "It must be possible if I order it" (Williamson and Van Wyk 2003: 106), and he did. Later in the day when Grey backed off, the Kaiser threw in the towel and told Moltke "Now you can do what you want" (McMeekin 2013: 349).

The Russian mobilization, which was intended to pre-empt the German war plan, also pre-empted the only peace plan. The Tsar was

---

[29] See Williamson and Van Wyk (2003: 138–141) for a selection and Mombauer (2013b: 417–422, 447–448, 491–492) for a fuller set.

the last person who could have avoided the war. Once he had decided to re-order the mobilization and now a full one at the insistence of his civilian and military advisors – Sazonov and Sukhomlinov, the war minister – talks ended. The coercive game trumped the Concert of Europe game.

These scripts were theoretically significant because they guided the actions of decision-makers and gave them a logic that made them meaningful at the time and after the fact. In the end the very real fear of being pre-empted by the other side's preparation created an overwhelming sense of insecurity that led the Kaiser to reciprocate.[30] The outcome was that the coercive game ended in a spiral to war rather than a prevention of war. War came about because both sides got caught in a *security trap*, which made each take measures to defend themselves from a military attack that would pose a grave threat or give a great advantage to the other side. A security trap can be defined as when both sides go to war because of extreme threat perception due to fear of an imminent attack. Insecurity rather than substantive grievances is the main motive guiding decisions.[31] It was this fear and the resulting insecurity rather than specific grievances that brought the dyad to war.

The contrast between this dyad and Austria-Hungary–Serbia or even France–Germany is stark in this regard. Likewise, insecurity, rather than planning a preventive war, was the key factor bringing Germany–Russia to war. This intense insecurity brought about, in part, by the proximity of powerful armies just over the border also played a role in getting the Tsar to mobilize. The militaries of both sides, due to this contiguity, became very anxious and focused on defense and winning the war, with much less concern for avoiding it. In this regard the time-pressure element of contiguity was a contagion process that was at work here.

The coercive game was not the only cause. The alliances formed an underlying structure that made the war spread rapidly and inexorably to the other major states, a phenomenon that was aggravated by the adoption of the offensive as the main military strategy (see Christensen and Snyder 1990). This is why, after declaring war against Russia, Germany attacked France. In particular, the long-existing Franco-Russian alliance made the Tsar more resolved than he would otherwise have been

[30] For a very different view that sees Bethmann-Hollweg manipulating the Kaiser to bring about a preventive war see Copeland (2000: Chs. 3 and 4, 2014b).

[31] This dyad is a classic case of a security trap. For a glimpse of how the security trap evinced itself during decision-making in Russia and in Germany see Otte (2014: 424, 443, respectively).

and put the Kaiser under a time pressure that made it imperative that he act once the Tsar mobilized.

The Austro-Hungarian–Serbian war can be seen as a local war that could have been the Third Balkan War. Instead it expanded to become a world war. If the Austro-Hungarian–Serbian war can be seen as the first epicenter of the world war, the German–Russian dyad can be seen as the second epicenter. Its eruption spread the war to most of the rest of the major states in Europe. This is another way of saying that, if Germany and Russia had not joined the local war, it would have been unlikely that France and Germany, let alone Britain and Germany, would have fought each other. By joining the local war, Germany and Russia made it probable that the other major states would intervene. They in turn joined because of the insecurity produced by the prospect of mobilization. Mobilization was the single most crucial decision taken in the July crisis that brought war about in the sense that there was no turning back.[32] The decisions surrounding mobilization, however, were a function of the alliance structure. The underlying alliance structure made the second epicenter the dangerous fault line it was.

The Role of Previous MIDs   Prussia and Russia had a rivalry, according to Thompson, going back to 1744 and lasting to 1807 (Thompson and Dreyer 2012: 79–80). During this time they fought each other both for positional and for territorial gains. Prussian troops were part of Napoleon's 1812 invasion, although this was not an entirely voluntary decision on Prussia's part. Prussia and Russia, however, joined forces in the Grand Coalition that eventually defeated Napoleon in 1814 and 1815. Prussia was part of the Congress of Vienna along with Russia and shared in the governance of the Concert of Europe. In the post-Napoleonic period the first MIDs between the two were in 1848 and 1850, as can be seen Histogram 2 (in the middle of the book). Both of these were connected with the First Schleswig-Holstein War. In 1848 Prussia invaded Denmark in support of German speakers in the two provinces. Russia, along with Britain and Sweden, threatened intervention unless Prussia withdrew, and it did. The war did not cease until 1850 and another great power MID aimed at Prussia occurred (Carr 1991: 40).

After 1850, relations between Prussia and Russia became less hostile. Once Bismarck came to power, he was able to manage relations

---

[32] On the causal role of mobilization see the exchange between Trachtenberg (1990/1991) and Levy (1990/1991) and the recent H-Diplo symposium on "New Light on 1914?" centered on Trachtenberg (2017).

Text Box 2.2.   **Germany–Russia rivalry**

Enduring Rivalry	Issue
THOMPSON: 1890–1945 SENESE AND VASQUEZ: 6th MID: 1936 ARMS RACE HORN: 1935–1938	Dominant Issue: Policy 25% (+) Territory THOMPSON: Positional and Spatial

with a series of alliances that kept Germany, Russia, and Austria at peace (see below). Thompson, as can be seen in Text Box 2.2, dates the modern Germany–Russia rivalry from the removal of Bismarck in 1890 and regards it as lasting through until the end of the Second World War.

In terms of the First World War, the most important MID preceding the war was the 1908–1909 Bosnian crisis. The 1914 coercive game was played the way it was because psychologically previous iterations of the game went the way they did; namely, the Tsar backed down and the Kaiser and several others thought he would back down again if sufficiently pressed. This was because Russia had not recovered from its defeat in the Russo-Japanese War. At the same time, the previous humiliation made the Tsar vow that he would never back down again, and he began a major military buildup, which itself was seen by certain German actors, namely Moltke and those in his entourage, as highly threatening. The arms buildup in and of itself provided a separate incentive for hostility and insecurity that made Moltke and others in the military push for war now rather than later, when they would be comparatively weaker. The data, however, show no severe arms race prior to 1914 between Germany and Russia. Despite the arms buildup after 1909 and of the "Great Program," this did not result in a mathematical arms race as measured by Horn, in part because the Great Program would not be completed until 1917 at the earliest (Levy and Mulligan 2017: 743).

Repeated crises and militarized disputes fueled hostility and at some point a sense of rivalry. The data in Text Box 2.2 show that the Thompson measure, which is based more on historians' assessments of whether the states saw themselves as principal enemies, sees Germany and Russia as rivals. The more behavioral measures that look at explicit

---

Text Box 2.3.   Germany–Russia territorial claims

1940–1945: Western Soviet Union (Claim Dyad 37801)
GMY–RUS
1943–1945: Königsberg/East Prussia (Claim Dyad 29401)
RUS–GMY

---

uses of militarized force do not indicate that a rivalry is present because there had been only four MIDs by 1914.

It is significant that, of the major players in July 1914, Germany–Russia had fewer MIDs than others, e.g. France and Germany, Britain and Germany, or Italy and Austria-Hungary. Likewise this dyad had had fewer arms races than France had had with Germany. Nor did Germany and Russia have any territorial claims against each other at this time.

Later as the territorial claims in Text Box 2.3 and the histogram show, territory became a key issue, with German conquests in the First World War and especially with the imposition of the treaty of Brest-Litovsk, which resulted in the secession of the Ukraine. This territorial claim carried over into the Second World War with Hitler's plans for *Lebensraum*. Before the First World War, however, there were no territorial disputes. To the extent that they were rivals before 1914 their rivalry was, as Thompson characterizes it, a struggle for position, and this was intimately involved with Germany supporting Austria-Hungary (and later the Ottoman Empire) and the competition for the allegiance of certain East European states, including Romania and Bulgaria.

Theoretical Analysis   All of this suggests that there were limited grievances. Unlike many of the major state dyads that entered the war, these two countries did not have many substantive disagreements. Rather they entered the war because they got caught up in a process of power politics. There were several elements at play: a strategy of coercion that followed a clear script and rules, alliances and alignments, previous learning that affected resolve, the prospect of an arms buildup that generated insecurity and hostility that made for hardliners, repeated crises that fueled rivalry and hostility, and lastly a set of military plans that created time pressure to decide quickly because of the contiguity of the armies.[33] Of these various factors, the failure of the coercive game was fundamental, and the alliances and alignment promoted the playing of the coercive game in the toughest way possible. For this reason contagion is seen in this dyad as resulting primarily from the first of the six contagion processes – contagion through alliances due to coercion failure. Contiguity played an added but subsidiary role in that the proximity of the armies made the military on each side hardliners who pressed for measures, namely mobilization, that not only increased the probability of war, but brought it about. Nonetheless, alongside these war-promoting factors, there were countervailing factors – vectors that pushed the decision-makers away from war – the most important being the personal desire of both the Tsar and the Kaiser to avoid war. Both, however, were willing to risk war, in the Tsar's case a world war that would involve both France and Britain and in the Kaiser's case a continental war where he hoped Britain would stand aside.

Because these two states were major states, this increased the probability that other major states would intervene (for the general pattern see Yamamoto and Bremer 1980). The initial joining broke the ice for both major and minor states and promoted further contagion. Grey was committed to defending France, and once the German army had attacked Belgium he had a moral issue that would bring on board some of those in the Cabinet reluctant to fight. The intervention of the major states made for a breakdown of the political order so that now major states were willing to let minor states use violence to bring about fundamental change through territorial shifts that they were not willing to permit in the past. Each of the major states attempted to entice a number of minor states, as well as Italy, to enter the war on this basis. As more states entered the war, it became more difficult for others to stay out. They entered because of the opportunity the war provided to gain stakes they could not gain during peacetime.[34]

The analysis of this dyad is based on a more revisionist position of Germany's role (see Vasquez 2014a). The conventional analysis places emphasis on Germany being responsible for the war and is best represented by the Fischer (1967, 1975) thesis (see also Mombauer 2013a). He sees Germany as starting the war and even deciding for war as early

[33] See Snyder (1984) and Van Evera (1984, 1999) for classic statements on some of these factors.
[34] As it became clearer that the war might change the world, it was important to take part in shaping the peace to protect one's own interest. This was one, but not the only, motive that may have played a role in the decision-making of some states, for instance, in Wilson's decision to join the war (see Stevenson 2011: 175; Cooper 2003: 439).

as the December 1912 war council. According to this analysis, Bethmann-Hollweg and others basically used the assassination as a way of getting the war they had always wanted. Fischer sees domestic German politics as important in the decision to go to war, including the timing of the war. Bethmann-Hollweg was concerned that the Social Democrats be convinced that Russia had started the war. Copeland (2000: Chs. 3 and 4, 2014b), who is a political scientist, places emphasis on Germany's desire to fight a preventive war and Bethmann-Hollweg's manipulation of the Kaiser and Austria-Hungary to bring about that war.[35] The most recent work, like that of Williamson (2014) and Clark (2012), has gone beyond this "German paradigm" and sees the war as having been brought about by a variety of factors and countries and not necessarily the responsibility of German decision-makers alone. In addition, these authors have seen Moltke as primarily pushing for a preventive war and the Kaiser and Bethmann-Hollweg as having a variety of aims that changed during the crisis itself. The present analysis is more reflective of this approach than of the preventive war hypothesis. Likewise, the analysis here sees the Kaiser in the last few days before the war as making a sincere effort to avoid the war. This is different from the view of Röhl (1994, 2012, 2014), who places much more blame on him for the onset of the war.

Outcome Both Germany and Tsarist Russia lost this war. Russian losses in the war ignited the internal forces that had long been agitating for revolution. In February–March 1917 the democratic Russian revolution overthrew Tsar Nicholas II, and he abdicated. Kerensky, who eventually became the head of this new government, continued the war, even initiating a new offensive in June, which resulted in another battlefield defeat (Keegan 1998: 338). This was a mistake, because one of the reasons for the revolutionary fervor was to end the war. At this time the Germans helped Lenin get to Helsinki in the hope that he would bring about a revolution. Within a matter of days of his arrival many responded to him, and a system of Soviets was created that overthrew the government in the October 1917 revolution. The Tsar was eventually executed along with all members of his family in order to prevent the Romanov dynasty ever returning to power. Lenin and Trotsky moved to end the war, but had to sign a very harsh peace at Brest-Litovsk. With this, the allies intervened to keep the

---

[35] Elsewhere (Vasquez 2014b) I attempt to provide a specific refutation of Copeland's position, so I will not discuss this here.

Eastern Front open and eventually were drawn into supporting the White Russians in the civil war.

In Germany, social unrest propelled by war weariness helped bring the war to an end. Starting with the mutiny of sailors at Kiel on November 3, rebellion spread to other cities, including Munich, and reached Berlin, where on November 9 Prince Max of Baden, who had been appointed as Chancellor in October, announced the Kaiser's abdication without his permission. A few hours later Philipp Scheidemann, a leading Social Democrat, declared a republic from the Reichstag balcony (see Röhl 2014: 177 for details). The war ended on the Western Front with an armistice at the eleventh hour of the eleventh day of the eleventh month. At Versailles, the new government was forced to sign a very harsh peace, even though foreign troops never conquered its territory. This would later come to haunt Germany in the form of Hitler and the charge that the German Army had been stabbed in the back by the new government.

Germany–France, August 3, 1914

As soon as Germany had declared war on Russia, it attacked France, going through Belgium. For those unfamiliar with the events, let alone German war plans, this seems a bit strange since the enemy was Russia and the crisis interactions of Germany and Austria-Hungary versus Russia and Serbia had involved France only in a secondary and supporting role. The fact that a war that had its origins in the Balkans and the East resulted in an initial military assault in the West illustrates the power of contagion, in particular the power of alliances as a contagion mechanism.

The Role of Alliances   After having his Halt-in-Belgrade plan fail in light of the Tsar's mobilization (see the Germany–Russia dyad above), the Kaiser turned matters over to Moltke and the army. One of the purposes of the Franco-Russian alliance was to intimidate Germany by facing it with a two-front war. Moltke and his predecessors had long planned for a two-front war by attacking France quickly, taking Paris while Russia slowly mobilized, and then swinging back to meet the Russian threat. This plan, which was initially conceived by the Chief of the German General Staff, Count von Schlieffen, and known by his name, was amended and revised over time by Moltke and is most accurately described as the Moltke–Schlieffen plan.[36] The plan illustrates

---

[36] Zuber (2002) has challenged whether the Schlieffen Plan was actually a war plan. See Lieber (2007) for an analysis of the implications of Zuber's thinking for explaining the First World War. See Mombauer (2006) for criticisms of Zuber's position and a review of the debate over his claims.

Text Box 3.1.   Germany–France alliances

Germany Alliances	France Alliances
1879–1918: AUH 2065	1893–1917: RUS 2075
1881–1887: AUH, RUS 2067	1902–1918: ITA 3001
1882–1918: AUH, ITA 2068	1907–1915: SPN, UKG 3005
1883–1918: ITA (–1915), ROM (–1916), AUH 2069	1912–1918: UKG 3013
1887–1890: RUS 2072	1915–1918: ITA, RUS (–1917), UKG 3019
1914–1918: TUR 3015	1916–1918: ITA, ROM, RUS, UKG 3022
1915–1918: AUH, BUL 3020	

how an alliance, by trying to reduce the power of an opponent by presenting it with a two-front war, encouraged war to spread and expand. Although France and Russia had plenty of allies at this time as Text Box 3.1 shows, this alliance was the key alliance that plunged the world into war. Moltke's military plan was responsible for spreading the war. There was no immediate substantive reason for Germany to attack France. Their grievances, although they existed on France's part, were not central to the July crisis. Nor was France directly involved in the coercive game that was being played by Germany, Austria-Hungary, and Russia, although it was indirectly involved in an important way. The Franco-Russian alliance had always been in the background, and the failure to successfully coerce meant that the alliance's contingency plans made the war spread rapidly.

So this dyad, like the German–Russian dyad, came to war because of contagion through alliances due to coercion failure. However, the details of the process and the roles of specific factors were slightly different. France was not a direct player in the crisis bargaining. The decision to go to war was not in the hands of Poincaré, the President, or Viviani, the Prime Minister. Whether the crisis escalated to war depended on the bargaining between the Kaiser and the Tsar and their ability to have gotten Austria-Hungary and Serbia to make some concessions. France's role was ancillary, particularly given the fact that both Poincaré and Viviani were at sea returning from their visit to St. Petersburg.

The Role of France in Spreading the War   Nonetheless, Poincaré and the French ambassador to Russia, Maurice Paléologue, played a critical role in activating the French commitment to Russia. From the very beginning they assured the Tsar that they were at his side, that France would go to war over a Balkan issue (Clark 2012: 350–353). They did not do what would have been beneficial for avoiding the war – namely, they did not tell the Tsar to support the Kaiser's or Grey's proposals for avoiding the war. Nor did they buttress the Tsar in resisting the advice of his military generals or moderate Sazonov by pointing out the risks of mobilization (see, for example, Otte 2014: 422). At a deeper level and for a much longer period they had increased the danger Russia posed to Germany by financing the construction of railways to make mobilization much faster. This, of course, was in France's interest in that it diminished the ability of Germany to win a war against France if it came about, but at the same time it increased the time pressure on German decision-making in a crisis.

If any pressure for peace was to come from the French government, it would have had to be from René Viviani. As both Prime Minister and Foreign Minister, he could have played a more forceful role, but the precise division of responsibilities between him and the President was not clear, neither constitutionally nor by precedent. Poincaré, most likely because of his personality, dominated. Still, Viviani softened positions here and there, and he hoped right to the end that war would be avoided; whereas Poincaré seemed to have made up his mind long before.

This has led some to argue that Poincaré really wanted war. Such a position was articulated early on in the 1920s by French Socialists and to a limited extent by the American revisionist H. E. Barnes (1970 [1926]). Mombauer (2002: 103) summarizes the French socialist view as follows: "Having been born in Lorraine, it was alleged that the former French president had been motivated by *revanche* ideas and had encouraged revanchist thoughts among the French people." This view is contrary to the common view in the last two decades that, because both leaders were literally at sea, France played no major causal role in bringing about the war (Keiger 1983). There is little direct evidence, in terms of documentary quotes, that Poincaré explicitly declared his preference for war, but there are some contextual factors consistent with this view. The thrust of the argument is that France could only hope to regain Alsace and Lorraine, which had been lost in the Franco-Prussian war, by having another war. A war with Germany in 1914 – with Russia and perhaps Britain as allies – could provide such an

Text Box 3.2.   Germany–France territorial claims

1849–1871: Prussian Rheinprovinz (Claim Dyad 22601)
FRN–GMY
1870–1871: Alsace-Lorraine (Claim Dyad 22401)
GMY–FRN
1875–1919: Alsace-Lorraine (Claim Dyad 22402)
FRN–GMY
1911–1911: French Congo (Claim Dyad 50801)
GMY–FRN
1911–1911: Logone River Triangle (Claim Dyad 51201)
FRN–GMY
1914–1919: Neukamerun (Claim Dyad 50802)
FRN–GMY
1917–1920: Saar (Sarre) (Claim Dyad 22604)
FRN–GMY
1918–1919: Eastern German Togo (Claim Dyad 43802)
FRN–GMY
1918–1919: French Cameroon (Claim Dyad 50402)
FRN–GMY
1920–1935: Saar (Sarre) (Claim Dyad 22605)
GMY–FRN

opportunity. Whether this was a hidden or simply a psychologically latent motive cannot be easily determined. Poincaré was born in Lorraine and both a hardliner and a nationalist, but he never expressly put forth the territorial objective during the July crisis, although it remained an official claim, as can be seen in Text Box 3.2. The fact that he did not mention it, however, is consistent with former Prime Minister Léon Gambetta's aphorism regarding the two provinces, "Y penser toujours, ne parler jamais" (Think of it always, speak of it never).

Barnes (1970 [1926]: 654–655) charges that Poincaré knew that France was not strong enough on its own to re-capture the lost provinces, but needed a general war to do that: "Both [Izvolsky and Poincaré] recognized that the chief objects of Russian and French foreign policy, the seizure of the Straits and the return of Alsace-Lorraine, could be realized only through a general European war." The only explicit quote he provides of Poincaré having this as his chief object, however, is a 1920 speech to university students, where he says "I could discover no other reason why my generation should go on living except for the hope of recovering our lost provinces" (Barnes 1970 [1926]: 386).

Still, this attack on Poincaré has not been sustained by recent historians. The most critical of France has been Schmidt (2007). He argues that Poincaré believed that a strong Franco-Russian alliance and firm resolve would avoid a war and perhaps even lead Germany to back down. He therefore is seen as risking war, but not necessarily welcoming it. His key concern and that of the French military was that Russia attack quickly so Germany would have to pull back troops from the West. To do that, Poincaré and Paléologue consistently took a hard line (see Trachtenberg 2010).

The Pattern of Previous MIDs Whatever the motives of Poincaré, what is clear, on comparing the conflict data for France and Germany with those for Germany and Russia, is that the former dyad had real grievances and a hostile relationship that put them at a greater risk of war. As Histogram 3 shows, France–Germany had had 12–14 MIDs by 1914, compared with the 4 for Germany–Russia. They were also rivals on all four measures, especially the behavioral (Diehl and Goertz, Klein *et al.*, and Senese and Vasquez) measures of repeated disputes. In addition, they had several territorial claims, compared with none for Germany–Russia. Many analysts feel that the modern rivalry between France and Germany had its origins in the loss of territory in the Franco-Prussian war. There is certainly a jump in hostility after that. Text Box 3.3 shows that the dominant issue is policy, but that 25% of the MIDs for the entire rivalry going back to 1830 are over territory. Likewise Thompson sees this as a spatial rivalry in part.

Nonetheless, it must be pointed out that Napoleon III was hostile to Prussia and Bismarck before the loss of Alsace and Lorraine. He had

---

Text Box 3.3.   Germany–France rivalry

Enduring Rivalry	Issue
KLEIN, GOERTZ, DIEHL: 1830–1940 DIEHL AND GOERTZ: 1830–1887; 1911–1945 THOMPSON: 1756–1955 SENESE AND VASQUEZ: 6th MID: 1866 ARMS RACE HORN: 1870–1873, 1913, 1933–1937	Dominant Issue: Policy 25% (+) Territory (1911–1945) THOMPSON: Positional and Spatial

sought to humiliate Prussia over the Spanish succession issue in 1870. In that sense there is an issue of status, and Thompson also classifies this as a positional rivalry. This positional struggle was joined with the other territorial issues that Napoleon III had pursued, namely his attempt to reclaim France's natural borders after the defeat of Napoleon I. The loss of Alsace and Lorraine raised the territorial question to a new height of nationalism and emotion.

Defeat in an important war and repeated crises no doubt had an impact on France re-building its military and the risk of arms races, which as the arms race data show were ongoing in 1870–1873 (related to the Franco-Prussian war, including its aftermath) and in 1913 and 1914.[37] The latter arms races were important because they raised tensions and fears in France regarding its physical security and being overrun by such a powerful and proximate neighbor. Despite these structural predispositions to war, however, it must be pointed out that France and Germany avoided war in the First and Second Moroccan Crises in 1904 and 1911 (Agadir). The latter, with its use of "compensation," showed the importance of diplomatic practices that could resolve territorial issues and avoid war. The latter crisis was also important because the Kaiser and Bethmann-Hollweg overruled the hardliner Kiderlen, the German State Secretary (foreign minister). Even so, the depth of the rivalry and the hostility residing within each nation was demonstrated by the fact that the peaceful resolution was resented in important sectors in both societies – the French government fell and in Germany the Kaiser was criticized in the press and Chancellor Bethmann-Hollweg jeered in the Reichstag. Moltke wrote privately to his wife that

If once again we crawl out of this affair with our tail between our legs ... Then I shall quit. But before that I shall propose that we do away with the army and place ourselves under the protection of Japan ... (Letter to Eliza, August 19, 1911 reprinted in Williamson and Van Wyk 2003: 91).

Theoretical Analysis   Contagion had three sources in the Franco-German dyad. The most fundamental was the Franco-Russian alliance structure, which pre-ordained a German attack on France if war broke out between Germany and Russia. The second was the chance to do something about the territorial claims and territorial rivalry over Alsace and Lorraine, which was, if not a source of war, a welcomed consequence of war. Lastly, joining a war provided an *opportunity* for revanche. The presence of one and most likely two other

---

[37] For 1914, see Histogram 3.

allies – Russia and Britain – reduced Germany's relative capability and thus lifted a barrier to war. A greater war provided a change in capability that favored France in that Germany was now considerably weaker than it would be in a bilateral war. Without an ongoing war the two states were less likely to go to war despite the grievances, especially those of France. These three contagion processes explain how and why these two major states came to war, even though they were not directly involved in the dynamics of the crisis bargaining in July 1914.

The involvement in the First World War of Germany–France as a dyad was a direct result of the escalation of the German–Russian crisis. The latter can be regarded as the second epicenter of war, with the first being Austria-Hungary and Serbia. This second earthquake brought in all the other major states in Europe with the exception of Italy. The Franco-Russian alliance insured that the French–German dyad would be the third dyad in the war once the coercion game had failed.

France got its war of revanche, but, just as the peace ending the Franco-Prussian War set the stage for the First World War, so too did the Peace of Versailles set the stage for the Second World War. By the early 1930s it would be Germany and Hitler that sought a war of revanche.

Germany–Belgium, August 4, 1914

Contagion by Contiguity   Belgium was a victim of this war primarily because of its physical location. Geography determined destiny. Theoretically this can be inferred because not only did Germany plan to go through Belgium to get to France, but also the French military wanted to do the same thing to get to Germany. The idea of going through Belgium came out of the war planning of each side – Moltke in Germany and Joffre in France. The Schlieffen plan modified by Moltke was a product of two considerations. The first was the tactical consideration of going around the heavily fortified border at Alsace and Lorraine. The second was the more strategic consideration of the Franco-Russian alliance. To deal with a two-front war, Schlieffen and then Moltke conceived of the plan of counting on the slow mobilization of the Russians to put the bulk of their force in the West to knock out France quickly and then swing back to the East.

The location of Belgium and its relatively weak defenses compared with the heavily fortified Franco-German border also made Joffre, the Chief of the French general staff, propose going through Belgium, even though he planned to attack Alsace and Lorraine frontally. For political reasons Poincaré vetoed this idea, because he knew invading Belgium would alienate Grey and the English (Williamson and Van Wyk 2003: 189; see also Clark 2012: 306–307).

Belgium was attacked, then, mostly because it was seen as an easy route to the enemy and its frontiers were less fortified because it was a buffer state. For Germany, however, and to a lesser extent France, Belgium was attacked because it was "in the way." It blocked Germany from getting to France, which was the ally of Russia. The reason Belgium was "in the way," however, was that the Franco-Russian alliance put Belgium in the way. Without that alliance it would not have been necessary for Germany to attack France because of a war with Russia. Contiguity played a crucial role, but it did not act alone. The opportunity and threat posed by Belgium's contiguity were activated by the war plans, which in turn were a function of the alliance structure. The alliance structure itself reflected a checkerboard pattern and, as in most such cases, was designed to make the enemy fight a two-front war.

This dyad came to war because of contagion, not grievances. Contagion is a better explanation than grievances or the issue and the steps-to-war explanation. One way of assessing this is by counterfactual reasoning. If the contagion explanation is correct and one takes away the ongoing war, then this dyad should not have gone to war. That seems to be a reasonable expectation. This is not to say that issue disagreements and some steps to war were not present in the dyad, only that they were not a significant causal force. Such inferences are difficult to make from statistical analyses, but in a case analysis they are easier to "see," although not necessarily to confirm by evidence.

What can be seen in Text Box 4.1 is that Belgium and Germany had five conflicting territorial claims, but only two dating from before 1914.

Text Box 4.1. Germany–Belgium territorial claims

1841–1919: Neutral Moresnet (Altenberg) (Claim Dyad 21601)
GMY–BEL
1909–1910: Lake Kivu Area (Claim Dyad 52801)
GMY–BEL
1916–1919: Ruanda-Urundi (Claim Dyad 52802)
BEL–GMY
1917–1919: Eupen and Malmedy (Claim Dyad 21801)
BEL–GMY
1919–1940: Eupen and Malmedy (Claim Dyad 21802)
GMY–BEL

One, Neutral Moresnet, was a border area, and the second was colonial. Both claims were made by Germany, with the first stemming from earlier Prussian claims. Neither of these produced a MID.

Neutral Moresnet as a border area might appear more salient because it could involve homeland territory, but neither country ever owned it in the post-Napoleonic period. It was created at the Congress of Vienna as a neutral area as a result of a dispute over a zinc mine between Prussia and the newly independent Netherlands (Belgium did not exist until its revolt from the latter in 1830). When Germany invaded in 1914, it treated the area as an occupied military territory in the same way as it treated Belgium as a whole.[38] The other territorial claim that was made by Germany was in East Africa, where Belgian and German interests collided on the ground. It was not a stake that would produce a war.

Histogram 4 also shows that there were limited grievances, with only one MID, and that in 1832 involving Prussia. This was a result of a multiparty dispute associated with the independence of Belgium from the Netherlands in 1830 that involved Belgium, France, Britain, and the Netherlands, as well as Prussia. By 1914 it was no longer an issue. Generally, then, Belgium and Germany had peaceful relations until the 1914 July crisis broke out. There was no rivalry until the war, as can be seen in Text Box 4.2, and this is indicated only by the Diehl and Goertz and the Senese and Vasquez measures, which are reflecting the MIDs after the war.

Of the other various steps to war, only arms races appear as a factor. Here we see arms races in the period 1868–1873, and more relevantly in 1913 and 1914. The latter two reflect Belgian realization that, because Belgium is surrounded by large neighbors, like Germany as well as France, it should have some defense.[39] In fact, during the July crisis its leaders felt that it had sufficient strength to defend itself, although this was not the case for outside observers, like Britain, France, and Germany (see Albertini, 1952 Vol. 3: 448). The arms race in 1913 shows some recognition of the threat posed by Germany (on the arms race see Stevenson 2007), but this was a result of a threat to

---

[38] The dispute over the zinc mine was resolved by creating this independent entity that had its own municipal officials, flag, etc. even though at one point it had a population of only 256. Prussia and the Netherlands had certain shared privileges in the country (such as conscription) that were taken over by Belgium after 1830. Once the zinc ore had been depleted there was little reason for its independence. Starting around 1900, Germany put more pressure on Belgium for negotiations. In 1915 Germany absorbed it during the war. At Versailles it was given to Belgium, see Sweers (2016).

[39] The data also show arms races for Horn between Belgium and France in 1870–1873 and in 1912–1913.

```
┌─────────────────────────────────────────────────────────────────────┐
│  ┌─────────────────────────────────────────────────────────────────┐ │
│  │                                                                   │ │
│     Text Box 4.2.    Germany–Belgium rivalries                        │
│  ═══════════════════════════════════════════════════════════════════  │
│  Enduring Rivalry                          Issue                       │
│  ─────────────────────────────────────────────────────────────────── │
│  DIEHL AND GOERTZ: 1914–1940              Dominant Issue: Territory and│
│  KLEIN, GOERTZ, DIEHL: 1914–1940          Policy                       │
│  SENESE AND VASQUEZ: 6th MID:                                          │
│  1936                                                                  │
│  ARMS RACE                                                             │
│  HORN: 1869–1873, 1913, 1933, 1934, 1936                              │
│  ═══════════════════════════════════════════════════════════════════  │
│  │                                                                   │ │
│  └─────────────────────────────────────────────────────────────────┘ │
└─────────────────────────────────────────────────────────────────────┘
```

invade Belgium with the intent not of conquering it, but of attacking France.

The threat of invasion was a result of a contagion process, not so much from the logic of the steps-to-war theory that focuses on the use of power politics to settle issues. The Germany–Belgium dyad went to war because of an ongoing war that had just started. The narrative of events makes that abundantly clear in that Bethmann-Hollweg asked permission to enter the country to fight the French. He did not want to have a war with Belgium.

Decisions for War   After the Kaiser had agreed to turn Moltke loose on August 1, the war plans were put into action by invading Luxembourg. Earlier versions of the Schlieffen–Moltke plan had called for attacking the Netherlands as well, but it was decided to forgo this and keep it as a windpipe for trade. This made Belgium the focus. Bethmann-Hollweg began by asking Belgium on August 1 for permission to enter her territory to engage the French, whom he (falsely) claimed had deployed forces by the Meuse. The tone was not overbearing in that it stated that "no acts of hostility against Belgium" were intended, that they would evacuate the territory as soon as there was peace, leave all its territory and colonies intact, and compensate Belgium in cash for any damages (see Albertini 1952, Vol. III: 452–453; Clark 2012: 549). At the same time, it was threatening in that it was an ultimatum with a twelve-hour deadline, and it said that if Belgium resisted it would be treated as an enemy (for more details see Clark 2012: 549–550). Following the invasion, Bethmann-Hollweg addressing the Reichstag on August 4 was even more apologetic, saying that the Germans had committed a wrong and violated international law, but they were forced to do so and would try to make it right as soon as

---

Text Box 4.3.   Germany–Belgium alliances

Germany Alliances	Belgium Alliances
1879–1918: AUH 2065	1920–1936: FRN 3024
1881–1887: AUH, RUS 2067	
1882–1918: AUH, ITA 2068	
1883–1918: ITA (–1915), ROM (–1916), AUH 2069	
1887–1890: RUS 2072	
1914–1918: OTM 3015	
1915–1918: AUH, BUL 3020	

---

they had met their military aims (quoted in McMeekin 2013: 377; see Mombauer 2013b: 571–572, doc 416 for excerpts). Of course, these remarks were made with an eye to the domestic Social Democrats and to the international audience, especially Britain. Nonetheless, they reflected the intention to pass through Belgium and not to conquer it.

King Albert, along with the entire government, decided to resist, despite the overwhelming force they were facing. To do any less, they said, would go against their honor as a nation. Still, they had no allies (Text Box 4.3) to aid them, a mistake they would not make again.[40] Nonetheless, the resistance was more than token, and the Belgians took heavy casualties at Liège,[41] but in the process delayed the German army, which may have denied the Germans the possibility of attaining ultimate success by taking Paris. Early on, the Germans were enraged by the resistance and committed a number of atrocities and reprisals, including the destruction of Louvain and the burning of its historic library (Keegan 1998: 81–83), which the British exploited for propaganda purposes.

The Bargaining Theory of War: An Anomaly   The heroic resistance of King Albert and the Belgian army is an anomaly for the bargaining theory of war. From the perspective of that theory, the resistance and war should not have occurred and the Belgians should have done the rational thing, which was to give in or try to negotiate a

---

[40] On the lessons learned by the Belgians from the failure of neutrality to protect them see Reiter (1996: 124–135).

[41] Conservative estimates are 2,000 to 3,000 Belgian dead and wounded with another 4,000 prisoners (www.en.wikipedia.org/wiki/Battle_of_Li%C3%A8ge). Herwig (2009) estimates the number as much larger.

deal at the margins. The bargaining theory of war maintains that, if the outcome of the war is known, then states should be able to reach a bargain that will avoid the costs of the war (Reiter 2003: 29, citing Fearon 1995). Each side knew the outcome of this war, so if the bargaining theory is correct the war should not have occurred. Fearon (1995) argues that there are three conditions under which a war might be fought and a bargain not reached – if information about capabilities is unclear (and hence the outcome uncertain), if there is a commitment problem where one side fears signing an agreement because future changes in capability may lead the side that gains considerably in power to renege on it, or because the issue is indivisible. The latter he relegates as considerably less important than the others. The Belgian decision to fight does not fit under any of these three exceptions.

First, the outcome is clear and the power differential enormous. The Belgians knew they would be defeated and that it would be a very costly defeat. The King "warned the members [of the Cabinet] that hostilities would assume a character of violence undreamed of ..." [that it] "would be a terrible ordeal for Belgium, and that it was essential not to do anything in a moment of passion ..." (Albertini 1952, Vol. 3: 458, quoting from the report of Galet). In addition, the outcome of fighting was much more disastrous for them than what the Germans were offering; namely, to keep their territory and independence intact, and pay for damages, as well as laying out the prospect for future friendly ties that would "grow stronger and more enduring" (quoted in Clark 2012: 549).

The "commitment problem" is not relevant here, since a future change in power is not a consideration.[42] Belgium was so low in power compared with Germany that fighting would mean it would lose and only be in a weaker position in the future. The main question was whether Germany might go back on its pledge and absorb Belgium. One decision-maker raised the possibility that Belgium would be annexed to the Reich (Albertini 1952, Vol. 3: 458). This possibility was not really taken that seriously, or at least was not discussed. There are two pieces of evidence that refute the commitment problem explanation. The first is that the Belgians never discussed the proposal in those terms. They were outraged by it and rejected it in principle as a great insult to their honor. In fact, it is the question of honor (and all the emotion associated with it) that produced the decision. The second is

---

[42] It is always difficult to determine whether one side will go back on its agreement, so one needs to see whether there is some way of enforcing it – normally this would be the future ability of the other side to punish non-compliance by going to war. This was not an option for the Belgians, since they would lose that war as they might this one, but agreement now would at least postpone the war.

that they made no effort to modify the bargain to make German commitment more enforceable. For example, they could have permitted German transit, but kept the army and made Germany stay away from certain other areas, including Antwerp, where the British could send aid.

What is even more remarkable is that after the fall of Liège the Germans repeated their offer on August 9: "Now that the Belgian army has upheld the honor of its arms by its heroic resistance to a very superior force, the German Government begs the King ... to spare Belgium the further horrors of war" (Albertini 1952, Vol. 3: 472). This was again rejected. Even after the Battle of the Marne the Germans made proposals "again and again" asking for some understanding between the two states, even offering recovery "of the Flemish regions of France" (Albertini 1952, Vol. 3: 472). By that time, however, the Belgians had joined the war effort of the Entente.

These repeated offers provide further evidence against the bargaining theory of war. First, there was now additional information on the outcome of the war, and, after the Battle of the Marne, the Germans improved their offer to get the Belgians out of the war. Second, the repeating of offers several times in light of increased information and that the Germans improved the offer should have increased the incentive to accept it, if Belgian decision-makers were thinking primarily in terms of costs and benefits. This did not happen. These additional offers after the German initial victory provide further evidence that it is not "rational" problems that made the Belgians reject the proposals, but their moral indignation.

Lastly, Fearon (1995) talks about the issue at stake as a source of bargaining failure. The issue in the ultimatum is divisible, and so not a reason for obviating a bargain, but note that the question of honor is not. Because none of the exceptions to making a bargain applies, this case is an anomaly for the bargaining theory of war.[43] The fact that honor is the key reason for rejecting the proposal out of hand suggests that a political psychology explanation that better explored the biological basis of the role of emotions in making decisions would be more applicable than the rational choice model.[44]

---

[43] Honor and moral indignation were also factors in the Melians rejecting the demands of Athens during the Peloponnesian War (see Thucydides, *The Melian Dialogue*). This is another and similar anomaly centuries before for the bargaining theory of war, suggesting that the Belgian case is hardly unique.

[44] One could hypothesize that the rational choice criteria utilize a different part of the brain and are associated with different chemical states than decisions based on value-laden criteria, like honor, that spark strong emotions.

What is more relevant theoretically is not why the decision to reject the proposal was made, but why the proposal (i.e. the ultimatum) was made in the first place. Here it is clear that Germany's war plans, going back to Schlieffen, were a key factor. The ongoing and future war is what prompted the German action; contagion is what brought this dyad to war. The contagion theory is a much better explanation of this case than the bargaining theory of war.

Third Parties   There were two third parties in this case – France and Britain. France's military also saw the advantage of going through Belgium. Joffre advocated this as far back as 1912. Going through Belgium was easier and would make for an early success for the offensive strategy to which he was committed. Because of Belgium's comparative weakness, he and others thought that the Germans would also go through Belgium, so they should go first. Like the Germans, Joffre felt they should reach a prior agreement with the Belgians; he also felt that they should seek British support.[45] As noted above, Poincaré blocked this for fear of losing British support. Nonetheless, the proposal was floated during the 1912 negotiations with the British, but even the British hardliner Henry Wilson thought unfavorably of it (Williamson and Van Wyk 2003: 191).

The Belgians were equally opposed to French intervention as to German, and early on warned that they would oppose either country if it violated Belgian neutrality. The doctrine of neutrality prohibited granting permission for troops to cross one's territory for the purpose of invading another. Despite concerns about France, the ultimatum focused Belgian attention on Germany. Nonetheless, the Belgians refused to let the French come in to meet the Germans and they rejected the offer of joint military actions with the French. Later, as things grew worse when Liège was attacked, King Albert asked for aid, but not much was forthcoming, at that time, as Joffre had his own war plans (Keegan 1998: 85).

A much more important third party than France was Britain, and in particular Grey. Grey was the main actor of whom Bethmann-Hollweg and the Kaiser were afraid. Several times they changed policy or phrasing, including wording in the ultimatum, in order to avoid antagonizing England (see Albertini 1952, Vol. 3: 454–455).

The integrity and neutrality of Belgium were a key issue for Grey because he hoped to keep the Cabinet together with this justification

---

[45] See the relevant section of Joffre's memoirs reprinted as a document in Williamson and Van Wyk (2003: 190–191).

and get them to agree to war. It was he who made the 1839 treaty protecting Belgium a focal point. It was he who asked both Germany and France on July 31 whether they would respect Belgium's neutrality (see Mombauer 2013b: 499–502, docs 355, 359). This public stance was a bit late since Germany was about to go to war, and, as noted in the Britain–Germany case study, this delay may have been because Grey feared that Germany might not attack Belgium and he would lose his rationale for the Cabinet.

Conclusion   The Germany–Belgium case is unlike the previous ones that have been examined to this point in that it represents an extension of the spreading of the war beyond the major states and the principals playing the coercive game. All the major states – Germany, Russia, France, Britain, and Austria-Hungary – came to war with each other because they were playing a coercive game that failed. When no one backed down, the dominos fell. This is a particular kind of contagion – one that drew these states into the local war between Austria-Hungary–Serbia – contagion through alliances.

That was not the case with Germany and Belgium. This dyad came to war because Germany had just declared war on Russia and France. War in this dyad was a product of an ongoing war. An ongoing war drawing in another party is the hallmark of contagion. The local dyadic war that expanded to bring in the major states in the first week of August fits this definition, but the Germany–Belgium dyad is the first that was brought into war that was not playing the coercive game. It reflects a different contagion process – war spreading through contiguity; specifically, war came to Belgium because it was in the way and not for any other reason.

Tragically for Belgium, it remained in the way and much of the combat on the Western Front was fought on its soil with it having no real say. Its land was scarred and its people had no voice as the war raged over what was once a proud and independent country.

Britain–Germany, August 4, 1914

The Crucial Role of Grey and the Decision for War   Like many of the other states that entered the war, Britain did so because of an individual decision-maker. In this case, it was Edward Grey, the Foreign Secretary. He was no straightforward hardliner, like Moltke or Berchtold, and he was the author of one of the better plans to avoid war; nonetheless, in the end he manipulated his fellow decision-makers, parliament, and the public into the war because he saw it as in the best interest of Britain.

For Grey there was only one reason for going to war – to protect France. He had hardly any interest in Russia (see Mombauer 2013b: 129, doc 83)[46] and even less in Serbia (McMeekin 2013: 204). As Sazonov contemplated war as early as July 24 and called in the French and British ambassadors for lunch, Buchanan – the British ambassador – told him, point blank, that Britain "had no interests in Serbia, and public opinion in England would never sanction a war on her behalf" (McMeekin 2013: 181). For Grey, Britain had an interest in maintaining a strong France, despite their previous colonial rivalry, which had only been put to rest a mere ten years ago in the 1904 Entente Cordiale. Deep down he was moved by the realist logic of the balance of power: France needed to be preserved against Germany. In his speech to the House of Commons, after talking at length about the importance of the neutrality of Belgium, he refers to this deep concern, although he does not mention the "balance of power." He says it is necessary to prevent Europe from "falling under the domination of a single Power" (sic) (Mombauer 2013b: 555, doc 401).[47] Other factors, like the naval arms race, the Kaiser's Kruger telegram, and the colonial rivalry played a role, but paramount was this conception of Britain's interest.

Unfortunately for Grey, only some of his colleagues accepted this proposition – Asquith, the Prime Minister; Churchill, head of the Admiralty but an outlier in the Cabinet, and a few others. Most of the Cabinet did not, and the risk of the government falling was real. Nonetheless, Grey believed he knew where the interest of the country lay, and he was determined that, if Germany attacked, Britain would stand at France's side. Yet he knew this reason would not garner the necessary votes in the Cabinet, so, when it became clear that Germany might attack France through Belgium, Grey seized upon that issue as a justification for war. This moral and legal issue he thought would carry the day among some of his Radical colleagues and hesitant Liberals.[48] It was not, of course, that Grey did not believe in preserving Belgian neutrality, it is just that in his mind it was not the real reason for going to war. To argue as he did was a kind of manipulation of his colleagues and of Parliament. Grey was willing to go so far, according to Williamson and Van Wyk (2003: 245) as not to openly threaten Germany with war if they attacked Belgium because he feared they

---

[46] On sentiment in Britain even after the 1907 agreement, see Clark (2012: 236).
[47] My thanks to Sean Lynn-Jones for bringing this passage to my attention.
[48] For a contemporary view of why Britain should not have entered the war see Ferguson (1999).

might, in fact, back down. Then they might attack another way and he would have no justification for going to war.

Realists would argue that, in order to prevent Germany from attacking, Grey needed not just to threaten Germany if they attacked Belgium, but to threaten them if they attacked France. The French ambassador, Paul Cambon, wanted an explicit pledge during the crisis, which he did not get, because Grey could not give one (Otte 2014: 457; McMeekin 2013: 314). Such a pledge would make Germany think twice. The argument that an explicit pledge might have deterred Germany and hence prevented the war has been made after the fact by political scientists as well (see Levy 1990/1991).[49] The domestic split, however, prevented Grey from doing this.[50] The Radicals were not only unwilling to go to war for France; even as early as 1912 Grey did not pursue the advice of those like Nicolson and Crowe to make an alliance with France as a way of dealing with the navy being overextended in the Mediterranean because he knew the Cabinet would oppose it (Williamson 1969: 270).

If invoking violation of Belgian neutrality as a *casus belli* was one way out of the domestic dilemma, there was also a more accommodationist way out – avoid the war through some sort of peace plan. Grey embraced this and pushed for some diplomatic settlement – either through four-power mediation based on the legacy of the Concert of Europe or by means of direct negotiations between the principals, namely Austria-Hungary and Russia. Grey thought, mistakenly, that, even after mobilization, war might be avoided in this way (Williamson and Van Wyk 2003: 232).

As Germany declared war against Russia and France, Grey went to Parliament to make the case for entering the war. Meanwhile the Cabinet was falling apart beneath him. Burns, Beauchamp, Morely, and Simon had already resigned (Otte 2014: 494). Lloyd George, the Chancellor of the Exchequer and leader of the Radicals, had switched to supporting war. Still there were those who were opposed,[51] and many did not even believe that Britain was legally bound by the 1839 Treaty that Grey had brought out to make his case (Mombauer 2013b: 402). In the end, Britain gave an ultimatum to Germany to cease its invasion of Belgium, and when the Germans had not responded by 11pm on August 4, Britain went to war. The night before, as Germany entered Belgium, Grey was recorded as saying, while looking out

---

[49] On the advantages of ambiguity for British policy see Crawford (2003: Ch. 4).
[50] See Otte (2014: 520) on how this would have happened.
[51] Immediately after Grey's speech, twenty-eight Liberal Party Members of Parliament gathered to reject intervention (McMeekin 2013: 369).

from his office at dusk, "The lamps are going out all over Europe, we shall not see them lit again in our life-time" (Otte 2014: 500).

Why Britain Entered the War   Britain was the last of the "Great European Powers" to enter the war. That was not an accident. Unlike Serbia and Austria-Hungary, it had no grievances against the others that made it want war, and unlike Germany and Russia it faced no immediate threat that compelled it to act first. Its concern, as seen by Grey, was a more calculated and strategic assessment of what might happen to the balance of power if Germany were to overrun France. Given Grey's inability to openly align with France and thus warn Germany, he could only wait for an attack through Belgium to get a *casus belli* that would commit the rest of his polity. Hence, Britain was the last to join the "Great" war.

Compared with the other five nation-states, Britain's entrance seems singular. It had no real territorial rivalry, nor was the war an immediate opportunity, and there was no formal full-blown defensive alliance before the war (see Text Box 5.1). On July 31, during the fateful weekend before the war, Grey told the British Ambassador to France that "Nobody here feels ... British treaties or obligations are involved ... I have told [*sic*] French Ambassador that we cannot undertake a definite pledge to intervene in a war" (Mombauer 2013b: 499–500, doc 356).

Still, each of the steps of war played a role. Even though, unlike the Franco-Russian alliance, the British Entente did not legally commit Britain to defend France if it were attacked, Grey wanted to defend France because he saw this as paramount to Britain's interest. As with

---

Text Box 5.1.   United Kingdom–Germany alliances

United Kingdom Alliances	Germany Alliances
1902–1930: JPN 3000	1879–1918: AUH 2065
1907–1915: FRN, SPN 3005	1881–1887: AUH, RUS 2067
1912–1918: FRN 3013	1882–1918: AUH, ITA 2068
1915–1918: FRN, ITA, RUS (–1917) 3019	1883–1918: ITA (–1915), ROM (–1916), AUH 2069
1916–1918: FRN, ITA, ROM, RUS (–1917) 3022	1887–1890: RUS 2072
	1914–1918: OTM 3015
	1915–1918: AUH, BUL 3020

the Franco-Russian alliance, it was not the formal terms of commitment, but the underlying bilateral interest, that made the alliance promote war. Although the alliance was an Entente primarily resolving colonial rivalry, the alliance bonds tightened over time. This began with the First Moroccan Crisis in 1905–1906. Bonds were tightened further in the Agadir crisis of 1911, with more elaborate staff-level talks that even pinpointed where the British Expeditionary force might land. These talks were kept secret from Parliament (MacMillan 2013: 397–398; see also Williamson and Van Wyk 2003: 224–226; Williamson 1969: Chs. 12 and 13). The major military agreement between the two occurred in 1912 when Britain moved its Mediterranean fleet to the North Sea and France vice versa, with the understanding that each would protect these respective areas for the other (McMeekin 2013: 72–73). This left the French Atlantic coast unprotected in the event of war, other than by the Royal Navy, and this was a previous commitment that many saw as a reason for supporting France in July–August 1914. Indeed, the first public commitment to France by the Cabinet came on August 2, amounting to a pledge to defend its northern coast.

Ultimately, it must be emphasized that what actually brought Britain into the war was the failure of the coercive game. The reason Germany attacked France and went through Belgium was that Russia did not back down and the coercive game failed. From a causal perspective, Britain came into the war by the same causal process and contagion mechanism as Germany and Russia, and France, even though the specifics for each dyad differed. The structure of the alliance arrangement made each enter from the same underlying causal process. What differed were the motivations and particulars accompanying the failure of the coercive game.

The domestic political situation in Britain was more split, so Grey had to come up with a substitute reason to get dissenters on board.[52] In addition, he had to wait until the war had actually started for this substitute reason to get actualized. Also he was not interested in going to war for the other member of the Entente – Russia – or for its client – Serbia, the main reason why the coercive game was being played. This raises some questions about the adequacy of the realist concept of national interest as a guide to explaining foreign policy-making.

---

[52] It must be remembered, though, that Bethmann-Hollweg and the Kaiser also faced a Reichstag that needed to be convinced. They, however, were more successful than Grey in getting support.

Grey and the Idea of National Interest   While it is true that Grey acted in accord with the way realists understood Britain's national interest, what is troubling is that a majority of the Cabinet did not conceive of the national interest in this way. Starting with Morgenthau (1954, 1973: 5–8, his second principle of realism) the idea of the national interest has been seen as something that is a law of international politics that is objective and universal. For Morgenthau (1952) it goes beyond the particularistic interests of class, region, or ethnicity. Everyone can agree on the essential interest of survival taking precedence over everything else in foreign policy. Hence, he defines its irreducible minimum as "the integrity of the nation's territory, of its political institutions and its culture" (Morgenthau 1952: 973), or in short territorial integrity and political sovereignty. He goes on to say that "Thus bipartisanship in foreign policy, especially in times of war, has been most easily achieved in the promotion of these minimum requirements" (Morgenthau 1952: 973).

Knowing that state leaders are compelled to act in the national interest is a powerful theoretical tool. In Morgenthau's words (1954, 1973: 5), "We assume that statesmen think and act in terms of interest defined as power, and the evidence of history bears that assumption out. That assumption allows us to retrace and anticipate, as it were the steps a statesman – past, present, or future – has taken or will take on the political scene." This means that for a realist the national interest can be read as a script known to all. It is not subject to the bias of personal interpretation or judgment; all who are rational (broadly defined) will be able to discern what it is. This does not mean that there will not be delusions, misperceptions, or even mistakes. There will be, but these will be punished mercilessly by the system just as physics punishes those who flout the law of gravity.

The British and Grey's case raise the question of just how easy it is to "read" the national interest. The decision-making of the dyads that entered the war provides a body of evidence to address this question. Here we will focus not on the more normative question of whether decision-makers *accurately* derived their national interest, but on the simpler question of whether they could easily derive it from the circumstances they were facing. Certainly Morgenthau's second principle of realism permits us to anticipate Grey's actions, but not the position of the majority of the Cabinet, which appears anomalous to say the least. If Morgenthau's laws are correct, then most of the decision-makers of the time should have been able to agree on what the national interest was. Of course, they do not use Morgenthau's language, since he wrote over thirty years later, but, if he is correct, there should be a clear goal and policy that should be obvious to all and that would protect the territorial integrity and political sovereignty of the nation.

Grey follows what many realists both within and outside of Britain would expect British interests to be – defend France against Germany to maintain the so-called "balance of power," which is logically compatible with defending Britain's territorial integrity and political sovereignty.[53] Unfortunately, for Grey, he could not get the majority of the Cabinet to read Britain's interest that way. Instead, the Radicals and others abhorred war in general and saw no need in this particular circumstance to defend France. They were prepared to see the government fall if it came to that. Grey had no doubts about this, neither did the prime minister, Asquith.

To actually defend Britain's interest, Grey had to find a policy and reason they might consider worthy of war. He settled on the defense of Belgian neutrality. To get Britain to do what was in its interest he had to invent a different policy that would gain a majority. This involved manipulating the Cabinet and Parliament. This is a far cry from everyone reading the national interest and then pursuing it with maybe just minor squabbles over the means. The second principle of realism and the idea that the national interest can be read as a script are not borne out in this case. *What we see instead is severe disagreement.*

One of the lessons of this case is that the concept of the national interest is not as objective and universal as some have thought. It does not produce the easy consensus that one would want even within the very elite and similarly educated English decision-makers of 1914.[54]

What are the implications of this conclusion for the remainder of this study? It implies that, when there is a strong leader, the idea of the national interest can be used to re-trace the steps of the decision-maker in the way Morgenthau predicts, but when the government is split this will not work. Instead, the inability to agree on the national interest will make the decision to enter the war dependent on difficult-to-predict

---

[53] Morgenthau (1952: 972), making an analogy to the U.S. Constitution, says of the national interest that narrowly it is the state's territorial integrity and political sovereignty, "but beyond these minimum requirements its content can run the whole gamut of meanings which are logically compatible with it." For Britain this was usually interpreted as maintaining a balance of power on the continent, and for some Americans this was interpreted as defending Britain. Morgenthau (1973: 195–197) describes Britain as the classic example of a balancer (see also Lieven 2015: 9).

[54] It may be the case that the realist conception of the national interest was not borne out in many of the cases in the First World War. A large number show a decision-making unit or government severely divided about what the national interest is. These include Bulgaria, Romania, and – the most extreme case – Greece (see the respective dyad cases below).

contingencies, one of which will be outside influences, including auctions.

The Role of the Naval Race, Rivalry, and Previous MIDs All of this is not to say that certain background factors were not at play that made Britain and Germany hostile. That hostility is commonly acknowledged to have its major source in 1898 with the naval arms race with Germany. Kennedy (1980), in the best work on this question, maintains that prior to the naval race Anglo-German relations were more neutral. The naval race sparked the Anglo-German rivalry or antagonism, as Kennedy calls it. At the turn of the century British foreign relations went through a number of turning points that reduced competitions or rivalries with France (1898/1904), the U.S. (1895), Japan (1902), and Russia (1907). The idea that she was a weary Titan (Friedberg 1988), and had to reduce conflict, naturally suggested she could do the same with Germany, and Bismarck and later leaders were receptive to an improvement in relations.[55] The naval race and the attempt of the Kaiser to challenge British naval hegemony produced a step-level change in the relationship between the two polities, i.e. a change not only in leadership perceptions, but in public sentiment as well. Ironically, the naval race does not appear in Text Box 5.2 because the Horn measure is based on a calculation of mutual military expenditures, and these just do not meet the threshold, in part because the

---

Text Box 5.2.   United Kingdom–Germany rivalry

Enduring Rivalry	Issue
KLEIN, GOERTZ, DIEHL: 1887–1921 DIEHL AND GOERTZ: 1887–1921 THOMPSON: 1896–1918 (Positional and Spatial), 1934–1945 (Positional) SENESE AND VASQUEZ: 6th MID: 1899 ARMS RACE HORN: 1935–1938	Dominant Issue: Policy 25% (+) Territory THOMPSON: Positional and Spatial

---

[55] The alternate view is that she viewed Germany as the principal rival and reduced the other rivalries in order to be able to meet the German challenge (see Thompson and Dreyer 2012: 49).

competition is naval and much of the expenditures, especially on Germany's part, involved land expenditures. The naval race was accompanied by other acts and MIDs that increased hostility.

Some of the non-MIDs were flamboyant verbal acts, like the Kaiser's 1896 Kruger telegram supporting the Boers and referring to the "hordes that have invaded your country." Others, like the 1908 "interview" published in the *Daily Telegraph* were inadvertent remarks complaining (rather undiplomatically) of Britain not reciprocating his friendship.[56] Colonial competition accentuated this verbal hostility. While the naval race made the British more hostile, the unwillingness of Britain and France to make a place for Germany irked the Germans. The Kaiser and other Germans resented the extent to which Britain would not give even the smallest concessions, as in the Samoa dispute (the 1887 territorial claim and the related MIDs in 1887 and 1888 in Histogram 5). The rivalry boxes indicate that, with Diehl and Goertz dating the rivalry from 1887 with colonial struggles in Samoa and South Africa, and Thompson dating it from 1896 just before the naval race.

Histogram 5 captures the nature of this competition, as do the territorial claims. The first six MIDs go up through 1899 and some are fairly intense, often reaching level 4 hostility for the use of force. Concomitant with them were a series of territorial colonial claims. None of these or the MIDs associated with them really threatened all-out war. This was because the two states were not contiguous and Germany was no naval match for Britain. In part this was why the Kaiser decided to build a navy, starting in 1898. It was because of the prospect of increased military capability that could "reach" Britain and its Empire that the naval race made Britain see Germany as its principal enemy. Of course, the dramatic increase in Germany's economic capability and trade must also be seen as a key underlying threat as well (Organski and Kugler 1980: 57–60).

Nonetheless, the Kaiser and Bethmann-Hollweg wanted to create a more friendly relationship with Britain, and this had been a central component of Bethmann-Hollweg's foreign policy (McMeekin 2013: 276). In many ways he was an Anglophile, while the Kaiser could be seen, as in the *Daily Telegraph* interview, as a scorned suitor. Even more of an Anglophile was Prince Lichnowsky, the German Ambassador in London. He would often put the most positive face on proposals, as

---

[56] MacMillan (2013: 136–138) provides some nice background and details about the incident.

when he agreed to mediation in 1914. With the exception of the Grey–Lichnowsky relationship, which remained individual, sentiments of this sort appeared only on the German side and not among the British. They were at best more neutral and sometimes openly hostile. As the July crisis evolved, Bethmann-Hollweg and the Kaiser would do just about anything to avoid war with Britain. Bethmann-Hollweg went so far as to suggest to the Kaiser that they sacrifice the German navy by reducing planned spending "for an agreement with England" (McMeekin 2013: 275), a suggestion the Kaiser summarily rejected.

Even though the affect between the leaders was not reciprocal, they did have some positive relations in 1914, the most important of which was the signing in February of an agreement on the Baghdad railway between Berlin and Baghdad that brought in Britain in key parts and raised hopes for cooperation (Clark 2012: 338). Previously, they had settled some of the important colonial issues (see Text Box 5.3), like trading Heligoland for German concessions in Zanzibar, as well as in the Pacific, although these were associated with threats of force. Still, the important Haldane mission to regulate arms failed, mostly because

---

Text Box 5.3.   United Kingdom–Germany territorial claims

1884–1890: Heligoland (Helgoland) (Claim Dyad 25001)
GMY–UKG
1885–1911: Rooibank and Ururas Areas (Claim Dyad 63601)
GMY–UKG
1887–1899: German Samoa (Upola and Savaii) (Claim Dyad 98204)
UKG–GMY
1889–1893: Vanga (Claim Dyad 54201)
GMY–UKG
1895–1899: German Solomon Islands (Claim Dyad 98301)
UKG–GMY
1914–1919: German New Guinea (Claim Dyad 97601)
UKG–GMY
1915–1915: German South West Africa (Claim Dyad 63602)
UKG–GMY
1917–1919: Western German Togo (Claim Dyad 43801)
UKG–GMY
1917–1919: British Cameroon (Claim Dyad 50401)
UKG–GMY
1917–1919: German East Africa (Claim Dyad 54202)
UKG–GMY

Haldane thought the British had won the arms race (which they had) and needed little from the Germans (Clark 2012: 319). Yet, when all is said and done, Grey and the Kaiser were on the same page – both worked hard to avoid war, both were sincere, and their two plans were compatible.

Their main difference was that Grey was committed to going to war if Germany attacked France, whereas the Kaiser and Bethmann-Hollweg wanted to avoid war only with Britain. This background in part helps explain the bizarre incident that occurred on August 1. Just prior to that, on July 29 Bethmann-Hollweg met with Goschen, the British Ambassador, to try to get Britain to remain neutral, especially if Russia attacked Austria-Hungary. He and the Kaiser had some hope of accomplishing this because an earlier message from King George V had raised the possibility of being neutral (McMeekin 2013: 276). Goschen asked whether Germany would respect Belgium's neutrality and Bethmann-Hollweg waffled. Grey replied through Lichnowsky that evening and now gave the explicit commitment he had so often avoided before; namely, that Britain would enter the war.[57] The wishful thinking of the Kaiser and Bethmann-Hollweg came to an end, and the Chancellor at 3am sent the telegram to Vienna threatening to withdraw support if the Austrians did not enter talks.[58]

It was in this context of having given up all hope about Britain that on August 1 Lichnowsky wrote saying that Grey had called him in, saying that, if France were not attacked, Britain would remain neutral, and he suggested that France might remain passive as well if the war were confined to Russia (Otte 2014: 474; McMeekin 2013: 330–331, 341–342). The Kaiser and Bethmann-Hollweg were delighted, and the Kaiser forced Moltke to abandon his war plans, much to his consternation and vehement objection (see the Austria-Hungary–Serbia case above). That night, soon after the Kaiser had gone to bed, news came from King George V that there must have been some misunderstanding about what Grey said and that was the end of the matter. Moltke was called in, and in light of the events in the East (see the Germany–Russia case) the Kaiser threw in the towel and set him loose to follow the military plan of going through Belgium.

Theoretical Analysis Although Germany brought Britain into the war by going through Belgium, the decision for war within this dyad

---

[57] On these events see McMeekin (2013: 277–280).

[58] It was the realization that Britain would definitely enter that gave Bethmann-Hollweg cold feet and made him much more active in pressuring Austria-Hungary (see Stevenson 1996: 402–403).

was really a one-way entry where Britain, and specifically Grey, decided for war, while the Kaiser and Bethmann-Hollweg did not want to go to war with Britain. Of course, Grey was responding to their attack on France, but that in turn was the result of the failure of the coercive game. Thus, contagion in this case must be seen as a result of the failure of the coercive game and the Entente that bound Grey to France. Despite the atypical one-way nature of the war decision, the dyad still fits the pattern of the other major states. The alliance and the underlying interest as interpreted by Grey brought the British into the war as a result of the outcome of the failed coercive game. Alliances were the contagion process that brought in Britain, even though Grey refused to actively play the coercive game.

It should also be noted that the crucial role Grey played in bringing Britain to war while averting the government from falling shows the very contingent nature of Britain's entry into the war.[59] Nonetheless, various structural factors played a role that made Grey and others willing to go to war. Among the most important were the naval arms race, hostility, rivalry, alliance ties, and repeated confrontations, all of which were self-reinforcing.

Montenegro–Austria-Hungary, August 5, 1914; and Montenegro–Germany, August 8, 1914

It is not surprising that Montenegro should have been among the initial countries to declare war. It was a staunch ally of Serbia and was ethnically Serbian. After the Second Balkan War there was serious talk of a political union of the two. It did not declare war against Austria-Hungary because the Habsburgs were the enemy of its friend, but because Austria-Hungary was its enemy. Serbian nationalism pervaded the country, and King Nikola I was no exception. Montenegro was a founding member of the Balkan League, and it was the first to declare war against the Ottoman Empire in the First Balkan War on October 8, 1912, with Serbia, Bulgaria, and Greece not joining in until over a week later. It was also very firm in the crises with Austria-Hungary during the two Balkan Wars, especially that over Scutari in 1913, where Austria-Hungary threatened and was prepared to go to war if Montenegro did not withdraw from its siege of it (see MacMillan 2013: 492–493 for details).

Montenegro can be seen as going to war because of its previous hostile interactions and MIDs with Austria-Hungary, its territorial grievances

---

[59] See Otte (2014: 504ff) for an argument on the importance of individual interactions and their contingent nature in the outbreak of the First World War.

due to its Serbian nationalism, and its alliance with Serbia. Montenegro is not in the Correlates of War data set because it does not meet the minimum population threshold of 500,000 to be included as a system member (Sarkees and Wayman 2010: 16), but there is no doubt that all of the above factors are present. Conversely, its declaration of war against Germany two days later on August 8 can be seen as valence balancing.

In 1916, with Serbia being overrun, its army, along with integrated Montenegrin units, retreated through Montenegro to Corfu. The retreat led to disagreements, and Montenegro splintered internally, with the King forming a government in exile and divided from those on the ground who would eventually try to depose him by calling a national assembly. With the conclusion of the war, the issue of the future of Montenegro was left to the great powers at Versailles, with Wilson supporting self-determination, but no one was clear on what that meant in this instance. Ultimately, Montenegro became part of Yugoslavia and King Nikola I died in exile in 1921 not long after France and Britain had withdrawn their support (MacMillan 2001: 119–120).

Austria-Hungary–Russia, August 6, 1914

Austria-Hungary and Russia are at the core of the coercive game that failed and brought about the First World War. Tsar Nicholas II tried to prevent Austria-Hungary from fighting a war against Serbia by threatening war against it if it did so. This was not the first time that either side had been involved in a coercive game. The main precedent was in 1908 and the most recent in 1912 during the Balkan Wars. In the first, Russia had to back down because it was still recovering from the Russo-Japanese War of 1904–1905. In the second, both sides pulled away from the abyss after each had mobilized on their mutual border. Each of these precedents had legacies for the relationship as they went into 1914.

The Role of Previous MIDs and Crises As Histogram 6 shows, these two states had confronted each other from the middle of the nineteenth century on. It was not always that way. They were staunch allies in the war against Napoleon, and they formed the core of the conservative–monarchical wing of the Concert of Europe as indicated by the Holy Alliance of 1815 of Russia, Austria, and Prussia of the three leading emperors. In 1849 when the new Emperor Franz Josef was threatened by revolution in Budapest, Tsar Nicholas I sent in troops to

---

Text Box 6.1.   Austria–Hungary–Russia rivalry

Enduring Rivalry	Issue
THOMPSON: 1768–1918	Dominant Issue: Policy
	THOMPSON: Positional and Spatial
ARMS RACE	
HORN: 1878, 1879	

---

put down the revolt. In 1852 as the liberal Napoleon III and England under the influence of Palmerston challenged Russia in the prelude to the Crimean War, Austria led the Concert to resolve the crisis, first with the Vienna Note and then with the Olmütz Proposals. These efforts should have prevented war, but they did not because of hardliners in England, leading some to argue that the Crimean War was an unnecessary war (see Richardson 1994; Rich 1985). Austria resisted British efforts and enticements to get her to intervene. However, in 1854 she threatened to intervene if Russia did not withdraw from the Ottoman provinces of Moldavia and Walachia, which Austria then occupied upon their withdrawal. The Crimean War produced the two MIDs in 1854 in Histogram 6. Toward the end of the war, Austria threatened Russia with armed intervention if she did not enter negotiations to end the war. These two actions represented a turning point in the relations of the two states that had been basically friendly since the Napoleonic era.

Thompson and Dreyer (2012: 40), however, date their rivalry to 1768, as can be seen in Text Box 6.1, although they also state that their relations fluctuated between alliances, mutual assistance, and confrontation. Of the confrontations, the most important resulted from their competition over the Ottoman areas of Europe. The Diehl and Goertz measure, which does not begin until 1816, does not indicate a rivalry because there were not six MIDs by the time Austria-Hungary collapsed in 1919.

The competition over Ottoman territory reached a highpoint in the 1908–1909 Bosnian crisis.[60] Izvolsky, the Russian Foreign Minister, thought he had reached an agreement with Aehrenthal, the Austrian

---

[60] For technical reasons this is listed not as a MID between Austria-Hungary and Russia in the Correlates of War data, but as a MID between Germany and Russia; see Histogram 2 for that case.

foreign minister, whereby Russia would recognize the Austrian annexation of Bosnia and Hercegovina and in return Austria would support Russia's desire for free passage of its warships through the Straits. Austria went ahead with the annexation. As the second part of the deal became public, Britain raised objections and Aehrenthal back-pedalled, denying there was ever a *quid pro quo*. Meanwhile Serbia protested, mobilized, and threatened war. During the crisis Conrad mobilized forces against Serbia and "made preparations to mobilize forces in Galicia near the border with Russia" (MacMillan 2013: 430), which the Russians publically accused the Austrians of actually implementing, while Izvolsky complained directly to Berchtold (Stevenson 1996: 125).[61]

Germany intervened by sending, in effect, an ultimatum saying that if Russia went to war with Austria-Hungary it would go to war in its defense. Tsar Nicholas II had to back down, given that Russia was still recovering. The Serbian government also had to back down and accept a harsh settlement, including giving up its territorial claim and agreeing to end agitation for the territory, as nationalists outside the government raged for war (see MacMillan 2013: 429).

Izvolsky was also personally humiliated and removed as foreign minister. As a consolation he became ambassador to France, where he was in 1914. He had never forgotten his humiliation by Austria-Hungary, and with the prospect of war he pushed the French on. McMeekin (2013: 55–56) states that, when Russia mobilized, "Izvolsky reportedly exclaimed, 'This is my war!'" His ranting about Austria-Hungary and his desire for revenge were well known, and some, like socialist leader Jean Jaurès, who was assassinated just before war broke out on July 31, complained of his undue influence and personal motives for war (McMeekin 2013: 322).

Part of the legacy of the Bosnian crisis, which fits a general pattern (see Leng 1983), is that it increased the number of hardliners and led to more intense and hostile crises in the future. This happened foremost in Russia with the vow by the Tsar not to be humiliated again. In Austria-Hungary and Germany it led to the lesson that Russia would back down if they were firm. On a personal level, Izvolsky became a dangerous hardliner, given his position as ambassador in Paris where he was not only receptive to the hard line of Poincaré, but also pushed for hardline actions against Austria-Hungary and Germany.

---

[61] Stevenson (1996: 126) believes that Conrad never actually increased the deployment of troops, but does note that "Conrad told the German attaché in Vienna ... 'in Galicia we are, so to speak, prepared.'" This is very close to being a MID, and it was certainly perceived as a threat by Izvolsky.

The next crisis came during the Balkan Wars, as indicated by the 1912 MID in Histogram 6. Rather than being the principal belligerents as in 1908–1909, Germany and Russia were third parties in the confrontation between Austria-Hungary and Serbia. There were several issues during the two wars that raised tensions, but the central one was when Serbia tried to gain access to the Adriatic and was on the verge of doing so militarily when it was blocked by Austria-Hungary by the latter proposing the new state of Albania. To gain his objective, Berchtold had to eventually issue an ultimatum threatening war to get Serbia to cease and desist (MacMillan 2013: 496). Simultaneously, he got agreement from the major states for a diplomatic solution favoring Austria-Hungary. Russia was not prepared to go to war for Serbia's larger demands and eventually supported the agreement of the major states; not before the Winter Crisis of 1912–1913, however.[62]

The Winter Crisis started with the announcement by Russia of a "trial mobilization" near the Galician border and the calling up of troops. It occurred in the context of Sazonov accepting in principle the creation of Albania, but this devolved into crucial differences over specific areas from which Serbia and Montenegro had to withdraw (Clark 2012: 284).

Clark (2012: 266–267) attributes the firmer Russian move to Sazonov embracing a new policy of coupling diplomatic actions with the threat of force. This in turn was associated with a decline in the influence of Kokovstov, the accommodationist Chair of the Council of Ministers, and an acceptance of more of Sukhomlinov's position by both Sazonov and the Tsar. However, the mobilization proved financially onerous for both sides, especially Austria-Hungary,[63] and both gradually reduced their strength, with the end of the crisis coming in March 1913 with a public announcement of troop withdrawals. Austria-Hungary was the first to move back, starting in late January (Clark 2012: 269–270).

The Winter Crisis and the two Balkan Wars represented another playing of the coercive game as in 1908–1909 and later in 1914, even though there were important differences in each case. Although the major states feared war might occur, and the mobilization had its own dynamic, ultimately both sides de-mobilized. Austria-Hungary basically got what it wanted from Serbia. It blocked Serbia's access to the sea

---

[62] The main crisis over the Balkan Wars ended for the two with the May 1913 agreement of the major states. The Winter Crisis preceded this from December through March.

[63] Even the Kaiser referred to this in July 1914 in that he did not want Austria-Hungary to endure another expensive mobilization without some sort of victory. See where he outlines his Halt-in-Belgrade proposal (Mombauer 2013b: 408, doc 277).

and created the new state of Albania. Serbia, although it lost, nonetheless had much to absorb from the two Balkan Wars, and Russia, although it de-mobilized and saw Serbia pushed back, still had accomplished much with the creation of the Balkan League and the liberation of more Slavs. Still, it was forced to choose between Bulgaria and Serbia in the Second Balkan War and went with the latter. Meanwhile Austria-Hungary flirted with supporting Bulgaria, but did nothing for the time being.

These two crises set the stage for 1914. Here a coercive game was played, but unlike in the previous two crises no one backed down. Most of the dynamic of the chicken game, however, took place between Germany and Russia and not between Austria-Hungary and Russia. In fact, part of Grey's effort was to try to get direct talks between the two principals, to no avail. This was mostly because Berchtold did not want talks, as indicated by his ignoring the last plea of Bethmann-Hollweg on July 30.

The Onset of War   The 1914 MID between the two reached a highpoint starting on July 23 when Austria-Hungary delivered the ultimatum to Serbia. As Sazonov and Poincaré (who was in St. Petersburg at the time) got wind of this, they separately warned Berchtold not to send an ultimatum (McMeekin 2013: xvii, 168–169). This came too late. After a short delay, once the ultimatum had been received, Sazonov urged the Pašić government to resist, which they did on July 25, even though they accepted all but one demand. The next highpoint of tension was on July 28 when Austria-Hungary declared war. There was then a rush by the two allies of the dyad principals to avoid war. The Kaiser failed to deliver Austria-Hungary and Grey was unable to deliver Russia. On July 29, Berchtold, worried about the Kaiser's second thoughts, bombarded Belgrade.

Ironically, Austria-Hungary and Russia were the last dyad among the major states to declare war. It was not until August 6 that Austria-Hungary declared war on Russia. By this time all the principals which had played the coercive game, plus Belgium, were at war. By August 5, however, Austria-Hungary was still only at war with Serbia. Part of the reason for this was that Berchtold and Conrad were not ready for war and wanted only to fight Serbia, not Russia. They were hoping that they could avoid any major battle with Russia so they could concentrate on the Serbian front. Moltke needed them in Galicia to hold the Russians, and it was this military pressure that eventually prompted them to declare war. Still, the delay indicates the extent to which war between the two was a result of the Austria-Hungary–Serbia conflict rather than of any direct grievances between the two of them. The way they went to war indicates that it was third parties that were crucial to bringing them to war.

Third Parties The chief goal of Berchtold, Conrad, and Franz Josef was to fight a war with Serbia in order to end the nationalist threat once and for all.[64] The local war was paramount for them, and they hoped to keep Russia out by relying on Germany to intimidate it, as had happened in 1908–1909. That was the entire point of the von Hoyos Mission and why Franz Josef insisted on German support as a pre-requisite to the war. They, along with a host of German decision-makers starting with the Kaiser, thought that Russia would back down because it was not ready for war. Moltke was the main exception, because he did not want Russia to back down, but intended to take advantage of the "better now than later" situation that the July crisis posed. For Austria-Hungary, Germany was the main third party.

Germany was not, however, just a blind hardline supporter. After he had read the Serbian reply, the Kaiser wanted to avoid a wider war with Russia. This worried Berchtold, and on at least two occasions, the declaration of war and then the bombardment, he rushed to local war to make sure that Austrian interests would not be sacrificed in any plan to avoid the larger war. He and the other Austrian leaders also refused to consider the Halt-in-Belgrade plan, because they were not interested in satisfying the unfulfilled article of the ultimatum that Pašić had rejected. They wanted to defeat once and for all the nationalist–territorial threat they had been facing. Germany was not only a supporter, but also something to worry about and a major state that could block their major foreign policy objective.

For Russia, Serbia was the third party that was the focal point. The Tsar and Sazonov were committed to supporting it. Pašić in turn needed that support, although he was prepared, because of the great difference in power with Austria-Hungary, to give in at the beginning. Why the Tsar and Sazonov were so willing to stand by Serbia when they had backed down before is an important question. In part, the Tsar had vowed never to back down again as in 1908–1909 and proceeded on a major military buildup, which was now continuing with the Great Program. It was this buildup that so worried Moltke. In the Balkan Wars, Russia had disengaged again, but there was no

---

[64] For a review of conflicting goals within the government and concerns about Romania, Albania, and Bulgaria see Fried (2014: Ch. 3).

humiliating defeat. Indeed, from the perspective of a preventive war logic, it made sense for them to bide their time until the Great Program was more completed (see Levy and Mulligan 2017). Be that as it may, their reputation as patron of Serbia and protector of the Slavs held sway, even though Izvolsky had sold them out in the 1908 deal with Aehrenthal. In this way, Serbia was the third party that made the Tsar and Sazonov go to war.

Serbia, however, was not the third party that made Sukhomlinov, Yanushkevich, and the military go to war. For them it was not Serbia and Slavic affinity that made for war. For them, as noted earlier, it was the security trap posed by German war plans and potential rapid mobilization that made them enter the war. Serbia and its goals were entirely secondary. Mobilization was also critical for Sazonov, but, unlike Sukhomlinov, he also had Serbia in the forefront of his thinking and calculating.

The other major third party for Russia was France, in the persons of Poincaré and Paléologue. They were constantly seeking to firm up the Tsar, constantly saying they were at Russia's side, constantly referring to their commitment to their alliance. Longer term, they had provided the loans and funding for the railways to undercut the German advantage in mobilizing. This was clearly in their interest, but at the same time it fueled an arms race and it made Moltke think in terms of "better now than later."

What Poincaré could have done, instead, was support Grey's effort more and push for the Halt-in-Belgrade plan. He also could have pointed out to the Tsar the dangers of mobilization and the likely reactions within the German decision-making circle. Such actions, however, were more consistent with the stance of Viviani, who was more accommodationist than Poincaré. He, however, was overwhelmed or overshadowed by Poincaré, even though from a constitutional perspective there was not a basis for this. In the end, France was an important third party supporting war.

Thus, the third parties played mixed roles. Germany made war between Austria-Hungary and Russia possible by providing a blank check that in turn made the playing of a chicken game possible. Even though the Kaiser and Bethmann-Hollweg tried to withdraw that check on July 30, Berchtold cashed it in. Serbia sought Russia's help as it had in the past. The Tsar, through Sazonov, stood by Serbia to provide the other main player of the chicken game. As the game between Germany and Russia was played out and engulfed by a security trap, the Austria–Hungary–Russia dyad went to war as a kind of *dénouement*. Poincaré stood on the sidelines, cheering on the Tsar, and Grey stood wringing his hands, unable to get his mediation efforts off the ground with no cooperation from Poincaré or Paléologue.

The Role of Alliances and Alignments   The main third parties reflected the underlying alliances. As can be seen in Text Box 6.2, these were Germany and France. These two countries embodied the heart of the Triple Alliance–Triple Entente antagonism that was the third party underlying the Austria-Hungary–Russia dyad.

Text Box 6.2 also shows that this fault line did not always exist. Bismarck with his foresight had tried to employ the practice of alliance-making to manage and control Austria and Russia. He did this in three pacts. The first was in 1873 with the Convention of Schönbrunn, the second in 1881 with the League of the Three Emperors, and the last indirectly in the 1887 Reinsurance Treaty between Germany and Russia. This was meant to undercut the latent threat of the 1879 alliance between Germany and Austria-Hungary. When Bismarck was pushed out by Kaiser Wilhelm, this left open the possibility of a Franco-Russian alliance that was signed in 1893.

Serbia, of course, had no formal alliance with Russia, but the two were drawn into a firm alignment by their Slavic affinity. Serbia, being considerably weaker and facing two powerful opponents – the Ottoman Empire and Austria-Hungary – needed whatever patron it could get. Russia was drawn in by its support for Pan-Slavism and was aligned to the Serbs while they were still part of the Ottoman Empire. This stemmed in part from its self-appointment as protector of Christian

---

Text Box 6.2.   Austria-Hungary–Russia alliances

Austria-Hungary Alliances	Russia Alliances
1879–1918: GMY 2065	1881–1887: AUH, GMY 2067
1881–1895: SER 2066	1887–1890: GMY 2072
1881–1887: GMY, RUS 2067	1893–1917: FRN 2074
1882–1918: GMY, ITA 2068	1909–1917: ITA 3009
1883–1918: GMY, ITA, ROM 2069	1910–1916: JPN 3010
1904–1908: RUS 3003	1914–1916: ROM 3018
1914–1918: BUL 3017	1915–1917: FRN, ITA, UKG 3019
1915–1918: BUL, GMY 3030	1916–1917: JPN 3021
	1916–1917: FRN (–1918), ITA (–1918), ROM (–1918), UKG (–1918) 3022

subjects within the Ottoman Empire and its special attachment to Serbia because of St. Cyril, the Serbian monk associated with the promulgation of the Cyrillic alphabet used in both Serbian and Russian. Russia had supported Serbia in 1804 when it rebelled from the Ottoman Empire, and it had occupied Serbia in 1808, raising alarm in Austria. The Ottomans returned after Napoleon's invasion of Russia in 1812. In 1815 Russia helped Serbia gain some autonomy, and then helped Serbia to acquire independence in 1878 after the Russo-Turkish War. Just prior to the First World War, its ambassador, Hartwig, had tremendous influence in Belgrade, and he is often credited with founding the Balkan League, which engineered the First Balkan War. Russia's role in creating the Balkan League was seen as a direct challenge to Austria-Hungary's aims in the Balkans and intensified Austrian rivalry with Russia.

Despite the rivalry, Austria-Hungary and Russia had few direct grievances with each other. This is indicated in Text Box 6.3, which shows they had no territorial claims against each other until the war, and that was over the main field of battle in Galicia. This lack of territorial claims makes explicit what has already been implied in the above analysis, namely, that this dyad went to war because others were fighting. Austria-Hungary started the war it wanted and preferred to keep that war local because that way it would win, but it was not interested in the wider war. It was really drawn into that war by the German failure to win the coercive game against Russia. In that sense this dyad was as much a product of contagion through alliances and the failure of the coercive game as was the Germany–Russia dyad.

The Role of Arms Races   The lack of a direct set of grievances is also underlined by the absence of arms races between the two during the five years prior to 1914. The main reason for this was not on the side of Russia, which began the Great Program just prior to the war, but on Austria-Hungary's side. The Hungarian parliament was very resistant to any increase in military expenditures or in the size of the

---

Text Box 6.3.   Austria-Hungary–Russia territorial claims

1914–1917: Eastern Galicia (Claim Dyad 29001)
RUS–AUH

army (Clark 2012: 292). As a result, of the major actors in the First World War, after Italy, Austria-Hungary spent the least (Stevenson 1996: 1–9).

The other arms races occurred at the time of the Russo-Turkish War of 1877–1878. These arms races were not so much direct confrontations, but mostly a function of Russia dealing with other conflicts. All in all, although the 1909 Russian decision for a buildup and subsequent buildups by Russia prior to 1914 were a concern for the Austrian elite (as opposed to the Hungarian), there was no intense anxiety comparable to that of Moltke in Germany or that in England during the naval race. A one-sided military buildup did not provide a step-wise increase in threat perception as in some of the other dyads. If there was no arms race effect and no territorial claims between the two, what made for war?

What Made for War?   The key factor was that Russia supported the territorial claims of its Serbian client even in the absence of a formal alliance. This alignment, however, was as strong as any alliance. Russia was willing to play the coercive game and Franz Josef, knowing this, made sure that the Kaiser and Germany would support the Austrians in a larger game.

Berchtold believed that Germany would take care of this larger game, although at times he needed to make sure of this by pre-empting, as in the July 28 declaration of war. The game he was playing was to promote a local war that would end the territorial and nationalist threat to the Empire. The Austria-Hungary–Russia dyad was a secondary consideration for him and others in the Austrian decision-making elite and for Russia, as well. Russia was not threatened by Austria-Hungary's capability, but by Germany's. Russia's foreign policy objective was to keep Germany out so that it could successfully intimidate, or, failing that, defeat, Austria-Hungary and save Serbia.

This dynamic of Russia preferring the interests of its client over those of the other major states in the former Concert of Europe can also be seen as an additional factor that brought about the war in general. Schroeder (2007) argues that the First World War came about because Russia was no longer willing to look at the collective interests of all the major states but pursued its own particularist interests. He maintains that Austria-Hungary had legitimate concerns regarding Serbia, and these should have been a concern of the major states in a functioning Concert of Europe. The breakdown of the prevailing peace system, then, can be seen as a structural factor that was a pre-requisite of a number of the interactions that brought about war.[65] Grey, of course, tried to follow the Concert of Europe script. The Kaiser and Germany were less wedded to this collective action because the 1905–1906 Algeciras conference that ended the First Moroccan Crisis taught them that the system was rigged against them. If the Concert had been working, the Austria-Hungary–Russia rivalry over the Ottoman Empire lands and Serbia might have been managed in such a way as to avoid a larger war. The breakdown of the Concert was relevant not only for dealing with Austria-Hungary and Serbia, but also for the larger management of the decline of the Ottoman Empire and the various territorial stakes that decline put on the table.[66]

To summarize, war between Austria-Hungary and Russia was a side effect of the broader coercive game being played by Germany and Russia. The existing alliances and alignment encouraged the playing of that game. The territorial stakes that the Serbian non-state actor put on the table and the Serbian government held were indirect, but important, causal factors. The rivalry between Austria-Hungary and Russia reflected both a spatial (territorial) and a positional struggle for the territory that the Ottoman Empire was no longer able to control.

Alongside the above, the failure of the Concert to manage this new set of territorial stakes served as an indirect cause. One factor built upon another. Of these, three were indirect territorial effects – Serbian objectives, the rivalry over the Ottoman Empire, and the breakdown of the Concert. The immediate cause of war between Austria-Hungary and Russia, however, was a result of a contagious process that came out of the existing alliance structure and the failure of the coercive game. The Austria-Hungary–Russia dyad played two roles in this contagious process. First, it started the larger coercive game by bringing in the Germany–Russia dyad. Second, the failure of this game brought them into war with each other.

Outcome   Both Austria-Hungary and Tsarist Russia lost this war not so much as a direct outcome of their own battlefield encounters, although these were not inconsiderable in the beginning, with Russia having the advantage, but from battles with others. In the end Russia lost to Germany and Austria-Hungary to a combined Italian–British–French force. Both monarchies were lost; both empires came to an end. Franz Josef and Tsar Nicholas each feared that the war could

---

[65] For a detailed historical analysis on how this happened during the years 1911–1914 see Mulligan (2014: Ch. 2).

[66] See Vasquez (2002) for this argument.

lead to revolution. For each there was a sense of foreboding, and this made them much more accommodationist than their advisors, but in the end they went forward with hardline advice and to a mutual disaster.

The Guns of August   The first week of August saw the rapid spread of war to every major state in Europe. All of this was the product of the coercive game. The key dyad in this game was the German–Russian dyad. This dyad that had fewer long-term grievances than other dyads, such as Austria-Hungary–Serbia or France–Germany, went to war because mobilization engulfed the Kaiser and the Tsar in a security trap even though both wanted to avoid war. Just as coercion was unable get the Tsar and Sazonov to stop backing Serbia, so was an explicit ultimatum from the Kaiser unable to stop the Tsar from mobilizing on July 31. With that Germany entered a state of *Kriegsgefahrzustand* (imminent danger of war), and on August 1 declared war on Russia.

With the fall of this domino the main supporter of France – Grey – was fully prepared to fulfill its alliance, but because of domestic opposition he waited. The Germans planned to attack first by going through Luxembourg and Belgium. The Germans, being sticklers for declaring war, did so, and declared war on France on August 3. Germany then declared war on Belgium the following day after it did not grant permission for German troops to transit its territory. The Germans' going through Belgium gave Grey the rationale he needed to keep the cabinet together to go to war, but not before another ultimatum had failed – this one the British demand that German forces withdraw from Belgium. The British duly declared war on Germany in the last hour of August 4. Grey was able to get Britain to live up to its unstated commitment to defend France and its implicit but officially unrecognized role in the coercive game. Finally, Austria-Hungary completed the circle and declared war on Russia on August 6.

The rapidity of the spread of the war demonstrates the power of contagion. Decisions were made with little hesitation once the other side had failed to back down or had attacked an ally. Grievances, like Alsace-Lorraine or the naval race, may have played a background role in generating rivalry, but it was the dynamic of the playing of the coercive game that led each of the major states to intervene in the war. The underlying alliance structure shaped the contagion and made the war diffuse the way it did.

The only dyad not to come to war through the contagion process of alliances and the failure of the coercive game was Germany–Belgium. Belgium came to war because it was in the way. Contiguity brought this dyad to war. But Belgium was in the way because of the Franco-Russian alliance and indirectly because of the failure of the coercion game. Friendly coercion (threats combined with lots of carrots) and another implicit ultimatum to pass through its territory resulted in war. The week was rounded out with the German declaration of war on Serbia on August 6. This was done in support of Austria-Hungary but not with any intention of immediate fighting. This last intervention was an example of valence balancing.

The three key contagion processes that occurred at the beginning of the war also followed a certain order in terms of which kinds of actors they brought in. Alliances and the coercive game brought in the initial interveners, which were the major states. Next came contiguity, which was a function of the war plans and the failure of the coercive game to prevent war. This brought in Belgium. Lastly, the allies of the belligerents declared war against the enemies of their friends, making valence balancing the third contagion process working in the initial phase of the war.

The next six days saw no new interventions, then, from August 12 to the end of the month, five more dyads entered the war. With the exception of Japan, all of these entered because of valancing balancing.

The Role of Alliances: Early Valence Balancing

The key thing about valence balancing is that these dyads come to war almost entirely because of the ongoing war. A dyadic war between them is not in the cards. The main reason for this is that they lack sufficient grievances to go to war. This is not to say that they have no grievances whatsoever or that some dyads do not have more than others. Nor is it to say that they have not had hostile relations or even MIDs. On the whole, none of these is sufficient to warrant the costs of war or fall within the rules of the prevailing order that provide reasons for going to war. Some dyads, as will be seen, exemplify the essence of valence balancing in that they have no grievances at all.

Another reason why they are not likely to go to war is that they are not contiguous. This means at one level that it is difficult for them to reach each other. As has been shown in general through statistical studies, dyads that are farther apart are less likely to go to war. Of course, distance is less a barrier for major-state dyads than it is for others, but it is a physical obstacle. It means that it is physically difficult for armies to meet, and for the three dyads being analyzed here when they declare war it is not expected that their armies would actually meet. As a result, the decision to go to war was considerably less deliberate than the decision to go to war in the first instance, for example the decision of Britain to go to war with Germany as opposed to Austria-Hungary. In fact, the decision to go to war in these instances is almost an after-thought. Leaders go to war because they have already made the more difficult decision to go to war with those with whom they have serious grievances.

The difficulty of armies meeting has a more important theoretical effect – it lowers threat perception. Lack of contiguity provides a source of security. Threat perception is lower because the opponent cannot easily attack. This makes defense easier because there is more warning time and thus more time to prepare. This is seen in the most extreme case in America's relying on its two oceans for defense. Lack of contiguity means lack of severe time pressure. Of equal importance is that non-contiguous states are not likely to have terri-torial grievances.[67]

By definition, lack of contiguity also prevents another source of con-tagion from operating, namely what the geographers call contagious as opposed to hierarchical diffusion (Gould 1969: 12, 14). Contagious dif-fusion results from contact and requires contiguity, whereas hierarchical diffusion follows some pecking order. The lack of contiguity means that wars spread to these dyads through some other contagion process. This means that all the factors that promote the spread of war through conti-guity are not operating here.

In summary, the absence of contiguity has three effects that reduce the probability of war. First, it makes it difficult for armies to reach each other, and this makes for less time pressure. Second, threat per-ception is also likely to be lower because lack of contiguity makes for fewer issues or grievances, especially territorial grievances. Third, this means that, if contiguous or contagious diffusion is not the process by which war spreads, then it is likely to be hierarchical diffusion that will bring these dyads to war, or they will remain at peace.

It turns out that it is hierarchical diffusion that brings these dyads to war, and this is well illustrated in the three cases at hand. These dyads came to war through alliances. Each of the belligerents was allied to those already at war. The process is hierarchical in that the existing alliance structure determined who would declare war with whom. In addition, the rank of importance in the alliance structure determined the timing of when these dyads went to war. They came to war only

---

[67] Vasquez (1995) argues that contiguous states are more likely to fight wars because they are more likely to have territorial disputes and not so much because they are adjacent. Vasquez and Henehan (2001) demonstrate this empirically.

after the principal alliance partners had gone to war. This also means that the logic of alliance membership also differs between the principal members in the alliance structure and the lesser parties. For the principals, alliances encourage them to play the coercive chicken game to the hilt because they believe they can rely on their alliance commitments (Italy being the exception).

For those brought to war through valence balancing this is not the case. Here alliances bring dyads to war by an entirely different logic. They come to war because the enemy of their ally is their enemy. This is not just a norm, but a behavioral principle that has shaped behavior for eons, and it works in the First World War to bring to war dyads that do not have grievances and typically cannot reach each other.

The reason for this was suggested in Chapter 1. Affinity involving psychological affect implies that actors want to have consistent relations across those with whom they interact. Thus alliances should all involve friends, and opponents should all be enemies. Neutrality is possible, but uneasy. What is very discordant is being a friend of your friend's enemy. Presumably in a polarized world this would be even more difficult psychologically. Of course, in rare cases actors may take concrete measures, like threats, to reduce their friend's relationship with another if psychological affect is not sufficient to balance the triangle.[68]

If this theoretical rationale is correct, it would be expected theoretically that dyads brought to war through valence balancing should have certain characteristics. First, they would be allies of belligerents who have already declared war. Second, they would not have very salient grievances and thus would be highly unlikely to have a dyadic war. Less generally, the dyads are not likely to be contiguous. The three dyads in question all fulfill these conditions.

Valence balancing was the third contagion process at work in the First World War. Chronologically, the war spread in 1914 first by alliances and the failure of the coercive game, then through contiguity because of Belgium being in the way. This accounted for five dyads. Then four more dyads entered through valence balancing.[69] They would herald a number of "lesser" dyads that would enter the war all the way down to 1917.

---

[68] France and Britain will do this to Italy when it lags in declaring war against Germany. This seems to have been necessary because of the positive affect Italy and Germany had with each other previously.

[69] The five are Serbia–Germany, France–Austria-Hungary, Britain–Austria-Hungary, France–Ottoman Empire, and Britain–Ottoman Empire.

Serbia–Germany, August 6, 1914

In many ways one would not expect Serbia to declare war on Germany, given its inferior power. It did this because Austria-Hungary had declared war on it, and Germany was Austria-Hungary's main ally. Normally, one would not expect a war between these two countries because they had no direct grievances. They came to war not just because of the local war, but because of the ongoing world war. By August 6 all the main belligerents were in the war, with Austria-Hungary declaring war on Russia the same day Serbia declared war on Germany. Serbia declared war on Germany because it was the ally of its mortal enemy – Austria-Hungary. Germany was the only country Serbia declared war on in the summer of 1914. This was valence balancing since, *if* Germany had not been allied to Austria-Hungary, Serbia would not have declared war on it. Secondarily, Serbia declared war against Germany because Germany had declared war against its patron and protector – Russia. Germany was consistently Russia's opponent whenever the latter defended Serbia against Austria-Hungary, hence it was also Serbia's enemy indirectly. In this variation of valence balancing Germany was not simply Serbia's enemy because Germany was an enemy of Russia, but also because the reason why Russia was an enemy was because it was defending Serbia. For Serbia not to have declared war against Germany once the latter two had gone to war would have made Serbia an ingrate for not having reciprocated the great support that Russia was providing in its hour of need.[70]

Serbia did this within the initial week because the logic of "the enemy of my friend is my enemy" was so compelling that Serbia saw this as part of what was entailed in going to war, and in doing so it rounded out the sides. For other parties that entered the war through valence balancing there was more of a time lag.

One could also argue that Serbia declared war because it was hostile toward Germany for supporting Austria-Hungary and thereby not permitting Russia's support working to prevent the local war. While such hostility was surely generated, it was tempered by the fact that such coercive games were not uncommon. The ultimatum the Kaiser had given Tsar Nicholas in the Bosnian Crisis resulted in both Russia and Serbia being humiliated, but still at other times the Kaiser was sympathetic to Serbia. As recently as the First Balkan War, the Kaiser did not see Serbia's demand for access to the sea as a reason why Germany would go to war. Further, he did not support Austria-Hungary on this issue (Clark 2012: 289), although he supported the demands of Grey

---

[70] Serbia would have failed to pay its debt to its patron, which in certain cultures would have been a great sin.

and the London Conference that Serbian troops leave Albania (Clark 2012: 286). It was this sort of lack of support that made Franz Josef send von Hoyos to Berlin on July 5–6 to make sure that Germany would stand at their side. Likewise, when the Kaiser read, belatedly, the Serbian reply to the ultimatum on July 28, he immediately saw no reason for war, as he noted in the margins. Here he seemed to be pulling back and coming up with a way of avoiding an all-out local war that might provoke Russian intervention.

Another piece of evidence that this dyad went to war because of valence balancing is that at the time, and despite the declaration of war, Serbia had no plans to fight Germany on the battlefield, and did not want to do so for obvious reasons. More importantly, Germany had no plans of actually fighting Serbia. Instead, Moltke undercut Conrad's efforts to fight the war he wanted in the South and pressured him to abandon that effort in order to swing his troops north to Galicia. This would allow Germany to follow the Schlieffen Plan in the West. Eventually, German troops did help Austria-Hungary to fight Serbia in 1915, with an agreement with Bulgaria to invade Serbia. Such plans were not developed until over a year later in October 1915.

The theoretical expectations about war contagion through valence balancing are fulfilled by this case. First, one would not expect a dyadic war between Germany and Serbia to break out. There were no direct grievances between the two. As can be seen in Text Boxes 7.1 and 7.2,

---

Text Box 7.1. Serbia/Yugoslavia–Germany territorial claims

No territorial claims

Text Box 7.2. Serbia/Yugoslavia–Germany rivalry

Enduring Rivalry	Issue
KLEIN, GOERTZ, DIEHL: 1992–2000	Dominant Issue: Policy
SENESE AND VASQUEZ: 6th MID: 1998	25% (+) Territory
ARMS RACE	
HORN: 1934–1938	

there were no territorial claims and there was no rivalry, although Klein, and Diehl and Goertz, identify one starting in 1992 with the Kosovo War. Likewise, as Histogram 7 shows, the first MID between the two was in 1914. Rivalry and repeated disputes did not emerge until later – during the Second World War and in the 1990s with NATO's and the U.S.'s disputes with Serbia as a result of the Yugoslav Civil War. In 1914, however, this was not the case.

Second, the two countries were not contiguous and it was difficult for them to reach each other except through third parties. Because of the lack of contiguity their armies, as expected, did not pose immediate threats to each other. The lack of contiguity also meant limited issues, especially territorial issues.

Third, the one indicator of hostility and threat that was evinced is in the arms race indicator. There is evidence of an arms race in 1914 (see Histogram 7) but not in the Balkan Wars. In 1914 what was really going on was Serbia building up its arms against Austria-Hungary rather than Germany per se. Likewise, Germany's arming was a result of its naval buildup against England and its land buildup against Russia and France.

What made for war were third parties, namely Germany's alliance with Austria-Hungary and Russia's alignment with Serbia as its patron that involved it in the coercive game first against Austria-Hungary and then against Germany. Without these alliances (see Text Box 7.3) and alignments, the coercive game would not have brought about war among the principals, and without that war Serbia would not have declared war on Germany. Once Germany had declared war against its patron – Russia – and Russia's ally – France, Serbia had to declare war against Germany; in this way the valences were balanced. Nonetheless,

---

Text Box 7.3.   Serbia–Germany Alliances

Serbia Alliances	Germany Alliances
1912–1913: BUL 3011	1879–1918: AUH 2065
1913–1918: GRC 3014	1881–1887: AUH, RUS 2067
	1882–1918: AUH, ITA 2068
	1883–1918: ITA (–1915), ROM (–1916), AUH 2069
	1887–1890: RUS 2072
	1914–1918: OTM 3015
	1915–1918: AUH, BUL 3020

valence balancing in this dyad was complicated because Russia was the patron of Serbia, and Germany was the main ally of Austria-Hungary. Germany became the enemy of Serbia not solely because it was an enemy of Russia, but also because it had made Austria-Hungary's war possible by nullifying Russia's support. Despite the complexities, all the parties were cognizant of the underlying dynamics. Serbia, in severing diplomatic relations with Germany, stated that, "in view of the state of war which now exists between Serbia and Austria-Hungary, and of that between Russian and Germany, the ally of Austria-Hungary, the Royal Serbian Government, *in view of the solidarity of her interests with Russia and her allies,* considers the mission of Baron Gieslingen, the imperial German Minister … to be at an end" (emphasis added).[71]

France–Austria-Hungary, August 12, 1914

The next week, six days after Serbia's declaration on Germany and the Austro-Hungarian declaration of war on Russia, Britain and France declared war on Austria-Hungary. Both of these were declarations on their opponent's main ally – Austria-Hungary, which became their enemy only because Germany was their primary enemy. The case of Britain–Austria-Hungary coming to war is an example of valence balancing *par excellence,* whereas that of France has more of a history behind it. France–Austria-Hungary will be dealt with first, because of this history.

Unlike the other dyads in this section which came to war because of valence balancing, France and Austria-Hungary had more long-term hostility. Thompson sees them as having a rivalry going back to 1494. Much of this early rivalry had to do with colliding Habsburg and French expansion, as Thompson and Dreyer (2012: 30) put it. Our interest, however, begins with the Napoleonic period. Austria became a mortal enemy of the French Revolution with the beheading of Marie Antoinette, wife of Louis XVI and daughter of Maria Theresa, Empress of Austria. The Austrians then fought Napoleon, were defeated in 1809, and in the end triumphed in coalition with the other great powers. With the Bourbon restoration in 1814 there was once again an alignment with France, with it being admitted formally to the Concert of Europe in 1818. For their alliances, see Text Box 8.1.

Histogram 8 shows that their first MID in the post-Napoleonic period was in 1840. As with Britain and the other great powers of the

---

[71] Serbian Blue Book, doc No. 50 (https://wwi.lib.byu.edu/index.php/The_Serbian_Blue_Book).

Text Box 8.1.   France–Austria-Hungary alliances

France Alliances	Austria-Hungary Alliances
1893–1917: RUS 2075	1879–1918: GMY 2065
1902–1918: ITA 3001	1881–1895: SER 2066
1907–1915: SPN, UKG 3005	1881–1887: GMY, RUS 2067
1912–1918: UKG 3013	1882–1918: GMY, ITA 2068
1915–1918: ITA, RUS (–1917), UKG 3019	1883–1918: GMY, ITA, ROM 2069
1916–1918: ITA, ROM, RUS, UKG 3022	1904–1908: RUS 3003
	1914–1918: BUL 3017
	1915–1918: BUL, GMY 3030

Concert, Austria became alienated against France because it supported Muhammad Ali in the Second Eastern Crisis. Austria used armed force together with Britain to defeat Ali. When Thiers responded by threatening war on the Rhine and mobilized troops, this led to the 1840 MID depicted in the histogram.

Both sides got caught up in the 1848 revolutions, which resulted in their second MID, but the real armed confrontation took place with the 1859 War of Italian Independence. Here Napoleon III plotted war with Cavour of Piedmont against Austria to redeem the provinces of Lombardy and Venetia for the Italians. This resulted, in part, from the desire of Napoleon III for Savoy and Nice, but he was also trying to break the strictures of the Congress of Vienna Peace system that had eliminated the natural frontiers of France. This was certainly fuel for a rivalry, but it was not of the same order as the intense hostile long-term interaction it had been during the pre-1815 period. In the War of 1866 between Prussia and Austria, with Italy allied to the former, Napoleon III supported Italy and, as a "mediator," assisted it in getting Venetia.

By this time France was becoming much more concerned with Prussia and Bismarck. In 1870, with war on the horizon, Napoleon III felt that relations with Austria were neutral enough that he could count on Austria as an ally against Prussia in the hope of it rectifying its defeat in 1866. This proved to be wishful thinking, since in 1867 Austria had combined with Hungary to form a dual monarchy and the latter would not support a return to a foreign policy focused on geographic Germany.

The MID in 1888 saw a return to more hostile interactions, but these had more to do with France and Italy than France and Austria–Hungary.

The former were involved in a trade dispute and France imposed a tariff. In July, in response to a French newspaper report, Italy feared a French naval attack on Spezia. The MID also involved Britain because it said it would defend Italy and sent in the navy. The 1888 MID was mainly between France, Italy, and Britain. Austria-Hungary was much more marginal, but met up with Britain off the coast of Barcelona in a show of support.

If there was a rivalry throughout the post-Napoleonic era, it was of a much different sort than what we normally think of as a rivalry, where states are willing to cut off their nose to spite their face (see Vasquez 1993: 77, 82). Instead they came into conflict because of some common rival or because they were allied with some state which was involved in a dispute with their ally. Austria was frequently on the other side of France, but its main opponent was not France per se but some other actor. This was even true in 1859, when Italian nationalists were the main cause of war, although France did a great deal of the fighting. Still, Napoleon III was willing to reach a peace with Franz Josef at Villafranca, and later hoped he would be an ally.

At the turn of the century, as Schroeder (1999: 74) points out, Austria tried to find a solution to the First Moroccan Crisis between France and Germany, and in the 1908–1909 Bosnian crisis France was "reasonably friendly" to Austria. Schroeder goes so far as to say that this reflected a policy option for Austria-Hungary, trying to gain financial and diplomatic support from France to make it less dependent on Germany in the Balkans. Poincaré, however, put an end to this, preferring a more consistent two-bloc approach.

What this brief history of previous interactions suggests is that, because both France and Austria-Hungary were active major states involved in the ruling of the system through the Concert of Europe, they were mutually involved in all the main crises of the day. Often they were on opposite sides, but not always, and in most cases, except when they directly fought each other, as in 1859, there was not the deep hostility that characterized most rivalries.

By 1914 Austria-Hungary was far from a rival of France. France's main opponent was Germany and its main ally was Russia. Austria-Hungary was a concern because it was in conflict with Russia. They came to war because Austria-Hungary was an ally of Germany, France's main rival, and because Austria-Hungary was an enemy of Russia, France's main ally. The French declaration of war on Austria-Hungary is seen here as coming as a result of valence balancing. In its declaration of war France mentioned three reasons for its going to war.

The first was that Austria-Hungary initiated hostilities in Europe and the second was that it intervened in the conflict between Germany and France by declaring war on Russia, which was allied to France. Thirdly, it stated that Austria-Hungary had sent troops to the border of Germany and France, which constituted a direct threat to France. This, as Albertini (1952, Vol. III: 539–541) discusses, was based on a false report. The declaration made it clear that without the ongoing war France would not be at war with Austria-Hungary. The lack of enduring hostility was further indicated by the fact that legacies of the Austro-Hungarian sentiment that France was not an implacable foe persisted even during the war. As things became more desperate, Austria-Hungary tried in 1916 to bring about an end to the war by getting Germany to give up Alsace and Lorraine.

The lack of contiguity also played a role. At the time of declaration, France did not really envisage a direct battlefield confrontation. In addition, the absence of contiguity meant there were few bilateral grievances. There were no territorial claims, for instance, as can be seen in Text Box 8.2. Most of their interactions resulted, as noted before, from both being major states and part of the governing structure of the Concert of Europe and the great power politics being played as that Concert fell apart.

The hostility generated by the Concert interactions is reflected in the arms race indicator in Text Box 8.3. There are mutual arms races

---

Text Box 8.2.   France–Austria-Hungary territorial claims

No territorial claims

Text Box 8.3.   France–Austria-Hungary rivalry

Enduring Rivalry	Issue
THOMPSON: 1494–1918	Dominant Issue: Policy
	THOMPSON: Positional and Spatial
ARMS RACE	
HORN: 1912, 1913	

during the Balkan Wars and in 1914. In the Balkan Wars, France and Austria-Hungary were always on the sidelines. The same was true in 1914, and the declaration of war could have come from either side. However, unlike Britain and Austria-Hungary, there was more of a long-term rivalry present. In the end it was the alliance structure and valence balancing that brought about the expansion of the war.

Britain–Austria-Hungary, August 12, 1914

Early on, Grey made it clear that Britain would not go to war for Russia and especially not for Serbia. He told Buchanan, his ambassador to Russia, that the British people would not be drawn into war because of Serbian concerns. Buchanan related this to Sazonov, when the latter pressed him for support on July 24. Of course, what Grey meant was that Britain would not go to war because of Russia or Serbia unless it involved a war where France was attacked by Germany. It was this form of contagion that led Britain to declare war against Austria-Hungary. France was the key for Grey, and in writing to declare war on Austria-Hungary on August 12 he stated that "A rupture with France having thus been brought about, the Government of His Britannic Majesty is obliged to proclaim a state of war between Great Britain and Austria-Hungary, to begin at midnight."[72] No other particulars were given, only that the state of war between Austria-Hungary and France obliged Britain to declare a state of war. This was valence balancing on Grey's part, and much more so than why France declared war on Austria-Hungary. Grey declared war solely because Austria-Hungary was an ally of the state that attacked France, whereas France, although it declared war because of valence concerns, had more of a history to its interactions with Austria-Hungary.

Britain's previous relations emphasize that it was purely valence balancing that led to war. Both Britain and Austria-Hungary were major states and part of the Concert of Europe that governed major-state relations in the post-Napoleonic era. As major states they interacted with each other on great-power business. As Histogram 9 shows, this resulted in only one MID before 1914. This was in the 1863 crisis that led to the Second Schleswig-Holstein War of 1864. Here Britain threatened Prussia, as well as Austria, and said it would stand by Denmark (see Carr 1991: 79). The cabinet was split on going to war, so this

---

[72] *Declarations of War: Severances of Diplomatic Relations, 1914–1918* (1919: 33), quoted from the Austro-Hungarian Red Book, doc LXV, Count Mensdorff to Count Berchtold.

threat did not lead to armed intervention, but the British were active diplomatically.

At other times, many of Britain's and Austria's interactions as major states were cooperative. Britain and Austria were key allies in the war against Napoleon. They had acted together in the use of force in 1840 against Muhammad Ali and saved the Ottoman Empire from being overthrown from within. Their joint action irritated France, which under Thiers had threatened war, only for Thiers to be forced to resign in October 1840 by the more cautious King Louis Philippe. Several years later, when the Crimean War broke out, Britain sought Austrian intervention into the war, but was rebuffed. Instead, in 1854 Austria threatened armed intervention unless Russia withdrew from Moldavia and Walachia, which it did, and Austria occupied these territories until the end of the war without participating in the war.

Other than the one MID in 1863, which was aimed as much against Prussia as against Austria, there were no other threats or use of force until 1914. This was because most of Britain's interactions with Austria were as part of its interactions with the Concert powers and not bilateral. This is not surprising, since they did not have any bilateral grievances per se. As Text Box 9.1 shows, they had no territorial claims against each other. This was a function not only of the lack of contiguity, but also of the fact that Austria-Hungary, despite it being a naval power, had no overseas empire. In addition, there was no rivalry (Text Box 9.2). The lack of MIDs implies that there was no rivalry, but

---

Text Box 9.1.   United Kingdom–Austria-Hungary territorial claims

No territorial claims

Text Box 9.2.   United Kingdom–Austria-Hungary rivalry

NO ENDURING RIVALRY
NO ARMS RACE

Thompson's measure shows that there was no perception of rivalry either. Nor were there any arms races. In short, one would not expect a dyadic war between the two states. At the actual declaration of war, Albertini (1952, Vol. III: 544) reports that the British ambassador confessed to Berchtold "that there were no differences between England and the Monarchy which could in the least justify the conflict," and Berchtold went on to say "that the two states ... were closely associated politically and morally ..."

In the end, Grey made it clear that the only reason for England to go to war with Austria-Hungary was if the latter went to war with France. He said "it would be difficult for England, as France's ally, to co-operate with her in the Atlantic and not in the Mediterranean" (Albertini 1952, Vol. III: 535).[73] Similarly, according to Albertini (1952, Vol. III: 542), Crowe mused that once England was at war with Germany the fiction of peace between Austria-Hungary and England "was illogical." England went to war because it was allied to France, and both went to war against Austria-Hungary because it was the ally of Germany and they were at war with Germany (Text Box 9.3). Albertini (1952, Vol. III: 545) concludes as much when he says that for the two states the war "was mainly against Germany and the conflict with Austria ... a side issue."

Text Box 9.3.   United Kingdom–Austria-Hungary alliances

United Kingdom Alliances	Austria-Hungary Alliances
1902–1930: JPN 3000	1879–1918: GMY 2065
1907–1915: FRN, SPN 3005	1881–1895: SER 2066
1912–1918: FRN 3013	1881–1887: GMY, RUS 2067
1915–1918: FRN, ITA, RUS (–1917) 3019	1882–1918: GMY, ITA (–1915) 2068
1916–1918: FRN, ITA, ROM, RUS (–1917) 3022	1883–1918: GMY, ITA (–1915), ROM (–1916) 2069
	1904–1908: RUS 3003
	1914–1918: BUL 3017
	1915–1918: BUL, GMY 3030

---

[73] These were his comments to Mensdorff, the Austro-Hungarian ambassador to London.

Normally, the absence of contiguity would reduce the likelihood of fighting. However, since both countries were major states during the period of the Concert of Europe and former allies against Napoleon there was plenty of contact and interaction. They saw themselves as part of a system of Global Governance. Unlike the Serbia–Germany dyad, this meant that a declaration of war might entail some direct military confrontation. This possibility was enhanced because of the Austro-Hungarian naval presence in the Mediterranean.

A potential naval clash with both Britain and/or France was of concern in Austria. Just before the declaration of war by the Entente states in 1914, Germany was pressuring Austria-Hungary to declare war against Britain and deploy its navy. Conrad resisted the German pressure, saying the Navy was not yet ready and any declaration must wait or the Navy would be lost.[74] Thus, both in Austria-Hungary and in Britain declaring war was not done with the feeling that no contact was likely. This, however, was a concern in the Mediterranean and not on land.

A land confrontation was less likely, since Grey had in the beginning not even planned an extensive presence in France. Nonetheless, the exigencies of the land battles brought important fighting in 1917 on the Italian front. This was done in conjunction with France and Italy, underlining the importance of alliances in spreading the war because of ongoing battlefield contingencies. These resulted when the Austrians broke the line at Caporetto with German help. Because battlefield conditions made for the British and French confrontation of Austria-Hungary, this overcoming of contiguity must be seen as a contagion effect of the ongoing war. The role of alliances is further indicated by the fact that the British and French action was a response to the German armed forces that were in the Alps actively fighting alongside the Austrians. Ultimately, British and French troops fighting alongside the Italians after Caporetto in the 1918 Battle of Vittorio Veneto enabled the Italians to win against Austria-Hungary and occupy Innsbruck. Valence balancing, then, may begin as a logical exercise that makes affinities consistent, but it can have an impact on the outcome as it did with Austria-Hungary–Italy, a dyad that was not even at war when Britain and France declared war in the second week of August.

---

[74] On German pressure and the Austrian reaction see Albertini (1952, Vol. III: 542). Naval concerns were also felt by Poincaré, who felt that the alliance with Russia required some French naval action against the Austro-Hungarian navy in the Adriatic (Albertini 1952, Vol. III: 541).

Conclusion on Valence Balancing in 1914

What we learn from contagion in these three dyads is as follows. First, valence balancing can make countries that have few grievances and that are not likely to fight a bilateral war declare war on each other. They do this because they treat an enemy of their ally as their enemy. Second, they go to war without hesitation and without much deliberation, with no qualms. This may be because they do not expect to actually encounter the other side on the battlefield. Third, they seem almost *compelled* to round out the sides based on a logical deduction of the alliance structure. The logic underlying this, however, is really a psychological balancing of affinities, making them consistent. Fourth, valence balancing makes the war spread very rapidly. As soon as the main allies had come to war due to the failure of the coercive game, these more distant dyads went to war. We will see whether this hypothesis also holds for later instances of valence balancing after the initial two weeks. Lastly, alliances can overcome the lack of contiguity in terms of permitting the stationing of troops typically near the battlefield of a threatened ally. This means that eventually the interests of an ally coupled with ongoing battlefield contingencies can produce grievances and reasons for war when there were none at the time of the declaration of war. These processes are best illustrated in British and French actions against Austria-Hungary on the Italian front after the battle of Caporetto in 1917, but they also are illustrated by German actions against Serbia in 1915.

In addition to the above, what *new* things do we learn from these cases? First, valence balancing is nuanced and differs across cases. Britain and Austria-Hungary went to war primarily because Austria-Hungary was an ally of Germany, which attacked France. Similarly, Serbia declared war on Germany, because it was an ally of Austria-Hungary and because it had declared war against Serbia's patron – Russia. In each, the enemy of my friend became my enemy. With France and Austria-Hungary the same principle held, but here there was more of a history of negative interactions and even early rivalry. Second, dyads do not expect to fight a land war, but often do because of battlefield contingencies associated with a long war and what became a total war of attrition. Many expected a short war, which was more typical of the past. Third, the absence of contiguity reduced threat, but this pacifying condition can itself be reduced when states have navies. Britain and France did not expect to have to fight Austria-Hungary, but Austria-Hungary feared the navies of Britain and France and expected that in a war it might be attacked. Still, not expecting land contact made them not expect the danger that would emerge as the war dragged on. Fourth, these cases show that valence balancing may make dyads become part of an ongoing war because of a logical exercise, but this can have a real impact on the outcome of the war. This happened not only on the Italian front, but with Serbia and Germany as well. Fifth, when states do not balance immediately or are in the process of considering valence balancing, their allies push them along. Germany did this to Austria-Hungary. Later on, France and Britain did this to Italy in 1916 by pressuring it to declare war on Germany after it had declared war on Austria-Hungary in 1915.

Opportunity

Japan–Germany, August 23, 1914

By the third week of August 1914, Japan had entered the First World War. It was the first non-European state to do so and the third last major state to enter (with Italy and the U.S. being the last two). With Japan's entry the war became global, keeping in mind, as noted below, that the use of Dominion and colonial troops made the war spread worldwide, albeit not among recognized nation-states. The reasons why Japan entered and how a war thousands of miles away spread to it provide some important insights into how contagion works.

The Decision to Go to War   The decision to join the war was made primarily by one man, Katō Takaaki, the foreign minister. The Prime Minister, Count Ōkuma, who was seventy-five, had only become prime minister in April, and followed the lead of Katō, with whom he had long been close. Katō had chosen most of the cabinet, and was the leading figure in the key Dōshikai party. He presented the cabinet and especially the Army elite and *genrō* (the elder statesmen) with a *fait accompli* as Dickinson (2003: 309) puts it.

Katō had a clear vision and strategy based on seizing the moment. For him, this was a golden opportunity because the ongoing war lifted a barrier to Japan's long-held ambition to increase its imperial empire. Beginning with the 1894–1895 Sino-Japanese War and the later 1904–1905 Russo-Japanese War, Japan had extended its holdings and sphere of influence beyond the Japanese islands into China, Taiwan, and Korea. Katō saw the time as ripe for picking off German holdings in Asia – especially within China, but also the German islands in the Pacific.

For Katō, the war in Europe was an opportunity to take advantage of German local weakness (see also Stevenson 2011: 171) and, much more importantly, to avoid the opposition of the other major states, especially Britain and Russia, but also France, to Japanese expansion. The major states had stripped Japan of the Liaotung peninsula, including Port Arthur, after its victory over China in 1895. Then, when Germany seized Kiaochow in 1897, Russia demanded compensation in 1898, and the major states approved a twenty-five-year lease of (the warm water) Port Arthur to Russia. This irritated Japan endlessly, but underlined the fact that the ruling political order had to be taken into account in any Japanese expansion. For Katō the war in Europe provided an opportunity to overcome a number of obstacles that would occur in peacetime; namely, Germany was in no military position to fight in Asia in 1914, but also the other major states were in no position to interfere diplomatically with Japan's initiatives in the way they had done in 1895. Even so, after the war the major states forced Japan to retract at the 1922 Washington Conference some of the Twenty-One Demands Japan had placed on China and even to turn Kiaochow over to China.

To gain major-state support, Katō immediately couched Japan's entry into the war as fulfilling an obligation to the 1902 Anglo-Japanese Alliance. Edward Grey of Britain played into his hands, by requesting Japanese military assistance especially if Germany should attack British Hong Kong and/or Weihaiwei. Katō exceeded the request by announcing that Japan would declare war. Once Katō suggested this, Grey tried to pull back (Stevenson 2011: 171; Dickinson 2011: 193), but Katō would have none of it and Grey realized his mistake, but nothing could be done.[75] Katō's immediate demand from Germany was Kiaochow, a key German enclave on the Chinese mainland.

Drawing on the alliance with Britain also provided the entry into the war with a legal justification both internationally and domestically. A number of groups had favorable inclinations toward Germany and admired its military tradition, including the elder statesman and former prime minister and field marshal Yamagata Aritomo, Katō's main rival. He and others in the Army even thought Germany might win the war.[76] Grey's request, however, was the key external catalyst that shaped the

---

[75] On the interactions between Japan and Britain see Nish (1972).

[76] Yamagata and others in the Army had earlier favored an alliance with Germany in 1911 and an abandonment of Britain. As Dickinson (2003: 321) speculates, it was even possible that Katō wanted to head off this group for fear that they might push for a German alliance that would have Japan attack British imperial interests in China rather than Germany's. In the end Katō's quick maneuvers to declare war made the Army jump at the prospect of fighting on the mainland in the immediate future and all the bureaucratic benefits that would bring them.

agenda (see Dickinson 2003: 307), and Katō used it to pursue his own larger foreign policy objectives.

The Japanese cabinet decided to go to war on August 8, only four days after Britain went to war with Germany, and a day and a half after Grey's request for assistance. This decision was approved by the *genrō* and the Emperor himself. Katō sent an ultimatum to Germany demanding the withdrawal of its navy from Chinese and Japanese waters and the delivery to Japan of Kiaochow, with the idea that it would eventually be returned to China. Germany was given seven days to reply, a much longer time than usual. Germany, of course, did not accept the ultimatum, and the declaration of war came on August 23, 1914.

Theoretical Analysis The chronological order of this legal entry compared with the previous ones by the European states is interesting theoretically. It came after the initial wave of major states that entered due to the failure of coercion to provide a non-violent victory (August 1–6) and after another wave of joining where major states rounded out their enemies through valence balancing (August 6–12). The entry of Japan is the first instance of contagion through opportunity, and the case provides a succinct illustration of how opportunity spreads war.

Although opportunity was the primary contagion process, it did not work alone. Clearly the underlying imperial rivalry with competing territorial stakes provided the objectives Katō was pursuing. Except for the insult in 1898 after Russia demanded compensation for the German acquisition of Kiaochow, there was no explicit rivalry between Germany and Japan, as the rivalry measures show (see Text Box 10.1). The fact that Germany was at war with Britain, and Britain was Japan's only real diplomatic supporter, made German colonies the obvious target. It could just as well have been French colonies in a different diplomatic circumstance, as it would be in 1940–1941. Territorial competition was important, but it was not focused on Germany specifically. Katō's policy was primarily opportunistic (for a discussion of other diffusion factors see Dickinson 2011: 192, 195). In Most and Starr's (1980) terms, imperial ambitions provided the willingness and the ongoing war the

---

Text Box 10.1.   Japan–Germany rivalry

NO ENDURING RIVALRY
NO ARMS RACE

Text Box 10.2.   Japan–Germany territorial claims

1914–1914: Shandong (Claim Dyad 80302)
JPN–GMY
1914–1919: Caroline–Marshall–Pelew–Mariana Islands (Claim Dyad 98104)
JPN–GMY

Text Box 10.3.   Japan–Germany alliances

Japan Alliances	Germany Alliances
1902–1930: UKG 3000	1879–1918: AUH 2065
1910–1916: RUS 3010	1881–1887: AUH, RUS 2067
1916–1917: RUS 3021	1882–1918: AUH, ITA 2068
	1883–1918: ITA (–1915), ROM (–1916), AUH 2069
	1887–1890: RUS 2072
	1914–1918: OTM 3015
	1915–1918: AUH, BUL 3020

---

opportunity. As a result, it should come as no surprise that Japan had no territorial claims prior to 1914, as the territorial claims data in Text Box 10.2 show. All its claims were a result of the decision to go to war. These sprang from the ultimatum in 1914. Nor were there any arms races.

Histogram 10 also shows that there was limited conflict between the two states. Likewise, alliances played a key role, but again they were secondary. Katō used the alliance domestically, and it added legitimacy. As with other states that subsequently entered (e.g. Italy) territorial concerns/interests trumped alliances. Nonetheless, alliances provided an underlying structure, and they explain how a war in far-flung Europe diffused all the way to Asia. Alliances provided for hierarchical diffusion in precisely the way we would expect after the initial spatial diffusion in Europe proper (see Text Box 10.3).

Lastly, Japan as the penultimate 1914 major state that entered the war illustrates Yamamoto and Bremer's (1980) finding that the more major states join an ongoing war the greater the pressure and likelihood that other major states will enter; see also Stevenson (2011: 176–178) on the difficulty of being neutral even for minor states. Japan's interests, in this case its imperial interests, were so intertwined with the imperial interests of other major states that just a few days after all the European major states went to war its cabinet was looking at entering the war, and Katō seized his opportunity.

That Katō was being opportunistic is supported by the fact that he and later his successors (he resigned in 1915) resisted demands to send troops to Europe. They did live up to their agreement to provide naval assistance, by supplying armed escorts to ANZAC forces all the way to Aden, and in March 1917 they even provided a cruiser and eight destroyers for use in the Mediterranean (Hunt 2017; Dickinson 2003: 301–302). Generally, however, their armed action was to gain colonial territory in East Asia and not to fight in Europe.

The war began with an ultimatum for Germany to leave Kiaochow, and when that did not happen Japan declared war on August 23. In the same month, as the Germans left, Japan took over the Caroline, Marshall, and Mariana Islands. They attacked Tsingtao (the capital of Kiaochow) with 50,000 troops (along with 2,000 British troops) in November, overwhelming the German force of just fewer than 5,000.

Conclusion   The Japanese went to war against Germany and joined the First World War primarily because it provided an opportunity to extend their imperial interests and gain German territory. The 1902 alliance with Britain provided an important justification, but it was not the main causal factor bringing about the *decision* to enter the war. The alliance, however, brought about a hierarchical diffusion of the war across continents, and the fact that Japan was a major state in the central system also promoted its joining the ongoing war.

Despite these factors, the decision had a contingent element to it. Without Katō's forceful leadership his rival, Yamagata, might have been supported by the Army and made Japan favor Germany. As with cases that occurred in 1915, there was in Japan a division between Anglophiles, in this instance Katō, who had spent a number of years in England, and Germanophiles, like Yamagata, who had spent time in Berlin.[77] Similarly, some consideration was given to who would win the war. However, unlike in later cases, this calculation did not play a great

---

[77] It is interesting to note how living in a foreign state where one is representing one's own state often makes diplomats and military officers sympathetic to that state. Of course, state bureaucracies are well aware of this tendency and try to pre-empt it by rotation. One wonders what brings it about, however, and, specifically, whether the affinity created by extended living in another country is sparked by some territorial bond.

role, most likely because the war in Europe had just been declared. Still, contingency affected Japan's choice of target; namely, whether Japan would go to war against Germany or Britain. An interesting observation provided by this case is that the Japanese leaders seemed unable to resist contagion, i.e. the temptation that opportunity provided. That is an important inference that is supported by this case analysis.

In the end, Katō must be seen as opportunistic, and the underlying structural factors made this possible. The dual opportunity of Germany being at war in Europe and therefore completely vulnerable to attack in East Asia and the breakdown of the global major-state political order that could oppose Japanese action was key in motivating Katō. This, coupled with Japanese imperial ambitions and the low-hanging territorial fruit, was too much to resist. The very same factors – low-hanging territorial fruit and opportunity – played a similar role in the Japanese decision to join the later Allied Intervention in Russia by sending troops to Siberia.

Interlude: Contiguity, Japan–Austria-Hungary, August 25, 1914   This dyad goes to war simply because Austria-Hungary is in the way. What is unusual, however, is that it is not the country that is in the way, but a cruiser that makes for the contiguity of the two navies. Contiguity is the reason why the war expands, but it is the contiguity of two militaries. Japan planned to attack Tsingtao, which was a port held by the Germans, and in the port there was a single Austro-Hungarian cruiser, the SMS *Kaiserin Elisabeth*, under German command. The Japanese were aware of the ship and there was an attempt by both sides to make an arrangement that would avoid war,[78] but this came to naught and the Japanese declared war on August 25, two days after the declaration on Germany.

The ship is the main reason the two states came to war and if it were not there, war would not have been declared. In this sense contiguity in terms of the *Kaiserin Elisabeth* being in the way of the Japanese siege of Tsingtao brought about the war between the two states. Even though the logic of this contiguity is the same as that of Belgium being in the way, it is different in that the *Kaiserin Elisabeth* was not a geographical space that was preventing an army from reaching its principal enemy.

In one way the war seems almost inadvertent. But one can go further and ask why the cruiser was there. Clearly the alliance between Germany

---

[78] Statement by Foreign Minister Katō, quoted in www.firstworldwar.com/source/tsing-tau_kato.htm (accessed March 5, 2015).

and Austria-Hungary was a main reason. Alliance, then, was an indirect reason for contagion. Theoretically one can speculate that the Japanese knew they would engage in combat with the Austro-Hungarians and felt legally compelled to declare war, but not without trying to get them to surrender first. The Austro-Hungarians, for their part, were no more going to give in than the Germans, and certainly they were not going to betray their ally which had supported them in Europe. Alliances played a very limited role, but still an indirect one. This explains why the ship was there and in part why the Austro-Hungarians were not about to give in.

However, Japan did not appear to declare war because of valence balancing. The Japanese did not declare war as a logical afterthought to balance their relations because Austria-Hungary was an ally of their enemy. We can infer this in part because of the short time between the two declarations and in part because the main motive discussed in the diplomatic record is the ship and the planned military attack on Tsingtao. The role of alliances then is different from the main two discussed in this book – valence balancing and the failure of the coercive game.

The inference that contiguity is the main factor bringing about contagion is further supported by the fact that the other factors did not play any role; in particular, there were no grievances between Japan and Austria-Hungary. As the data show, there was no rivalry between the two; nor were there any territorial claims. Specifically, Austria-Hungary had no significant imperial possessions in the Far East that were of interest to the Japanese. Consequently, there were no prior MIDs. Nor were there any arms races.[79] In the end this would be the only war between the two.

By early September the Japanese had launched their offensive with 50,000 troops, with the aid of 2,000 British imperial troops. The *Kaiserin Elisabeth* saw action in the beginning and in the middle of the siege, with half its crew manning the ship and the other half serving as part of the German land forces. Once the shells for its heaviest guns had been expended, the ship was scuttled and its lighter guns were stationed on land. This limited Austro-Hungarian contingent went down to defeat with their German allies. Later, however, Austria-Hungary got its revenge when one of its submarines torpedoed the Japanese destroyer *Sakaki* in the Mediterranean in June 1917, killing sixty-eight of its crew.

---

[79] For this reason the text boxes on these indicators and the histogram have not been included.

This case shows how an inadvertent (but not random) placement of a battle cruiser put Austria-Hungary in the way and brought it into the war even though there were no grievances between it and Japan. This contiguous stationing of the militaries best explains how contagion occurred in this case.

Interlude: Valence Balancing, Austria-Hungary–Belgium, August 28, 1914 This dyad is also a classic example of valence balancing. Germany attacked Belgium because it was in the way, and did not want to go to war with it. Austria-Hungary declared war on Belgium only because Germany had. It said in the first line of its declaration of war that, in view of the fact that Belgium had refused to accept the propositions made to her by Germany on several occasions and that she was now cooperating with Britain and France, Austria-Hungary was compelled to consider herself in a state of war with her (letter from Count Berchtold to Count Clary, Brussels).[80]

Even less so than for the Germany–Belgium dyad, Austria-Hungary had no long-standing grievances with Belgium. There were no territorial claims, whereas Germany–Belgium had some colonial conflicts. Neither was a rival with each other on any of the three measures, and the only MID they had was the 1914 crisis. The single exception in the data to this pattern is the arms race indicator, where Horn finds an arms race in the years 1912–1914. This indicator probably does not mean that the two were directly arming against each other. It does, however, indicate that ongoing military expenditures in the European system as a whole were affecting this dyad in such a way that a mathematical correlation between the two sides' military expenditures is being unearthed. It may also suggest that Belgium was in the outer part of some network that tied the two dyads into the war that occurred. This arms race indicator, however, is clearly less obvious than the explicit alliance structure, which everyone knew about and was made reference to in the declaration of war.

Russia–Ottoman Empire, November 2, 1914

The Ottoman Empire was the last key entrant into the First World War in 1914, coming in on November 2, a little over two months after Japan. As with Japan, opportunity was the primary process that brought about intervention, with territorial rivalries playing an important

---

[80] *Declarations of War: Severances of Diplomatic Relations, 1914–1918* (1919), "Austria-Hungary," p. 11.

Text Box 11.1.   Russia–Ottoman Empire rivalry

Enduring Rivalry	Issue
DIEHL AND GOERTZ: 1876–1921 KLEIN, GOERTZ, DIEHL: 1817–1829, 1876–1921, 1993–2000 THOMPSON: 1668–1918 SENESE AND VASQUEZ 6th MID: 1827 ARMS RACE HORN: 1876, 1928, 1929, 1936–1938, 1975, 1976, 1994	Dominant Issue: Policy THOMPSON: No Thompson Issue

---

secondary role. The breakdown of the political order combined with territorial rivalries, as is often the case. Unlike for Japan, however, these processes were not so much motivated by aggrandizement as an attempt to ward off a steady decline and get some stable security in a hostile environment. Whereas Japan's decision-makers were confident and could take advantage of the ongoing war, the leaders of the Ottoman Empire were struggling to just stay afloat. All of the nearby European states were potential wolves, and even the potential allies among them, like Bulgaria, could just as easily become deadly enemies.

The decline of the Ottoman Empire can be traced back at least to Peter the Great, who modernized Russia and encroached upon the Black Sea, which was an Ottoman lake. Catherine the Great furthered this process. This territorial rivalry is typical between neighbors who have long-term power transition. It is no surprise that Thompson identifies this rivalry as going back to 1668 (see Text Box 11.1).

The Sick Man of Europe The struggle between these two neighbors was slightly different than the European decline of the Empire in the Balkans, which can be traced back to the Greek Revolt of 1821. Gradually, but steadily, one after another of the European possessions revolted and/or were stripped away, followed by the creation of a new Balkan state. The pattern often involved Russia protecting Christians or just intervening to fight one bilateral war with the Turks after another, which they typically won. The one exception to this pattern was the multiparty Crimean War, where the Ottoman Empire was able to declare war on Russia with the support and eventual intervention of England and France. Here, and only in this case, were the Turks able to halt and temporarily reverse a trend, which by the early twentieth century had made them the "sick man of Europe."

Beginning in 1878 the Ottomans lost, among other territories, Cyprus, Batum, Montenegro, Romania, and Serbia. Austria-Hungary also occupied Bosnia and Hercegovina in that year. These losses were followed by the imposition of protectorates or occupations by France in Tunisia (in 1881) and by Britain in Egypt (in 1882), Crete (in 1898), and Kuwait (in 1899).

By July 1908 these losses, coupled with domestic complaints, led to the revolt of the Young Turks. They pushed out Sultan Abdulhamid II and re-established the constitution of 1876, with elections for a new parliament. This resulted eventually in the Committee of Unity and Progress (CUP) ruling alongside the new Sultan Mehmed V Resad, a constitutional monarch. As the Young Turks were consolidating their control, crises came repeatedly and in quick succession in the period leading up to the First World War. Just three months after the Young Turk revolt Bulgaria declared its independence on October 5 (having been autonomous since 1878), and on October 6 Austria-Hungary formally annexed Bosnia and Hercegovina. In March 1910 there was a revolt in Kosovo. In 1911 there was a revolt in Yemen and then one in Northern Albania (Trumpener 2003: 338–339). These revolts were followed in September of 1911 by Italy invading Tripolitania and Cyrenaica; when the Ottoman Empire encouraged resistance in the interior in 1912, the Italians bombarded the Dardanelles and took Rhodes and the Dodecanese islands. This ongoing war led the Balkan League, consisting of Montenegro, Serbia, Bulgaria, and Greece, to declare war against the Ottoman Empire in the fall of 1912. The Ottomans were defeated badly, with Bulgaria coming within thirty-seven miles of Constantinople (McMeekin 2011: 23). This pushed them almost entirely out of Europe except for a tiny strip of land by Constantinople. Almost half of the population of the Empire resided in this area, known as Rumeli. The Empire was flooded with Muslim refugees, and their stories of atrocities sparked a desire for revenge (Aksakal 2008: 14).

The Bulgarians, however, became disaffected with the Serbs and Greeks because of the status of Macedonia, and attacked them. This led to the short Second Balkan War, that the Ottoman Empire entered to regain Adrianople (Edirne) and part of Western Thrace – a move that was successful and very popular in Turkey as a way of redeeming part of its honor.

The Decision-Making Context These events from 1908 on set the stage for the decisions the leaders of the Ottoman Empire took in 1914. The Young Turks rightly felt that they needed to stop this pattern of defeat and decline if they were to survive, and that to do so they would have to modernize their military and their nation (see Aksakal 2008: 13, 17). The onset of the war provided an opportunity to achieve these long-term goals. The ongoing war provided two things – an alliance that would increase the Ottoman Empire's power quickly and a breakdown of the existing structure that might permit it to reverse some of the territorial losses it had suffered.

Unlike Japan, which side the Ottoman Empire would choose was not clear. Japan's main objective was Germany's colonies and its main ally was Britain going back to 1902, so the side on which it would enter was not so much in question, at least for Katō. In addition, Japan was a powerful and rising state, and its enemy – Germany – was far away and weak locally. For the Ottoman Empire, things were quite different. It had no ally, and whichever side it spurned would likely attack it. This made for two difficult decisions – whether to enter and on which side (and then when). This set of decisions was not unlike what other minor states in the Balkans would face.

At the center of this decision was Enver Pasha (also known as Enver Bey) who became the Minister of War only in January 1914. He is sometimes portrayed as the key player who single-handedly engineered Turkey's entry into the war, but see Aksakal (2008: 10), who disagrees with this view. Although he was a pivotal figure, he had an essential ally – Talat Pasha or Talat Bey. He and Talat Pasha were the dominant figures in an elite that also included Cemal (Djemal) Pasha, who was initially more pro-French and later became more oriented to Germany, and Cavit (Djavit) Pasha. Enver Pasha was often opposed by the Grand Vizier Said Halim. In addition, the German Ambassador Baron Wangenheim and Otto Liman von Sanders played important roles in the capital, as did the German Admiral Souchon, commander of the *Goeben* and *Breslau*.

Alliance Decisions On August 1 Germany declared war on Russia, and on August 2 the Ottomans signed an alliance with Germany. This tight temporal connection suggests that these events were highly connected. Nonetheless, the decision was in the making for over a month and far from a forgone conclusion. The actual onset of war seemed to precipitate a final decision that the Ottomans kept delaying, mostly for bargaining purposes.

In the immediate aftermath of the two Balkan Wars the Ottoman Empire attempted to improve its capability. This took two forms – reform of the military and the search for allies. Both Britain and Germany were seen as agents that could aid military reform. Naval ties with Britain had existed before the Young Turks, and in 1914 Sir Arthur Limpus, a Rear Admiral, was head of a mission to improve the Navy. More importantly, the Ottomans had ordered two major battleships from Britain that would make a dramatic difference. The German mission, under Otto Liman von Sanders, arrived in December 1913 with the purpose of overhauling the military. This led to a crisis with Russia, which now saw the "Germans on the Bosporus" as Clark (2012: 334) put it, and considered going to war. War was avoided because of a lack of British and French support, and a face-saving solution was adopted.[81]

From the beginning, the Turkish decision-making elite wanted some alliance to protect itself from the series of reversals that reached a height in the First Balkan War. As early as 1911 it had sought an alliance with Britain, but was refused (Haldi 2003: 138). Just before the July crisis France, Russia, and Britain were all approached. In order to curry favor and in the hope of getting some sort of alliance, Russia was given permission to supervise reforms regarding the Armenian population in Eastern Anatolia. Subsequently, Talat Bey proposed an alliance to Sazonov that was rejected. Cemal Pasha in July proposed an alliance to Viviani, Prime Minister of France, in return for French support for Greece's return of islands in the Aegean that the latter had seized in the Balkan War, but he received no response as Viviani rushed off to St. Petersburg with Poincaré to meet the Tsar.[82] During this time the Ottomans also tried unsuccessfully to get several loans from both Britain and France (Aksakal 2008: 60).

An alliance with Germany was always a consideration, and this received new emphasis in light of the Entente response. It began with Austria-Hungary, which actually suggested an alliance as it contemplated war with Serbia.[83] As early as July 14, Berchtold had his ambassador raise the possibility of a German alliance with the Ottoman Empire, but this was brushed aside by the Germans. Jagow, Germany's foreign minister, had given this some thought and felt that the

---

[81] The crisis was resolved by making Liman von Sanders a marshal and an inspector general in the Ottoman army. The crisis had two important domestic impacts within Russia. Sazonov moved toward a more hardline position from his previous more mixed stance, and the crisis saw Kokovstov, the accommodative Chair of the Council of Ministers, losing much of his influence (Clark 2012: 345–346). He would be removed by the Tsar in January 1914.

[82] On these attempts see Trumpener (2003: 344).

[83] Austria-Hungary was concerned that if Turkey joined the Entente that would make Bulgaria unlikely to attack Serbia because it would then be surrounded by enemies.

Ottomans were not strong enough to provide much military support, and they would need German support from a likely Russian invasion of Eastern Anatolia (see Aksakal 2008: 93–94 for details).

In the next few weeks, however, Turkish military capacity and Turkey's willingness to use it in the Black Sea would become the focus of the two main German representatives on the ground – Ambassador Baron Wangenheim and Otto Liman von Sanders, head of the German military mission. Enver Pasha was the key figure pushing for an alliance with Germany.

Beginning as early as mid July 1914 when Austria-Hungary was seeking support from Turkey as well as Bulgaria against Serbia, Enver Pasha would go back and forth with Wangenheim about whether and when to have an alliance with Germany (Aksakal 2008: 96–97). Wangenheim was hesitant about an alliance because he felt the Ottomans were too weak. Jagow agreed with this position. The Kaiser, however, was very enthusiastic about an alliance because he thought it would inflame Muslim subjects in the Entente's empires, especially in the Arab world. Bethmann-Hollweg was initially on the fence, but felt if there was an alliance then the Ottomans had to immediately attack Russia so as to divert troops from the Eastern Front.

Enver Pasha felt the Germans were a better option than the Entente because of the danger that Turkey might become "Russia's vassal," as he told Ambassador Wangenheim on July 22 (Trumpener 2003: 345). He also told Wangenheim that he thought Germany and Austria-Hungary were stronger and they would win (Trumpener 2003: 345). In addition, the British and the French had been encroaching systematically on Ottoman possessions in North Africa and the Middle East. The Germans even encouraged the Ottomans to attack the British in Egypt. From the perspective of the Ottomans, an alliance with Germany provided a better defense and would permit them to regain territory in the Caucasus. At the same time, however, making the Entente their enemy meant that the areas that Britain and France had encroached upon, like Egypt and Tunisia, would be at risk in a war, as might control of the Straits and Constantinople itself.

It took numerous interactions to reach an agreement. These reflected German hesitancy and internal disagreement on the utility of having the Ottomans as allies, and the Ottoman attempt to drive the best bargain, as well as the desire to get an alliance without actually entering the fighting. These two elements – who would give the best deal and who was the likely winner – are the key theoretical elements in the contagion model that explain which side a country will join. Enver Pasha and his internal allies spent most of their time trying to get the best possible deal they could from Germany. Germany was a better choice because Enver Pasha believed they would be more apt to provide a long-term reversal of Turkey's decline (Aksakal 2008: 13, 17, 152; 2011), and they were not as direct a threat to the Straits. In addition, they had not rebuffed the Young Turks they way the Entente had. Still, would they and the Ottomans win?

Once war with Russia had broken out on August 1, the Germans provided some strategic advantages that tipped the scale. The most prominent of these was the acquisition of the *Goeben* and *Breslau*. The *Goeben* was a dreadnought that would give the Ottomans an edge in the Black Sea. With the final signing of the alliance on August 2, Wangenheim and Liman von Sanders supported Enver Pasha's request for the two ships, which were being pursued by the British and French navies, to enter the Straits (Aksakal 2008: 103). The Grand Vizier objected and tried using their entry as a bargaining chip to get Germany to pressure Bulgaria into an alliance with the Ottomans (Aksakal 2008: 114–115). The ships finally entered the Straits on August 10. The Ottomans ended up announcing the purchase of the ships pre-emptively before the Germans had fully agreed, but they went along with it (Aksakal 2008: 116, 118). Nonetheless, the German commander of the two ships remained in place, albeit now as an Ottoman commander. The acquisition of the two German ships, albeit under German command, made up for the fact that Churchill, head of the Admiralty, had blocked on August 1 the delivery of the two ships of dreadnought class – the *Sultan Osman* and *Reşadiye* – the Ottomans had purchased, and confiscated the ships.

Even though the alliance was signed, Enver Pasha had additional and more specific demands that he would impose before he would agree to enter the war. The day after the alliance was signed, the Ottomans declared their neutrality on August 3. The Germans did not want to readily concede to any of these specific demands and had to be forced into granting them by the bargaining situation. The first was a rescinding of the capitulatory privileges, special concessions including economic exemptions from Ottoman law that permitted foreign states to control custom duties, postal services, etc. These were unilaterally abrogated on September 8 after the signing of the alliance, but before entry into the war. The Germans even joined Italy and the other major states in opposing this, but did little else (Trumpener 2003: 350). Second, the Ottomans demanded a payment of five million Turkish pounds in gold before they would actually enter the war. This they got in two shipments in October in return for an agreement (of which the Grand Vizier was not a party) to send Souchon into the Black Sea. Third, although not a demand for entering the war, the Ottomans wanted

Germany to encourage Bulgaria and Romania to ally with them and join the Central Powers as a way of protecting their rear, if they went to war with Russia (see Aksakal 2008: 119–123 for details).

The Decision to Go to War   The actual declaration of war was a convoluted affair, with "Turkish" actions provoking a Russian declaration of war on November 2.[84] The Ottoman decision to go to war involved a struggle between Enver Pasha (and his supporters) and Grand Vizier Said Halim and between the latter and the German actors on the ground, who played an important role. Early on Enver Pasha had "ordered" Souchon, commander of the *Goeben* and *Breslau*, to take the two ships into the Black Sea on maneuvers, which the Germans had been demanding. Said Halim confronted Enver Pasha on September 16 at a secret cabinet meeting and forced him to withdraw the order, much to the irritation of the Germans, who, reacting to Bethmann-Hollweg and the Kaiser, were planning to use the excursion to entangle Russia into a war.[85]

Bethmann-Hollweg and the Kaiser wanted the Turks to attack the Russians as soon as possible for strategic reasons. They wanted to divert Russian troops from the Eastern Front so as to aid their efforts as well as Austria-Hungary's. As early as mid September (Aksakal 2008: 151) pressure was put on Admiral Souchon to enter the Black Sea. Despite the reversal Enver Pasha had suffered from Said Halim, he was able to give "secret" orders to Souchon to enter the Black Sea (Aksakal 2008: 176–177), which he did on October 27. This was done with an understanding that if he encountered Russian ships he could engage them. Souchon exceeded these orders and actually bombarded Sevastopol and other ports, as well as sinking some Russian warships on the way. This provoked the Russian declaration of war. How much he exceeded his orders or followed Enver Pasha's true intentions is still a scholarly controversy, but Enver Pasha and the Germans were not unhappy about the outcome, and Said Halim accepted it after protesting it in the cabinet.[86] In this way both the hardliners in the cabinet and Germany

---

[84] Sources differ on the date of this declaration, with some having it as November 3 and others as November 5. I have gone with Goldstein (1992: 214).

[85] For details on this incident see Aksakal (2008: 158); see also Fromkin (1989: 71–73).

[86] The orders involved an elaborate plan whereby Enver Pasha authorized the maneuvers and then once at sea they would be radioed to open a sealed order from Enver to attack Russian ships. This would be contingent on Enver getting cabinet approval. If he could not get approval then he would radio Admiral Souchon not to open the second order and go ahead on his own authority. In fact, no radio message was ever sent, apparently to protect Enver (see Aksakal 2008: 176–177 for this analysis). All along Souchon was not acting on his own, but was in direct contact with Ambassador Wangenheim.

used the naval action to force a war. Britain and France followed up with a declaration of war on November 5. Turkey soon attacked Russian positions in the Caucasus, and the Russians had to deploy troops there.

The Role of Territory, Previous MIDs, and Arms Races   That Russia became the immediate target is not entirely surprising given the long-term rivalry between Russia and the Ottomans. The history of previous MIDs and wars between the two was extensive and enduring, as can be seen in Histogram 11. Although most of these MIDs were over policy questions, the wars involved territorial shifts, with Russia expanding at the Ottomans' expense. These MIDs made Russia the principal enemy. A comparable histogram for Germany–Ottoman Empire would show only three MIDs – in 1876, 1880, and 1897, again underlying the stark difference between the threat posed by Russia and that posed by Germany. Likewise, an examination of MIDs for Britain–Ottoman Empire and France–Ottoman Empire, while indicating nothing like the contention with Russia, still shows numerous MIDs prior to 1914, with both Britain and France having had nine MIDs with the Ottoman Empire.

The territorial claims before the First World War illustrate this, as can be seen in Text Box 11.2. These started with Russian demands and then an Ottoman demand when the Russians took over a piece of territory. Although there were no explicit territorial claims between the two after 1878, the fear that Russia sought greater influence or outright control of the Straits was very real. A more immediate threat was that Russia would seek control over Armenia in Eastern Anatolia. Once the war had broken out, these claims were made formally, as shown in Text Box 11.2.

The pattern of MIDs and wars was not associated with arms races before the war. The insertion of the *Goeben* and *Breslau*, however, did change the distribution of naval power in the Black Sea to the Ottomans' advantage, so it spurred a Russian reaction. The Russians had in fact as early as July 1912 gotten the Duma to approve funding to increase the size of the Russian navy to one and a half times that of the Ottomans' (Aksakal 2008: 111), but not much came of that. In the immediate aftermath of the Liman von Sanders crisis, the Russians held a conference in St. Petersburg and planned to enlarge the Black Sea fleet for an offensive in the Near East (Steiner and Neilson 2003: 128). After the war and preceding the Second World War there were arms races between Turkey and the USSR, as can be seen in Text Box 11.1. This reflects, in part, the impact of the First World War on relations.

Text Box 11.2.   Russia–Ottoman Empire territorial claims

1828–1829: Western Georgia (Claim Dyad 85801)
RUS–OTM
1855–1856: Kars (Claim Dyad 85802)
RUS–OTM
1856–1857: Southern Bessarabia and Serpent's Island (Claim Dyad 37401)
OTM–RUS
1870–1878: Southern Bessarabia (Claim Dyad 37402)
RUS–OTM
1877–1878: Eastern Anatolia (Claim Dyad 85803)
RUS–OTM
1878–1878: Alashkert and Bayazit (Claim Dyad 85804)
OTM–RUS
1915–1917: Constantinople/İstanbul (Claim Dyad 38401)
RUS–OTM
1916–1917: Eastern Anatolia (Claim Dyad 85805)
RUS–OTM
1916–1918: Kars–Ardahan–Batum (Claim Dyad 85806)
OTM–RUS
1920–1921: Batum (Claim Dyad 85807)
USSR–TUR
1945–1953: Kars and Ardahan (Claim 85808)
USSR–TUR

The data suggest, however, that arms races did not play a role in why these two parties went to war with each other in 1914.

Lastly, the pattern of alliances suggests, as in fact was the case, that the Ottoman Empire could in 1914 have swung either toward the Entente or toward the Triple Alliance, since neither side had any formal ties to the Ottoman Empire, as Text Box 11.3 shows. The decision of which side to ally with, however, was complicated by potential minor allies, namely, Bulgaria and Romania, as well as Italy. What each of these might do would affect what the Ottoman Empire would do.

The Russian Perspective   Sean McMeekin (2011: 28–30) argues that the real motive for Russia entering the war was to gain control of the Straits and Constantinople (compare with Bobroff 2006). He begins his argument by saying that Russia did not go to war to protect Serbia, and that, indeed, it had not supported her vigorously in the past, including in 1908 and most recently in the Balkan Wars, where it really

Text Box 11.3.   Russia–Ottoman Empire alliances

Russia Alliances	Ottoman Empire Alliances
1881–1887: AUH, GMY 2067	1854–1856: FRN, UKG, ITA[a] (1855–) 2031
1887–1890: GMY 2072	1854–1856: AUH 2034
1893–1917: FRN 2074	1914–1918: GMY 3015[b]
1909–1917: ITA 3009	1914–1918: BUL 3016[b]
1910–1916: JPN 3010	
1914–1916: ROM 3018	
1915–1917: FRN, ITA, UKG 3019	
1916–1917: JPN 3021	
1916–1917: FRN, ITA, ROM, UKG 3022	

[a] Prior to 1860, ITA refers to Piedmont.
[b] Not included in the histogram because the alliance was made within three months of the war.

did not want Serbia to have access to the sea and instead supported the creation of Albania. In addition, he rejects the notion that major powers ever go to war to support minor states. Next, he points out that the Straits were an important question in the Cabinet. As recently as December 1913–January 1914 during the Liman von Sanders affair Sazonov was prepared to use the crisis as an opportunity to finally get the Straits and partition the Empire (McMeekin 2011: 31; 2013: 59–60). Hardliners, such as Krivoshein, had wanted this because of trade concerns. More importantly, the hardliners felt they must act now before Germany established a firm presence in the Straits. Already in October 1912 during the First Balkan War, Bulgaria had come close to taking Constantinople.

All of these events, according to McMeekin (2011: 30), made Russian decision-makers see the war as an opportunity to get what they wanted and to do so before others stepped in and the window would be lost. The Ottoman Empire was the sick man of Europe and it was only a matter of time before it fell apart. He states that Sazonov first "mooted the idea of provoking a European war over the Straits question" in January 1914 (McMeekin 2011: 31).

Instead of McMeekin's view, the position taken here is that in the end Russia entered the First World War not because it sought a war to get the Straits, but because of the failed coercive game with Austria-Hungary and Germany. Even the generals, like Sukhomlinov, put aside these other objectives and got caught up in the exigencies of a possible war and the fear of what a German mobilization might mean as the July crisis came to a head. The Tsar, in particular, but also Sazanov, were focused on this crisis and were caught up in its dynamic. Russia entered the war because of the mobilization question, which was a reaction to the fear of what the German military might do if war broke out.[87] The Ottoman Empire was not part of this immediate decision, at least not for the Tsar, the foreign ministers, or the generals in command. It may have been for certain hardliners, such as Krivoshein, but he did not play a major role in the mobilization decision.

As for the war with Turkey, once the general war had broken out, Russia sought to avoid a war with Turkey for the same reason Germany and Austria-Hungary wanted one – it would mean opening another front that would strain the Russian military on the Eastern Front and force it to move troops (see Bobroff 2006: 100–101). Russian decision-makers would later seek the very objectives McMeekin sees as critical, but not in the fall of 1914. War with the Ottoman Empire was not opportune for them at that time. It would mean naval action in the Black Sea and deployment of troops in the Caucasus. Even more importantly, it would mean a closing of the Straits and greater German influence in the Bosporus.

It was the Young Turks and not the Tsar who considered going to war. They saw the ongoing war as an opportunity to reverse their decline and protect themselves from further encroachment. They wanted an alliance with the Central Powers for this purpose, and if they avoided a war so much the better, but that was not likely. All the German decision-makers pushed for Ottoman military action, which Enver finally approved, although not openly and not with the support of the Cabinet or even their full knowledge. Given the open attack, Russia had no choice as a major state but to declare war.

The *Goeben* and *Breslau* tipped the naval balance in the Black Sea decidedly in the Ottomans' favor. As a result, the Entente Powers could not supply Russia, and Russia could not export through the Straits. Churchill decided on the ill-fated attack at Gallipoli to open the Straits. This led to a major Turkish success under the command of Mustafa Kemal, later to become the first President of the Republic of Turkey.

---

[87] McMeekin (2013: 395–401) in his later book also sees the Russian early mobilization as an important reason why the war started.

Theoretical Analysis   The entry of the Ottoman Empire into the ongoing European war is very much a story of contagion in that without an ongoing war the Ottoman Empire would not have fought Russia, let alone Britain and France allied with Russia. Even though Russia declared war, it did so because it was provoked through a military attack. In doing so, Russian decision-makers played into the hands of the Germans, who wanted to open another front. Bethmann-Hollweg and Jagow wanted Turkey to live up to its alliance and attack Russia. The strategic necessities of the ongoing war spread the war to the Ottoman Empire.

Significantly, little was done by any of the principals to prevent the war. Instead, the key decision-makers in the Ottoman Empire debated how to take advantage of the war. This fact underlines the conclusion that the key contagion process that spread the war was the *opportunity* it provided to Ottoman leaders. The opportunity, however, was somewhat vague – it was an opportunity to reverse a long-term decline rather than to gain specific territories, as with Japan and later as with Italy.

Even though various factors pushed decision-makers in the Ottoman Empire in different directions, and unanticipated events – such as decisions in Germany to have local actors like Admiral Souchon take matters into their own hands – played a crucial role, the overall confluence of variables made both the decision of Ottoman leaders to enter the ongoing war and the side on which they would enter predictable. The decision-makers were split between those who wanted war and those who resisted. Still, certain goals were important to all. First, Russia was the Ottoman Empire's main rival and principal enemy; Germany, on the other hand was not a threat. In addition, its former protectors in the Crimean War – Britain and France – were now encroaching on its territories in North Africa. Second, Russia posed the major threat – it was contiguous and its navy and land army were nearby. Third, if the Empire's decline could be reversed, this would involve building up its military and its economy. Britain and, to a lesser extent, France could do this, but so could Germany. As the war approached, Churchill's decision to cut off the sale of the promised ships and Germany's willingness to have the *Goeben* and *Breslau* get safe haven in the Straits were significant contingent acts that pushed the Ottoman leaders toward Germany. So too, was the Triple Entente's spurning of an alliance early on, and the Kaiser's willingness, as well as Austria-Hungary's, to entertain one. Lastly, reversing decline ultimately meant regaining territory, and this could best be done in the Caucasus at Russian expense and in the Balkans with Bulgaria's and Austria-Hungary's support, which an alliance with Germany would help. In the end the war gave the

Ottoman leaders an opportunity to break out of restrictions the power order and the normative order had placed upon it that made it the sick man of Europe. All they had to do was seize it.

Seizing the opportunity, however, did not come without risk, because if they lost the war, they could lose everything. Hence, an alliance with Germany without actually going to war was attractive. The Kaiser and top decision-makers in Berlin would not accept this. With what appears to have been the connivance of Enver Pasha, German decision-makers had Admiral Souchon take naval action that exceeded his orders and made Russia declare war, thereby taking the final decision out of the hands of the split government at the Porte. Except for this last act of how they would enter the war, the actual entry and the decision to oppose Russia and support Germany were very much in the cards.

The main theoretical lesson that can be derived from this case is that opportunity will determine whether a side will enter an ongoing war, and territorial rivalry will determine which side a state will join. Opportunity in terms of a second front was important especially for Germany, but for the Ottoman Empire the key was not so much the role of a second front, but that the *ongoing war* provided an opportunity for it to fight its own private or parallel war. The ongoing war provided the Ottoman leadership with a window to reverse its decline and at the same time perhaps regain territory. The war with Germany and Austria-Hungary meant that Russia could not easily engage on a second front. The ongoing war provided the Ottomans with enhanced military equipment, including a dreadnought that shifted the distribution of power in the Black Sea. At the same time, the fact that Russia at best could divert only a limited part of its army to the Caucasus meant that the Ottoman army could have a real chance of increasing Turkey's territorial mass and bringing fellow Muslims into the Empire. Likewise, German support provided it with an ability to attack British positions in Egypt. The German alliance, however, meant not only military support, but also diplomatic allegiance that limited the normative prohibition against territorial change and war, especially by a minor state. The ongoing war, then, not only opened a window that reflected a major shift in capability, but also precipitated a breakdown in the prevailing political normative order that limited change.

From the Russian perspective a major war could have had a similar effect in terms of the breakdown of the political order that prevented it from gaining control of the Straits. Sazonov realized this, and McMeekin (2011) makes much of this in his analysis of the Russian origins of the First World War. However, it is argued here that this potential was not actualized before the war broke out because the danger of

German invasion focused decision-makers' attention on mobilization issues and not on the utility of provoking a war to gain the Straits. Once the war had occurred, however, the Straits became a goal, as did other Russian territorial ambitions, such as in Armenia. Russia's allies recognized this formally in 1915 in a secret treaty with Russia that gave them the Dardanelles and Constantinople, although that would be a free port. Thus, the First World War and the breakdown of the political order finally provided Russia with the opportunity to re-draw the map to resolve the Eastern Question in its favor.

The Russian–Ottoman dyad is an important case for the study of war contagion because it provides nuances and contingencies on how contagion actually works when contradictory vectors are in place and a side can swing either way. The East European dyads that entered in 1915 provide similar insights.

Outcome and Aftershocks Ultimately, despite the collapse of Tsarist Russia and the Bolshevik Revolution, the Ottoman Empire had chosen the wrong side. With the collapse of Bulgaria, coupled with defeats in the Middle East portions of the Empire, its position was not defensible and it began to crumble, as simultaneously did Austria-Hungary. The Young Turks abandoned rule on October 13, 1918, with Enver Pasha and others leaving on a German warship on November 2. A caretaker government then sued for peace with the British, which resulted in the Armistice of Mudros, which came into effect on October 31, 1918. On November 13, troops from Britain, France, and Italy occupied Constantinople.

With the end of the fighting in Europe, the various allies attacked the Ottoman Empire, and it collapsed as the new government tried to save Turkey proper. As the Entente victors decided its fate at Versailles in 1919, Greece and Italy attacked separately. The May 1916 Sykes–Picot Agreement was put into effect by Britain and France. The 1920 Treaty of Sèvres partitioned Turkey so that non-Turkish areas were given to Greece and to Italy, as well as others. Nationalists led by Mustafa Kemal, who had established a new capital at Ankara, resisted through force of arms and were able to save all of Anatolia, Constantinople (İstanbul), and even parts of European Thrace. All that took to 1923 with the Treaty of Lausanne.

Interlude: Valence-Balancing, Britain–Ottoman Empire, November 5, 1914; and France–Ottoman Empire, November 5, 1914 Three days after Russia declared war on the Ottoman Empire, both Britain and France declared war on the Ottomans on November 5, 1914.

The swiftness of this declaration, given their earlier uncertainty, makes it clear that it was the alliance obligation that was the key factor. There was no long deliberation and internal debate. In terms of the contagion models being examined here, this makes it a clear case of valence balancing in both instances.

This is not to say that territorial ambitions had no role in the overall relations of the countries. Both Britain and France had been nibbling away at the outer boundaries of the Ottoman Empire, first in North Africa and more recently, especially for Britain, in the Persian Gulf. By the time of the war Britain had several territorial claims and France one, as can be seen in Text Boxes 12.1 and 13.1, respectively. Unlike Sazonov, however, the major decision-makers in each country did not seek a war for territorial goals. In both instances there was ambivalence. Britain, especially, but also France, still wanted to preserve the Ottoman Empire and keep Russia out of the Straits. Each in its own way had supported the efforts of the Young Turks to modernize the country – Britain especially, with the naval mission led by Admiral Limpus and even the selling of two dreadnoughts. Russia objected to these British actions vehemently, particularly during the Liman von Sanders crisis, and it was the lack of enthusiasm on the part of Britain and France that made Sazonov back off from the idea of attacking the Straits at that time (Clark 2012: 346). Both countries had been protectors of the Ottoman Empire in the Crimean War, and this legacy still affected Grey. So neither went to war to carve up the territory of the Ottoman Empire; valence balancing was the key.

Text Box 12.1.   France–Ottoman Empire territorial claims

1885–1910: Wad al-Mukta and Biban (Claim Dyad 68601)
FRN–OTM
1915–1920: Greater Syria (Claim Dyad 71201)
FRN–OTM/TUR
1916–1920: Cilicia (Claim Dyad 70601)
FRN–OTM/TUR
1920–1921: Cilicia (Claim Dyad 70602)
OTM/TUR–FRN
1936–1939: Hatay (Alexandretta) (Claim Dyad 71601)
TUR–FRN

Text Box 13.1. United Kingdom–Ottoman territorial claims

1857–1858: Perim Island (Claim Dyad 77801)
OTM–UKG
1878: Cyprus (Claim Dyad 36801)
UKG–OTM
1892–1906: Sinai Peninsula (Claim Dyad 73601)
UKG–OTM
1901–1920: Kuwait (Claim Dyad 72601)
OTM–UKG
1915: Kamaran Island (Claim Dyad 77601)
UKG–OTM
1915–1920: Basra and Baghdad (Claim Dyad 72001)
UKG–OTM/TUR
1916–1920: Palestine and Transjordan (Claim Dyad 75001)
UKG–OTM/TUR
1918–1920: Mosul (Claim Dyad 71401)
UKG–OTM/TUR
1919–1923: Cyprus (Claim Dyad 36803)
OTM/TUR–UKG
1920–1926: Mosul (Claim Dyad 71402)
OTM/TUR–UKG
1955–1959: Cyprus (Claim Dyad 36805)
TUR–UKG
Third Party: GRC

The Underlying Structure As can be seen from Histograms 12 and 13, France and Britain had a long history of MIDs with the Ottoman Empire going back to the independence of Greece. These conflicts, although numerous, were not as frequent as those with Russia (Histogram 11) and did not have as many wars. In addition, both Britain and France sometimes intervened after the wars with Russia to reduce the harshness of the peace terms. The height of their friendliness, however, came with the Crimean War, when both supported the Ottoman Empire, indeed enabled it – especially Britain – to gain some leverage. It was this legacy that still lingered in 1914 despite all the MIDs that had transpired since then.

Nonetheless, both France and Britain had a rivalry with the Ottoman Empire according to the behavioral indicators but not Thompson, as can be seen in Text Boxes 12.2 and 13.2. These see the dominant issue as policy as opposed to territory, and the MIDs do not reach a 25%

Text Box 12.2.   France–Ottoman Empire rivalry

Enduring Rivalry	Issue
DIEHL AND GOERTZ: 1897–1938 KLEIN, GOERTZ, DIEHL: 1880–1938 SENESE AND VASQUEZ 6th MID: 1881 ARMS RACE HORN: 1862, 1912, 1913, 1934, 1936, 1937	Dominant MID Issue: Policy

---

Text Box 13.2.   United Kingdom–Ottoman Empire rivalry

Enduring Rivalry	Issue
DIEHL AND GOERTZ: 1895–1934 KLEIN, GOERTZ, DIEHL: 1827–1934 SENESE AND VASQUEZ: 6th MID: 1897 NO ARMS RACE	Dominant MID Issue: Policy

---

threshold on territory. France had arms races with the Ottoman Empire in 1862 and at the time of the two Balkan Wars, whereas Britain had none. This profile, in conjunction with that of Russia (and compared with Germany's), was enough to push the Ottomans toward the side of the Central Powers. It was also a profile that might spur imperial wars or incursions on the part of France and Britain toward the Ottoman Empire, but not enough for them to have had a major two-party war. This they avoided despite the recurring MIDs. The Ottoman Empire, which had the real grievances, was too weak to do anything. Its weakness is emphasized by its lack of alliances (as can be seen in Text Boxes 12.3 and 13.3). Meanwhile, France and Britain had a variety of involvements that kept their attention (and commitments) to the Ottoman Empire limited.

Once the war had occurred, the territorial ambitions of the two liberal imperial states, which had been present since the late nineteenth century, came forth. They both agreed in 1915 to give up the long-held goal of keeping Russia out of the Straits and made a secret treaty to give Russia that. They then proceeded with their own partition in the

Text Box 12.3. France–Ottoman Empire alliances

France Alliances	Ottoman Empire Alliances
1907–1915: SPN, UKG 3005	1854–1856: FRN, UKG, ITA[a] (1855–) 2031
1912–1918: UKG 3013	1854–1856: AUH 2034
1915–1918: ITA, RUS (–1917), UKG 3019	1914–1918: GMY 3015[b]
1916–1918: ITA, ROM, RUS (–1917), UKG 3022	1914–1918: BUL 3016[b]

[a] Prior to 1860, ITA refers to Piedmont.
[b] Not included in the histogram because the alliance was made within three months of the war.

Text Box 13.3. United Kingdom–Ottoman Empire alliances

United Kingdom Alliances	Ottoman Empire Alliances
1902–1930: JPN 3000	1854–1856: FRN, UKG, ITA[a] (1855–) 2031
1907–1915: FRN, SPN 3005	1854–1856: AUH 2034
1912–1918: FRN 3013	1914–1918: GMY 3015[b]
1915–1918: FRN, ITA, RUS (–1917) 3019	1914–1918: BUL 3016[b]
1916–1918: FRN, ITA, ROM, RUS (–1917) 3022	

[a] Prior to 1860, ITA refers to Piedmont.
[b] Not included in the histogram because the alliance was made within three months of the war.

1916 Sykes–Picot agreement. Valence balancing would also prove to be an important reason for contagion in Italy declaring war against the Ottoman Empire after it went to war with Austria-Hungary in 1915, but with Italy the territorial rivalry played a more prominent role, thereby illuminating the more limited role territorial ambitions played in the case of Britain and France vis-à-vis the Ottoman Empire.

It should also be noted that Serbia declared war on the Ottoman Empire the same day that Russia did. Serbia had long regarded the

Ottoman Empire as the enemy, ever since it was conquered, and as a rival once it had gained independence, so it is no surprise that it declared war. Since it had its hands full with Austria-Hungary and could not fight Turkey, this must be seen as an act primarily of valence balancing. The valence balancing is foremost in support of Russia, but secondarily also a declaration of war against the ally of Austria-Hungary. Thus, while territorial rivalry is a variable, it must, because of the ongoing battles, be seen as a latent or dormant variable. This is further evinced by the fact that Serbia did not expect to face the Ottomans in battle in the near future.

The Global Spread of the War to Colonial Areas

From the very beginning of the war in August 1914, fighting was spread to colonial areas. These entities had no legal say in their participation because they had no sovereignty in the International System. The spread occurred in two ways – first, European belligerents fought each other within their colonial spheres; and second, they drew upon their colonies for troops, especially when these, like India, had armies. In this way a good part of the globe was affected, not only in terms of being drawn in but also in experiencing battles far from the European center.

Even before the British Expeditionary force had fully arrived on the continent in late August 1914, British troops in co-ordination with French troops attacked German Togoland on August 7, 1914. By August 26 it had fallen and was divided by the two. At the same time, on August 8, Britain bombarded German East Africa and then invaded with Indian forces. This would become typical of how contagion moved hierarchically through the British and French empires, where colonial or Dominion troops were used to do a significant portion of the land fighting. South African troops were brought in, and Portugal was also involved in this arena. The fighting in East Africa continued until the end of the war, with Germany counter-attacking in Rhodesia a week before the Armistice in November 1918.

In the Pacific on August 20, 1914, New Zealand seized Samoa, and twelve days later, on September 11, Australia attacked the Bismarck Archipelago and had defeated German forces in New Guinea by September 21. In September British and French troops invaded the Cameroons from the North and South, respectively. British troops also entered German Southwest Africa, and the Union of South Africa took over the campaign, defeating the Germans by the summer of 1915.[88]

---

[88] Documentation of the above events may be found in Stearns and Langer (2001: 662); see also Keegan (1998: 205–211).

Thus, as the Battle of the Marne was being played out in September, Britain attacked the major German colonies in West Africa, East Africa, and Southern Africa, often using Dominion or colonial troops and with the cooperation of its allies – France and Portugal.

Once Britain and France had declared war on the Ottoman Empire, we see further evidence of this sort of diffusion. Britain began by immediately tightening its control where it was already influential if not dominant. By December 1914 the British had annexed Cyprus, occupied Basra, and imposed a protectorate over Egypt. In March–April 1915 France and Britain promised Russia Constantinople and the Straits, which was followed a year later by the Sykes–Picot Agreement dividing most of the remaining Ottoman Empire between Britain and France. Early in the summer of 1915 the British got the Sharif of Mecca to call for an Arab Revolt, promising self-rule after the war. By the end of the year British troops had moved into the Sinai and in March 1917 they had also occupied Baghdad. During August 1916 Italy was promised Smyrna (İzmir), Adalya and Konya in Anatolia in return for recognizing the Sykes–Picot Agreement. In July 1918 Arabs led, in part, by T. E. Lawrence took Aqaba, and in December British troops occupied Jerusalem. Just before the Armistice on November 7, the British occupied Mosul.[89] While all these actions were obviously military attempts at aggrandizement that are well known, they also show how the war diffused down the imperial "ruts in the hill." Britain and France would now replace the imperial Ottomans, with bribes along the way to the Arabs, the Italians, and the hapless Tsarist Russians.

The second way in which the war spread was by the European states using colonial and Dominion troops in their fighting, typically directly, but sometimes as laborers. In terms of sheer numbers, India accounted for 1.5 million troops, most of them going to the Middle East, but some to East Africa (Raghavan 2016: 34). On the French side, there were upward of 450,000 troops from North Africa and Sub-Sahara Africa, with another 115,000 or so drawn from settlers or others of European extraction. These fought on the Western front alongside the metropolitan French forces, with the colonial forces often serving as shock troops and taking heavy casualties. The numbers are uncertain, but figures anywhere from 42,000 to 278,000 have been mentioned,[90] although the latter is hard to believe. From Indo-China approximately

---

[89] These events are documented in Stearns and Langer (2001: 656–659).
[90] These numbers for both the size and the casualties are taken from Koller (2014 [updated 2017]: 2–3).

43,000 were recruited into the military and another 49,000 brought over as workers (Brocheux 2015: 7). The involvement of these troops must also be seen as hierarchical diffusion through the Imperialist System.

As for the Dominions, the most famous involvement was that of ANZAC forces at Gallipoli starting in April 1915. In Europe proper, Canada participated in great numbers with an expeditionary force of upward of 600,000 fighting first under British command and later under Canadian command on the Western Front, taking heavy casualties at major battles. South Africa played a leading role in nearby German colonies.[91] The Chinese people also played a role in that Britain paid to bring in approximately 100,000 laborers and France another 43,000–44,000 (Stevenson 2017: 290), all of this separate from the Chinese government, which was fractured. Such transactions were possible only because of imperial relationships with China.

How can this contagion be explained? The six models presented in Chapter 1 seem inadequate. One of the new things learned in this study that was not explicitly understood before is that the Imperialist System itself provided a structure that primed countries for contagion. This structure was similar to the alliance structure in that it provided ruts in a hill by which the war spread through hierarchical diffusion. As will be seen later, this Imperialist System was similar to other hierarchies in the system that made for order through hegemony (as discussed by Lake 2009). Imperialism/Hegemony will be added as a seventh model of contagion, the only one that was not explicitly anticipated before the fact. Since this is an *ex post* finding, it will be discussed in more detail in the concluding chapter.

Early on in the war, contagion brought in much of the globe outside of Europe that was not part of the legal system of sovereign states. It did this through a system of hierarchy that made the world far from anarchic. This started in 1914, but would continue through 1917. We turn now to the second wave of contagion that began in 1915.

---

[91] Participation in the war effort was sometimes very unpopular in the Dominions. There was a significant Afrikaner rebellion and a failed coup d'état with an attempt to get German support, including a joint German–Boer incursion from South West Africa (Stapleton 2016). In Canada, French-speaking Québec was hostile to aiding Britain, even though France was an ally.

Opportunity

Italy–Austria-Hungary, May 23, 1915

Background   The Italian states and Austria-Hungary had fought three wars against each other before 1915 when Italy entered the First World War. All of these were for the same reason – *irredenta* – the liberation of the unredeemed from foreign rule. Italy went to war in 1915 because of this territorial rivalry with Austria originating in 1848. The Thompson and Senese–Vasquez measures identify Austria and Italy as rivals, and territory at the heart of that rivalry (Text Box 14.1). Histogram 14 shows that territory is the modal issue (three of ten), especially early on, and that 25% of their total MIDs are over territory. Such a percentage generally is associated with an increased probability of going to war and that is confirmed in this case. Thompson also sees this rivalry as territorial (spatial) as well as positional – a struggle for status.

Going back to Mazzini and Garibaldi, the ideology of nationalism was constructed to claim that people of the same nation – defined in this case as those who spoke the same language – had a right to self-rule. Nationalism was linked with self-determination and, in 1848, the idea of a republic. None of these ideas were part of the legitimate norms within the system. At the time, territory (and the people on it) was owned by monarchs who had that ownership as a divine right. Dynastic succession (including marriage) and international agreements were the only means by which territory could legitimately be transferred. The Austrians – Austria-Hungary was not constituted as a Dual Monarchy until 1867 – and their ruling Habsburg family had the Italian lands as part of the Congress of Vienna settlement ending the Napoleonic Wars. Their legal and "moral" right (for the time) was unimpeachable. This meant that the newly emergent nationalists had no real non-violent way of gaining their territorial ends.

```
┌─────────────────────────────────────────────────────────────────────┐
│                                                                       │
│     Text Box 14.1.    Italy–Austria-Hungary rivalry                   │
│   ════════════════════════════════════════════════════════════════   │
│   Enduring Rivalry                      Issue                          │
│   ────────────────────────────────────────────────────────────────   │
│   THOMPSON: 1847–1918                   Dominant Issue: Not Available  │
│   SENESE AND VASQUEZ: 6th MID:          25% (+) Territory              │
│   1877                                                                 │
│                                         THOMPSON: Positional and       │
│                                         Spatial                        │
│   ARMS RACE                                                            │
│   HORN: 1849–1851, 1859, 1860, 1912, 1913                             │
│   ════════════════════════════════════════════════════════════════   │
│                                                                       │
└─────────────────────────────────────────────────────────────────────┘
```

Instead the goals of national liberation, self-determination, territorial acquisition, and rule by the people as a republic were seen as attainable only by revolution. In Europe, 1848 was a year of revolution, and the Italians were in the lead, with revolutions in Sicily in January, Venice in March, and Rome in November. But revolutions spread throughout Europe, in Berlin, in Paris, in Budapest, among other places, and most importantly in Vienna, the capital of the Austrian and Habsburg Empire. Metternich, state Chancellor and architect of the Congress of Vienna, was forced to flee. With that, the people of Milan revolted in March. As a result Piedmont, the one independent Italian state, intervened to help them. Revolts spread to Venice, Tuscany, and Rome. The latter was ruled by the Pope, but under the protection of French troops.

One by one, the Northern Italian revolts (i.e. not including Rome) in each of these geographically separated cities were suppressed by the Austrians under their new king – the eighteen-year-old Franz Josef – who was put in power by the family to replace his limited uncle Ferdinand I. General Radetzky – of the famed Radetzky March by Strauss – after a strategic retreat crushed the numerically superior army of King Carlo Alberto of Piedmont and forced him to abdicate in favor of his son, Victor Emmanuel II. Venice under the leadership of the charismatic Daniele Manin was starved into submission. Most dramatically of all, the Roman Republic with Garibaldi and Mazzini at hand was crushed by French troops supporting the Pope.

The main lesson of the wars of 1848 was the refutation of the revolutionary slogan *L'Italia farà da sé* – Italy will do it herself. In other words, Italy, more properly the Italian people, will bring about her own liberation and redemption without outside foreign help. After 1848, it was clear that Italy was no match for Austria and that an outside ally would be needed. Leadership shifted away from Garibaldi, who supported a republic, to Cavour and King Victor Emmanuel II of Piedmont. They sought an outside ally – Napoleon III of France, who helped defeat Austria in Lombardy in 1859. Under Cavour's diplomacy, revolts in the Habsburg provinces of Tuscany, Modena, and Parma as well as parts of the Papal States erupted, and they were eventually liberated. Garibaldi, working with Cavour, brought about a revolt and the independence of the two Sicilies under the rule of the Spanish Bourbons, so that by 1860 most of geographic Italy was liberated except for Venice and Rome.

Along with the search for allies, there were military buildups that led to arms races between the two states (see Text Box 14.1). These followed the 1848 revolutions and occurred along with the 1859–1860 wars. They also clearly preceded the First World War, with arms races occurring during the two Balkan Wars (fought by their neighbors) in 1912 and 1913 and as the First World War itself was approaching in 1914 and 1915 as Italy was deciding on which side to enter (see Histogram 14).

The War of 1866 would be the third war with Austria, and, with Bismarck as an ally, Venetia was acquired. This left Rome, which was taken in 1870 by force of arms against the Pope, who could no longer be defended by Napoleon III. He withdrew his troops, which were needed for the Franco-Prussian War. This left only the small contingent of Austrian troops led by General Kanzler, who could not prevent the walls of the Vatican from being breached, and who was told by the Pope to surrender to save lives once they had been breached.

Almost forty-five years before 1914 all of Italy was considered unified, but there were still some pockets of Italian-speaking areas under Austro-Hungarian rule – Trentino and Alto Adige (Südtirol) in the Alps and Trieste with its exceptional naval base and the nearby Italian-speaking areas of Northern Dalmatia. These claims, as Text Box 14.2 shows, were made by Italy going back to 1866 for Alto Adige, while for Trieste the claim was not made until war broke out in 1914.

The Decision to Go to War   Italy's decision to enter the war was different from those of all the other major states, and it set a precedent for the way minor states, especially in Eastern Europe, would join the war. Of all the states that entered the war, Italy was the one that did not have to enter to meet at least some of its territorial objectives. This was the case because of a clause in the Triple Alliance treaty; Article VII that said that if Austria-Hungary gained territory Italy should be compensated.

Text Box 14.2.   Italy–Austria-Hungary territorial claims

1848–1866: Lombardy–Venetia (Claim Dyad 25801)
ITA[a]–AUH
1866–1918: Trentino–Alto Adige (South Tyrol)
(Claim Dyad 26601)
ITA–AUH
1866–1876: Venetia and Giulia (Julian March)
(Claim Dyad 33201)
ITA–AUH
1914–1918: Dalmatia (Claim Dyad 33401)
ITA–AUH
1915–1918: Venetia and Giulia (Julian March)
(Claim Dyad 33202)
ITA–AUH

---

[a] Prior to 1860, ITA refers to Piedmont.

Antonino di San Giuliano, Italy's foreign minister, under the new government of Antonio Salandra had served under the previous government of Giovanni Giolitti (the major figure in Italian politics before the war). San Giuliano was the central decision-maker with regard to the July crisis, especially once General Pollio, Chief of the General Staff, had died on July 1. Pollio was an adherent supporter of the Triple Alliance. San Giuliano took a more flexible approach to satisfying Italy's long-held *irredentismo*. He began by declaring Italian neutrality on August 3 as war was breaking out.[1] On August 4, Poincaré addressed the French National Assembly to cheers when he said that assurances were such that France could move troops away from its Southeastern border with Italy. This meant that the French no longer had to worry about fighting a two-front war, which was one of the main purposes of the Triple Alliance. San Giuliano was able to declare neutrality because he argued that the alliance was a defense pact and Austria-Hungary had not been attacked but was attacking Serbia, which was technically correct. He then went on and invoked Article VII and demanded compensation. Initially the hope was that Italy could get this without joining the war effort of its allies, but by simply assuring Austria-Hungary that it would not join the other side. As it was, Italy had signed a secret

---

[1] Neutrality also protected Italy's military position since it was still recovering from, indeed still bogged down in, its war in Tripolitania and Cyrenaica.

Text Box 14.3.   Italy–Austria-Hungary alliances

Italy Alliances	Austria-Hungary Alliances
1882–1915: AUH, GMY 2068	1879–1918: GMY 2065
1888–1915: GMY, AUH, ROM 2069	1881–1895: SER 2066
1902–1918: FRN 3001	1881–1887: GMY, RUS 2067
1909–1917: RUS 3009	1882–1918: GMY, ITA 2068
1915–1918: FRN, RUS, UKG 3019	1883–1918: GMY, ITA, ROM 2069
1916–1918: FRN, ROM, RUS (–1917), UKG 3022	1904–1908: RUS 3003
	1914–1918: BUL 3017
	1915–1918: BUL, GMY 3030

agreement with France in 1902 (as noted in Text Box 14.3), which, although mostly a colonial agreement over North Africa, contradicted and made moot much of Italy's reason for joining the Triple Alliance, namely, its colonial rivalry with France.[2]

Bethmann-Hollweg pressed Berchtold of Austria to accept the Italian demands. If the Italians joined the other side this would be bad for the Triple Alliance. It would mean that Austria-Hungary would now be involved in a three-front war – Russia, Serbia, and Italy. The dispersal of its armies would weaken it considerably, especially on the Russian front, where they were needed to help Germany. Meanwhile, as was already happening, even Italian neutrality would free the French from a two-front war, which would also be detrimental to the Germans. Trading land was worth the price to Bethmann-Hollweg, but of course it was not his land. To the Austrians the demands were an act of perfidy.

The demands might have had some chance of succeeding if they had been confined to Trentino and Alto Adige, which after all had long been on the agenda and had in parts at least a sizable Italian-speaking population, but the Italians had added the demand for Trieste. This was a strategic port and the major naval base of the Austro-Hungarian navy. Without it they would have difficulty maintaining their naval presence in the Mediterranean. It was a stake over which the Austrians would never budge.

---

[2] See Gibler (2009: 212), who treats the exchange of letters as a neutrality pact. The agreement says that, if France is the object of aggression, "Italy will maintain a strict neutrality." The Italians do not see this as inconsistent with the Triple Alliance in that both it and this 1902 agreement are defensive.

San Giuliano died on October 16, and Salandra, who had worked closely with him, now was in sole control. He talked to both the French and the British about joining their side. In effect what was going on now was an auction for Italy's loyalty. Salandra was guided by two factors: which side would give him the most and which side was likely to win. The Entente was always able to promise him more, because it was not their territory. Still, they had to be somewhat careful of Serbia and its concerns about the Dalmatian coast and Russia standing up for Serbia. But Italy also had territorial concerns in the Ottoman Empire, which also affected Russia's interests and tempered what could be promised. Nonetheless, the constraints were nothing compared with what faced Austria-Hungary and Germany.

The prospect of territorial gains had to be discounted by the probability of winning. There would be no point in going with the side that gave them the most if they lost. At the same time, if he held out too long his aid might not be needed or the price he could demand would be less. At the very end, in March 1915, Grey was spurred on to make a deal with the Italians by a military setback and the hope that an Italian entry would encourage other neutrals to enter on the Allied side (Hamilton and Herwig 2003: 382). Additionally Salandra had to weigh the costs of war against a future opponent. If Italy decided to actually fight Britain, its long coastline would be very vulnerable to the British Navy and its extensive imports from Britain, including coal, subject to blockade. In addition, the Ottoman Empire had joined Germany and Austria-Hungary in November 1914, and they were a rival with which Italy still had territorial ambitions and claims.

Nonetheless, as time dragged on Berchtold finally was moved to grant compensation. He decided to offer Trentino, but this was vehemently opposed by Conrad, Chief of Staff, and Tisza, the Hungarian Prime Minister and former dove. The two of them forced the once all-powerful engineer of the war to resign. The Italians signed the Pact of London on April 26, 1915, which met their territorial demands and avoided the British naval threat. There was then a period of domestic turmoil, with the King even thinking of abdicating. Ultimately, the Italians declared war on May 23, 1915, but they held off declaring war with Germany, which had supported their efforts for compensation.

Theoretical Analysis   The Austro-Hungarian–Italian case raises some interesting theoretical issues that tell us a great deal about the contagion process in general and specifically in the First World War. A clear inference is that, when territorial objectives and rivalry push a state in one direction and alliance ties in another, territory is much more potent. The long-term irredentist territorial quest always pushed Italy in this direction. The only real question was whether it could satisfy it diplomatically through compensation and remain in the Triple Alliance. Contagion worked in this dyad because of territorial rivalry, and this factor overwhelmed any alliance effect that would make Italy join the war because of its previous commitments to the Triple Alliance.[3]

A second factor that brought Italy into the war was the *opportunity* the war provided to attain this long-held claim to Trentino and Alto Adige that went back to 1866. The breakdown of the political order meant that Concert of Europe opposition to this claim, which had been sustained for almost fifty years, would now be obviated. Instead of opposing this territorial shift, both sides were willing to entertain it to gain Italy's adherence to their coalition. Ongoing war lifted a barrier to political change and made possible shifts in territory and changes in issue position that were not possible before. Violence, which major states usually do not endorse when it is done by other states, was now permitted. That is what is meant by an opportunity: a window that has been closed in the past is now opened, and it is not known how long it will remain open, so states must act while they have the chance. The war in 1914 provided Italy with a unique opportunity to gain territory that it had no chance of gaining diplomatically before and for which it could not use force without being defeated (in this case by Austria-Hungary).

The opportunity created by the ongoing war produced an auction. Ongoing wars do not always do this, but it did so in this instance because Italy had assets desirable to both sides. They therefore bid for its support, and Italy encouraged this from the very beginning. Italy's decision would create important precedents and a demonstration effect for subsequent decisions to join the war in Eastern Europe.

In terms of assessing the relative potency of territory and opportunity, the distinction between sufficient and necessary conditions clarifies matters. Opportunity in terms of the ongoing war itself was the most powerful contagion factor in this case because it served as a necessary condition for the sufficient condition of territorial rivalry. This combination of opportunity with territorial rivalry would become the hallmark for how contagion worked in the second wave.

Italy–Ottoman Empire, August 21, 1915   Italy did not declare war on the Ottoman Empire with the others because in 1914 it was still not in the war, trying to get from Austria-Hungary what it could

---

[3] See Weitsman (2004: 88–97) for further analysis on Italy leaving the Triple Alliance.

through the principle of compensation. Once it did enter at the end of May 1915, it took only to the end of the summer to declare war on the Ottoman Empire. On the surface this was valence balancing, but it also reflected opportunity and Italy's long-term territorial rivalry with the Ottomans. This can be seen in Text Boxes 15.1 and 15.2 and in the many MIDs recorded in Histogram 15. The alliances of both sides are listed in Text Box 15.3. The arms races reflect military buildups associated with the 1911 war as well as the Balkan Wars. Despite the

---

Text Box 15.1.   Italy–Ottoman Empire territorial claims

1911–1912: Libya (Claim Dyad 69001)
ITA–OTM
1912–1915: Castellorizzo (Claim Dyad 36405)
ITA–OTM
1912–1920: Dodecanese Islands (Claim Dyad 37001)
ITA–OTM/TUR
1915–1920: Antalya and Konya (Claim Dyad 70801)
ITA–OTM/TUR
1917–1920: Smyrna (İzmir) (Claim Dyad 71002)
ITA–OTM/TUR
1920–1921: Antalya and Konya (Claim Dyad 70802)
OTM/TUR–ITA
1920–1923: Dodecanese Islands (Claim Dyad 37002)
OTM/TUR–ITA
1939–1945: Dodecanese Islands (Claim Dyad 37006)
TUR–ITA

Text Box 15.2.   Italy–Ottoman Empire rivalry

Enduring Rivalry	Issue
DIEHL AND GOERTZ: 1880–1924 KLEIN, GOERTZ, DIEHL: 1880–1924 THOMPSON: 1884–1943 SENESE AND VASQUEZ: 6th MID: 1905 ARMS RACE	Dominant MID Issue: Policy THOMPSON: Positional and Spatial
HORN: 1861, 1862, 1912, 1913, 1928, 1929, 1934, 1936–1938	

Text Box 15.3.   Italy–Ottoman Empire alliances

Italy Alliances	Ottoman Empire Alliances
1882–1915: AUH, GMY 2068	1854–1856: FRN, UKG, ITA[a] (1855–) 2031
1888–1915: GMY, AUH, ROM 2069	1854–1856: AUH 2034
1902–1918: FRN 3011	1914–1918: GMY 3015[b]
1909–1917: RUS 3009	1914–1918: BUL 3016[b]
1915–1918: FRN, RUS, UKG 3019	
1916–1918: FRN, ROM, RUS (–1917), UKG 3022	

[a] Prior to 1860, ITA refers to Piedmont.
[b] Not included in the histogram because the alliance was made within three months of the war.

ongoing rivalry, which is indicated by all the measures, the actual declaration of war was mostly an act of valence balancing, since Italy was fully occupied with Austria-Hungary. Once the First World War ends, this will change, and Italy will take the opportunity the victors provide to invade Turkey.

Bulgaria–Serbia, October 14, 1915

Bulgaria became independent as a result of the Russo-Turkish War of 1877–1878, and the ensuing treaty of San Stefano gave it most of the borders it wanted from the Ottoman Empire. The major states, however, felt that this was too large a state for one that would likely be under heavy Russian influence, so they restored areas, especially in Thrace, to the Ottoman Empire. From that time on the Bulgarian elite was fixated on bringing all its nationals within its country and getting back to the San Stefano borders. The earliest tension regarding Bulgaria's borders happened in 1885 while Bulgaria was still an autonomous entity and not yet independent. King Milan of Serbia, fearing that Bulgaria's absorption of Eastern Roumelia from the Ottoman Empire might lead it to seek Macedonia, invaded Bulgaria. He was repulsed, and Bulgaria had to be stopped from overwhelming Serbia by the threat of Austrian intervention (Sarkees and Wayman 2010: 260–261).[4]

---

[4] Since Bulgaria was not an independent nation-state at the time, this war is not recorded as an interstate war in the Correlates of War data and thus does not appear in the MID histogram. It is listed as an extra-state war.

The Macedonian question led Bulgaria to fight three wars – the First Balkan War, which was against the Ottoman Empire; the Second Balkan War, which was initially against Serbia and Greece; and then the First World War, where it attacked Serbia. Each of these wars was driven by a territorial rivalry. The first and last were sparked by the opportunity of an ongoing war that weakened its opponent by splitting its army on more than one front. Bulgaria's entry into the First World War can be best explained by a combination of its fierce nationalism coupled with the opportunity of the ongoing war, which made it possible for this nation that was badly beaten in the Second Balkan War to regroup and seize its dream.

The combination of opportunity and territorial rivalry as two powerful factors making for contagion affected several dyads in the First World War. This was seen in the cases of the Ottoman Empire–Russia and Italy–Austria-Hungary, and it will be seen again in the case of Romania–Austria-Hungary. Each of the cases is slightly different, however, and this permits the observer to derive tentative inferences about the relative importance of different variables.

In the case of the Ottoman Empire–Russia it was not so much irredentist claims that motivated it joining the war as it was long-term decline and a desire to increase its territory regardless of nationalist sentiment. This in turn was coupled with a fear that, without change, insecurity would increase and the Empire might fall apart. The ongoing war, by diverting the military of its rival, permitted the Ottoman Empire to engage in a war where it had a chance of being on the winning side and even winning specific engagements if these were wisely selected.

For Bulgaria–Serbia nationalism was the motivating force for the territorial rivalry, and it is a powerful drive for war either when there is a good opportunity for war, as in the First Balkan War, or when there was not, as in the Second Balkan War. Bulgaria fought in the Second Balkan War because of its nationalism (and a sense of betrayal by its ally) and obviously gave insufficient attention to the possible coalition of forces it would face. It was likely that it would just keep coming whenever it could, and that it would attack Serbia again even if there were no opportunity provided by an ongoing war. In this sense one can think of territorial rivalry as more powerful and opportunity as secondary, whereas in the Ottoman–Russian case the opposite seems to have been the case. Still, for Bulgaria the ongoing war in 1914 was a great opportunity because it weakened its rival, and it would not likely have another chance to reverse its situation for some time to come.

Two other cases also had this combination, but again with slight differences. With Italy–Austria-Hungary a strong formal alliance was at play that should have prevented a war. This factor was also present in Romania–Austria-Hungary, but what was more important here was the role of divided government in shaping the final decision. All four cases, however, had two common forces at play: major states sought to buy the allegiance or neutrality of the potential joiner, and the joiner tried to determine who would ultimately win as a key consideration in making its decision. For the Ottoman case, the major states were not very active in soliciting an alliance, whereas in the three others the ongoing war did push them to seek allies and the belligerents were so anxious to have them that the potential joiners could conduct an auction. Likewise, later joiners could take advantage of the ongoing battlefield to assess who was likely to win, although this often led to misjudgments. The Ottomans had to be more deductive.

Background   Historically, Russia was the patron of Bulgaria. In the Russo-Turkish War of 1877–1878 Bulgaria had gained its autonomy, and in 1908 it had gotten its independence, while Russia defended it from a possible invasion from the Ottoman Empire. For these reasons the government and elites felt obligated to Russia. Russia also set up the Balkan League, which was a way for Bulgaria to capture parts of Thrace and Macedonia that had been taken away by the major states in the Treaty of Berlin. Part of the Balkan League involved an agreement that if the allies disagreed they would accept Russian arbitration.

Prior to the dispute Serbia and Bulgaria had a similar history – both had been occupied by the Ottoman Empire for a long period and both had Russia as a patron and liberator which had fought its occupier. Both saw the Ottoman Empire as the main enemy. One would normally expect them to have cordial relations, but the question of Macedonia prevented that. This was indicated early on with the 1885 war. In 1912, however, in the First Balkan War, they became military allies against that Ottoman Empire in the hope that both of them could gain at the expense of the Ottoman Empire. They agreed that Bulgaria would attack in Thrace and that Serbia and Greece would fight in Macedonia. They would then split the spoils. At the end of the war, however, Bulgaria had no troops in Macedonia, which was occupied by Serbia and Greece. The Bulgarians felt the Serbs were reneging. Sazonov was approached to arbitrate the dispute, but he was hesitant. By the time he agreed to arbitrate, the Bulgarians had decided to attack Serbian and Greek positions in Macedonia, which bordered on Bulgaria, and the Second Balkan War was under way. General Savov of Bulgaria attacked on the night of June 29, 1913. At the beginning of that month, on June 1, 1913, Serbia and Greece had signed an alliance, so they were prepared. The war was a disaster for Bulgaria, as Romania soon attacked Bulgaria to gain Dobrudja, a disputed area between the two. The Ottoman Empire then entered the war to regain some of the territory it had lost to Bulgaria in the First Balkan War and re-captured Adrianople and the surrounding area in Thrace.

As a result of this war Bulgaria saw Serbia as its principal enemy, and Macedonia became the main focus of its territorial objectives. In addition, large parts of the government and elite saw Russia as betraying it and moving closer to Serbia and away from Bulgaria.[5] With the Second Balkan War, the government of Stoyan Danev fell, and Vasil Radoslavov, who was not pro-Russian, became Prime Minister.

Having been badly beaten by a strong coalition of its neighbors and completely isolated, there was little Bulgaria could do. Then the assassination of the Archduke occurred. As Austria-Hungary thought of war, it naturally saw Bulgaria as a potential supporter, just as it saw the Ottoman Empire, the other major enemy of Serbia, as an ally. The prospect of a war between Austria-Hungary and Serbia provided an opportunity to gain Macedonia that in its present defeated condition Bulgaria had no hope or strategy for gaining. Previously, both Austria-Hungary and Germany had tried to attract Bulgaria by offering loans right after the Second Balkan War. Austria-Hungary was the first to do this when Bulgaria stood alone, but that was not enough to meet its needs. Germany came forward with a substantial amount of money, and when it did, this brought in the French, who were prepared similarly to give a large sum, so long as the loan was backed by Russia. Bulgaria went with Germany, which signaled a shift (see Clark 2012: 276–278). The loans began a turn in foreign policy that the July crisis accentuated. As Russia moved to defend Serbia against Austria-Hungary, Bulgaria felt more estranged. The feelers from Vienna for an alliance illuminated a path by which Bulgaria might recover from its great losses in the recent war.

Still Bulgaria was in a weakened position. It had other enemies besides Serbia. Romania was right on its border, and the Ottoman Empire had retaken part of Thrace. Also there could be no siding with Austria-Hungary until it was clear what Russia would do. Once the larger war between the major states had broken out things were somewhat

---

[5] On Sazonov's dilemma, see Clark (2012: 272–281).

clearer. The Ottomans in particular sought an alliance with both Bulgaria and Romania to protect their rear if they went to war with Russia. Such an alliance would also protect Bulgaria's rear if it went to war against Serbia. To do so, however, also meant going to war with Russia. Such were the dilemmas facing the new government as the crisis broke.

Internal Politics The Bulgarian government, while not as divided as some, for instance Romania, still had divisions and separate bases of power that prevented it from being a centralized unitary decision-making unit. At the center was Tsar Ferdinand, from Saxe-Coburg (which made him Austrian–German), but he was also the grandson of Louis Philippe, the former citizen king of France (Hall 2003: 390). He was born a Catholic and raised in Austria, but had his son baptized as Orthodox to gain recognition from Russia. He was brought to power as an outside constitutional monarch in a military coup in 1896. In 1908 he declared Bulgaria independent. He played a central role in decision-making until the end of the war in 1918. Prior to 1915 he would swing between those who were more pro-Russian and those who were pro-German (Clark 2012: 273). During this time Russia had only been irritated with Tsar Ferdinand on two occasions – in 1908 when he declared independence unilaterally without gaining Russian approval and then in 1913 as Bulgaria came close to taking Constantinople and Sazonov had to send a warning telling the Bulgarians, in effect, not to advance. Ferdinand actually had regalia made for himself to be Emperor at Byzantium (McMeekin 2011: 25).

The Prime Minister, who was the key legal authority, was Radoslavov, who had succeeded Danev after the disastrous Second Balkan War. He and many others in the elite were bitter about Russia's lack of support. A third actor was the military, which was a bit of a wild card. They had brought Ferdinand to power, displacing the previous popular Alexander Battenberg (Hall 2003: 390), and, more relevantly, General Savov had ordered the attack in 1913 without waiting for Sazonov's diplomacy. The nature of this decision is still controversial regarding the extent to which the General acted on his own. Hall (2003: 394–395) reports that Ferdinand's role was obscure, even though technically he was commander in chief, and afterwards the Prime Minister denied knowing of the order, but Savov denied that. Although the extent of Savov's independence is not clearly established, he did advocate the attack and give the order, and the policy was certainly consistent with Prime Minister Danev's overall stance and the pervasive nationalist sentiment of the time. Hall (2003: 394) also says "the impetus for the attack came" from the General and not Tsar Ferdinand, but that he "certainly ... approved of the order."

With the outbreak of war between Germany and Russia, and Russia acting as the patron of Serbia, the sentiments of the Bulgarian masses and elites were somewhat torn. With Radoslavov as Prime Minster there had been a definite shift away from the pro-Russian policy of the past. Russia was seen as having chosen Serbia over Bulgaria in the Second Balkan War. Still, there were many who retained the old affections. Hall (2003: 397) relates how the Bulgarian ambassador in St. Petersburg, a former war hero, resigned and accepted a position in the Russian army. Others of much lesser note did the same. The decision-making elite did not feel that way. Radoslavov was the key figure, and he focused on Macedonia and bided his time. Officially, Bulgaria remained neutral, but in August as the Great War broke out Bulgaria supported anti-Serbian guerillas in Macedonia (Hall 2003: 397).

The Decision to Go to War Both Radoslavov and Tsar Ferdinand tended to favor the Central Powers over Russia – Radoslavov because of his political position and Ferdinand because of his birth. In this sense, the division within the decision-making elite was not sharp, as in Romania or Greece. The key element was whether they could get what they wanted in Macedonia and maybe parts of Thrace from one side at lower costs than from the other. Although sentiment favored the Central Powers, a deal with Russia might get them most of Macedonia if Serbia, because of its desperate situation, would make a major concession. This would be highly attractive, if Serbia and Russia could be trusted. This would permit Bulgaria to remain neutral and avoid another war, which would be welcomed since they were still weakened from the last two.

The other option was to intervene in the war on the side of Austria-Hungary and Germany and seize Macedonia by military force. They could gang up on Serbia the way Serbia and Greece had ganged up on them in 1913. Early on this was a live option. Conrad, the Austro-Hungarian Chief of Staff, on July 29, the day after the Austro-Hungarian declaration of war on Serbia, urged Bulgaria to enter the war against Serbia before the general spreading of the war to the European major states the next week. This was too soon for Radoslavov.

The decision-making went on into 1915, with the key elements being who could offer the best deal and who was likely to win. These elements reflect the major theoretical factors in the contagion models outlined in Chapter 1. The desire of both sides to gain Bulgaria as an ally permitted Bulgaria to conduct an auction for its loyalty. Russia and the

Entente had difficulty in making a reasonable offer because they could not get Serbia to meet any of the Bulgarian demands over Macedonia in return for Bulgaria's neutrality. Instead, Russia wanted Bulgaria not to remain neutral but to attack the Ottoman Empire in return for territory in Thrace. Nonetheless, in the spring of 1915 the Entente had important successes on the battlefield that made Radoslavov think they might win (Hall 2003: 398). They had landed at Gallipoli and the Russians had made advances against the Austro-Hungarians. However, it was not until May 29, 1915 that they finally were able to make an offer on Macedonia that would also give Bulgaria Eastern Thrace, but by then the Entente's military situation was worsening, with defeats in Galicia and the Turks having counter-attacked at Gallipoli (Hall 2003: 398).

The enhanced military position of the Central Powers made Bulgaria lose interest in the Entente, but what really made the Bulgarians more interested in the other side was that they could offer them all they wanted vis-à-vis Serbia and Macedonia. Then, what really capped the deal was that Germany and Austria-Hungary agreed to a joint invasion, with their forces attacking from the north and Bulgaria attacking from the east. This would permit Bulgaria to take Macedonia immediately. The government agreed to this, and Ferdinand announced Bulgaria's entry into the war on October 14. With this, Serbia's allies declared war – Britain on October 15, France on the 16th, and Russia and Italy on the 19th. Interestingly, Russia was tardy compared with the other Entente powers, in part, no doubt, because of its former patronage coupled with Slavic affinity. Bulgarian troops would meet the armies of all of these allies of Serbia, including Russia as the war came to an end. All of these are examples of the role of alliances in spreading the war and of valence balancing in particular. With Bulgaria joining the Central Powers, the Ottoman Empire also got its long-sought alliance with Bulgaria to protect its rear from attack.

Territorial rivalry coupled with an assessment of who was likely to win was responsible for Ferdinand and Radoslavov taking this decision. However, underlying this was the opportunity of the ongoing war that made this decision even possible. Without the ongoing war, Bulgaria was not in a military position to take on Serbia. Serbia was now more powerful and had more people and resources than it did before the two Balkan Wars. In these wars Bulgaria had taken tremendous casualties and was financially in desperate straits. It was simply incapable of fighting, let alone winning, a third Balkan War by itself. The ongoing war changed that; now it could have allies and financial support. In addition, the auction between the two sides provided it with an opportunity that might not come again. Even though it was not as prepared as it could have been later on, it needed to take this opportunity because there was no telling when another might arise.

What exactly did the opportunity provide? First, it provided for a two-front war that would split and weaken Serbia's military. Second, it provided two powerful military allies and, even more importantly, it provided for a joint invasion that had a high probability of succeeding in short order (and it did). Third, the opportunity also consisted of the breakdown of the prevailing political order that normally would provide a constraint on minor states fighting among themselves for territorial gain.

The Role of Territory, Previous MIDs, and Arms Races   The data profile of Bulgaria–Serbia sheds some light on the power of the variables pushing Bulgarian decision-makers to war with Serbia. Text Box 16.1 shows the importance of Macedonia for Bulgarian–Serbian relations. It began in 1913 and continued right up until the Versailles settlement in 1919, which was imposed on the defeated Bulgaria. It then arose again in the Second World War and was only settled in 1948 as the Cold War imposed itself (see Text Box 16.1).

Text Box 16.1.   Bulgaria–Serbia/Yugoslavia territorial claims

1913: Serbian Macedonia (Claim Dyad 34204)
BUL–SER
Third Party: GRC
1914–1919: Serbian Macedonia (Claim Dyad 34206)
BUL–SER
Third Party: GRC
1919: Strumica Valley (Claim Dyad 34215)YUG[a]–BUL
1941: Serbian Macedonia (Claim Dyad 34207)
BUL–YUG
1944: Serbian Macedonia (Claim Dyad 34208)
YUG–BUL
Third Party: GRC
1944–1948: Pirin Macedonia (Claim Dyad 34216)
YUG–BUL
Third Party: GRC

---

[a] Until 1929 Yugoslavia was officially called the Kingdom of Serbs, Croats and Slovenes.

Text Box 16.2.   Bulgaria–Serbia/Yugoslavia rivalry

Enduring Rivalry	Issue
DIEHL AND GOERTZ: 1913–1952	Dominant MID Issue: Policy
KLEIN, GOERTZ, DIEHL: 1913–1952	25% (+) Territory
THOMPSON: 1878–1955	THOMPSON: Spatial
SENESE AND VASQUEZ 6th MID: 1941	
ARMS RACE	
HORN: 1912, 1925, 1926, 1936–1938, 1940, 1950–1951, 1973–1974	

The more behavioral Diehl–Goertz measure shows this rivalry beginning in 1913 with the Second Balkan War, but the more historically
sensitive Thompson measure dates the rivalry from 1878, the date
Bulgaria became autonomous within the Ottoman Empire, and he sees
Macedonia as the main issue (Text Box 16.2). Thompson and Dreyer
(2012: 91–94) see Bulgaria simultaneously in rivalry from 1878 with
the Ottoman Empire, Romania, and Greece. During the First World
War it ended up fighting the latter two.

The only arms race preceding the 1915 entry was in 1912, which
reflects their joint arming in preparation for war with the Ottoman
Empire, but such arms races are fungible and are used later in the war in
1913. Thereafter, Bulgaria was too weak to engage in an arms race with
any of its rivals. Text Box 16.2 also reveals the likely impact of the First
World War on subsequent perception of threat between the two, as well
as hostility derived from the ongoing rivalry. Arms races erupted in the
1920s and in the 1930s as the Second World War loomed. They stopped
as the Soviet Union dominated Eastern Europe at the war's end, but
were resurrected in 1950 as Yugoslavia defected from Stalin's sphere.

Text Box 16.3 indicates the limited allies these two minor states had
and the fact that they were brought together temporarily in the Balkan
League in 1912, only to turn on one another because of a dispute over
the territorial spoils of war. This again indicates the power of territorial
rivalry over alliance commitments when push comes to shove, a pattern
more dramatically revealed in Italy's and later Romania's entry into the
First World War despite their long membership of the Triple Alliance.

Lastly, Histogram 16 shows that the 1913 war was the start of a series
of MIDs that continued through the early Cold War. This is an example of what has been seen several times in this analysis – territorial

Text Box 16.3.   Bulgaria–Serbia alliances

Bulgaria Alliances	Serbia Alliances
1912–1913: SER 3011	1912–1913: BUL 3011
1912–1913: GRC 3012	1913–1918: GRC 3014
1914–1918: OTM 3016[a]	
1914–1918: AUH 3017	
1915–1918: AUH, GER 3020	

[a] Not included in the histogram because the alliance was made within three months of the war.

disputes produce a rivalry and then a war that does not result in an overwhelming victory but leads to more MIDs and even wars. This is a recursive relationship in which certain events, typically a war, produce a step-level jump in hostility. For the minor states and late entrants in Eastern Europe this was not an uncommon pattern.

   Outcome   The short-term outcome was very successful for Bulgaria. Serbia was quickly overrun and Bulgaria got Macedonia, thereby revising both the 1878 Treaty of Berlin and the 1913 Treaty of Bucharest. The Serbian army was pushed out and had to retreat. After taking Macedonia, Bulgaria invaded a section of Greece to keep the Serbian army separated from the British. The British Navy, however, bombarded Bulgarian positions at Doiran in April 1918, and it fell to the British and Greeks as the Bulgarians retreated on September 20, 1918. The defeat by the British Navy led to mutinies and revolts in the capital. Five days later British troops entered Bulgaria. With defeat, Tsar Ferdinand abdicated in favor of his son, Boris, and retired to his estates in Austria-Hungary, where he lived until 1948. Alexander Stamboliski, leader of the Agrarian Party, became Prime Minister in 1919 and accepted the peace, which was discussed at Versailles but embodied in a separate Treaty of Neuilly. Bulgaria lost Macedonia, Dobrudja, and Thrace, becoming land-locked. In a coup in June 1923 Stamboliski was killed by Macedonian nationalists, who first cut off the hand that had signed the March 1923 Treaty of Niš with the Kingdom of Serbs, Croats and Slovenes (MacMillan 2001: 142). These losses of territory to Serbia, Greece, and Romania would later become issues during the Second World War.

Conclusion   The main driving force of Bulgarian foreign policy since 1878 was restoration of its San Stefano borders. This led it to have rivalries with first the Ottoman Empire and then its main competitors – Serbia and Greece – for Macedonia. The fourth rival in line was Romania, also because of its conflicting territorial claims. Bulgaria would fight wars with each of its rivals, and the rivalries continued after the First World War and into the Cold War, with vestiges in certain instances still present today.

Territorial rivalry over Macedonia became the compelling motivation for Bulgaria's entry into the First World War. Unlike some cases, indeed the Serbian case in June 1914, it was not so much that non-state nationalist groups had to push state decision-makers to pursue this agenda; rather, state decision-makers themselves embodied this irredentism, as much as any. This was true of prime ministers Danev and Radoslavov, who had different stances on Russia, Tsar Ferdinand, and the military. What this means is that, regardless of opportunity, Bulgaria would have likely gone to war over Macedonia at some point. Territorial rivalry must be seen as the key factor pushing Bulgaria into the war.

Opportunity played a role in that it permitted Bulgaria to use the ongoing war to achieve its main foreign policy objective in a circumstance when it otherwise would not have done so. Bulgaria had just been badly defeated in 1913. It was isolated diplomatically and incapable militarily and financially from getting involved in another war.

The July crisis provided an opportunity in three regards. First, it gave the Bulgarians powerful allies, like Austria-Hungary that actually approached them. Second, it permitted them to conduct an auction for their allegiance since both sides sought them as allies. Siding with Russia and the Entente even offered the prospect of gaining large parts or most of Macedonia while remaining neutral. Radoslavov was ultimately swayed by a calculation of who was likely to win, given the battlefield outcomes. Third and finally, the idea of a joint invasion tipped the scale, because it assured victory over Serbia at minimal military cost. Going in this direction also was consonant with the negative psychological affect toward Serbia as a result of the Second Balkan War. It also had better guarantees since Bulgaria could rely on its own military strength to gain what it wanted, and not some diplomatic deal where Russia and the other Entente allies would pressure Serbia to give up Macedonia against its will.

While the latter could not be predicted since it depended so much on contingences, like diplomatic skill and the military conditions, the vectors associated with these contingencies favored the Central Powers since they had no constraints on what they could promise. They could offer the reward almost immediately, and they had the local military advantage on their side.

The opportunity of the war insured that Bulgaria even in its weakened condition would take advantage of it. In October 1915 the playing out of the pro-Entente vectors was not in the cards, but the *ex ante* probabilities that pro-Central Powers vectors would play out the way they did were in the cards. As soon as Bulgaria entered the Entente states declared war, first Britain on October 15, then France the next day, with Russia and Italy bringing up the rear on October 19. Of these valence-balancing decisions the most difficult was that of Russia, which had been Bulgaria's patron since its first days. Russia's declaration cemented the gradual displacement of Bulgaria by Serbia in this triangular relationship going back to the Second Balkan War. All of this is consistent with the contagion models laid out in Chapter 1.

Interludes: Valence Balancing and Opportunity

Germany–Portugal, March 9, 1916

Portugal and Britain had been allies longer than any other two states in the system, with their alliance going back to 1386 and having been renewed periodically (see Text Box 17.1). It was this alliance and the tight relationship between the two that led Portugal to enter the war. At the outbreak, Portugal said it would enter the war, if Britain wished. The alliance permitted Britain to use Portugal's ports and, when the war broke out, Portugal extended this privilege to France. It did not

---

Text Box 17.1.   Germany–Portugal alliances

Germany Alliances	Portugal Alliances
1879–1918: AUH 2065	1816–Ongoing: UKG 2000
1881–1887: AUH, RUS 2067	
1882–1918: AUH, ITA (–1915) 2068	
1883–1918: ITA (–1915), ROM (–1916), AUH 2069	
1887–1890: RUS 2072	
1914–1918: OTM 3015	
1915–1918: AUH, BUL 3020	

extend this privilege to the Central Powers; in fact, it interned German ships in Lisbon. Portugal also sent a delegation to Britain to co-ordinate action, including in the colonies in Africa, where it permitted British troops to cross Mozambique to attack German colonies.[6]

While Portugal was extremely friendly with Britain, it had certain grievances with Germany, mostly of a colonial nature. The two had several territorial disagreements and conflicting claims, as can be seen in Text Box 17.2. Germany had taken Kionga at the end of the nine-teenth century, and Portugal would later use its entry into the war to regain it. Still, there was no rivalry between the two according to Thompson and according to Diehl and Goertz (see Text Box 17.3). However, there was an arms race with the approach of the First World War (see Histogram 17).

These colonial problems suggest why Portugal was so willing to aid Britain. In August of 1914, even though Portugal and Germany were not officially at war, Germany had attacked several Portuguese positions

---

Text Box 17.2.   Germany–Portugal territorial claims

1894: Kionga Triangle (Claim Dyad 60801)
GMY–POR
1904–1915: Kavale Rapids Border (Claim Dyad 61401)
GMY–POR
1916–1919: Kionga Triangle and Southern German East Africa (Claim Dyad 60802)
POR–GMY

Text Box 17.3.   Germany–Portugal rivalry

Enduring Rivalry	Issue
SENESE AND VASQUEZ 6th MID: 1941 ARMS RACES HORN: 1937	Dominant MID Issue: Policy

---

[6] These facts are taken from Shirkey (2009: 146–147).

in Angola and along the Mozambique border. Germany had desires to gain territory in Angola, and Britain had transported Portuguese troops to Africa to meet this challenge. Portugal had been using the alliance as an insurance policy to help protect its far-flung empire, which included not only Africa, but also East Timor and Macau.

Despite Portugal being willing to enter the war earlier, both Britain and France were hesitant. This was because they did not think very highly of Portugal's armed forces, and their performance in East Africa lent much credence to this view.[7] The Entente Powers did not regard Portugal's army as necessary until 1916. At that point submarine warfare was taking its toll, and Britain asked Portugal to seize the German merchant ships it had interned and use them to trade with the Entente (Shirkey 2009: 149). The Portuguese did this on February 16, and Germany declared war on March 9, with Austria-Hungary following a few days later. Once they were in a legal state of war, Portugal coordinated its military actions in East Africa with Britain. Prior to that their actions had been independent. It was at this time that Portugal regained Kionga. Portuguese troops did not fight in Europe until after Verdun. The first troops arrived in January 1917 and were put under British command. Their number eventually rose to around 60,000.

Theoretical Analysis   While this case is fairly minor, it involves several contagion processes. Germany, and even more so Austria-Hungary, were not interested in going to war with Portugal, and Portugal for its part was not interested in going to war with Germany in Europe despite tensions in Africa. The ongoing war brought them to war because of four factors – alliances, colonial contiguity, colonial territorial disagreements, and opportunity – all of which interacted to make this an example of how the structure of the global imperial hierarchy diffused the war. One key factor in this mix was Portugal's *alliance* with Britain. The alliance was important to Portugal over the years because Britain guaranteed its independence, and the alliance was useful to Britain because it gained access to Portugal's ports, including the Azores. The formation of a republic in 1910 coincided with doubts about the long alliance since it was made with the Crown. This meant that the new government had something to prove, so it went out of its way to declare its support (Paige 2007: 136–137). Because Portugal was not directly threatened there was no reason for her to go to war, so in effect the alliance produced a kind of *valence balancing*. Portugal ended up at war because Germany was an enemy of its friend and ally.

---

[7] See for instance Paige (2007: 136–144).

At the same time, it must be kept in mind that Portugal was willing to do this to curry favor with Britain because of its colonial disagreements with Germany.

Technically this was not valence balancing, because it was Germany and not Portugal that declared war. Nonetheless, Portugal was doing things – interning German ships and then seizing them – that insulted Germany and made it declare war. What is important is that the things that Portugal did were done because it regarded Germany as an enemy of its ally. This produced three MIDs – one in 1914 and two in 1916 when war was declared (see Histogram 17).

Two other aspects of this case also make the valence balancing that was going on here different from that in 1914. First, Portugal knew that in doing Britain's bidding there was a good chance it would see combat with Germany. Typically in valence balancing the third party does not really think direct combat will come about because of the absence of contiguity, although as we have seen in the 1914 cases combat did result despite the absence of contiguity. Second, Portugal and Germany had real colonial grievances in Africa where their possessions were *contiguous*. In fact, they were already in combat long before the incident in Lisbon harbor that led to the German declaration of war. The *territorial disagreements* meant that the ongoing war could provide an *opportunity* for Portugal, as well as Germany, to settle claims in their own private or parallel war. This colonial war was not so private, however, because it became part of an integral colonial front that Britain was systematically conducting against Germany's few colonies since it first entered the war.[8] Thus the global imperialist structure was a very important part of the contagion.

In this process, battlefield conditions also played a role, although a supplementary one. It was the success of German submarine warfare that led to Britain's initial request, and it was the stalemate on the Western Front and the losses at Verdun that led Grey to relent and accept Portugal's offer of troops (Shirkey 2009: 149).

Lastly, once Germany had declared war, Austria-Hungary soon followed. Its ships too had been interned and seized along with Germany's, but this had been done simply because they were there with Germany's. In that sense "naval" contiguity played a role, similarly to the way it had with Austria-Hungary and Japan. This declaration of war was more an incident of true valence balancing in that Austria-Hungary declared war only because Germany declared war. Additionally, it did

---

[8] One of Britain's first military engagements with Germany, for instance, was over Togoland on August 7, 1914.

not really expect to go to war with Portugal on land, and it had no grievances with Portugal. They had no territorial claims with each other, no rivalry, no arms races and no MIDs until 1916.[9]

Romania–Austria-Hungary, August 27, 1916

Of all the cases of war contagion in the First World War, the case of Romania is the one most torn by contradictory forces combating each other: (a) Romania had multiple territorial ambitions that pushed it in opposite directions, (b) the government was more divided than most at the outbreak of the war in 1914, and (c) as the war spread this had an impact on Romanian decision-making – something that the entrants in 1915 did not have to worry about very much. Certain unforeseen events, such as the death of the King, and battlefield contingencies pushed Romania's decision-making in a direction that made the opportunity of the ongoing war too hard to resist. In this process territorial rivalry was to play a key role in making Romanian decision-makers seize the opportunity, but it was battlefield conditions and the decisions of previous entrants that more shaped which side it would eventually join. Like the other cases, the decision-making should be analyzed as two separate decisions – the one to enter and the one choosing which side to join.

Territorial Objectives   As with Italy and Bulgaria, Romania had territorial goals that were based on nationalist and irredentist concerns. These were not as rabid as those of Bulgaria, in part because of the absence of strong nationalist non-state actors and in part because there were diverse territorial objectives. The latter were significant in making Romanian foreign policy less fixated than that of Bulgaria or even Italy. The largest territorial objective was Transylvania, which was in the heart of Austria-Hungary and had a large Romanian population. This concern was salient to many in Romania because the minority was often openly repressed by the Hungarian government. This objective against Austria-Hungary was supplemented by a territorial claim to Bukovina, which was to the North, but also within Austria-Hungary. The nature of these claims, however, had been contained because Romania had been a secret member of the Triple Alliance of Austria-Hungary, Germany, and Italy since 1883, and it had renewed this alliance in 1913.

[9] There was an arms race as recently as 1909 and there had been arms races earlier in the nineteenth century, but our coding rules do not include arms races outside the first and last MID that occurs in order to reduce the number of false positives.

Text Box 18.1.   Romania–Austria-Hungary alliances

Romania Alliances	Austria-Hungary Alliances
1883–1916: AUH, GMY, ITA 2069	1879–1918: GMY 2065
1914–1916: RUS 3018	1881–1895: SER 2066
1916–1918: FRN, ITA, RUS, UKG 3022	1881–1887: GMY, RUS 2067
	1882–1918: GMY, ITA (–1915) 2068
	1883–1918: GMY, ITA (–1915), ROM (–1916) 2069
	1904–1908: RUS 3003
	1914–1918: BUL 3017
	1915–1918: BUL, GMY 3030

Text Box 18.2.   Romania–Austria-Hungary territorial claims

1914–1918: Banat (Claim Dyad 32201)
ROM–AUH
Third Party: SER
1914–1918: Bukovina (Claim Dyad 37601)
ROM–AUH
1916–1918: Transylvania (Claim Dyad 32601)
ROM–AUH

Romania had joined the alliance out of fear of Russia (see Text Box 18.1). As Text Box 18.2 shows, there were no territorial claims until 1914, and the claim to Transylvania was presented only in 1916, the year of the war entry. Still these did not result in a rivalry for either Diehl and Goertz or Thompson (as noted in Text Box 18.3). Nor were there many MIDs before the war; there was only one in 1883, and that was at a low level, as can be seen in Histogram 18, and in the same year as they signed the alliance.

The only indicator of tension in the data is the Horn arms race measure, as can be seen Text Box 18.3. This shows mutual military buildups in 1909 after the Bosnian Crisis between Austria-Hungary and Russia/Serbia and then in 1912 and 1913. Both of the latter were

---

Text Box 18.3.   Romania–Austria-Hungary rivalry

Enduring Rivalry	Issue
NO ENDURING RIVALRY ARMS RACE HORN: 1909, 1912, 1913	

---

associated more with the Balkan Wars than with any direct confrontation, but of course armaments are fungible.

A territorial objective that pulled Romania in a different direction was its desires in Russian Bessarabia to the East. Here there were Romanians as well, albeit they were less self-aware than the population in Transylvania. However, the Romanian population in Moldavia that bordered Russia was hesitant to go to war with its giant neighbor because it would bear the brunt of an attack. A third territorial concern was the recent taking of Dobrudja from Bulgaria during the Second Balkan War. Of the three objectives this was the most salient to Romanian decision-makers because it had recently been won in the Second Balkan War and they did not want to lose it at all costs (something consistent with prospect theory).[10] Thus, while it was unclear whether to make Austria-Hungary or Russia an enemy, there was no ambivalence about Bulgaria, which was seen as an enemy because of Dobrudja. These various territorial objectives meant that Romania could not satisfy all of them by entering the war, but had to choose which of its territorial rivalries it would focus on, and hence which neighboring states it would make its war-time enemies and which it would befriend. The contradictory territorial objectives also meant that Romania was surrounded by enemies, a strategically perilous situation during an ongoing war.

Divided Government   Other than Greece, which ended up in civil war, Romania was the most divided state in Europe when war broke out in August 1914. King Carol was German and a Hohenzollern, who was invited to be king by landowners who overthrew his predecessor, Alexandru Ioan Cuza in 1866. King Carol was an historic figure, having led the Romanian army in the Russo-Turkish War of 1877–1878

---

[10] See Levy (1992, 1996). Prospect theory hypothesizes that actors are more willing to take risks to prevent losses than to attain gains they do not yet have.

and proclaimed Romania independent of the Ottoman Empire at the end of the war. He had significant power and influence, despite being a constitutional monarch. He had negotiated Romania's entry into the Triple Alliance as a fourth party. During the July crisis, but before the war, he told the Austro-Hungarian ambassador that Romania would stay in the Triple Alliance (Hall 2003: 401). A meeting of the Crown Council on August 3, soon after Germany and Russia had gone to war, would not support the King in his pro-German views.

Prime Minister Ion Brătianu was anti-Austria-Hungary, but the two major parties were split. His Liberal Party was more firmly in the anti-Austria-Hungary camp and prepared to work with Russia and the Entente. The Conservative Party was pro-Austria-Hungary, but became fragmented over the contradictory territorial objectives.[11] Although King Carol and Brătianu were very divided on the issue of which side to favor, this was not a bitter rivalry. As the July crisis unwound Brătianu, although he favored the Entente, was held back by a fear of being attacked on two sides by Austria-Hungary and Bulgaria, but also, according to Albertini (1952, Vol. III: 558), "by a certain reluctance to flout the King's feelings ..." These splits of course were also a function of whether Transylvania or Bessarabia should be the focus of Romanian foreign policy.

The military, unlike in Bulgaria, was not an independent player that would threaten the civilian order. It was, however, mostly pro-Russian (Albertini 1952, Vol. III: 570). The government itself was based on the large landowners, with little attention to the peasants. They had revolted in 1907, and had been suppressed in a bloody affair. They were nonetheless nationalistic when it came to irredentist claims.

When the war broke out Serbia, Greece, and Romania were mainly concerned that this might give rise to Bulgaria, with Austro-Hungarian support, trying to overturn the Treaty of Bucharest, which gave Romania Dobrudja at the end of the Second Balkan War. Above all, Romanian decision-makers, including both Brătianu and King Carol, wanted to prevent a victorious Austria-Hungary creating a Big Bulgaria by stripping Serbia of territory it had won in the Second Balkan War. Romania and Greece quickly re-asserted their alliance with Serbia, and stated that they would defend the Treaty of Bucharest against any moves that Bulgaria might make, but they indicated that this did not mean they would go to war with Austria-Hungary. Instead both declared their neutrality.

---

[11] For more on the domestic situation, see Hall (2003: 400–401).

Neutrality made sense, given the contradictory ways in which their territorial claims pulled them and the division of the government. It also prevented an open break between the King and Brătianu. Of course, even better would be to prevent a wider war altogether, and this became the tack of the government when the Austro-Hungarian ultimatum was delivered to Serbia. Brătianu recommended to Serbia that she accept all the conditions. When an invasion seemed likely, according to Albertini (1952, Vol. III: 559) there were reports that he proposed on July 25 a variation of the Halt-in-Belgrade plan that the Kaiser would propose three days later. The King also pushed this proposal directly to both countries (Albertini 1952, Vol. III: 570).

Thus, in the early days, Brătianu and the King worked together, but at the Crown Council meeting of August 3 as Germany and Russia went to war it became more difficult to avoid an open disagreement. The King began by making a plea to adhere to the long alliance with Austria-Hungary. This was supported only by Petre Carp, the former Prime Minister. A telling argument against the alliance was made by Alexandru Marghiloman of the Conservative Party. He argued, as the Italians were to do, that the *casus foederis* of the alliance was not fulfilled because Austria-Hungary was not attacked, but was in fact going to attack Serbia. A telegram arriving in the middle of the meeting, informing those present that Italy had declared its neutrality, reinforced this argument. The King, having lost the argument, warned that they would regret their decision, but declared that as a constitutional monarch he would implement it. Brătianu favored a policy of waiting to see how events developed, which was what prevailed not only in August 1914, but for two more years.[12]

King Carol died in October 1914, and was succeeded by King Ferdinand, who had considerably less strong views. This left Brătianu completely in charge of foreign policy, with a large pro-French sentiment at his back. He managed to gain a written promise from Russia that it would support the Romanians' nationalist claims against Austria-Hungary in return for their neutrality (Hall 2003: 403).

The Decision to Go to War   Territorial rivalry was a key element in the decision to go to war. The outside parties realized this and made things more difficult by proposing territorial incentives to lure Romania into the war early on. The first to do so were the Central Powers. As fellow members of the Triple Alliance, they were concerned with the potential consequences of Romania defecting, and they put pressure on

---

[12] Details on the August 3 meeting are taken from Albertini (1952, Vol. III: 572–575).

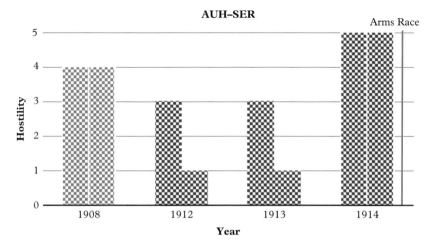

Histogram 1.

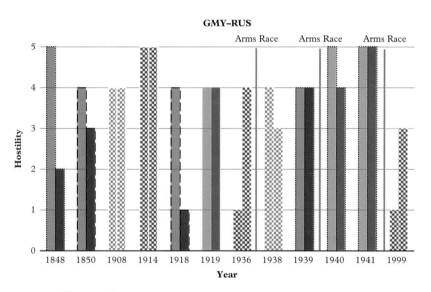

Histogram 2.

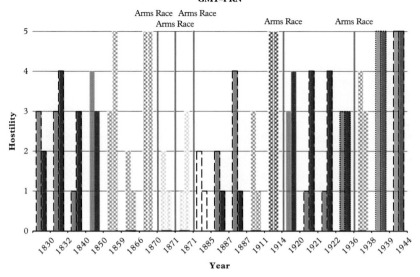

Histogram 3.

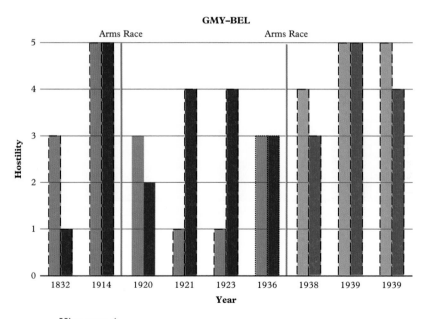

Histogram 4.

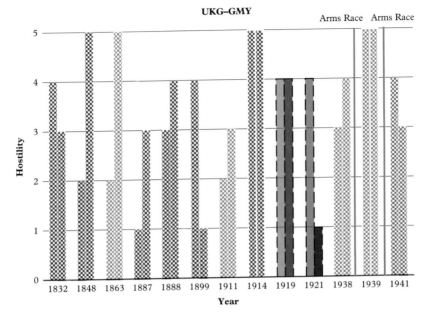

Histogram 5.

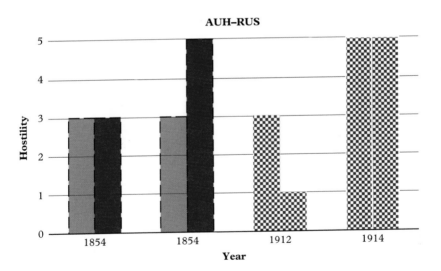

Histogram 6.

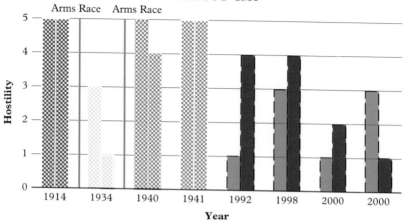

Histogram 7.

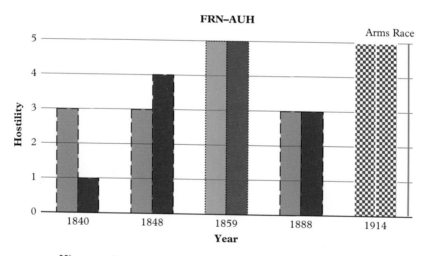

Histogram 8.

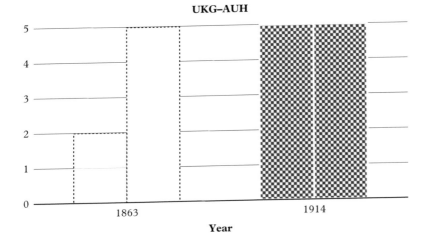

Histogram 9.

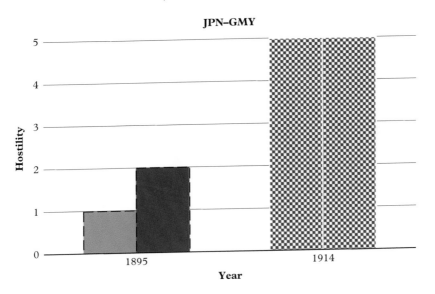

Histogram 10.

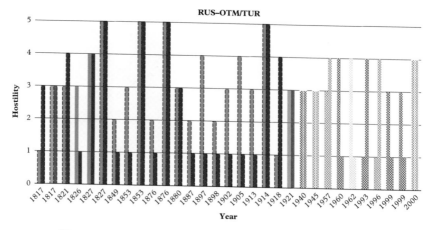

Histogram 11.

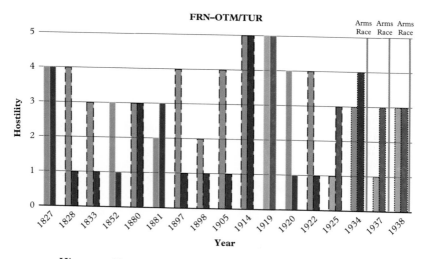

Histogram 12.

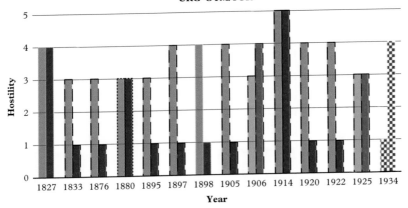

Histogram 13.

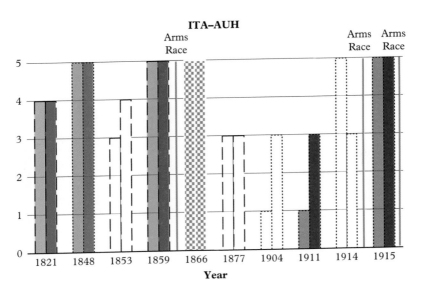

Histogram 14.

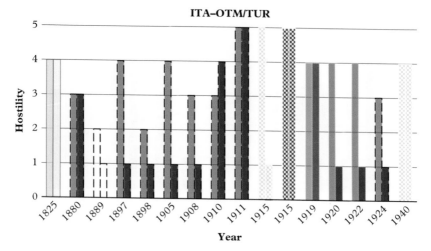

Histogram 15.

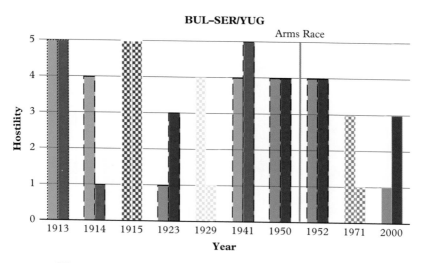

Histogram 16.

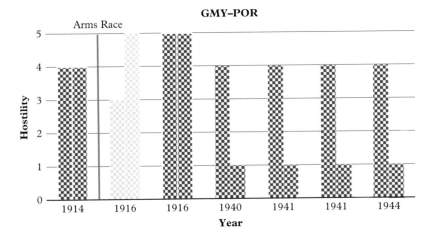

Histogram 17.

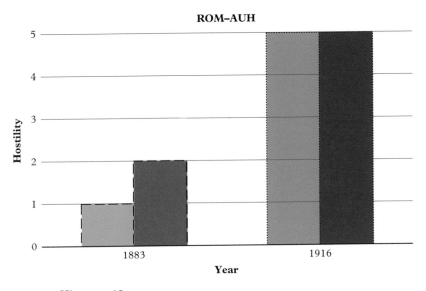

Histogram 18.

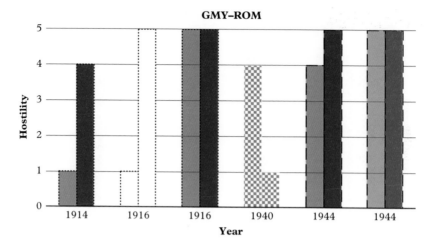

Histogram 19.

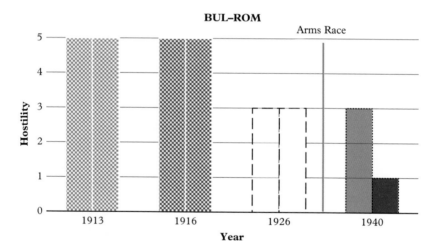

Histogram 20.

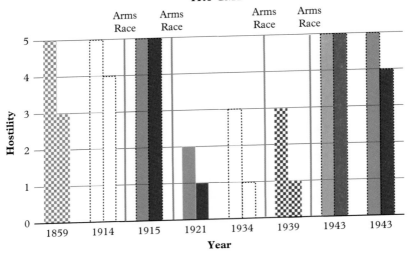

Histogram 21.

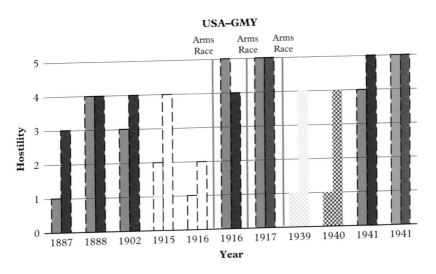

Histogram 22.

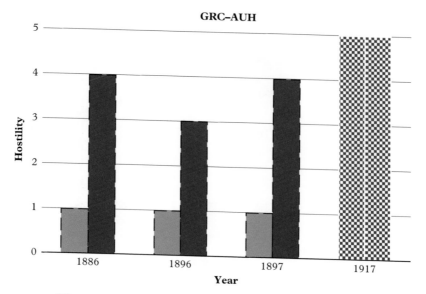

Histogram 23.

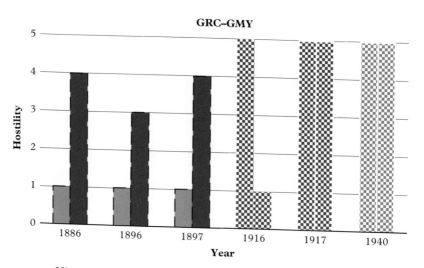

Histogram 24.

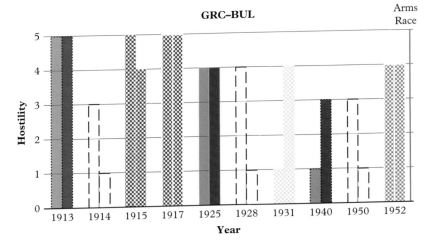

Histogram 25.

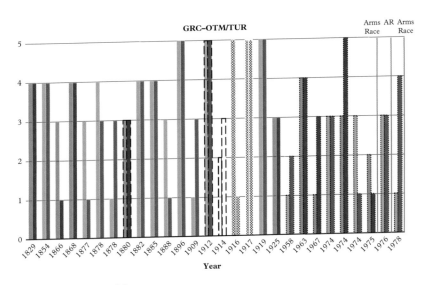

Histogram 26.

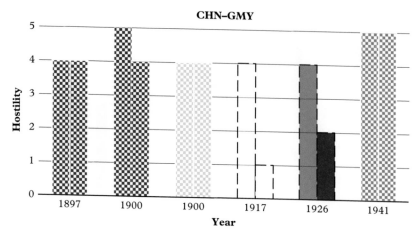

Histogram 27.

King Carol to fulfill his obligations and pro-German proclivities. The Kaiser on July 30 sent a telegram drafted by Bethmann-Hollweg directly to King Carol, invoking the blood tie and the pervasive German prejudice against the Slav. He said that "In this grave hour my thoughts fly to you … who have erected a dam against the Slav tide. I am confident that as King and Hohenzollern you will remain loyal … and fulfill your engagements under the alliance to the utmost" (quoted in Albertini 1952, Vol. III: 566). The next day Jagow had the German Chargé d'Affairs make a promise that if the Romanians joined the war against Russia they would get Bessarabia. As war broke out and Bethmann-Hollweg wanted Romanian mobilization to help on the Eastern Front, he had King Carol told of efforts to get Bulgaria to join the Central Powers and that, if Romania would join the war against Russia, Bulgaria would recognize the loss of Dobrudja (Albertini 1952, Vol. III: 568). At the same time, the alliance with the Ottoman Empire was announced, putting pressure on both Romania and Bulgaria to align with the Central Powers.

The Russians were also active during the July crisis. On July 30–31, pivotal days during the mobilization crisis, Sazonov telegraphed Brătianu supporting Romania gaining Transylvania, and this was followed up with face-to-face discussions, with Brătianu even inquiring whether France and Britain would support this proposal (Albertini 1952, Vol. III: 569–570).

The possible territorial gains were clear to Brătianu and Romanian decision-makers once war had broken out in August 1914, but they resisted joining either side because doing so would pit them against one of the two major states that were contiguous to them. The risks were great, so inertia proved to be the safer course. Nonetheless, of the key territorial goals, the primary one was to keep Dobrudja and prevent the formation of a Greater Bulgaria. Closely following was the nationalist desire to enlarge Romania with the acquisition of Transylvania with its large number of discontented Romanians. Furthermore, these two goals reinforced each other in that Austria-Hungary and Bulgaria were naturally aligned against Serbia, Romania's steadfast ally in the last war. This meant that the territorial vectors favored the Entente. By joining Russia, Romania could gain more territory, and territory that was of greater nationalist and strategic value.

Although neutrality held sway for some time and there was a consensus in favor of the territorial goals that could be provided by the Entente, the ultimate decision to enter the war centered on two factors. The first was the same factor that would influence the Ottoman Empire, Italy, and Bulgaria – who would win? The second was the impact of other states deciding to enter the war. The latter factor was not present in the decisions of states that had previously entered, but was new and unanticipated from a theoretical perspective.

First, in terms of who would win, it was immaterial whether Russia and the Entente supported Romania's claims to Transylvania if they lost the war. Of more importance was that Romania was no military match for Austria-Hungary. Brătianu felt Austria-Hungary had to be almost on the verge of collapse in order for Romania to attack. The Hungarians, in particular, could be expected to mount a fierce fight to keep such a large part of their domain, and Tisza, the Prime Minister, had expressed concern about Transylvania to Conrad and Berchtold during the discussions about going to war with Serbia in July 1914.

Brătianu was patient. He was not moved by early Russian success in Galicia, which proved correct when the Germans defeated Russia at Tannenberg (Shirkey 2009: 105). Likewise the British reversal at Gallipoli made him wary. The key event for him was the Brusilov offensive launched by Russia in June 1916 (Shirkey 2009: 107–108), almost two years after the war had started. This success, coupled with diplomatic moves, made him think Austria-Hungary was close to collapse (see Shirkey 2009: 109). This meant that the window was closing and, if Brătianu did not jump through it, the Romanians could not be part of the peace settlement and thus would no longer be entitled to any territory.[13] This diplomatic insight on his part was coupled with an explicit threat by Britain and France that, if the Romanians did not act now to aid Russia's current offensive in the East to relieve pressure on the Western Front at Verdun, then they might lose the prospect of making territorial gains (Hall 2003: 404). So in the end it was not just Romania's opportunity to take advantage of Austria-Hungary's multifront war that made for contagion, but also the battlefield demands of the Entente that made them pressure Romania. The British and French also pointed out that their planned joint offensive at Salonika would pin down Bulgarian troops, thereby protecting Romania's rear as it attacked Transylvania. Brătianu was still quite short of munitions and held out until mid August, when he signed a military convention.

The Romanian leaders had gotten promises for all of their territorial demands – Transylvania, Bukovina, the Banat, and parts of Galicia (see Text Box 18.2), but they did not know that the Entente Powers had secretly agreed not to be held to all of this (see Keegan 1998: 306). Romania declared war on Austria-Hungary on August 27, 1916, and

---

[13] A similar concern about being at the peace conference may also have later played a role in Wilson's decision to have the U.S. enter the war, see below.

Germany declared war on Romania the next day. The Ottoman Empire and then Bulgaria declared war on Romania a few days later, on August 30 and September 1, respectively.

While timing and battlefield factors were key in bringing Romania into the war, a second factor was the impact of the decisions of previous neutrals to join the war, in particular Italy and Bulgaria. Italy's intervention was critical because it set the precedent that an ally could declare its neutrality and then switch sides. Like Romania, it too argued that the *casus foederis* was not satisfied by the July 28 war and it declared its neutrality. Unlike Romania, however, Italy had a compensation clause in its alliance, so it began bargaining almost immediately. From the first week of August until May 23, 1915 it, in effect, conducted an auction for its participation. Then it switched sides, shattering any external or domestic normative restraint on Romania doing the same thing.

Several months later, in October, Bulgaria made an agreement with Austria-Hungary, which had supported its cause against Serbia, and with Germany for a joint invasion of Serbia. Bulgaria entering on the side of the Central Powers without any agreement vis-à-vis Romania made it more difficult for Romania to subsequently join this coalition. Doing so would have meant allying with its more recent enemy and a territorial rival. Such a coalition was also complicated by the fact that victory by this side meant that Serbia, Romania's natural ally against Bulgaria, would be weakened and perhaps destroyed, while its natural enemy would be increased in territory and population. Bulgaria joining the Central Powers limited Romania's latitude.

With these two examples we see how contagion builds on contagion. The decision of some neutrals to join the fray encouraged others to join. This worked in two ways. First, it established precedents that further broke down the existing political norms, thereby making it easier for states to switch sides. Second, the configuration of the sides meant that one side would be in a better position to grant the territorial objectives of remaining neutrals and guarantee their future security.

Outcome   Despite never getting the needed munitions because of logistical difficulties, Romania was able to take advantage of Austria-Hungary now having to fight on what would amount to another front (it was already fighting Russia, Serbia, and Italy), and it was able to almost walk into Transylvania. Despite the stretching of its forces, however, Austria-Hungary was not near collapse, and it was able to counter-attack along with Germany. Of equal or more importance, the joint British–French offensive at Salonika was stymied by the Bulgarians (with aid from the Germans and the Turks), and the Bulgarians were able to attack Romania in its rear in Dobrudja. The army was pushed back all the way to Moldavia, where it sought Russian protection. The defeat was rapid and convincing, with the capital being occupied, but a key military remnant held on with a new coalition government under Brătianu, and King Ferdinand remained in power. This remnant fought in conjunction with the Kerensky offensive in 1917, but with the Bolshevik revolution in October they were isolated and negotiated an armistice in December 1917, with a formal surrender in May 1918 accompanied by a harsh treaty signed by the new prime minister, Alexandru Marghiloman, but which King Ferdinand refused to sign. Romania re-entered the war the day before the armistice on the Western Front on November 10, 1918, with Bulgaria already out of the war. In late November and early December, as Austria-Hungary fell apart, Bukovina and then Transylvania voted for union with Romania. The Versailles meeting subsequently ratified this shift. However, before a final agreement could be reached, the new Soviet state of Hungary, which had control of the territory, was attacked by Romania and Czechoslovakia in 1919, and Romania occupied Budapest. In the process the Béla Kun regime collapsed and he fled (for details see MacMillan 2001: 265–268). Although Romania had made a very costly miscalculation, it was able to recoup at the expense of its territorial rivals and enlarged considerably because it had joined the side that won.

Conclusion The ongoing war provided an opportunity for Romania to gain, but also a serious threat that it might lose important territory it had just acquired through force of arms. For the longest time, Transylvania had remained a nationalist desire – both the Romanians and the Hungarians knew this, but the weakness of Romania and the alliance politics of the time made this an aspiration that was out of reach. Recent Hungarian repression and mistreatment of the Romanians kept the issue in the forefront of the agenda, however. The ongoing war raised the prospect that now something could be done that might get Romania out of the straitjacket of the prevailing political order that had tied and bound its deep nationalist objective. The exigencies of wartime coalitions, however, also provided an opportunity for its main revanchist enemy – Bulgaria, which had lost Dobrudja in the last war. Romanian decision-makers knew Austria-Hungary saw Bulgaria as a natural enemy of Serbia and had recently supported it diplomatically. A world war raised the prospect that Bulgaria might be favored by Austria-Hungary over Romania.

Opportunity lifts obstacles by changing the capability of actors and breaking down the normative constraints of the prevailing political order. A wider war provided Romania with the prospect of a weakened Austria-Hungary and the aid of powerful allies, especially Russia. By 1916 Austria-Hungary was fighting on three fronts – Russia, Serbia, and Italy. Her armies and resources were not only split, but strained to the limit, leaving little to defend Transylvania against an invading neighbor and a restless population. The ongoing war also broke down norms that prevented great territorial change. Russia and the Entente sought Romania's allegiance and promised it what it wanted – the diplomatic structures of the past were broken.

The same was true, however, for Romania's territorial objectives against Russia in Bessarabia. Germany and Austria-Hungary were quick to offer this territorial objective. In August 1914 the fighting on the Eastern Front already was all Russia could handle. The Ottoman Empire was soon to enter the war, producing a second front, and the Central Powers hoped that Romania would add another. All the while, they played on Romania's obligation to its alliance of over thirty years' standing.

The salience of the two major territorial goals of Romania – keeping Dobrudja and gaining Transylvania, along with Bukovina and the Banat, made switching sides and joining Russia the more lucrative choice. The territorial rivalries and the unequal balance of the rewards made a tilt toward the Entente the more obvious choice from the very beginning. Contingencies like King Carol's sentiments and family ties, as well as the party split, delayed this, but only while he remained on the scene.

The main factor preventing this choice was determining who would win. The general weakness of Romania made this factor the key. It accounts for why, compared with Italy and Bulgaria, it took so long for Romanian decision-makers to enter the war. They waited until what they saw was the last moment and even then made a decision under the threat that the Entente would abandon them if they did not decide now. They thought Austria-Hungary was on the verge of collapse, but in this they miscalculated. Battlefield conditions were a crucial factor in the timing of Romania's war joining, and this happened to coincide with the territorial factor in terms of which side to join, making the decision somewhat easier. The ongoing war provided an opportunity for Romania to fight its own private war, but too much of the burden was on it alone and the battlefield worked horribly against it. The irony of chance, however, worked in its favor, and in the end it got what had seemed impossible before the war. Still, to get everything it had to attack the new state of Hungary in 1919.

The lateness of Romania's entry also meant that this was an instance of contagion building upon contagion. Romania's choice was conditioned by Italy's and by Bulgaria's. Even before then, the entry of the Ottoman Empire had an effect, if only slight. The ongoing war in August 1916 was not the same as the ongoing war in May and October of 1915. Neutrals now faced more pressure to enter to seize what might otherwise be lost opportunities.

Germany–Romania, August 28, 1916   The day after Romania declared war on Austria-Hungary, Germany declared war on Romania. This may seem like a case of valence balancing (and it is technically), but a strong one in that Germany was not just balancing but strongly supporting its ally. In that sense this is really a case of contagion through alliances (Text Box 19.1). Nonetheless, Germany had no major disagreements with Romania. There were no territorial claims until after the war, as can be seen in Text Box 19.2. Likewise there was no rivalry before the war, as can be seen in Text Box 19.3. Additionally,

---

Text Box 19.1.   Germany–Romania alliances

Germany Alliances	Romania Alliances
1879–1918: AUH 2065	1883–1916: AUH, GMY, ITA (–1915) 2069
1881–1887: AUH, RUS 2067	1914–1916: RUS 3018
1882–1918: AUH, ITA (–1915) 2068	1916–1918: FRN, ITA, RUS (–1917),
1883–1918: ITA (–1915), ROM (–1916), AUH 2069	UKG 3022
1887–1890: RUS 2072	
1914–1918: OTM 3015	
1915–1918: AUH, BUL 3020	

Text Box 19.2.   Germany–Romania territorial claims

1941–1944: Serbian Banat and Timoc Valley (Claim Dyad 32208) ROM–GMY

Text Box 19.3.   Germany–Romania rivalry

Enduring Rivalry	Issue
SENESE AND VASQUEZ 6th MID: 1944	Dominant MID Issue: Policy 25% (+) Territory
ARMS RACE HORN: 1890, 1893, 1913, 1934, 1936, 1937	

Histogram 19 shows that their MIDs were related to the onset of the war and did not constitute a history of conflict. While the number of MIDs is more extensive than that with Austria-Hungary, this is only because of the impact of the First World War on subsequent relations. The only indicator of conflict is the arms race indicator. These arms races, however, were really echoes of arms races with other parties, especially those occurring around the Balkan Wars.

As Germany declared war on Romania, the Ottoman Empire followed suit two days later. This can be seen as a case of valence balancing given the closeness in time and the fact that the Ottomans were fully occupied defending their Empire and not likely to attack Romania. This was not the case with Bulgaria, however. For it this was an opportunity for a revanchist war.

Bulgaria–Romania, September 1, 1916 When Romania attacked Austria-Hungary it immediately created an opportunity for Bulgaria to retake Dobrudja and gain revenge for its initial loss in the Second Balkan War when Romania literally stabbed it in the back. As can be seen in Histogram 20, this was the major MID that shaped the relations between the two countries. Romania listened to its new allies' claim that Bulgaria would be preoccupied in Macedonia, and British and French troops in Salonika could hold it down there, so it would be unable to take revenge if Romania turned on Austria-Hungary. This turned out not to be the case, and on September 1 Bulgaria attacked.

The opportunity was too great to miss, because Romania was not that strong to begin with and, once Austria-Hungary was able to re-deploy its forces, Bulgaria could take advantage of this new military situation and get help from all its Central Powers allies to boot (Text Box 20.1). Austria-Hungary, with the aid of Germany, pushed the Romanians out of Transylvania, while Bulgarian forces combined with German and Ottoman troops attacked from the other side through Dobrudja.

Text Box 20.1.   Bulgaria–Romania alliances

Bulgaria Alliances	Romania Alliances
1912–1913: SER 3011	1883–1916: AUH, GMY, ITA (–1915) 2069
1912–1913: GRC 3012	1914–1916: RUS 3018
1914–1918: OTM 3016	1916–1918: FRN, ITA, RUS (–1917), UKG 3022
1914–1918: AUH 3017	
1915–1918: AUH, GER 3020	

Text Box 20.2.   Bulgaria–Romania territorial claims

1913–1913: Southern Dobrudja (Claim Dyad 35801)
ROM–BUL
1914–1918: Southern Dobrudja (Claim Dyad 35802)
BUL–ROM
1918–1919: Southern Dobrudja (Claim Dyad 35803)
ROM–BUL
1938–1940: Southern Dobrudja (Claim Dyad 35804)
BUL–ROM

Text Box 20.3.   Bulgaria–Romania rivalry

Enduring Rivalry	Issue
THOMPSON: 1878–1945	Dominant MID Issue: Policy 25% (+) Territory THOMPSON: Spatial
ARMS RACE HORN: 1912, 1925, 1926, 1936, 1937	

As can be seen from Text Box 20.2, the major territorial claim was to Dobrudja in 1913, but Thompson puts the rivalry back to 1878 when Romania became independent (Text Box 20.3).

Romania opposed the big Bulgaria that Russia favored and there was disagreement over their border. Romania wanted Silistra, which Russia had given Bulgaria (Thompson and Dreyer 2012: 92). Silistra later became a secondary issue after Dobrudja in the Second Balkan War.

Valence Balancing, 1916

Italy–Germany, August 28, 1916

This was one of the few cases where a side valence balances against its will. Italy did not want to declare war against Germany, but was coerced into it by Britain and France. In this way this case is similar to the Brute Force model, but armed intervention was not used. Instead there was simply hard bargaining. What occurred was that Italy had very positive relations with Prussia after its 1859 war with Austria. This war that produced the first MID between the two (see Histogram 21) did not end badly for Italy. Indeed, Prussia refused to send troops to aid Austria, which led Franz Josef to agree to negotiations. Afterward, they became allies in the 1866 war.

Bismarck wanted to be prepared to deal with Austria, and sought an alliance with Italy for a war against Austria in return for supporting Italian claims to Venetia. The Italian alliance proved instrumental in bringing about the 1866 war because, when the Italians mobilized, Franz Josef was forced to mobilize, and this forced the reluctant Kaiser Wilhelm to mobilize at Bismarck's insistence. Italy got Venetia for its efforts, although the Austrians gave it to Napoleon III, who turned it over to them as part of his "mediation." The Alliance with Prussia was invaluable in getting the prize that had proved elusive in the previous war. It generated a positive affinity for Prussia.

This occurred a second time in 1870 with the outbreak of the Franco-Prussian War. This time Napoleon III begged Italy to send troops, but they refused even when he promised not to stand in their way should the Italians act against the Pope, who was protected in part by French troops, to take Rome. The ongoing war permitted Italy to attain the last of its major territorial goals, thereby uniting the whole peninsula. These two events solidified the Italian–German alignment, which was eventually embodied formally in the Triple Alliance of 1882. Here Italy's irritation with France taking Tunisia, which it saw as its natural sphere for colonization, led Italy to form an alliance against France. In the alliance treaty Germany and Austria-Hungary agreed to defend Italy if it were attacked by France (see Text Box 21.1).

The positive relation between Italy and Germany is also showed by the absence of any territorial claims (see Text Box 21.2). They had no direct grievances with each other. Their overall affinity prior to war is

Text Box 21.1.   Italy–Germany alliances

Italy[a] Alliances	Germany Alliances
1855–1856: FRN, OTM, UKG 2031	1879–1918: AUH 2065
1859: FRN 2041	1881–1887: AUH, RUS 2067
1864–1870: FRN 2049	1882–1918: AUH, ITA 2068
1866: PRU 2052	1883–1918: ITA (–1915), ROM (–1916), AUH 2069
1882–1915: AUH, GMY 2068	1887–1890: RUS 2072
1888–1915: GMY, AUH, ROM 2069	1914–1918: OTM 3015
1902–1918: FRN 3001	1915–1918: AUH, BUL 3020
1909–1917: RUS 3009	
1915–1918: FRN, RUS, UKG 3019	
1916–1918: FRN, ROM, RUS (–1917), UKG 3022	

[a] Prior to 1860, Italy refers to Piedmont.

Text Box 21.2.   Italy–Germany territorial claims

No territorial claims

further indicated by the rivalry indicator, which shows a rivalry only once the war has started (see Text Box 21.3). This is somewhat misleading, however, since the behavioral measure goes to six disputes and then automatically goes back to the first dispute, which in this case involved Italy mobilizing at the start of the war and not really taking direct action against Germany proper. Note that Thompson does not see the two as rivals. There were two arms races, but the more serious one was associated with the Balkan Wars and not directed toward Germany.

This affinity to Germany and its past history made Italy not declare war against Germany in 1914. It preferred to see its involvement as a local war between it and Austria-Hungary. This was even more so since Bethmann-Hollweg had supported Salandra's effort at gaining compensation through Article VII during the beginning of the war. These

Text Box 21.3.   Italy–Germany rivalry

Enduring Rivalry	Issue
DIEHL AND GOERTZ: 1914–1945	
KLEIN, GOERTZ, DIEHL: 1914–1943	Dominant Issue: Policy
SENESE AND VASQUEZ: 6th MID: 1939	25% (+) Territory
ARMS RACE	
HORN: 1888, 1913–1915, 1933–1938	

political bonds were reinforced by strong economic ties. German investors had significant holdings in Italian banks. In addition, there was important overland trade, which Germany, suffering from the British blockade, needed and from which Italian firms benefited.

The Entente Powers did not like this situation, and wanted Italy to enter the war against Germany. As the fighting at Verdun raged on, they wanted some assistance to break the deadlock and insisted that Italy declare war or they would retaliate. Italy had no choice but to comply since its fate and territorial goals were tied to Britain and France. In the end, this turned out to bite the Italians when German troops helped the Austro-Hungarian army break the deadlock at Caporetto in 1917.

5   1917: The Third Wave

The United States

United States–Germany, April 6, 1917

The last of the world powers or major states to enter the war was the U.S. This lateness was not unexpected, given the disdain of Europe that its City on the Hill perspective gave it and George Washington's Farewell Address reinforced. The fact that a country with such a vibrant isolationism, led by a President who had just been re-elected with the slogan "he kept us out of war," would eventually join the war is testimony to the power of contagion to overwhelm obstacles and countervailing factors. Why it eventually entered gives us some insight into how contagion worked in conditions that were not initially favorable.

The U.S. lacked three conditions that had brought in so many of the previous entrants. First, it was not a player in the coercive game that initially made the local war a world war. Second, it lacked the territorial ambitions and rivalry that motivated so many of the joiners, especially after the initial expansion. Lastly, it was not contiguous to any of the belligerents; most of the states that joined the ongoing war had states bordering them that were already in the war. Yet it entered, albeit quite late in the game.

The Underlying Structure

The underlying structure of territorial claims, alliances, rivalry, arms races, and MIDs supports some of this image of limited conflict, but potential competition. First, the territorial claims that existed between the U.S. and Germany were colonial and relatively minor, e.g., the conflict over Samoa that included Britain as a third party (Text Box 22.1). The German colonial rivalry with the U.S. was definitely of secondary status. Samoa was not the kind of competition that would give rise to war or even rivalry.

Text Box 22.1.   United States–Germany territorial claims

1887–1899: German Samoa (Upola and Savaii) (Claim Dyad 98201)
USA–GMY
Third Party Claim: UKG
1887–1899: American Samoa (Tutulia and Manu'a) (Claim Dyad 98202)
GMY–USA
Third Party Claim: UKG

Text Box 22.2.   United States–Germany alliances

United States Alliances	Germany Alliances
1908–1910: JPN 3008	1879–1918: AUH 2065
1921–1931: FRN, JPN, UKG 3031	1881–1887: AUH, RUS 2067
1936–1945: ARG, BOL, BRA, CHL, COL,	1882–1918: AUH, ITA (–1915)
COS, CUB, DOM, ECU, SAL, GUA, HAI,	2068
HON, MEX, NIC, PAN, PAR, PER, URU,	1883–1918: ITA (–1915), ROM
VEN 3036	(–1916), AUH 2069
	1887–1890: RUS 2072
	1914–1918: OTM 3015
	1915–1918: AUH, BUL 3020

Another obstacle to entering was the pattern of alliances (Text Box 22.2). The U.S. did not have any alliance aimed at Germany, nor was it tied to any country that did. This was because the U.S. did not have many alliances until after the war, and the key one was with Latin American states. This meant that the U.S. could not be drawn in because of its alliance commitments.

Despite the importance of the absence of these contagion factors, there were some red flags. Some of the conflict measures – that of Thompson and that of Senese and Vasquez – indicate a rivalry between the two, with Thompson seeing it going back to 1889 (Text Box 22.3). Senese and Vasquez indicate that the sixth MID between the two was in 1916, with the first being in 1887. Both of these measures then date the beginning of the rivalry around the time of the Samoa dispute and the emergence of the U.S. as a world power at the time of the

Text Box 22.3.   United States–Germany rivalry

Enduring Rivalry	Issue
THOMPSON: 1889–1918, 1933–1945 SENESE AND VASQUEZ: 6th MID: 1916 NO ARMS RACE	Dominant MID Issue: Policy THOMPSON: Positional

Spanish–American War. The latter is seen as more causal and the former as more of a consequence of global competition than a cause of rivalry. Thompson, in particular, sees the conflict as a positional rivalry between the two, as both were competing with Britain for world hegemony.

Thompson sees the long-term structural power shifts as key to the rivalry, as well as a factor bringing about the First World War generally (Thompson 1992, 2003; see also Geller 1992). For him, the involvement of the U.S. would not be surprising, although its late entry would need to be explained.

Also somewhat ominous was the presence of arms races between the two. Starting with Theodore Roosevelt, the U.S. was building a Great White Fleet. As can be seen in Histogram 22, this led to an arms race with Germany, which was also engaged in a naval buildup aimed at Britain, in 1916 and 1917.[1] The arms race in 1916 was a direct reaction by Wilson to the sinking of the *Lusitania* in 1915 (see Stevenson 2017: 44; Cooper 2003: 434). Wilson even talked to Congress of building "the greatest navy in the world," while at the same time greatly expanding the merchant marine (Tooze 2014: 35).

The pattern of MIDs was the most dangerous indicator that suggests war might come about and ultimately it predicts the war. The four MIDs from 1915 on all involved conflict over German use of submarine warfare and the sinking of ships that in one way or another involved neutrals, typically as passengers in allied ships. This is the issue that will bring the U.S. to war, and how and why it did so provides the answer as to why a country like the U.S., with so many ideational factors keeping it neutral, eventually succumbed to entering the war.

---

[1] Readers should remember that arms races that occur during a war in the system are shown in the histogram and not listed in the table.

Initial Pressures and Wilson's Resistance

The key event that raised the possibility of war was the sinking of the *Lusitania* on May 7, 1915. This was still early on in the war; Italy was about to enter but had not done so yet. The *Lusitania* was a British passenger liner, and 128 Americans were killed out of 1,198 fatalities. The act was seen as a moral outrage because it was a passenger liner and not a cargo ship, and because submarines were seen as a cowardly and illegitimate form of warfare. At the time, it was claimed that there were no munitions on board, but subsequent investigations long after the war suggested otherwise.[2]

This was the kind of issue that touched Wilson's personal moral code and his foreign policy insisting on the rights of neutrals, including the right to trade. The sinking of the *Lusitania* raised an uproar in the American press and is still seared in the collective memory of the American people. It put pressure on Wilson to respond, but at the same time he did not want to enter the war if it could be avoided. His immediate reaction was to publicly declare that "There is such a thing as a man being too proud to fight," and "There is such a thing as a nation being so right that it does not need to convince others by force that it is right." Eloquent as this was, Teddy Roosevelt, who ran against Taft and Wilson in the 1912 election and was pro-English, derided Wilson as cowardly.[3]

To avoid war, Wilson decided to make demands on Germany regarding its use of submarines as a weapon. This led the populist William Jennings Bryan to resign as Secretary of State, because he saw the demands as risking war. The Germans did not respond, and in August 1915 another passenger liner was attacked, and Wilson "informally" threatened to sever diplomatic relations if attacks without warning continued (Cooper 2003: 434). The Germans relented, and said they would not attack passenger liners, but they would continue to attack merchant ships. The following spring in March 1916 (the year of the Presidential election) the Germans sank the *Sussex* in the English Channel, wounding several Americans. The informal threat now became a formal threat to break relations, a step often leading to war, especially during this period. The Germans decided to pledge not to attack merchant ships without warning, and submarine warfare was now restricted. This was a major breakthrough for Wilson, and indicated that the Germans no more than Wilson wanted the U.S. to enter

---

[2] See *The Guardian*, May 1, 2014, www.theguardian.com/world/2014/may/01/lusitania-salvage-warning-munitions-1982, last accessed June 16, 2017.
[3] The example and quotes are taken from Cooper (2003: 432).

the war. While it was a major victory, the *Sussex* pledge set the condition by which the U.S. would enter the war, namely, a return to some sort of unrestricted use of submarines. This happened in 1917.

Before then Wilson tried to avoid this occurrence by ending the war through his personal mediation of it. After winning the election, he made a major effort in his "Peace without Victory" campaign to bring both sides to the table. This attempt had three major advantages for Wilson. First, it would eliminate the future danger of unrestricted submarine warfare that might bring the U.S. into the war. Second, it would give the U.S., and Wilson in particular, a major role in world affairs as befitted a new major (and now rich) world power. Third, it would solve the domestic and external dilemmas of what he called his "double wish" to remain firm with Germany and yet not make demands that would risk war (see Cooper 2003: 432).[4]

The attempt to mediate failed for a variety of reasons, but the main catalyst was that German decision-makers, with the Kaiser's approval, decided on January 9, 1917 that Britain was near breaking point and that, if the trade support from the U.S. could be shut off, they would be broken. They knew this would bring the U.S. into the war (Stevenson 2017: 13), but they thought that before the U.S. could make a difference, Britain and France would be economically defeated. It was a gamble, and it was taken out of the desperation of the Western Front.

Presidential-directed Government

Unlike the East European entrants of 1915–1916 – Bulgaria and Romania – and the later Greek entrant of 1917, the U.S. lacked severe domestic divisions that hampered its decision to go to war. There were differences between hardliners and accommodationists, as there were in Germany, but nothing as severe as in the minor states, and nothing even approaching the domestic divisions that faced Edward Grey.

The main reason for this was that the U.S. presidential system gave Wilson almost authoritarian control of foreign policy, with the major exception of the right to declare war legally. Wilson did not have to listen to his cabinet, or to the press, and once re-elected he did not have to run for office again. There were still many reasons to listen and gain support, but he held the most important cards because the system gave them to him and everyone knew that.

---

[4] The peace option was similar to Grey's attempt to mediate and avoid war as a way of dealing with his dilemma of wanting to go to war if France were attacked, but at the same time knowing that this would make the Cabinet fall.

The decision-making struggle was mostly a struggle within Wilson himself. Divisions within the society undoubtedly had an influence, but he made the ultimate decision. Wilson always wanted to avoid war; nonetheless, he was pushed into it by factors that remained outside his control. He was not enthusiastic about going to war, but, once he had moved in that direction, he tried to re-define the war to make it more acceptable, indeed legitimate, to his sensibilities and character.

The differences between Wilson and other leaders in the American polity can be seen by juxtaposing his position with those of two of his opponents – the hardline progressive Teddy Roosevelt (TR) and the accommodationist long-time leader of the Democratic Party William Jennings Bryan. Teddy Roosevelt was the former progressive President, who in that sense was similar to Wilson, but he was different in that he believed in the use of force and in many ways exulted in the excitement of combat and war, as exemplified by his organizing of the Rough Riders and their charge up San Juan Hill. Today, he would be regarded as a realist and an internationalist. He had read Alfred Thayer Mahan, and was influenced by him in pushing the U.S. to become a global naval power. His position, like that of a number of Republicans and others, such as Senator Henry Cabot Lodge, was that the U.S. had to enter the war to preserve the balance of power by siding with Britain, a view that remarkably did not have much influence within the administration (Cooper 2003: 422). Wilson shared his Anglophile affinity, but not the realist political belief. Nor did he share TR's attitude toward war, if not outright pugnaciousness. Wilson was a Presbyterian, the son of a minister, and very religious, as well as moralistic. This religiosity made him easily embrace the idea that there was a special relationship between "the United States and Providence" (Knock 1992: 4). This all reinforced a kind of rigidity of style that made him see things as right and wrong and made him not open to compromise or realpolitik bargaining. As part of this worldview he found war abhorrent, although this did not stand in the way of his bombarding Vera Cruz in 1914 because Mexico refused to give an apology and a twenty-one-gun salute to the U.S. in connection with the arrest of some American sailors (Zinn 1980: 349). Nonetheless, early on he thought that some sort of world organization could be created to mediate disputes and eliminate the need for war.[5] So, although Wilson ended up taking the decision TR wanted, the reasoning and sentiments behind it were quite different.

---

[5] Knock (1992: 12) points out that as early as 1887 he had written about world federalism, and in 1908 he joined the American Peace Society.

He was also very different from Bryan, his Secretary of State, who had run for President three times and lost. If TR represented an extensive, especially East Coast, interventionist bloc, Bryan exemplified a large neutralist bloc. This position was also well represented in Congress by important Mid-West isolationists – Senator Robert La Follette of Wisconsin and Senator George Norris of Nebraska – and in the House by Democratic majority leader Claude Kitchin. Besides being a Democrat, the fundamental belief Wilson shared with Bryan was the idea that war was never in the interest of the common person or, as it was expressed at the time, the common man. War was in the interest of selfish leaders – monarchs like the Kaiser of Germany. The beauty of democracy was that the people realizing their interest would restrain their leaders from going to war. Bryan was an isolationist, a good deal of which stemmed from the pervasive ethos of American exceptionalism that saw Europe as the fount of power politics, Machiavellianism, and war, from which America should remain distant – a view that would find its way into Wilson's Fourteen Points of "open covenants of peace, openly arrived at." But, unlike Wilson, Bryan was very concerned not to take any action that might eventually put the U.S. in a position where it might become involved in a war. Thus, in 1914 he opposed not just trade with belligerents, but also private lending, a position Wilson overrode (Tooze 2014: 43).

This stance made Wilson concerned that the kind of situation that involved the U.S. in the War of 1812 not be repeated (Cooper 2003: 431). While he was insistent on the rights of neutrals, including the right to trade with belligerents, under international law, he was also hesitant to push these so hard that the risk of war would become highly probable. Thus, when the *Lusitania* was sunk he was morally outraged and felt he must get Germany to stop this kind of illegal and immoral form of warfare, but how to do that without making a demand, which if refused would push him into a corner that would bring about war, was a dilemma.

Bryan's opposition to taking any hostile action toward Germany was clear; he favored prohibiting or discouraging Americans from travelling on British ships. Wilson wanted instead to make some demand on the perpetrator, and this disagreement and difference in approach led Bryan to resign on June 9, 1915, just a little over a month after the sinking of the *Lusitania*. Wilson also knew that Congress did not support an aggressive response, nor was this supported by the Press (see Cooper 2003: 432–433).

Bryan was replaced by Robert Lansing, who would follow Wilson's lead, which made it easier for Wilson to seek his counsel. Other than the Secretary of State, Wilson had two main advisors on foreign policy – Colonel House and later the new Mrs. Wilson (from December 1915 on) – Edith Bolling Galt, who was his confidante, if not alter ego. The Cabinet was something Wilson would listen to and take advice from, but not something that he would permit to overly influence his own decision-making. The major exception was William McAdoo, the powerful Secretary of Treasury and Wilson's son-in-law, who was concerned about the economic boom wartime trade had brought about. Outside the cabinet, Walter Hines Page, the American ambassador to Britain, played a role. He was avowedly pro-Entente, and thereby somewhat discounted, but he reinforced Wilson's Anglophile stance.

After his re-election, as Wilson tried to mediate in early 1917, both Lansing and House became more hard-line about the need and likelihood of the U.S. entering the war, and more openly pro-Entente, while Wilson was still neutral on both counts. House as long ago as February 1916 in his European visit had told Grey and Jules Cambon, of the foreign ministry of France, that he expected the U.S. to enter the war on the Entente side (Knock 1992: 72). Near the end of the year, on December 20–21, 1916, Lansing sought to coach the Allies on the terms they would accept to end the war – territorial demands on Alsace-Lorraine, Belgium, and Serbia – that they and he knew would be rejected by the Central Powers and lead to unrestricted submarine warfare (Knock 1992: 110). By the time of Wilson's "Peace without Victory" speech both were concerned that Wilson was too neutral and not in the Entente camp, as they were.

The last division within the U.S. that should be mentioned was the ethnic dispersion of different groups who derived their ancestry from one of the two belligerent sides. Wilson and most of the elite shared a clear English bias. England had settled the original Thirteen Colonies. Most American university education was Anglocentric (see Cooper 2003: 491), especially in terms of the study of literature, and up until the 1830s with the coming of the Irish most immigrants were from England. By 1910 the dominance of those with English ancestry had changed, with German-Americans being the largest ethnic group, with 2.5 million having been born in Germany and another 5.8 million having at least one German grandparent.[6] In addition, there were many Irish Catholics in the U.S., especially on the East Coast, who were bitterly opposed to Britain, which opposition the 1916 Easter Rising accentuated. The German-Americans were not a pervasive influence within the culture, especially elite culture. Their main political effort

---

[6] These figures are from Stevenson (2017: 38).

was through the campaign to stop selling arms to the belligerents. Some in high quarters in Germany, like Zimmermann, felt that the fear that these German-Americans would revolt would keep Wilson from going to war (see Tuchman 1958; 103); this, however, was never in the cards.

Wilson's Decision to Go to War

The decision to go to war was Wilson's. Cooper (2003: 442) makes this argument strongly and concludes his case study as follows: "He and he alone took the United States into World War I." What were the events and the decision-making process that led Wilson to reach this decision, since it was one he was reluctant to take and one he tried to avoid?

The key factor that led to the U.S. entering the war was the German decision on January 9, 1917 to resume unrestricted submarine warfare. The sinking of the *Lusitania* in 1915 raised the issue, and the attack on the *Sussex* led Wilson to threaten to sever diplomatic relations, which led Germany to agree to restrict submarine warfare and no longer attack merchant ships without warning. In return Chancellor Bethmann-Hollweg expected Wilson to do something about the blockade (Stevenson 2017: 43), which he was never able to do. Nevertheless, for Germany to now go back on that pledge, which was a major victory for Wilson, would mean war.

Cooper (2003: 424) recognizes this, and states that "American intervention on the side of the Allies could not have happened if the Germans had not initiated submarine warfare." He goes on to call this decision "the indispensable precipitant to American intervention." What he does not tell us is why the Germans took this decision, and he denies that war entry was a result of outside "great forces at work," which he denigrates as a causal explanation (Cooper 2003: 421–424). Be that as it may, it can be agreed that, of the factors that weighed on Wilson's mind, unrestricted submarine warfare had a primary place, but other events also inserted themselves.

One of these was the failure of his peace offensive, which occurred at the same time that the German decision was being made. By the end of 1916 Wilson knew that the stalemate on the Western Front was bringing all sides close to a breaking point. The Battle of Verdun with its immense casualties had been going on since February 21. With his re-election Wilson decided that the time was ripe for bringing the war to an end through some sort of mediation. As the last major state that was not in the war and as someone who had been careful not to be too biased toward one side or the other, he was in a good position to do that, or at least he was the only powerful actor available.

In mid December he sent notes to each side asking them to outline their aims and what results might bring the war to an end. Just as he was planning to do this Bethmann-Hollweg, the German Chancellor, independently initiated a peace note of his own in December. Wilson's peace attempt came at an opportune moment, since it seemed to overlap with an opening on the German side. Wilson got replies from the Entente Powers, with the British a little more specific than the French. On this basis he addressed the U.S. Senate on January 22 with his "Peace without Victory" speech. This was after the secret meeting of the German Imperial Council on January 9, but before its public announcement on January 31.

Part of Wilson's purpose was to establish the leadership of the U.S. and play a role in shaping the peace terms, which the speech began to outline. The announcement of unrestricted submarine warfare did not scuttle the peace offensive, but on February 3 the U.S. broke diplomatic relations without following up with a declaration of war. Discussions between the two sides still continued.

In the midst of this, news of the Zimmermann Telegram broke at the end of the month on February 28.[7] The Telegram was intercepted by British intelligence and delivered to Ambassador Page by Foreign Secretary Arthur Balfour in a way that hid the source (Tuchman 1958: 151–152). Wilson, and just about everyone in the U.S., could not believe that the Germans would stoop to such a bizarre plan, even though the U.S. at the time had troops in Mexico chasing Pancho Villa for most of 1916. Nothing came of the plan on Mexico's part, and the telegram was not a justifiable reason for going to war, even though it made Wilson not trust the Germans and turned public sentiment even more against them (Knock 1992: 117–118).

With the sinking of ships just before the release of the Telegram and after the severance of diplomatic relations, war seemed to loom. Wilson made one more desperate attempt to ward it off. He supported the arming of merchant ships. The measure passed the House, but was filibustered in the Senate by La Follette and Norris. On March 4, the day of his second inauguration, Wilson implemented the measure by executive order. This bought some time. More importantly, and perhaps this was the real motive for the measure, it permitted the resumption of trade. The German announcement had led to an effective shut down of American trade, so much so that McAdoo as early as February urged

---

[7] Cooper (2003: 436 n33) provides a useful chronology of the dates from January 9 to April 6, when the U.S. declared war.

that measures be taken to alleviate the situation. Still, it was one more step closer to war.

Germany had exempted neutral ships from attack until March 4 to give them some breathing room; the newly armed ships set sail on March 18 and they were torpedoed. At this point both Colonel House and Lansing favored going to war, but Wilson resisted. He met with the Cabinet on March 20, and most of its members recommended war. He thanked them for their advice and left without telling him what he planned to do. Shortly after, he decided to recall Congress into session, the only purpose of which would be to declare war.

On April 2 he addressed Congress and asked for a declaration of war. In it he went over the reasons for war and the history of relations that led him to this recommendation. In addition to the normal reasons that states give for going to war, which in this case included the allegation that unrestricted submarine warfare meant that Germany was already at war with the U.S., he gave other reasons that laid out a different vision of the world and of world politics that the Entente Powers did not have as part of their war aims. Although he had long sought to create some kind of League and a collective security pact as part of peace plans that he put forth to both sides, now he enlarged his goals. For Wilson this war was now compelled to make the world safe for democracy. It would be a war to end all wars. It would bring about a revolution in international relations that would make for permanent peace.

Such heights of rhetoric were not new to Wilson, but for him it was not just eloquence, it was his personal justification for engaging in a violence that he no doubt found morally repugnant. By April 1917 the war on the Western Front had reached levels of slaughter unknown in the world.[8] How anyone could enter such a fray strained the imagination and seemed a kind of madness. Wilson could not become a part of such insanity. He had to change the war – re-define it into something noble, something worth dying for and presumably killing for. The fact that his rhetoric still moves many, especially political liberals, should not make us ignore the psychological needs that motivated it, even if they were not conscious. In a little over a decade the self-delusion would become increasingly clear.

Although Wilson shaped the way the war was viewed within the U.S. and had an impact at Versailles, was he necessary for U.S. intervention? The counter-argument is that great forces external to the U.S. would have pushed any President to go to war. Presumably his Republican opponents – Teddy Roosevelt, Lodge, and the 1916 Republican

---

[8] On this see Keegan (1998: Ch. 9).

Presidential candidate, Charles Evans Hughes – had already acceded to them. Wilson as an opponent to war in general and as an embodiment of at least some of the isolationist and moralistic sentiment of other opponents of the war was able to delay entry, but in the end succumbed to these outside forces. What were these forces, and how can the U.S.'s entry into the war be explained theoretically?

The German Decision

The outside force was the decision in Germany to resort to unrestricted submarine warfare after pledging not to. Without this decision Wilson, given his abhorrence of war, would likely not have gone to war. In this sense, Cooper (2003) is correct in placing so much emphasis on the individual. The U.S. decision to declare war was contingent on Wilson in that he would have avoided war in the absence of the German decision, whereas TR or Charles Evans Hughes would have most likely sought a declaration without the German resort to submarine warfare. However, the Germans were an outside force Wilson could not directly control. Why did they make this fateful decision?

By late 1916 the internal shape of German governance had changed from 1914 with the initial decision to go to war. Moltke had left early in the war as the Battle of the Marne led to a stalemate. His health, which was not good to begin with, combined with the stress of impending failure, led to him to be replaced and moved to the rear. Eventually, the battlefield victories in the East led to Field Marshal Hindenburg and his chief of staff Ludendorff being put in control of the war and much of the political decision-making associated with it. By 1916 Hindenburg overshadowed Bethmann-Hollweg and even the Kaiser himself, although the latter still made all appointments. Hindenburg in his mid sixties and a veteran of 1866 and the Franco-Prussian War had been appointed by Moltke just before the Battle of the Marne to salvage the situation in the East, which he did with the victory at Tannenberg. After the failure at Verdun, the Kaiser replaced Falkenhayn in August 1916 with Hindenburg and Ludendorff, who were appalled by the situation on the Western Front, especially after the British attack on the Somme (Tooze 2014: 47–48).

They decided on a more defensive posture in the West, but accepted the navy's long-advocated recommendation for unrestricted submarine warfare. Admiral Henning von Holtzendorff argued that, if they sank 600,000 tons, they would break Britain in less than six months (Keegan 1998: 351). Submarine warfare had many successes even while restricted (Cooper 2003: 425). During 1915, for instance, submarines sank 227 British ships (slightly over 800,000 tons) (Keegan 1998: 353), and the navy now believed that an all-out effort would strangle trade and bring Britain, and therefore France, to its knees. Submarine warfare was also needed to break the Entente blockade, which was slowly starving them.

Bethmann-Hollweg had always opposed the use of unrestricted U-boat warfare, because he believed it would bring in the U.S. He and others, like Jagow and Ambassador Bernstorff, held that the only way out was to get Wilson to bring peace as a mediator. Even the Kaiser wrote directly to Wilson urging him to hurry (Tuchman 1958: 110). In late December, Bethmann-Hollweg undertook his own peace offensive. Then, with Wilson's "Peace without Victory" speech, he tried to capitalize on that. Bethmann-Hollweg saw negotiation as the best way out because Germany was in a strong position on the ground – occupying a good part of northern France, as well as Belgium, and able to trade things, like parts of Alsace-Lorraine (on the latter see Mulligan 2014: 172). In addition it would assuage the Social Democrats, who were becoming restive.[9] Time was running out, however. He had his chance, and the navy was adamant. The Kaiser was undecided at first, but would not oppose Hindenburg, Ludendorff and the navy. In the last meeting at the castle of Pless on January 9, 1917, surrounded by this high-level military leadership, Bethmann-Hollweg stood alone. His hour-long speech before the Kaiser did not aid his cause, making the Kaiser impatient.[10]

The decision of January 9 to opt for unrestricted submarine warfare did not give Bethmann-Hollweg's plan, let alone Wilson's, enough time to work. Whether it would have is an interesting counter-factual question.[11] Kurt Riezler, Bethmann-Hollweg's secretary, thought that, without submarine warfare, Wilson would have limited financial credit to bring the Entente Powers to the table and that this would have been more effective than the naval move (Tooze 2014: 58). In the end, the Kaiser sided with the generals in the January Imperial War Council, and by July Bethmann-Hollweg had been pushed out of office by Hindenburg and Ludendorf.

[9] On this and other motives Bethmann-Hollweg had see Kennedy (2014).
[10] Tuchman (1958: 127–128) gives a detailed account of this meeting.
[11] The main obstacle to a negotiation was posed by the British and French, since their battlefield position was less advantageous. However, Bethmann-Hollweg had floated the possibility of withdrawing from Northern France and Belgium and maybe making concessions on Alsace-Lorraine. If Wilson had cut the credit available to the Entente Powers – as Lansing worried – when Wilson ordered the Federal Reserve to not permit Americans to continue to buy unsecured bonds, then they might have been brought to the table (see Knock 1992: 108; Stevenson 2017: 49).

This was now the second time the military had got a power politics script to supersede a peace script in Germany, the first being during the mobilization crisis. Nonetheless, Bethmann-Hollweg and his ambassadorial entourage continued to press this case with Wilson until the very end of January, just before the announcement. On January 31, late in the day, Ambassador von Bernstorff presented Lansing with the announcement and Gerard, the American Ambassador in Berlin, was given one in Berlin.[12]

It is one of the ironies of history that both the Chancellor of Germany and the President of the U.S. wanted to arrange a peace, but neither was able to do so, and they could not do so because of a single act – the announcement of unrestricted submarine warfare. Other factors, such as Wilson's desire to be at the conference table, may have played a role in his mind, but they are minor compared with his desire to avoid war, and of course as a mediator he would be at the head of the table. Wilson did not abandon the peace script; he was pushed off it by Germany's attack undersea.

Theoretical Analysis

Wilson decided in favor of war because of German unrestricted submarine warfare. After the sinking of the *Sussex* in 1916 he was able to secure a pledge that they would no longer attack ships without warning. Once they had withdrawn from that pledge he felt he had no choice but to recommend war to the U.S. Congress. The decision to go to war was then a result of the German decision to rely on submarines to win the war. The U.S. trade with the Entente had been extensive. It entered the war because its trade with the enemy made it an enemy of those who were hurt by that trade. Trade with a belligerent increases the probability of war and biased trade even more so. It was the war itself that brought in the U.S., making its entry a classic example of contagion. Trade had created an *economic dependence* of the Entente on the U.S., and Germany thought that severing that lifeline would give it an edge to end the stalemate on the Western Front. This was the main reason for this dyad coming to war.

The economic dependence model could also see the dependence of the state that sent the goods as giving it a vested interest in the outcome of the war and therefore as providing an additional or alternative reason

---

[12] Tuchman (1958: 136) notes that, after the meeting, von Bernstorff was dismayed, given all his personal efforts to get peace negotiations. She reports that later, when confronted by the American press, he said "I am finished with politics for the rest of my life."

for going to war. While this is a theoretical possibility, this does not seem to be the case in this instance. The economic relationship between the U.S. and the Entente was more complicated than it is often portrayed. The first thing to keep in mind is that in market economies countries do not trade, firms do. Second, this means that any economic interest regarding which side should be supported is initially produced by firms and creditors engaged in the disproportionate trade and not by state leaders. This gap means there has to be some connection between the two to transmit the interest. Lastly, in this case, the firms and the state did not seek to trade with one side over the other, but with both and to profit as much as they could. They ended up trading more with the Entente because the British blockade of Germany prevented a more balanced flow of goods. At least initially, trade was not meant to favor one side and certainly not to have an impact on the outcome of the war.

Nonetheless, the extensive trade had a substantial economic impact on the trading state. Wilson realized the economic effect of the war on the U.S. and seemed averse to taking any actions that might jeopardize the boom (see Stevenson 2017: 39). While America insisted on the rights of neutrals to trade with all, the British blockade on Germany was very effective and most trade was with the Entente. Early on Wilson was concerned with the British blockade, and this produced a low point for Anglo-American relations by the summer of 1916 when the British began to seize U.S. mail on the high seas and blacklisted U.S. and Latin American firms trading with the enemy (Knock 1992: 80), but submarine warfare became a more salient issue. Trade with the allies included not only foodstuffs, clothing, and raw materials, but also munitions. Trade was carried on by credit, and J. P. Morgan managed an increasingly large amount of credit and even floated Entente war bonds among Americans in 1915. These kinds of actions Wilson sought to regulate for fear of their implications. The implications were that such dependence would give the U.S. an economic motivation to favor victory by the Entente. The Left, as well as isolationists, would charge this. Even before the U.S. entered the war, it went from a debtor to a creditor nation.[13]

This trade gave the firms, and especially their creditors, represented best by J. P. Morgan & Co., a vested interest in the outcome. Wilson was not a supporter of Morgan, however, and the House of Morgan was a major supporter of the Republican Party, particularly in the 1916 Presidential campaign. Still, the collective polity had a vested interest in

---

[13] For more details on the financial connections, see Cooper (1976).

maintaining this boom, and McAdoo, the Secretary of Treasury, represented that interest. Wilson had early on opposed efforts to embargo arms because it would hurt industrial production (Stevenson 2017: 39), and later in 1915 he acceded to McAdoo's position that he should not prohibit the Allies from floating bonds in the US. (Stevenson 2017: 39). This was an indirect tie between Wilson and those who gave credit and shipped goods to Germany, but this concern does not seem to have been a factor in Wilson's decision-making. Without submarine warfare and the incidents it created, he would not have gone to war to just protect the economy and Morgan's and others' investments.

The implications of economic dependence and the role they played in U.S. entry into the war were a subject of discussion within American domestic politics at the time and subsequently. After the war the isolationists and the Left lectured the public and then Congress that these "merchants of death" had brought about U.S. intervention and such a path to war must be eliminated in the future. The result was a series of legislative acts, known collectively as the Neutrality Acts, 1935–1939. These prohibited trade with belligerent countries and American travel on their ships, when the U.S. was not at war, and further prohibited the extension of credit to those countries. They, in effect, outlawed the very rights of neutrals that Wilson had sought to defend. Franklin D. Roosevelt tried to limit such legal restraints to aid the Allies in the Second World War by such programs as "cash and carry" and later "lend-lease." These lessons derived by American isolationists show that domestic actors were aware of some of the contagion factors that could bring the U.S. into the war that are outlined by the economic dependence model. The evidence suggests, however, that it was more the structure of the trade in terms of how it hurt Germany and Germany's attempt to stop it, rather than the vested interests of the "merchants of death," that brought about intervention.

The U.S. entered late in the war and that was because it had few grievances against Germany until the war broke out. The comparatively limited nature of its grievances can be seen by comparing Histogram 22 of its MIDs with Germany with those France and Britain had with Germany (see Histograms 3 and 5).

An indirect factor that can play a role in the widening of wars has been brought to light by the data analysis of Yamamoto and Bremer (1980). They find that, as one major state joins an ongoing war, this increases the probability that another major state will join. This is a classic example of contagion, and elsewhere I have labeled it *bandwagoning* (Vasquez 2009: 263–265). They show that the decision to enter wider wars is not an independent decision where the choice of others has no effect, but one that is affected by what previous major states have decided – whether that be to join or to remain neutral. The analysis here goes beyond Yamamoto and Bremer (1980) in that it not only posits that as one major state joins an ongoing war it puts pressure on others to join, but delineates what specific contagion processes bring those major states into the conflict.

One of the rationales that Yamamoto and Bremer (1980) give for this kind of contagion is that, as more major states enter and the war goes on, more of the interests of states that have not entered become affected. Interests are affected in three ways during the war. Early on in terms of the failure of the coercive game the need to stand firm as a way of preventing the other side from attacking one's ally is seen as a prime interest. Another common interest provided by an ongoing war is the opportunity it creates for gaining territorial objectives that the prevailing political order had blocked. This can be seen early on with Japan and Italy, both major states if somewhat weaker than the initial major-state entrants.

Lastly, a war that so expands that it becomes a general war within the system, like the Thirty Years' War or the First World War, begins to appear to neutrals, especially major states, as one that may re-shape the international system by the peace it creates. This creates pressure to join the war to gain a seat at the peace table. Decision-makers in some minor states, like the Ottoman Empire, felt this even though it was not the main reason for entering the war. Similarly, this has been seen as a motive for Wilson to intervene. His various attempts to mediate a peace reflected this motive without paying the blood tax – this is one of the reasons why his role was resisted by the belligerents. Wilson realized the strategic advantage that being the sole major state that was neutral in a protracted war gave him, so the fact that he wanted to shape a peace is not at issue. What is at issue is how much of a factor this played in his decision to go to war. It seems to have been secondary, given his unwillingness to pay the blood tax, which in turn was a result of his abhorrence of war in general and European power politics in particular – a sentiment he shared with the isolationists.

The main evidence we have that his desire to gain a seat at the peace table was an element in his thinking was what he said in his February 28, 1917 meeting with Jane Addams, although he had not definitely made up his mind by then to enter the war. He said that if as President he were participating in the war he would have a seat at the table, but if he was head "of a neutral country he could at best only 'call through a crack in the door'" (reported in Knock 1992: 120).

Lloyd George, the new Prime Minister of Britain, was not about to accept American mediation, since he had been elected to bring about a knock-out blow; nonetheless, he knew of Wilson's desire for a leadership role and played upon this in a February 11 message to him asking him to enter the war so he could help to make the peace afterward (Knock 1992: 119). Conversely, Kaiser Wilhelm II unintentionally did the opposite and said in a message delivered through his ambassador on January 31 that Germany was willing to enter negotiations, but that Wilson "would not be welcome to participate" in any conference (Knock 1992: 116).

Link (1979: 68–71, summarized in Knock 1992: 118), after considerable study, reports that Wilson had three reasons for entering the war: unrestricted submarine warfare, the Zimmermann Telegram, and a desire for a seat at the table. Are these of equal weight? Knock (1992: 118) says the last two were "crucial factors ... once Germany demonstrated its intention to prosecute submarine warfare ..." The theoretical analysis here does not disagree with that assessment, but places emphasis on the economic dependence that the use of unrestricted submarine warfare was trying to end. Thus, it is not surprising that in his address to Congress asking for a declaration of war he began with submarine warfare and recounted incidents of it. While it is always difficult to discern the weight of what factors really go into an individual's decision, what is clearer is that unrestricted submarine warfare is a more justifiable reason to ask people to give up their lives than the Zimmermann Telegram and desiring a seat at the peace table. As such, it is given primary weight here, whereas the others are seen as secondary.[14]

Aftermath

Once in the war, Wilson tried to shape the peace with his Fourteen Points. His presence resonated with much of the public in Europe. He attained three important objectives – a major role for self-determination in re-drawing the map of Europe, the spread of democracy to the defeated monarchies of Germany and of Austria-Hungary, and the creation of a League of Nations. These were successes, even though realpolitik and interests still prevailed in much of the decision-making at Versailles because of Clemenceau, Lloyd George, and Orlando.

The centerpiece for Wilson – the League of Nations – however, led to a domestic battle within the U.S. Congress and a rejection of the

---

[14] Of the two, the Zimmermann Telegram is seen as idiographic to this case and the desire of wanting a seat at the peace table as more generalizable.

Treaty of Versailles. A leader more willing to compromise and make deals might have saved the treaty, but this was not Wilson's tack. Instead, he sought to go over the head of Congress and went on a grueling campaign across the country that ended in a stroke that disabled him for the remainder of his presidency. The rejection of the treaty led to a return to America's traditional isolationism, even though now it was the most economically powerful nation in the world. This absence is sometimes seen as resulting in the failure of the League. This is probably not accurate. Wilson had won at Versailles and got most of what he wanted. Moreover, the League was actually fairly successful in its first ten years, especially in resolving remaining territorial disputes in the volatile Balkans. Its collapse came as the territorial disputes of the major states were put onto the global agenda – first with Japan, then Italy, and ultimately Germany. The League could not deal with these territorial disputes, and these revisionist states left the League and its liberal global governance. It is not clear what the U.S. could have done to make the League work at that point. The League failed because the Treaty of Versailles was a harsh peace, and that treaty was already fully shaped by the time Wilson lost his battle with Congress.

As political scientists have documented, war leads to a centralization of the state (Tilly, 1975; Rasler and Thompson 1989; Gibler 2012). In democracies this takes the form of a diminution of civil liberties, and this occurred dramatically in the U.S. with the passage of the Espionage Act on June 15, 1917, which made illegal any attempt to oppose conscription or foment treason, including the use of the mails to disseminate such ideas. Under Postmaster General Burleson, and with Wilson's support, many socialist publications, including *The Masses*, were banned from the mails. A number of people who actively opposed the war, as well as German-American leaders, were incarcerated, and many were the subject of vigilante violence.[15] The most famous of those imprisoned was Eugene Debs, the socialist candidate for President who ran against Wilson in 1912. On June 16, 1918 he gave a speech opposing the draft and was arrested shortly after: he went to prison in 1919, and ran for the Presidency from his cell in the 1920 election. After the war, Wilson refused to release him from jail, saying that, "While the flower of American youth was pouring out its blood to vindicate the cause of civilization, this man, Debs, stood behind the lines sniping, attacking, and denouncing them … This man was a traitor to his country and he

---

[15] For some examples of these see Knock (1992: 133–134), who also documents less violent mass actions, like changing the name of sauerkraut to "liberty cabbage." See also (Meyer 2016: Ch. 12).

will never be pardoned during my administration" (quoted in Cronin 1989: 220). Finally, two days before Christmas 1921, the conservative Republican President Warren G. Harding commuted his sentence.

Just before deciding to ask for a declaration of war on March 19, 1917 Wilson had warned, "Once lead this people into war, and they'll forget there ever was such a thing as tolerance. To fight you must be brutal and ruthless, and the spirit of ruthless brutality will enter into the very fibre of our national life ..." (quoted in Cooper 2003: 437, from Heaton 1924: 268–270). Wilson may well have been speaking of tendencies he recognized might emerge within himself. Whatever the case, the actions against those who opposed the war led his progressive supporters, like Upton Sinclair, to complain "that while helping to win democracy abroad, we are losing it at home" (quoted in Knock 1992: 137).

Conclusion

The U.S. entered the war, like many others did, because it was attacked. In the larger scheme of things these attacks were marginal, with little loss of American lives, compared with the invasion of Belgium, for instance. Nonetheless, these losses were enough for Wilson and others, in part because the nature of these attacks was seen as an immoral and cowardly form of warfare. Once Germany had reneged on the 1916 *Sussex* pledge not to engage in unrestricted submarine warfare there was no turning back in their minds, and the country was united with those realists, like TR and Henry Cabot Lodge, who wanted to go to war for the balance of power, not to mention those like Morgan & Co. who had a vested interest in an Allied victory. The long-term Anglophile nature of the elite overwhelmed any affinity for Germany provided by the numerous German-Americans or the Irish. The vote in Congress was overwhelming, 82–6 in the Senate and 373–50 in the House.

German decision-makers had gambled that they could win before the U.S. could make a difference on the battlefield. Indeed, the U.S. firms were playing an important role in continuing the war by providing trade on credit.[16] The recent success of submarine warfare provided a reasonable option for making a difference, particularly after the failure of

---

[16] Rasler and Thompson (1983) show that in global wars, like the First World War, the side with greater access to credit tends to win. This is consistent with Rosen (1972), who shows that the side with greater government revenue tends to have a high probability of winning wars. Thus, the intuition of German decision-makers was correct.

Verdun to bleed the enemy to death. The economic dependence of the Entente on U.S. trade and the incentive this provided to Germany overcame the factors that had kept the U.S. neutral for so much of the war.

American troops and the morale and vigor they supplied to exhausted and at times mutinous troops on the Entente side had an important psychological impact, especially after the collapse of the Russian front. Their actual fighting at Château-Thierry also had an impact. In retrospect, the most important role the U.S. played in the Entente victory was the very economic trade and credit that Germany sought to sever. If this lifeline and especially the credit had never existed, then the British and French would have sought some sort of peace. As Paul Kennedy (1984: 11, 22, 26) argued, after Caporetto the Italians would have left the war, but the British and French kept them in with troops. After Verdun the French would have collapsed if they had been fighting alone. British finance played a large part in keeping France and Italy in the war. By late 1916 the U.S. was keeping Britain and France afloat (see also Vasquez 2009: 281).

Wars are tests of strength and from the beginning U.S. trade added to the material well being of the Allies and then, with the extension of credit, to its economic strength. German decision-makers attacked U.S. trade in the hope of crippling that economic strength. Instead, the official entry of the U.S. into the war enhanced that economic strength before the Germans could win on the battlefield.

United States–Austria-Hungary, December 7, 1917

After declaring war against Germany, Wilson considered asking Congress to declare war against Austria-Hungary, but delayed. He thought there might be a chance that the new Emperor Karl I, who had ascended to the throne when Franz Josef died on November 21, 1916, might be willing to accept his mediation. Wilson's attempt to negotiate a separate peace broke down, because Karl I would not break his alliance with Germany. When this became clear, the U.S. declared war on December 7, 1917, about eight months after the U.S.'s declaration of war against Germany.

Emperor Karl I had sought some sort of peace right after he came to power, approaching the French through his wife's brother, Prince Sixtus of Bourbon (Keegan 1998: 319) in March 1917. In the same month he moved Conrad, who was a hardliner, from Chief of Staff to commander of the Italian front, where he would have less political influence. The peace move came to naught and was seen by Germany as an attempt at a separate peace, which they opposed.

Despite delay in the U.S. declaration of war, this case was ultimately driven by valence balancing. The U.S. went to war because Austria-Hungary was an ally of Germany. Austria-Hungary was not part of the U-boat campaign around the North Sea that led to Wilson's decision to seek a declaration of war against Germany. Because of the belief that Austria-Hungary might be involved in peace talks, the declaration of war was postponed. Austria-Hungary, however, broke diplomatic relations two days after the U.S. declaration of war on Germany on April 8, but without a follow-up declaration of war.

The U.S. went to war with Austria-Hungary because it was an ally of Germany. In fact, Wilson's message to Congress asking for a Declaration of War was that Germany was controlling the actions of the Austro-Hungarian Empire. Wilson said to Congress that "The Government of Austria-Hungary is not acting on its own initiative or in response to the wishes and feelings of its own people, but as the instrument of another nation" (quoted in Scott 1918: 167).

The actual declaration referred to acts of war that Austria-Hungary had engaged in as a justification. As Scott (1918: 168–170) reports, these were detailed by the House Committee on Foreign Affairs as consisting of three types. First, giving verbal assent to, if not physical cooperation with, the German policy of submarine warfare after January 31. Second, possibly engaging in submarine warfare on its own in the Mediterranean that injured Americans. Third, engaging in propaganda activities and encouraging a strike in a munitions plant. To this was added the announcement that soon the U.S. would be aiding the Entente effort in Italy to repel the Austrian attack in the Alps and therefore it would be appropriate for the U.S. to be in a legal state of war before that happened (Scott 1918: 171). This last reference meant that, unlike in some of the 1914 instances of valence balancing, the U.S. did expect to have a combat involvement with a non-contiguous enemy.

What can be concluded about this case? The dyad went to war because of valence balancing. The U.S. would not have gone to war with Austria-Hungary if it were not at war with its ally, and Austria-Hungary broke relations with the U.S. and supported Germany's unrestricted submarine warfare policy (and likely engaged in it in the Mediterranean) only because it was an ally of Germany. Likewise, the U.S. active support of the Entente action in Italy was because it had joined them.

It should be noted that, although the U.S. declared war against Austria-Hungary, it did not declare war against the Ottoman Empire or Bulgaria, both of which were actively engaged in fighting and allies of Germany.

Greece

Greece–Austria-Hungary, Germany, Bulgaria, and Ottoman Empire, June 27, 1917

Among its neighbors Greece had two enemies and one ally, and all of these were the result of the Balkan Wars. By 1914 its most serious threat was the Ottoman Empire, which was contemplating war because of its dispute with Greece over certain Aegean Islands. The second enemy was Bulgaria, with which it had just won a war over Macedonia that Bulgaria started. Its only reliable ally was Serbia, by whose side it had fought in both Balkan Wars.

The prospect of an Austro-Hungarian–Serbian War and its possible spread to a general war posed dangers to Greece because it provided an opportunity for Bulgaria to attack Macedonian lands in Serbia with Austro-Hungarian backing. Additionally, the war and the uncertainty it might bring could provide external support for the Ottoman Empire in its conflict with Greece over the Aegean. Even though it was an ally of Serbia, the Serbs did not expect Greece to enter a general war. However, if Bulgaria were to attack, that would be a different matter, and its alliance did compel it to enter, although the real reason would be the threat a Bulgarian attack would place on Greek Macedonia. In short, the local war, and the prospect of a wider one, meant uncertainty and possible danger for Greek decision-makers, rather than an opportunity.

The relative lack of opportunity was because Greece had just won two successful wars that had increased considerably its territory and its population, by about two million. It still had ambitions, especially in Asia Minor, but the key tasks now were to keep what it had gained and defend itself from the opportunity a wider war provided to its rivals and potential enemies.

Divided Government

Greece was the last European country to enter the war, and this was no accident. From the start, half of the government considered intervention on the side of the Entente and the other opposed it. The interventionists were led by Venizelos, head of the Liberals and Prime Minister for most of the time. He had helped win the independence of Crete in 1905 from the Ottoman Empire, and he had come to power in 1910. He led Greece during the two successful Balkan Wars. Even though he would resign more than once, he was the dominant figure and would

lead the Greek delegation at Versailles. He was a nationalist and capti-
vated by the *Megali Idea* of uniting all Greeks within the Greek home-
land. This meant keeping Macedonia, continuing the ongoing fighting
in Albania, incorporating the Greek areas of Asia Minor, bringing in far-
flung islands, such as Cyprus, and maybe even taking Constantinople.
Except for the first two, however, these were not immediate objectives for
him, but ideals that might or might not come to the fore depending on
circumstances.

In opposition was King Constantine, a Dane by birth, and married to
one of Kaiser Wilhelm's sisters. He insisted on neutrality, a position
consistent with Germany's desires, though the Kaiser wanted Greece as
an ally (Albertini 1952, Vol. III: 635–638). The King was supported by
the military, especially its head – General Metaxas – and had considerable support within the society, particularly within the "older" pre-
Balkan War areas of Greece, whereas Venizelos had more support in
the newly acquired territories, although Venizelos was able to win elections during this tumultuous period. The King was popular, in part,
because he had led troops during the Balkan Wars along with General
Metaxas.

From 1914 until 1917 the King's position prevailed and Greece did
not intervene, but this was more because neutrality was the default position and not because it was the chosen policy. Greece stayed out of the
war because the government was stalemated and could not reach a
decision.

It must be emphasized that the decision on hand was to declare war
against Austria-Hungary and Germany and its allies. A decision to fight
against Bulgaria or the Ottoman Empire alone would not have been so
difficult, since Greece had serious grievances against them and one on
one was relatively equal to them. Joining an ongoing world war was a
different matter. Under normal circumstances it was not likely that
Greece would fight against these major states, nor would they necessarily attack her. This would only happen in the context of an ongoing
general war.

The Model

The inability of the two sides to reach a decision made Greece very different from the other states that had entered up to this point. In each of
the cases, divisions were resolved. Greece seemed to be closer to intervening on the Entente side, since the King, although sympathetic to
Germany, did not advocate joining the Central Powers, but only
neutrality. Nonetheless, Venizelos could not get his position accepted.

The King's ability and influence kept Greece out of the war for a long time; however, he never convinced his opponents, nor was he able to defeat them so that the entire polity accepted his neutral position.

The resulting stalemate left the door open for outsiders to make the decision. Battlefield events made this even more of a possibility as the war reached Greece's doorstep and foreign troops encroached on Greek territory. Ultimately, outsiders, namely, France and Britain, worked with Venizelos to engineer Greece's entry on the side of the Entente.

The model that explains Greek intervention is dissimilar from those that explain how the earlier dyads entered the war. Contagion here was the result of brute force by one side on a state unable to make up its mind. Contagion worked in this instance by outside armed intervention putting one faction in power and throwing out the other. This occurred primarily because of the battlefield conditions and the attempt by the Entente to break the stalemate on the Western Front, and the desperate situation on the Eastern Front and the Balkans, coupled with the sovereignty vacuum within Greece. Outside intervention in an emerging civil war resulted in a coup d'état that enabled a popular figure to take over and meet the Entente's demands and needs.

This contagion process differed from the way Greece's neighbors – Bulgaria and Romania – entered the war. In each of these instances these states were able to bargain and conduct an auction with the major states for their allegiance. This sort of thing did not happen in Greece, because neither of the domestic sides could "deliver" Greece. Instead the situation was reversed; now the outsiders determined who would rule internally and the domestic government had few objectives it could impose through a bargaining process. For the Entente this became a situation of "when all else fails impose one's will through brute force." Nothing quite like this had happened in the war previously. The closest thing to it would come soon when the Entente, again, would try to keep Russia in the war by intervening in support of the White Russians. Again battlefield contingencies, in this case keeping some sort of Eastern Front going to prevent the Germans moving more troops to the Western Front, were a major factor.[17]

---

[17] This case is an example of contagion resulting from interstate war producing civil war and revolution as is best illustrated by the Russian case. The connection between interstate and civil war has been demonstrated statistically by Bremer (1982). The typical explanation is that popular suffering leads to dissent and attempts to remove the war leadership and/or overturn the government; for a general discussion of war and domestic punishment as it relates to the First World War, see Goemans (2000). Russia illustrated this process, whereas the Greek civil war and domestic coup are clearly different from the typical scenario represented by Russia 1917.

What needs to be emphasized, however, is that armed intervention was not a long-term plan. Although the French had given some thought to getting their way by establishing a "protectorate" over Greece rather than pursuing an alliance (see Shirkey 2009: 144), even this tack grew out of battlefield contingencies rather than a long-term strategy. In this sense, the sixth model of how contagion works is a direct and immediate effect of the ongoing war. Without the ongoing war, such armed intervention would not have occurred, and its purpose was not so much imperialism as it was an attempt to win the wider war by widening it further.

The interests of France and Britain were for Greece to enter the war against the Central Powers, and thus Greece entered the war against all four of the immediate combatants, not just its traditional rivals – Bulgaria and the Ottoman Empire. This is further evidence that the decision was not fully in Venizelos's hands.

Early Factors

In the beginning a factor that had affected other minor states that considered intervening also played a role with the two main Greek decision-makers – Venizelos and King Constantine. Both were concerned about who would win. For King Constantine, although his main reason for being neutral was his ties to Kaiser Wilhelm, an added important reason was that he thought Germany and the Central Powers were stronger militarily and would win (Shirkey 2009: 140). Venizelos, conversely, was convinced that the Entente would win, although at certain junctures, such as after the initial Battle of the Marne and early Entente failures, he began to think the war would be long, so he wavered and shifted from a position of intervening on the side of the Entente to holding off or even being neutral (Shirkey 2009: 141).

Similarly, the interest of the Entente in Greece also wavered on the basis of battlefield events. Britain and Grey were more interested in Greece as they attacked the Ottoman Empire at Gallipoli than they were before or after the offensive. This wavering was a result of the fact that Greece was less important to the Entente than other countries, like Bulgaria or Romania, whose entry it was thought would be more helpful. So in the end, as with the other late entrants, considerations of who would win played a role in the decision to intervene. The King's view was fairly constant and less subject to the volatilities of the battle-field, mostly because he wanted to stay out. Venizelos's orientation fluctuated, since he actually wanted to enter the war.

As early as August 2, 1914, Venizelos expressed his sympathies for the Entente (Hall 2003: 407). He hoped that an alliance with them might allow Greece to pursue certain territorial objectives, but he was rebuffed because Russia distrusted Greek ambitions in Thrace, which was near Constantinople, and Grey did not want to pursue the matter until the military situation was clearer (Shirkey 2009: 141).

A more immediate concern, and one both Venizelos and the King could agree upon, was to meet the potential threat from Bulgaria, which might attack Serbia to reverse its losses in Macedonia with or without Austro-Hungarian support (Albertini 1952, Vol. III: 638). At the beginning of the war, both Greece and Romania announced that they would oppose any challenge to the 1913 Treaty of Bucharest. At the same time Venizelos made it clear to Serbia that the Greeks could not come to the aid of Serbia in its war with Austria-Hungary even though they were formal allies, but that they would aid them if they were attacked by Bulgaria. This commitment would later become a problem when in 1915 the Serbs were attacked by Bulgaria.

The August alliance of the Ottoman Empire with Germany and then its entry into the war in November 1914 added another element pushing Greece toward the Entente, since now one of its two main enemies had joined the fight against its main ally – Serbia. Germany had earlier offered territory in Serbia and Albania if Greece were to join them, but Venizelos was more focused on the lands within the Ottoman Empire and he feared the British Navy would wreak havoc on them if they were to join the other side, as did even King Constantine (see Albertini 1952, Vol. III: 639).

When the Entente seemed to have the upper hand against the Ottoman Empire with the landing on Gallipoli, Venizelos wanted to move quickly to join the war before the window closed. By 1917, as Stevenson (2017: 278) notes, he had also justified his actions before Parliament as wanting to enter to make sure Greece would have a seat at the Peace Congress. At the time of Gallipoli, Grey was more receptive to Greece, and offered territorial concessions in Asia Minor in January 1915 in return for active involvement both on the Serbian front and on the Ottoman front (Hall 2003: 408). However, Bulgaria, which was still neutral, was considered a more valuable ally by Grey and France, both of which were actively wooing her (Hall 2003: 409). Sazonov also raised objections to any Greek presence in Constantinople. With these problems Venizelos's effort collapsed, and he resigned on March 6, 1916, to be replaced by a government more to the liking of the King. New elections in June returned him to power with the divisions between his supporters and those of the King now intensified in the so-called *Ethnikos Dikhasmos* (National Schism) (Hall 2003: 409).

Earlier, Italy entered the war in May 1915, switching sides and joining the Entente. This made new efforts to join the Entente problematic because Italy and Greece had conflicting territorial claims in Asia Minor and in Albania, making Italy not an avid supporter of Greece joining.

Events Leading up to Armed Intervention

The key action that sparked the series of events that led to armed intervention was when Bulgaria mobilized against Serbia at the end of September as a prelude to entering the war on October 14, 1915, having made a pact for a joint invasion with Austria-Hungary and Germany. Bulgaria joining the Central Powers meant that Greece's two main rivals – Bulgaria and the Ottoman Empire – were on the same side, further reducing the uncertainty of future arrangements. During the interlude between Bulgaria's mobilization and its declaration of war against Serbia, Venizelos accepted the landing of Entente troops at Salonika to aid the Serbs. King Constantine had explicitly refused this request by Venizelos, although he had accepted a mobilization of the army against Bulgaria to protect Greece and possibly prevent the attack on Serbia. Venizelos's decision on Entente troops resulted in a close vote of no confidence in the parliament that Venizelos won, but the King still dismissed him (Shirkey 2009: 142–143). Elections in December that were boycotted by Venizelos resulted in a neutralist and pro-King government. Meanwhile, Bulgarian and German troops were on the Serbian border with Greece, and in May the Greek army surrendered Fort Rupel, which permitted Bulgarian troops to take Eastern Macedonia.

The situation of the Serbs quickly became desperate, and they were overrun. To aid them and their war effort, the French and British established a kind of territorial control of Salonika and stayed for over a year and a half before Greece entered the war. They had previously occupied Lemnos to facilitate the Gallipoli campaign and also occupied Corfu to aid the Serbian withdrawal. The British and French forces failed to relieve the Serbs when attacking southern Serbia, and were pushed back by the Bulgarians. Meanwhile, in Salonika they suffered the ravages of malaria, with their base reduced to a vast military hospital according to Keegan (1998: 255–256).

As a result of this and other actions, pro-Entente military officers in the Greek Army led a coup d'état in Salonika against the King on August 30, 2016 with the knowledge and support of Venizelos (Hall 2003: 410). On October 9, Venizelos went to Salonika, where he set up a separate army and government, recognized by the British, thereby starting a civil war. In December, French and British troops attacked the King and his supporters in Athens. They were pushed back and withdrew after many casualties. They then imposed a blockade on the King's government's areas and occupied more of the areas out of his control. In the summer of 1917, on June 10, the French minister Charles Jonnart issued an ultimatum demanding that the King abdicate.[18] To save lives, he did so in favor of his son, who accepted a united government under Venizelos. Greece then declared war on June 27.[19] Without the French ultimatum and earlier invasion of Athens, Greece would not have entered the war. Greece was coerced into entering the war by the brute force of France and Britain.

This does not mean that other factors played no role, but these were all secondary or at least indirect. There were four such factors. The two most important were contiguity and the ambition of Venizelos. Contiguity with the defeated Serbs and the presence of Bulgarian and German troops made the situation desperate. In this sense, Venizelos did not so much enter the war as the war entered Greece. Nonetheless, Venizelos did not sufficiently accept the constitutional structure, and when the opportunity arose he sought a unilateral solution through a coup d'état under the protection of foreign troops. These troops were then used to topple the King and his government.

Battlefield desperation in the Balkans, the stalemated Western Front, and the collapse of the Eastern Front and Tsarist Russia were a third factor that played a role by putting immense pressure on the Entente. The kinds of carrots and inducements which had been offered to get Italy and Romania to join were gone. The Entente resorted to armed force to put in place a government that would declare war. Contagion by brute force is what spread the war to Greece.

Lastly, the armed intervention was employed because the government was so weak and split that a decision could not be reached. The King's position of neutrality carried the day because it was the default position, but he could not get Venizelos and his supporters, who continued to win elections, to accede to that position, and, needless to say, Venizelos could not convince the King, his supporters, and most of the army. The internal deadlock, coupled with intrinsic military weakness, left the door open to armed intervention.

---

[18] For more detail on the role of the British in these actions see Stevenson (2017: 276–278).

[19] Details and documentation of these events may be found in Hall (2003: 410–411); see also Keegan (1998: 308).

The Underlying Structure

If the above analysis is correct in arguing that Greece entered primarily because of outside forces rather than internal ones, this should be reflected in the underlying grievances between Greece and Austria-Hungary and Germany. In fact there were no territorial claims between Greece and these two major states, as can be seen in Text Boxes 23.1 and 24.1. Nor was there any rivalry according to the two measures of rivalry (Text Boxes 23.2 and 24.2).[20] The main hostile alliance that Greece had that would affect relations with the Dual Alliance was its current alliance with Serbia and its broken alliance with Bulgaria (see Text Boxes 23.3 and 24.3).

Text Box 23.1.   Greece–Austria-Hungary territorial claims

No territorial claims

Text Box 24.1.   Greece–Germany territorial claims

No territorial claims

Text Box 23.2.   Greece–Austria-Hungary rivalry

Enduring Rivalry	Issue
NO ENDURING RIVALRY ARMS RACE HORN: 1913	

---

[20] The Senese and Vasquez measure indicates a sixth MID occurring only in 1940 during the Second World War.

Text Box 24.2.   Greece–Germany rivalry

Enduring Rivalry	Issue
SENESE AND VASQUEZ: 6th MID: 1940 ARMS RACE HORN: 1913, 1934, 1936–1938	Dominant MID Issue: Policy

Text Box 23.3.   Greece–Austria-Hungary Alliances

Greece Alliances	Austria-Hungary Alliances
1912–1913: BUL 3012 1913–1918: SER 3014	1879–1918: GMY 2065 1881–1895: SER 2066 1881–1887: GMY, RUS 2067 1882–1918: GMY, ITA (–1915) 2068 1883–1918: GMY, ITA (–1915), ROM (–1916) 2069 1904–1908: RUS 3003 1914–1918: BUL 3017 1915–1918: BUL, GMY 3030

Text Box 24.3.   Greece–Germany alliances

Greece Alliances	Germany Alliances
1912–1913: BUL 3012 1913–1918: SER 3014	1879–1918: AUH 2065 1881–1887: AUH, RUS 2067 1882–1918: AUH, ITA 2068 1883–1918: ITA (–1915), ROM (–1916), AUH 2069 1887–1890: RUS 2072 1914–1918: OTM 3015 1915–1918: AUH, BUL 3020

The arms race measures do indicate some tension between Greece and the two major states in 1913 at the time of the Balkan Wars, but none thereafter in this period. The absence of a later arms race reflects Greece's need to recover from the wars and its inability to engage in any arms race in 1914–1917.

Previous MIDs, however, do indicate more of a history of conflict, but there is a clear gap between the late nineteenth century and the beginning of the First World War (see Histograms 23 and 24). In the twentieth century there were no MIDs between these two major states and Greece until 1917 and 1916, respectively.

Although there are some MIDs, there is not the pattern of territorial claims, rivalry, and war there was between Greece, on the one hand, and Bulgaria and the Ottoman Empire, on the other. It can be seen from Text Boxes 25.1 and 26.1 that Greece and Bulgaria and the Ottoman Empire had a number of territorial claims (and vice versa) with each, and that Bulgaria and the Ottoman Empire were clear rivals of Greece, with Thompson seeing the former going back to 1827 and

---

Text Box 25.1.   Greece–Bulgaria territorial claims

1913: Greek Macedonia (Claim Dyad 34209)
BUL–GRC
1914–1919: Greek Macedonia (Claim Dyad 34210)
BUL–GRC
Third Party: SER
1918–1919: Western Thrace (Claim Dyad 36006)
GRC–BUL
Third Party: OTM
1919–1923: Western Thrace (Claim Dyad 36007)
BUL–GRC
Third Party: TUR
1941: Western Thrace (Claim Dyad 36008)
BUL–GRC
1944: Greek Macedonia (Claim Dyad 34211)
BUL–GRC
1944–1947: Western Thrace (Claim Dyad 36009)
BUL–GRC
1946–1947: Burgos and Rhodope Mountains (Claim Dyad 36010)
GRC–BUL
1948–1953: Alpha–Beta–Gamma Islands (Claim Dyad 35701)
BUL–GRC

Text Box 26.1.   Greece–Ottoman Empire/Turkey territorial claims

1828–1832: Samos (Claim Dyad 36401)
GRC–OTM
1828–1913: Crete (Claim Dyad 36601)
GRC–OTM
1840–1882: Thessaly (Claim Dyad 36201)
GRC–OTM
1844–1913: Macedonia (Claim Dyad 34201)
GRC–OTM
Third Party: SER, BUL
1853–1914: Epirus (Claim Dyad 33801)
GRC–OTM
1881–1914: Eastern Sporades (Claim Dyad 36402)
GRC–OTM
Third Party: ITA
1897: Thessaly (Claim Dyad 36202)
OTM–GRC
1912–1923: Dodecanese Islands (Claim Dyad 37003)
GRC–OTM/TUR
Third Party: ITA
1914–1923: Eastern Sporades (Claim Dyad 36403)
OTM/TUR–GRC
Third Party: ITA
1914–1923: Imbros and Tenedos (Claim Dyad 36404)
GRC–OTM/TUR
Third Party: ITA
1915–1920: Smyrna (İzmir) (Claim Dyad 71001)
GRC–OTM/TUR
Third Party: ITA
1918–1920: Eastern Thrace (Claim Dyad 36004)
GRC–OTM/TUR
Third Party: BUL
1920–1923: Smyrna (İzmir) (Claim 71003)
TUR–GRC
1920–1923: Eastern Thrace (Claim Dyad 36005)
TUR–GRC
Third Party: BUL
1964–Ongoing: Aegean Sea Islands (Claim Dyad 36406)
TUR–GRC

the latter going back to 1878 (see Text Boxes 25.2 and 26.2, respectively). Note that Klein, Diehl and Goetz see a rivalry only with Bulgaria, beginning at the time of the Second Balkan War. The main current alliance Greece had was with Serbia, and this was aimed at

Text Box 25.2.   Greece–Bulgaria rivalry

Enduring Rivalry	Issue
DIEHL AND GOERTZ: 1914–1952	Dominant MID Issue: Territory and Policy
KLEIN, GOERTZ, DIEHL: 1913–1952	THOMPSON: Positional and Spatial
THOMPSON: 1878–1947	
SENESE AND VASQUEZ: 6th MID: 1928	
ARMS RACE	
HORN: 1923, 1924, 1936–1938, 1951–1953	

Text Box 26.2.   Greece–Ottoman Empire rivalry

Enduring Rivalry	Issue
DIEHL AND GOERTZ: 1866–1925; 1958–1989	Dominant MID Issue: Territory
KLEIN, GOERTZ, DIEHL: 1866–1925; 1958–2001	THOMPSON: Positional and Spatial
THOMPSON: 1827–1930; 1955–Ongoing	
SENESE AND VASQUEZ: 6th MID: 1878	
ARMS RACE	
HORN: 1913, 1934, 1936–1938, 1975–1977	

Bulgaria both in the Second Balkan War and again in 1914 (see Text Boxes 25.3 and 26.3).

The territorial claims with Bulgaria went back to the Second Balkan War and focused on Macedonia, and they continued until after the First World War. The territorial claims with the Ottoman Empire were more diverse and went back to 1828, and have continued to the present.

The pattern of arms races with the Ottoman Empire is similar to that with the major states, showing only an arms race in 1913 associated with the Balkan Wars. There were no arms races with Bulgaria until 1923, after the First World War.

The pattern of MIDs for Bulgaria does not go as far back as for the major states or for the Ottoman Empire (see Histogram 25). This is

---

Text Box 25.3.   Greece–Bulgaria alliances

Greece Alliances	Bulgaria Alliances
1912–1913: BUL 3012	1912–1913: SER 3011
1913–1918: SER 3014	1912–1913: GRC 3012
	1914–1918: OTM 3016
	1914–1918: AUH 3017
	1915–1918: AUH, GER 3020

Text Box 26.3.   Greece–Ottoman Empire alliances

Greece Alliances	Ottoman Empire Alliances
1912–1913: BUL 3012	1854–1856: FRN, UKG, ITA[a] (1855–) 2031
1913–1918: SER 3014	1854–1856: AUH 2034
	1914–1918: GMY 3015[b]
	1914–1918: BUL 3016[b]

[a] Prior to 1860, ITA refers to Piedmont.
[b] Not included in the histogram because the alliance was made within three months of the war.

---

because Bulgaria entered the system late and because Greece and Bulgaria shared the Ottoman Empire as an enemy until the Second Balkan War. Thus, the pattern of MIDs for this dyad started in 1913 and then continued as a consequence of the First World War until the Second World War. The pattern of MIDs for the Ottoman Empire was more extensive and went back to 1829 with the Greek Revolt from the Ottoman Empire. The MIDs continued the rivalry until the present, with a respite after 1925, beginning again in 1958 and go through 2001, where the data end.[21]

The data indicate that the underlying structure was such that the grievances between Greece and Bulgaria and the Ottoman Empire were more salient in that these dyads had several territorial claims with each other and a pattern of rivalry, whereas none existed between Greece

---

[21] The histogram is truncated at 1978 for reasons of space. There were thirteen MIDs occurring regularly afterward, all over territory.

and Austria-Hungary and Germany. The set of MIDs with the Ottoman Empire was one of the most extensive of any of the dyads that entered the war (see Histogram 26), although these were more influential before 1914 and after 1917. Although there were MIDs between the major states and Greece going back to the nineteenth century, these were still nothing compared with the pattern of MIDs with the Ottoman Empire, or even the pattern with Bulgaria, which, although it consisted of only one MID, involved a bitter war, whereas there was no prior war between Greece and the major states. All of this suggests that the underlying grievances were not such as to give Venizelos the public support he needed for his choice. Instead it suggests that brute force was needed to overcome the lack of grievances.

Outcome and Aftermath

It took almost a year after the declaration of war for a Greek army to be deployed. In combination with the French and British they fought against the Bulgarians to retake parts of Serbia and by November 1918 had scored several victories that helped produce Bulgaria's surrender. In 1919, under the Treaty of Neuilly, Greece received Western Trace and Bulgaria lost its access to the Aegean.

In June of that year, during Versailles, the Entente Powers permitted the Greeks to land troops in Asia Minor at Smyrna.[22] This led to the Greco-Turkish war of 1919–1922, where the Greeks were initially successful in gaining many of the Greek enclaves and getting almost as far as Ankara. In the Treaty of Sèvres in 1920 Greece gained Eastern Thrace, several areas along the Asia Minor coast, and several Aegean Islands. For a while it looked like the *Megali Idea* would come to fruition. Nonetheless, 1920 saw Venizelos defeated in elections and King Constantine return.

The Treaty – which was also with Britain, France, and Italy – abolished the Ottoman Empire and partitioned it. This led to a nationalist revival under Mustafa Kemal, who reversed the situation through armed force, and Greece was badly defeated, with previous acquisitions having to be given up under the Treaty of Lausanne (1923). King Constantine abdicated a second time, and died shortly thereafter. As part of the peace, there was a misguided nationalist-inspired population exchange between the two states, with over one million refugees coming to Greece, where they suffered hardships and were not easily assimilated,

---

[22] On the diplomacy involved in this decision and its consequences, as well as how it was related to Italy, see MacMillan (2001: 431–436).

since many spoke only Turkish. The bitter failure in Asia Minor put to rest a great part of the romanticism of the *Megali Idea*.

Conclusion

Contiguity brought the war to Greece's doorstep, and without that it might not have entered the war. The key to Greece's entry was, however, that the decision was imposed from the outside on a Greek government that was unable to reach a decision because of sharp divisions. France and Britain intervened in collusion with one faction within Greece, pushing aside the reigning King and forcing Greece's entry. This makes this case unique in how the war spread and how contagion worked. The domestic faction that entered the war did so, however, to promote its territorial ambitions. Territorial rivalry and contiguity make the Greek case similar to other dyads, but the specific contagion process that brought about entry – brute force – was unusual. It occurred, in part, because of the lateness of the entry and the desperate effort the Entente exerted to break the stalemate on the battlefield.

Opportunity and the Breakdown of the Political Order: Siam and China

Theoretical Analysis

Both of these countries are different from many of the minor and late entrants in that alliances, territorial grievances, and opportunity created by changes in power were not the main factors propelling their declarations of war. As Stevenson (2017: 285) points out, both were motivated by their desire to eliminate the unequal treaties that the imperial powers had imposed by attending the peace conference that would follow the war. By 1917 when they entered, they rightly perceived the ongoing war as destroying the existing political order and the peace conference as making a new one. Their aim was to get what in the larger scheme of things was a minor change in the imperial order – the amelioration of the unequal treaty system. This had already been one of the conditions of the Ottoman Empire's entry when the Ottomans sought to eliminate capitulatory privileges, and they had implemented it unilaterally before even entering (see Russia–Ottoman Empire). The leaders of Siam[23] and of China saw the war as an opportunity, really a once-in-a-lifetime opportunity to change the prevailing political order to improve their

---

[23] Siam was officially renamed Thailand in 1939.

subservient position. Wilson's February 4, 1917 State Department call for all neutrals to do something about submarine warfare (Papers of Woodrow Wilson, Vol. 41: 116) provided the gateway for them to walk into the war several months later. In both cases they entered on the side of the Entente, and what is unusual is that it is these very allies – Britain and France – that were their main targets for reform. In addition, China had more extensive grievances against Japan involving the Twenty-One Demands.

The logic of the decision-makers in terms of the connection between attending a peace conference and obtaining what they wanted is unclear, since they had no substantial power on their side; nor did the Entente seek their support; nor did they ask the Entente to support a change in the unequal treaties as a condition of their entry. It is also clear that the Entente did not need their support in such a far-away location. In this way, contiguity worked against them, while it minimized the risk of their entry. Their belief in the importance of the peace conference seems to have rested on the assumption that they could only have a voice – a seat at the table, so to speak – if they entered the war, and so they did. This is similar to Wilson's concern that it was important to enter to shape the peace by attending the peace conference. The difference between the two cases is that for Wilson it was one of several elements (and, as argued above, a secondary one), whereas with Siam and China it was the primary motive. While this might be seen as a costly and risky decision of the two minor states, it was not, since they did not have any intention of becoming fully involved in armed conflict given their distance; in fact, they do not satisfy the Correlates of War threshold as participants in the war. Siam would send a small expeditionary force, including an aviation unit, whereas China would not. Siam suffered nineteen deaths, but the Chinese, who were commercially supplying upwards of 150,000 laborers, would see over 5,000 killed just in transit (Stevenson 2017: 290).

In their declarations of war neither would refer to their "real" reasons for joining (see Stevenson 2017: 292), but placed the blame on unrestricted submarine warfare and violations of international law. Submarine warfare did take over 500 Chinese lives (see Stevenson 2017: 292), and the Chinese focused on submarine warfare in their declaration of war.[24] While both countries had the above in common in their decision to enter the war, they were different with regard to other processes.

---

[24] See the Presidential proclamation declaring war on Germany and Austria-Hungary, 14 August, 1917 in *Declarations of War: Severances of Diplomatic Relations, 1914–1918* (1919: 18–19).

Siam–Germany and Austria-Hungary, July 22, 1917

The Kingdom of Siam was much less divided than China, which was governed by various warlords. It was an absolute monarchy, with King Vajiravudh, or Rama VI, generally pro-British, as was Prince Devawongse Varopakarn, the foreign minister, who was kept on from the previous ruler – King Rama V (1868–1910). Rama V is often credited with keeping Siam independent as a buffer zone between Britain and France. Only a few in the elite were pro-German, mostly those who had been educated there, but everyone was in favor of neutrality. By 1917, however, sentiment toward Britain increased when Wilson called upon all neutrals to enter the war and the prospects for Germany seemed less than they had been. The final decision was taken in the summer, with the King playing the major role (Hell 2015). Since there was no legislature, the King's decision was determinative. A major reason he gave was to overturn the unequal treaties, but he maintained this could not be stated officially (Stevenson 2017: 286; see also Pad 2017).

At the suggestion of the French, the King decided to send an expeditionary force to Europe, consisting of an aviation unit and a motor corps. In total a little over 1,200 volunteers were sent – none saw combat per se, but they were honored by playing a role in the occupation of Germany's territory (Hell 2015). Siam did get a seat at the table at Versailles and pushed for an end to the unequal treaties, to which the U.S. agreed in 1920, but Britain and France not until 1925.

China–Germany and Austria-Hungary, August 14, 1917

In China, the situation was more complicated. First, Japan had active armed forces in the country and was occupying territory it took from the Germans in 1914. Second, the country was very divided, not so much over the war in Europe, but because there was no centralized government but a set of warlords who controlled various parts of the country, and these divisions, which were a prelude to civil war, became associated with different positions on whether to enter the war and on which side.

Chinese leaders first considered war in 1914 when Japan attacked German positions in China and then followed up with the Twenty-One Demands on the official Chinese government. This was not so much a consideration of entering the First World War as it was of China defending itself from Japanese expansion on its territory, particularly in the Shandong Peninsula, and further infringements on China's sovereignty. The European major states that had intervened to limit Japan's gains after the 1895 Sino-Japanese war were not going to re-assemble since they were at war with each other and the prevailing political order was shattered. Only the U.S. publically opposed the Twenty-One Demands, and Grey, while sympathetic, was not about to oppose his Japanese ally. Given their military weakness, there was little the Chinese could do, and, according to Stevenson (2017: 289), President Yuan Shikai and the foreign ministry initially thought of using whatever peace conference would emerge at the end of the war as a way of raising the issue. The problem, however, was that the only option of entering the ongoing world war was to enter against Germany on the side of the Entente. Japan blocked this until 1917, when there was a change in the foreign ministry. By this time Japan had also gained secret agreements with its allies that after the war it would be permitted to take over Germany's treaty rights in Shandong, which China was opposing.

This meant that China's entry into the war would not achieve its main aims (Stevenson 2017: 296), although its fractured leadership did not know that. It also meant that the sending of very large numbers of Chinese laborers would not help China get what it ultimately wanted. This became more evident as it intervened in the war and demanded reductions in the large indemnity it owed from the Boxer Rebellion and an increase in its external tariffs. The Entente supported only an elimination of the indemnity owed to Germany and Austria-Hungary. Similarly, they would not permit China to increase its tariffs against their goods. Ultimately, China would get some change in the unequal treaties, but not until the Washington Naval Conference of 1922, which was after and separate from the peace conference at Versailles. The Washington Naval Conference was a partially successful attempt to bring in the U.S. to build a new political order, and in this order China's interests had more of an influence. The strategy that the breakdown of the prevailing political order in 1914 provided an opportunity for China (as well as Siam) to bring about change proved correct.

In the process, however, Japan's war against Germany inside of China and the attempt by various Chinese leaders to enter the war on the side of the Entente further strained the fragile internal situation. Before his death in 1916 Yuan had faced a separate government in the South that had opposed his attempt to replace the fledgling republic with a monarchy with him as the emperor. The South was the stronghold of the Kuomintang. Yuan was replaced as President by Li Yuanhong, who was acceptable to the South as well as to Japan. Duan Qirui, a powerful general, was Premier. The two came into conflict, with the latter wanting entry into the war and the former more hesitant. There was a series of struggles between the two that also brought in the cabinet and parliament and saw Duan briefly resigning in protest and Zhang Xun, a strong military governor, intervening. In the end, war was declared by parliament and a reorganized government led by Duan. Meanwhile the Kuomintang withdrew from parliament and re-established a separate government in the South that also declared war. The decision to enter the war accentuated the warlord system and the internal civil war that was gripping China. In fact, part of Duan's motive in wanting to go to war was that he believed he would in that case be able to obtain financial aid and loans, but ultimately only Japan came through with substantial funds (for more details on the Chinese domestic situation, see Stevenson 2017: 293–295). Thus, it was not only the attempt to overturn the unequal treaties which played a role in China's intervention, so did the jockeying for internal power, but given the fractured nature of the situation and the geographic vastness of China, nothing less could be expected. Nonetheless, the warlord system made China extremely different from the unified Siam.

The Underlying Structure

The underlying structure of MIDs, territorial claims, rivalry, and arms races showed more of a reason for conflict between China and Germany than Siam and Germany. Siam had only one MID with Germany, and that was in 1917 when it declared war. There was no rivalry according to Thompson or the other behavioral measures. Finally, there were no arms races. The situation with China was different, but still there is not much here to predict war. Thompson identifies a rivalry, but this was between 1897 and 1900 and reflected the imperial struggle. There were several MIDs, as can be seen in Histogram 27, with two of the three before 1917 related to the Boxer Rebellion. There was one arms race in 1937, associated no doubt with arming in China related to conflict with Japan. Upon examining only these data one would assume that China declared war out of some resentment because of German imperialism, but in fact the real imperial threats came from Japan, Britain, France, and Russia – the countries that it joined. Japan's occupation of the former German areas and its active involvement in Chinese internal conflicts made it the key threat. One must conclude, then, that the real motive in the declaration is not reflected in the profile of China–Germany.

An examination of the MIDs and rivalries with the Entente and its allies supports this claim. We see with Japan that it had thirteen MIDs by 1916 out of a total of thirty-eight by 1999. Thompson sees the

two as having had a rivalry during the years 1873–1945 and then
1996–ongoing. Klein *et al.* date the rivalry as 1873–1958 and then
from 1978 until their data end in 1999. There were also arms races in
1937, 1939–1940, and 1944. The interactions with France were somewhat less, but still more than those with Germany. There were six
MIDs before the First World War out of a total of eleven. Thompson
sees a rivalry during the years 1856–1900, slightly longer than that of
Germany's, and Klein *et al.* see one for 1870–1927. There were arms
races in similar years: 1937, 1940, and then 1952. The situation with
Britain was not unlike that of France, but with only two MIDs before
the First World War, but a total of fifteen. Thompson lists it as the rivalry that goes back furthest in time – to 1839 – but also ending in 1900
with the Boxer Rebellion. Klein *et al.* see one in the Cold War era for
1958–1968. The arms races are earlier than the others: 1900–1901, and
then in the Second World War period: 1937, 1939–1940. Likewise, the
relationship with Russia was not that different. Russia in the past was as
much an imperial threat as Japan. The alliance with Russia was actually
an indicator of that. The two states had fifteen MIDs before the First
World War and another eighteen through 1947. All of these indicate
that the underlying structure did not embody greater grievances toward
Germany than toward the Entente and its allies. It suggests instead
that some other motive was working here – the one given by the
decision-makers, namely, that they wanted a seat at the table to pursue
an end to unequal treaties and do what they could to ease their imperial
exploitation. This goal managed to remain intact as the Chinese worked
their way through their complicated internal political situation to bring
about a declaration of war. The imperial structure accounts for a good
part of both why and how China joined the war. This is emphasized by
the fact that the only territorial claim was over the Shandong Peninsula
(Text Box 27.1), and that claim was really related to the 1895 war with
Japan. See Text Boxes 27.2 and 27.3 for the China–Germany rivalry
and their alliances, respectively.

Text Box 27.1.   China–Germany territorial claims

1895–1898 Shandong (Claim Dyad: 80301)
GMY–CHN
Third Party: JPN

Text Box 27.2.   China–Germany rivalry

Enduring Rivalry	Issue
THOMPSON: 1897–1900 SENESE AND VASQUEZ: 6th MID: 1941 ARMS RACE HORN: 1937	Dominant Issue: Policy THOMPSON: Spatial

---

Text Box 27.3.   China–Germany alliances

China Alliances	Germany Alliances
1896–1900: RUS 2077	1879–1918: AUH 2065 1881–1887: AUH, RUS 2067 1882–1918: AUH, ITA (–1915) 2068 1883–1918: ITA (–1915), ROM (–1916), AUH 2069 1887–1890: RUS 2072 1914–1918: OTM 3015 1915–1918: AUH, BUL 3020

Conclusion

What is unusual about the cases both of Siam and of China is that opportunity played a role only because of the breakdown of the prevailing political order and not because of the change in political power. The entry of these two minor states was strictly a function of the ongoing war and evinced a spreading of the war to a faraway non-contiguous location. Neither state would have ever thought of fighting Germany, and in fact the target of their intervention was not so much Germany as the allies they were joining. What they wanted was not to fight one side, but to participate in the war so they could participate in the diplomacy of peace. By 1917, and with the entry of the U.S. and the call by Wilson for all neutrals to enter the war, it was clear that the old order was being rent asunder. The peace conference would build a new order, and the leaders of these countries hoped that they could participate in that peace conference and push an agenda that would permit them to end the system of unequal treaties to which they had been subjected.

But how did the war spread to them? This can be seen as an illustration of hierarchical diffusion that did not rely on alliances. These minor states were tied to the major states and the prevailing political order, by the system of imperialism. The Imperialist System can be seen as a network that tied together those that dominated the system and those that suffered under it. The ongoing war had broken down the diplomatic underpinnings of this system because it broke down the former Bismarckian peace system that managed imperial competition, which had most recently been exhibited in the major-state intervention in the outcome of the 1895 Sino-Japanese War. The prospect of creating a new world order by an actual face-to-face peace conference propelled these two minor states, which were not colonies, to seek a seat at the table.[25] In the case of China that system had brought the war to it, as Japan tried to supersede Germany's place in China. Germany had rights protected by the major states, and the desire of Japan to accede to those rights provided an opening for China to deal with it on a diplomatic playing field. Officially, China declared war because submarine warfare violated international law, and this was the subject in most of its legal declaration (*Declarations of War: Severances of Diplomatic Relations, 1914–1918* 1919: 19), following the lead of Wilson. This was of course a concern, but Stevenson (2017: 292) argues that it was not the main motivation.

Latin American States and Miscellaneous Declarations of War

On February 4, 1917 the U.S. State Department sent an official note to all neutrals asking them to join the U.S. and sever relations with Germany because of its violations of the rights of neutrals through the use of unrestricted submarine warfare. This can be seen as a form of contagion coming out of the battlefield conditions of the ongoing war, although at this point it was only a prelude to intervention. This was still an attempt to pressure Germany and Austria-Hungary to change their policy, but the severance of diplomatic nations usually preceded a declaration of war, and was often done simultaneously. The call in and of itself, then, must be seen as a way of promoting contagion. It had an effect in that a number of states seriously deliberated the note

---

[25] Colonies, though they were part of this system, could not legally enter the war, so they were inoculated from the contagion. Nonetheless, Wilson's fourteen points would later lead such members of the Imperial System to try to reform the prevailing order to eliminate colonialism in the name of nationalism. This is best illustrated by Ho Chi Minh approaching Woodrow Wilson at Versailles.

(Stevenson 2017: 285), including those far away from the U.S. sphere of hegemony – namely Siam and China. None of the states took that drastic step at this time. Those that did all waited until the U.S. itself entered the war. Even among those that did declare war, none was involved in combat except for Brazil. Thus, we are talking here about limited contagion.

Nonetheless, from a theoretical point of view it is interesting to analyze why these states joined the ongoing war and what processes drew them in. The analysis sees two factors operating. The first is valence balancing. Most of these states declared war out of loyalty to the U.S. This sort of diffusion can also be seen as hierarchical diffusion along the structure of U.S. hegemony in Latin America. The closeness of ties would explain both the degree to which they entered the conflict (e.g. severing relations only or declaring war) and the timing. The closer the ties, the more likely they were to declare war and the earlier, at least that would be the *ex ante* hypothesis.

An examination of Latin American declarations of war in Table 5.1 seems consistent with this hypothesis. Those that declared war in 1917 were Panama and Cuba, within ten days of the U.S. declaration on April 6.

Table 5.1. *Latin American and Liberian declarations of war*

Date	Country declaring war	Against country	Number of MIDs
April 7, 1917	Cuba 40	Germany 255	4 MIDs: 1914, 1941, 1942, 1942
April 7, 1917	Panama 95	Germany 255	4 MIDs: 1941, 1940, 1942, 1943
August 4, 1917	Liberia 450	Germany 255	Not in data until 1920, 1 MID: 1944
October 26, 1917	Brazil 140	Germany 255	4 MIDs: 1917, 1942, 1942, 1944
December 10, 1917	Panama 95	Austria-Hungary 300	No Data
December 16, 1917	Cuba 40	Austria-Hungary 300	0 MIDS
April 23, 1918	Guatemala 90	Germany 255	2 MIDs: 1918, 1941
May 8, 1918	Nicaragua 93	Germany 255	2 MIDs: 1918, 1941
May 8, 1918	Nicaragua 93	Austria-Hungary 300	1 MID: 1918
May 23, 1918	Costa Rica 94	Germany 255	1 MID: 1941
July 12, 1918	Haiti 41	Germany 255	5 MIDs: 1872, 1896, 1909, 1941, 1941
July 19, 1918	Honduras 91	Germany 255	3 MIDs: 1918, 1941, 1942

These states also declared war on Austria-Hungary within ten days of the U.S. declaration on December 7, 1917. Interestingly, the third state closely related to the U.S. to declare war was Liberia, on August 4. Liberia, which had been founded by former U.S. slaves, can be seen as part of the structure of U.S. hegemony that did not include colonies. The last Latin American state to declare war in 1917 was Brazil, and this was due, in part, to submarine warfare (see the discussion below).

The declarations in 1918 spread to the Central American states and one remaining Caribbean state: Guatemala, Nicaragua, Costa Rica, Haiti, and Honduras. Interesting, other than Brazil, no other South American states (those south of Panama) declared war. Several did sever relations in 1917, however: Bolivia very early severed relations on April 13; and then, about twenty days *before* Brazil declared war, Peru (October 6) and Uruguay (October 7) severed relations, and Ecuador followed on December 8.

A second factor that reinforced valence balancing was submarine warfare. Some states, for instance Brazil and Argentina, had ships that were sunk, and this encouraged Brazil to declare war. In addition, the substantial ethnic affinities in some states were an influence. For example, the large Italian immigrant populations in Argentina and Uruguay were important for generating sympathy for the Entente and its allies, whereas conversely the German immigrants in Chile, Bolivia, and southern Brazil tended to sympathize with Germany (Jiménez 2014). Also churches were sometimes anti-French because of that country's anti-clerical stance. These ethnic affinities were present from 1914 on, and seem less significant than valence balancing and hierarchy because it was only in 1917 when the U.S. entered that these states declared war or severed relations with Germany. Nonetheless, Argentina and Chile remained neutral.

Any analysis of Latin American states would be incomplete without a discussion of those that remained neutral. If the theory presented here is correct, then one would expect that the factors making for valence balancing would be absent or weak. This analysis will be conducted in Chapter 6 on neutrals.

Brazil–Germany, October 26, 1917

Just after the U.S. declared war, the President of Brazil announced that Brazil would remain neutral, but by May 22 he had sent a message to the Brazilian Congress saying that Brazil could not be neutral towards the U.S. when it was involved in the defense of her rights toward a foreign power. This was because "she was united to that country by the closest of closest friendship" (Boyle 1918: 6). The Brazilian government then sent a circular to friendly powers explaining its "revocation of neutrality" in terms of "Pan Americanism" and "continental solidarity" (Boyle 1918: 6, 39–40). Within a month Uruguay responded positively to the note, while Argentina and Chile did not and maintained their strict neutrality.

The initial reaction to the U.S. declaration of war seems to indicate that concerns about valence balancing played a role in the attitude of the government, as they did in the Brazilian Congress and wider public, with the exception of those of German descent and some intellectuals (Schulze 2015: 3). The problem with this interpretation is that the Presidential message to Congress occurred around the same time as the sinking of the *Paraná* by German U-boats on April 5 just before the U.S. declaration of war.

The actual declaration of war did not occur until October 26, by which time three more ships had been sunk and the country was up in arms. What is clear is that, even if Brazil would have followed others in declaring war out of Pan-Americanism and continental solidarity, it would have been unlikely that it would have gone beyond that and taken direct military action as it prepared to do. The sinking of her ships led her to make a conscious decision to seek reprisals, and she offered to be part of British naval patrolling, which in fact happened. Her navy saw some action, but this was limited because of the outbreak of the Spanish flu as they landed on the African coast and because, by the time the main force had arrived at Gibraltar, the November 11, 1918 Armistice had been signed.

Theoretically, then, the U-boat attacks played a major role in the decision to go to war. This roused both the Congress and the public at large. The attacks of course mean that economic dependence was the contagion process at work, along with any valence balancing. Germany attacked all neutral shipping. Brazil was not singled out, but part of the larger decision to attack U.S. trade. In this sense the ongoing submarine warfare against the U.S. became contagious to all the remaining neutrals trading with the Entente and its allies. Nonetheless, Argentina's shipping was also attacked, but it was able to remain neutral. Part of the reason for this, as will be seen in the analysis of the neutrals in Chapter 6, had to do with how Germany handled the situation, but part also had to do with Argentina's attitude toward the U.S. and its resistance to American hegemony.

Part III

Conclusions: Lessons from the First World War

6   The Neutrals

Most of the theoretical works on neutrality, including those from a legal or historical perspective, are of two sorts: those that look at the doctrine and practice of neutrality, including its evolution (e.g. Abbenhuis 2014a) and those that look at the impact of events on the ability of states to remain neutral (e.g. the classic study by Orvik 1953). The latter often deal with specific well-known countries that have been neutral (see Salmon 1997). Like some of these studies (e.g. Kruizinga 2014), this chapter tries to determine why states were neutral in the First World War. The main purpose of this chapter is to see whether the factors that made contagion spread are absent from those states which remained neutral. From the point of view of making inferences, the neutrals provide a comparison group for learning the extent to which the factors that have been discerned as producing contagion are causally important. If they are important, then they should be absent from those states that do not enter the war. This is the standard way of making social science inferences.

This book selected the case of the First World War, however, because it was an exemplary case of contagion. As such it should come as no surprise that there were few neutrals. From a methodological point of view this limits the confidence we can have in the inferences we can make, but that is a tradeoff in selecting a premier case of contagion. From a theoretical point of view – even though there were only a few cases – the neutrals are important for providing a benchmark.

Of course, the reality could be more complicated. Even if some of these factors are present instead of absent, there may be other factors that inoculate these countries from the contagion. For example, in an epidemic, people may be exposed to an infection (i.e. contagion factors are present), but they still do not get the disease. Identifying such factors, even in medicine, is difficult and requires a great deal of knowledge about the causes of the disease and why it spreads in the first place. In medicine the theoretical assumption is that there must be some antibody at work, or (even more wide-sweeping) there might be a genetic resistance. In this chapter, therefore, some attention will be given to examining not only whether certain contagion factors are absent, but also what actual factors might have produced neutrality and why decision-makers decided not to enter and belligerents decided not to attack. The second purpose of this chapter is to see what characteristics or decision-making processes these states may have had that made them neutral. The approach here is to learn something about the determinants of neutrality by comparing the few cases that did not go to war with the many that did. Before turning to these empirical analyses, it is best to spend some time conceptualizing neutrality to get a better sense of its different aspects.

Conceptualizing Neutrality

Neutrality in war can be defined as abstaining from active fighting in an ongoing war and not providing substantial support favoring one side over the other. Neutrality is a formal diplomatic practice recognized under international law, with important codifications taking place not that long before the war, beginning with the Hague Conventions of 1907 that outlined the formal rights and responsibilities of neutrals and culminating in 1909 with the Declaration of London that discussed neutrality and maritime warfare, defining what could be considered contraband goods.[1] Neutrality is a legal state and typically formally declared just as war is formally declared. Declaration is required so other states can recognize that this condition and its legal rights and responsibilities are now in effect. Of course, with the waning of declarations of war after 1945, so too have declarations of neutrality waned.

For this analysis, in order to explain pure examples of neutrality, states that sever relations with belligerents, as a number of Latin American states did at the behest of the U.S., are *not* considered neutral. When the First World War erupted a number of states formally declared their neutrality. Although states might be legally neutral, they sometimes also announced that they had benevolent neutrality toward one side, while others took pains not to engage in any acts that might jeopardize their strict neutrality of favoring neither side.

One important aspect of neutrality is that some states that declared their neutrality remained neutral only for a period of time, while others remained neutral throughout the conflict. What separates these two sets?

---

[1] For a full discussion of the evolution of neutrality under Western international law see Orvik (1953: Ch. 1).

Since the factors associated with temporary neutrality seem different from those related to neutrality that endured throughout the war, the two sets will be analyzed separately.

For those countries that were only temporarily neutral, an important distinction to make in conceptualizing neutrality is whether a state joined a war or was brought in by force of arms against its will. Contagion implies a loss of control; the concept suggests that the ongoing war draws you in. It is important to examine the source of this loss of control – whether it is self-generated or imposed from the outside. This aspect is also relevant for those that were always neutral – why were they not drawn in by the ongoing war? Why were they able to resist? Were they inoculated? Or were they literally on the sidelines because of their distance from the battlefield?

Involvement against one's will in the First World War could result through two very different processes. The most common was being attacked by one side. This is clearly how the U.S. became involved. Belgium also fits into this category, although it was offered a bargain. To a certain extent Russia's declaration of war against the Ottoman Empire also fits into this category because of the attack on Sebastopol and its ships in the Black Sea, which was meant to provoke a declaration of war. Nevertheless, all of these are clearly examples of contagion in that the battlefield contingencies of the war led a belligerent to expand the war. The second process was rarer. This is the armed intervention by one or more belligerents in a neutral to force it to enter by a coup d'état or some other action that makes it declare war. The best illustration of this is the use of brute force to bring in Greece. To a certain extent the Entente intervention against Soviet Russia to keep it in the war is similar.

Being attacked by a belligerent, even if it is a future ally, is a very different process from "joining" the fray voluntarily. Joining involves a combination of incentives and restraints and a balancing of risks and opportunities. These factors, when they are complicated, can account for delays in joining, but more often than not they interact with other factors that are pulling decision-makers toward neutrality. How this might work is best seen when examining specific cases rather than in the abstract. We turn to that analysis now.

The Temporarily Neutral

The states that entered in the second and third waves were all temporarily neutral. All but Portugal declared their neutrality. These included Italy, Bulgaria, Romania, the U.S., and Greece. Within this group there are two different types. The first are those that tried to make a bargain in return for their neutrality. Italy exemplified this. It first tried to get compensation from Austria-Hungary based on Article VII of the Triple Alliance. In return it was willing to remain neutral. This is significant in that if it were to enter the war against Austria-Hungary this would have added a third front – to those of Russia and Serbia. For this reason, Bethmann-Hollweg urged some sort of compensation. As Berchtold resisted, being pressured by Conrad and Tisza, Italy turned to the other side. Eventually an auction ensued and the Entente was able to offer a better deal because it was not their territory that they were giving away. The auction added to the length of the neutrality, but it eventually became clear that Italy would have to do more than just remain neutral to get what it wanted.

Bulgaria went through a similar process. It sought offers from each side. In the beginning its decision-makers hoped that it could gain something by remaining neutral. They hoped that Russia could get Serbia to make some concessions on Macedonia in return for their staying out. Conversely, Austria-Hungary right after it declared war was offering them incentives if they entered. The end result was an auction and Bulgaria went with the Central Powers, because again they could offer the better deal since they were giving away Macedonia – territory that belonged to their enemy and not their ally.

The bargaining process and end game were similar to that of Italy, but the start was quite different. Bulgaria declared neutrality in the beginning because its government was divided, with different decision-makers favoring different sides, and because it was still recovering from the two Balkan Wars, in the second of which it was badly beaten. This start game was similar to that of Romania, which declared neutrality because there was a division in the government. Capability was also a factor in that Romania was in between two major states – Austria-Hungary and Russia – and it had a third potential enemy – Bulgaria – at its back. These put it at greater risk. The bargaining process also reflected an auction as with the other two.

At a more profound level all three states were drawn into the war by a combination of opportunity and territorial rivalry. The opportunity of the ongoing war changed the existing distribution of power to give them an advantage that they did not have before. In each case their territorial rival was weakened by fighting on other fronts. In addition, the ongoing war brought about a breakdown in the political order so that now major states on each side were no longer restraining them from the use of war, but actively courting them. This combination of opportunity and territorial rivalry was a great temptation to these states and made their decision a function of the incentives the belligerents could provide as discounted by restraints. The incentives beyond the territorial offers could sometimes be very high. Bulgaria was offered a joint invasion of Serbia. Many would be offered munitions and money, as was Romania, although the munitions never came to fruition. In 1914 the Ottomans were sent large shipments of gold by Germany to enter the war.

There was basically only one restraint – the probability that the side that was chosen would fail to win. All three countries weighed this factor and discounted the respective offers by this. There was no point of getting a better deal if that could not be delivered. Weighing which side would win furthered delayed the decision as the neutrals waited to see whether they could discern trends in the battlefield outcomes. This proved difficult because of the fluctuations in the East and the stalemate in the West. In addition, individual decision-makers and groups within the neutral state often read the evidence differently. All the decision-makers tried to fine-tune their decision to gain the maximum leverage, but at the same time realized that, if the battlefield outcomes were tipped too far, they might not be needed. Thus, Italy thought the launching of the Entente campaign at Gallipoli would produce a victory, so it rushed to enter the war before it was too late, only to find later that the British and French along with the ANZAC contingent were pushed back.

Sometimes the belligerents themselves would become exasperated and set deadlines for a decision or they would pull offers off the table. Hence, the Entente told Romanian decision-makers in June 1916 in reaction to Verdun that if Romania did not enter soon the offer would be withdrawn. This tactic was also used to get Italy to declare war against Germany. Italy, if it had had its choice, would probably never have declared war against Germany. It did not see itself as entering the Great War as much as it saw itself as fighting against Austria-Hungary. Italy had no territorial grievances against Germany, nor any rivalry. In addition, it had been allied with Germany in 1866 and in return got Venetia. All of this made for a positive affinity that promoted a decision for long-term neutrality. The Entente, however, would not tolerate this situation, and after Verdun it put increasing pressure on Italy to declare war or face a cutting off of aid and support. So the Italians relented in August 1916. In a sense they were coerced, but not enough for it to be seen as an act of brute force; rather it should be seen as part of the bargaining process, albeit very hard bargaining.

In the end, the underlying structure of these temporarily neutral states made them primed for entering the war. They all ended up going to war because of the powerful combination of opportunity and territorial rivalry.

The latter was sufficiently strong to even make two of them – Italy and Romania – defect from their major alliance. The attempt to gain what they wanted by making a bargain in return for their continued neutrality was never realized by any of them and was most likely illusionary from the very beginning as the scope of the war became clear. One lesson from these cases of temporary neutrality is that these states gave up neutrality because they could not get what they wanted unless they entered the war. That was the price they had to pay at the auction in which they participated. Their entry was in a sense predictable and unsurprising even to the extent of which side they would enter. Often, the passage of time would make the decision easier. Sometimes the domestic obstacles of divided government resolved themselves internally – as with the death of King Carol of Romania. At other times the external situation was clarified as their enemies joined the other side, making the division between the blocs clearer. The latter happened with Romania as Bulgaria entered on the side of the Central Powers. This kind of predictability was not present with those that remained neutral throughout the war.

Somewhat different was the case of Portugal. It initially was neutral, but quite early on made it clear to Britain that it would do whatever the British wanted. This was mostly due to their long-term alliance going back to 1386. The two had a strong interdependent relationship with regard to their respective colonial empires, with Britain transporting Portuguese troops and at the beginning of the war Portugal permitting Britain and France to use its naval facilities. The formation of a republic in 1910 made the new regime anxious to solidify this old relationship. This was particularly so since Britain and Germany at one point had entered talks about splitting the Portuguese African Empire amongst themselves if it should default on its debt. It was their African empire that drew Portugal into the war on a de facto basis as early as August 1914 with German attacks on Angola (Rollo, Pires, and Ribeiro de Meneses 2017: 2). The actual German declaration of war in March 1916 was more of a de jure action than with other states that were temporarily neutral. The colonial disputes with Germany and the long-term alliance with Britain made Portugal's entry a result of the hierarchical diffusion brought about by the system's imperial and alliance structures.

The U.S. was the major neutral that held out until the end. It was immune from most of the contagion factors at play with the other temporarily neutral states. It had no alliance, was spatially distant, and had no territorial grievances for which the ongoing war provided an opportunity and thus could not really be persuaded by the belligerent states.

In addition, it had a strong leader who abhorred war. However, as head of a major state Wilson wanted to play a role and be at the peace table. He tried this with his mediation effort, which failed in part because of bad timing and Entente resistance. In the end, the economic dependence that the Entente had on U.S. trade by credit provoked an attack by Germany, without which the U.S. would have remained neutral. Economic dependence was the key factor from the beginning and this brought it in, once Germany thought it had enough submarines to strike a really crippling blow on Britain.

The Enduring Neutrals

These states were less likely to enter the war *ex ante*, although some almost did against their will by virtue of their being attacked. The most obvious explanation to account for these neutrals is that they lacked the contagion factors that were present in the other states. The remainder of this chapter will begin by examining the extent to which the seven main contagion factors were absent. The study will then examine each neutral individually to see what can be gleaned about why they remained neutral in this particular case. These two analyses will be conducted first on the European neutrals and then on the Latin American neutrals.

Table 6.1 lists the neutrals and whether certain contagion factors were present, beginning with the European neutrals. As can be seen in the table, many of the five neutrals, but not all, lacked certain key contagion factors, in particular they were in no alliance with a belligerent, had no rivalry, and were not proximate to the battlefield. The only factor they all have in common, however, is the absence of a rivalry as defined by Thompson (2001) or by Klein *et al.* (2006) and Diehl and Goertz (2012: 105–108). Another key and striking characteristic of the European neutrals is that most, with the exception of the Netherlands and Switzerland, were on the periphery of Europe. The Scandinavian countries were set above, with water being an important intervening factor. Spain was down at the tip. The Netherlands was central, but it was only not involved through a deliberate decision by Germany to keep it open as a windpipe for trade, and Switzerland had a tradition of its neutrality being respected. The absence of rivalry and their geographic position in combination appear to be key underlying structural factors that kept them out of the war.

Two other factors that promoted neutrality were the absence of an alliance with any of the belligerents and the lack of territorial claims. Only Spain had an alliance, and this was with Britain and France, which

Table 6.1. *Contagion factors within neutrals, 1914–1918*

Neutral	Alliance	Territorial claims	Rivalries	Land contiguity[a]	Proximity to battlefield[b]
EUROPEAN STATES					
Spain	1. UKG-FRN 1907–1915	1. 230–200 (UKG) Gibraltar 1816–2001 end of data[c] 2. 230–600 (MOR) Northern and Southern Morocco 1904–1912	None U.S. pre-1816–1819[c]	Yes: FRN, POR	Not
Sweden	None	None	None	Russia (Finland)	Not
Norway	None	None	None	Russia	Not
Denmark	None	1. Virgin Islands 2 (USA)–390 1865–1917[c]	None	Yes: GMY	Proximate, but separated by water
Netherlands	None	1. 210–200 (UKG) Corentyn/New River Triangle 1816–1966[c] 2. Maroni 210–220 (FRN) 1849–1975[c] 3. Oecussi Enclave Border 235 (POR)–210 1909–1914[c] 4. Palmas Island 2 (USA)–210 1906–1928[c]	None	Yes: GMY, FRN	Proximate
Switzerland	None	None	None	Yes: FRN, GMY, AUH, ITA	Proximate
LATIN AMERICAN STATES					
Argentina	None	1. Puna de Atacama 160–145 (BOL) 1814–1941 2. Falkland Islands (Malvinas) and Dependencies 160–200 (UKG) 1841–2001 end of data[c] 3. Beagle Channel 160–155 (CHL) 1904–1985 4. Rio de la Plata 160–165 (URU) 1882–1973	THOMPSON: ARG-BRA 1817–1985 ARG-CHL 1843–1991	No	Not

Country		Disputes	Source references		
Chile	None	1. Palena/Continental Glaciers 155–160 (ARG) 1903–1998 2. Antofagasta 145 (BOL)–155 1884–2001 end of data 3. Beagle Channel 160 (ARG)–155 1904–1985 4. Tacna–Arica 135 (PER)–155 1884–1929	THOMPSON: ARG–CHL 1843–1991 CHL–PER 1832–1929 BOL–CHL 1836–ongoing	No	Not
Mexico	None	1. Clipperton Island 70–220 (FRN) 1897–1934[c] 2. Rio Grande Bancos 70–2 (USA) 1884–1972[c] 3. El Chamizal 70–2 (USA) 1895–1964[c]	KLEIN–DIEHL–GOERTZ: CHL–PER 1852–1921 KLEIN–DIEHL–GOERTZ: USA–MEX 1911–1920	Yes: USA	Not
OTHER Ethiopia/ Abyssinia	None	1. Southeast Sudan 530–200 (UKG) 1898 2. Boran Galla 530–200 (UKG) 1898–1907 3. Gadaduma Wells and Minor Territories 530–200 (UKG) 1907–1936 4. Lake Rudolf Border 530–200 (UKG) 1909–1936	THOMPSON: ETH–EGY 1868–1882 ITA–ETH 1882–1943	Suez Canal: No Eritrea: Yes British Somaliland: Yes Djibouti: Yes Not contiguous to battlefield, distance approximately 500 miles	Approximately 1,500–2,000 miles

[a] Source Keegan (1998: 1914 map inside cover).
[b] Contemporary driving distance was used to calculate miles. This makes the proximity closer than it was at the time (www.distancecalculator.net).
[c] Factor present with a belligerent, e.g. alliance with a belligerent, territorial claim made against a belligerent.

accounts for its benevolent neutrality toward the Entente. The alliance, however, was countered by the territorial claim to Gibraltar. Other than Spain, only the Netherlands had any territorial claims, and these involved colonial disagreements. The one Danish claim was with regard to the Virgin Islands and the U.S., and was not relevant. The only claim that might have been a factor was the one over Gibraltar and that worked against neutrality.

Theoretically what can explain the neutrality of the European states? Their neutrality is important because it is only these five of all the European states that remained outside the conflagration. All the others succumbed. And that diffusion, with the exception of the case of Britain, occurred though direct land contiguity. All of them were contiguous with at least one belligerent, so what protected them? The Netherlands and Switzerland have already been explained away in that Germany decided not to attack Holland, and Switzerland had an historic role of being neutral. Once these two have been removed, it is clear that the remaining states were on the periphery. It was this location that protected them. The indicator of distance from the battlefield supports this inference. Only Denmark was within 500 miles, and its distance was greater than it appears because the separation by water made it farther from the battlefield that the miles suggest. Being far away was a key variable, and that becomes clearer once distance is properly measured.

Distance and being on the periphery also was relevant in that it suggests that these states were not needed by any of the belligerents. This was true of all five of the states. Their armies were of limited value, and what trade they could offer could also be provided if they remained neutral. Likewise, none of these states wanted to enter the war. The absence of any territorial grievances and rivalry did not make the ongoing war an opportunity for any of them. Finally, the general absence of alliance ties provided no draw either. In sum, upon close examination, the claim that these states were neutral because of the absence of the major contagion processes seems to hold for all the European neutrals except the Netherlands. Where they are present in a few instances, their lack of impact is easily explained. Does a similar pattern hold for the Latin American neutrals?

Distance and being on the periphery was accentuated for the Latin American states, and it is not surprising that none declared war until the U.S. did. They had no alliance with the belligerents and no rivalries with them. Two of the states did, however, have territorial claims – Argentina with Britain over the Falklands and Mexico with France over an island. The real question is why didn't the Latin American neutrals follow the U.S. by valence balancing? Here distance again seems to play a role. The two major South American states that were neutral – Argentina and Chile – were as far from the U.S. as one can get. Theoretically, valence balancing has been explained in this analysis through the structure of American hegemony. Distance serves as a rough proxy of this, but a more precise indicator of hegemony should be a subject of future investigation. The one neutral that was proximate to the U.S. was Mexico, and this case needs to be explained, and will be addressed in the in-depth analyses.

European Neutrals: Case Studies

The European neutrals will be dealt with by first examining those on the periphery – Spain and the Scandinavian countries – and then those at the heart of Europe – the Netherlands and Switzerland. All of the European neutrals, as well as the U.S., believed that the doctrine of neutrality would protect them, and if it were violated it would be violated only at the edges. The heyday of norm construction and progress in international law at the turn of the century was certainly grounds for optimism, but the war changed things. Britain encroached on the doctrine early on with the establishment of a blockade out by the North Sea. By 1915 Germany had initiated submarine warfare – a new weapon that many considered immoral, but whose main purpose was to deny the neutrals the right to trade. One of the main consequences of the war was that belligerents on both sides refused to abide by the norms of neutrality, and as the war became a war of attrition they openly engaged in economic warfare that completely destroyed the rights of neutrals and the international law of neutrality. They even went so far as to declare that there were "belligerent rights" that justified their actions (Kruizinga 2014: 542), though these had no legal standing.

The neutrals protested, and the Netherlands was particularly steadfast in objecting to specific violations (Hertog 2011). The European neutrals hoped the U.S. and Wilson would do more and lead a bloc of them, but he demurred, preferring to go off on his own. Wilson did protest strenuously against German submarine warfare and even got the Germans to stop after the sinking of the *Lusitania* in May 1915 and the *Sussex* in March of the next year, but the U.S. had little impact on the blockade imposed by Britain. Ultimately, the international law of neutrality was in shambles, and even after the war the U.S. Congress accepted this with its Neutrality Acts in the 1930s. All of this went to support the realist analysis (Morgenthau 1948: Ch. XVI) that international law was not a viable solution to war and could not be substituted for power.

Spain

Spain was a key country that stayed neutral throughout the war, and this was due to its location. In addition to it being on the periphery, there were three basic reasons for it being able to remain neutral. First, the government was divided between those that were pro-British and French and those that were pro-German. This division also ran along the domestic fault line that separated the two major political parties – the liberals and left, including workers, vs. the conservatives, aristocrats, and Catholics. The domestic divisions were accentuated by an active propaganda war conducted by the belligerents within Spanish society. The sentiments of these two sides were so intense that, if Spain had entered on one side or the other, it might have, in the view of some, provoked unrest, if not a civil war (Kruizinga 2014: 570). This in itself made neutrality seem the better course. Beyond the educated elites, however, most Spaniards were not aroused by the war going on abroad. Albertini (1952, Vol. III: 691–693) in his early analysis emphasized this, but he may have underestimated the sharp divisions within the elite and the role of the king.

In between the two parties was King Alfonso XIII, who sought to play a mediating role as a visible European neutral. The King was a strong figure and, although recognizing that Spain had a benevolent neutrality toward Britain and France, he would not support going beyond that. From early on the King engaged in humanitarian efforts. He tried to protect Belgians from the harshness of German occupation, and he even tried to get the Tsar released. He approached Wilson for a joint role as mediator, but was rebuffed, and after the U.S. had entered the war tried to go it alone. Given this disposition, he was not going to permit Spain to enter the war. Added to this was his positive relationship with the Kaiser that was reciprocated because of a monarchist affinity. Here a strong leader worked to inoculate Spain from the ongoing contagion.[2]

Second, and of equal importance, is that militarily Spain was weak. The army was not sufficiently trained to enter the Western

---

[2] For documentation on the role of the King in the above see (Ponce 2014: 9; 2011: 56–57).

Front and slightly over half of its soldiers – 76,000 of 140,000 – were stationed in Morocco dealing with unrest (Ponce 2011: 54). Spain's armed forces were not of much use to the Entente, and this utility decreased as Italy and Portugal entered. What the Entente Powers wanted from Spain was iron-ore and, although they had to put pressure on Spain to get more, Spain being neutral was actually better for trade since it would be less likely to be the target of an all-out attack (Ponce 2011: 10). What France wanted from Spain was for it to guard its southern frontier, and it got this early on when King Alfonso assured the French government that they could remove their troops from the Pyrenean frontier without fear (Albertini 1952, Vol. III: 692). These factors remained true even after the U.S. had entered the war and pressure increased for Spain to join as well.

From Germany's perspective, if Spain entered on their side they would have to protect it from attack with little in return. From Spain's perspective, siding with the Central Powers would be difficult because of the economic dependence of Spain on the Entente Powers. Nonetheless, the possibility of an alliance was explored, with Germany offering Spain certain territorial acquisitions, including the prized Gibraltar and Tangiers. The King at one point raised the idea of compensation in return for Spain's support of the Entente (Ponce 2014: 9). These lures, even though they were not pursued for long, were similar to the auctions conducted by the 1915–1916 entrants into the war, and this shows how contagion might have worked to bring Spain in. This did not occur, however, because neither side really needed or wanted Spain. Nor did the sinking of Spanish ships by German submarines, which had reached a crisis point by August 1918, bring Spain in, as it had Brazil, for example. Things were smoothed things over, with Germany striking a deal that Spain would be given six ships (see Ponce 2014: 8 for details).

Finally, it should be noted that the main difference between Spain and Portugal was the colonial factor. Portugal was drawn into a de facto war with Germany in Africa because it was adjacent to its colonies, whereas Spain's North African holdings were not. Contiguity again played an important, if negative, role.

As with Spain, the Nordic Scandinavian countries were on the periphery hanging over Germany and across the Baltic Sea from Russia; they were also distant from the main battlefields. This combination protected them from the contagion all around them. All three declared neutrality immediately, and had joined together by December 1914 to form a bloc.

Sweden

Sweden was the largest of the three and the only one that was previously a major state in the global system. As a former rival of Russia, and having been knocked out of the Great Power system by it in the Great Northern War of 1700–1721, it remained quite hostile to Russia and its power in the Baltic. This hostility was an important barrier to it leaning toward the Entente. Once Russia had been kicked out of the war, food shortages and a change in government led Swedish leaders to move closer to the Entente (Kruizinga 2014: 568).

More important were the extensive pro-German sentiments within the population and the government. The most visible proponents of such sentiments were the Activists, who openly called for entry and alignment with Germany. Two motives guided this movement. The first was an affinity for common Teutonic heritage and general pro-war sentiment. The second was a security concern that a Russian victory would give Russia control over the Eastern Baltic, but that a German victory with Sweden at its side would lead to more Swedish influence in Scandinavia after the war (see Kruizinga 2014: 571–572). The Activists had support in the conservative Hammarskjöld government and from King Gustav V, who was married to the Kaiser's first cousin. More broadly the military, as well as the upper and middle classes, were pro-German. In addition, many active in the socialist movement looked to the German Social Democratic Party for inspiration. Only the Activists, however, pushed for actual intervention. The seriousness with which they did so was to some extent a function of battlefield conditions, reaching a height with German successes in summer 1915 on the Eastern Front, but then subsiding with the stalemate in the fall. The end result was that Sweden maintained benevolent neutrality toward Germany early in the war.

This culminated with a secret agreement made by Wallenberg, Sweden's foreign minister, that involved keeping its lighthouses blacked out, mining the sound between it and Denmark to target the British, and banning the British from supplying Russia (Qvarnström 2014: 6–7). Still, there were those who opposed the Activists' agenda and the broader pro-German stance. The Social Democrats in particular warned against an adventurist foreign policy (Kruizinga 2014: 572). When the Hammarskjöld government fell in early 1917, they gained more influence. Nonetheless, throughout the war Sweden traded with both sides, which was in its economic interests, although the Hammarskjöld government maintained a pro-German trade policy. Nevertheless, both Germany and Britain attempted to block trade with their opponents. Despite its secret agreement with Germany, Britain was able to supply Russia across Sweden through an organization called Transito that the government was unable to control and which the Prime Minister called a state within a state (Orvik 1953: 51). The need to keep this line open, however, gave Sweden a bargaining tool to prevent Britain from trying to cut off Swedish trade with Germany completely (Kruizinga 2014: 568). Sweden lost approximately 700 sailors to British mines and German torpedoes (Qvarnström 2014: 6). This loss in trade coupled with reduction in imports created hardships and even food shortages as the war dragged on, and these eventually resulted in domestic protests.

The ability to trade with both sides worked to keep Sweden neutral since that trade, albeit reduced, was useful to both sides. The benevolent neutrality toward Germany, which was a function of domestic and elite attitudes, satisfied German needs. A naval war in the Baltic would also have over-extended Russia and Britain. While the Activists wanted to enter on Germany's side, as the severity of the war became clearer, this had a sobering effect (Kruizinga 2014: 572), and once the Hammarskjöld government fell they had lost their chance.

Norway

Soon after the beginning of the war in December 1914, the King of Sweden called a joint conference of the Nordic neutrals at Malmö. Norway, along with Denmark, came together with Sweden to make common cause for their rights as neutrals. They agreed to consult on all serious decisions regarding trade with the belligerents. On several other occasions in 1915 and 1916 the three – sometimes with Spain, Switzerland, and the Netherlands – tried to induce the U.S. to form some kind of league to defend the rights of neutrals, but these attempts failed, as did their effort to create a more effective Nordic neutral bloc.[3] Nonetheless, when in early 1917 Wilson called on all neutrals to sever relations with Germany the three Nordic neutrals saw this not as a way of maintaining their neutrality, but as a way of drawing them into a coalition that would enter the war. So they rejected it, unlike the Latin American states (Orvik 1953: 106–108). More like the action of a bloc of neutrals was when in that year Norway's two Nordic neighbors came to its aid during the fish crisis with Britain and Germany.

Of the three Nordic neutrals, Norway relied on maritime trade the most. Its merchant marine was the fourth largest in the world at the

---

[3] On these early events and those in 1915–1916, see Orvik (1953: 92–94, 104).

start of the war (Haug 2016: 1). It depended on trade both for import-ing needed resources, like coal, and for exports to maintain its eco-nomic well being. In short, it was economically dependent on trade for its survival, and this dependence made it vulnerable during the war, especially after it became clearer that it would not be a short war (Keilhau 1930: 297). Since most of its trade was with Britain, it was most vulnerable to it, and it was this economic dependence coupled with Norway's size that is key to understanding what occurred.

Almost immediately, the British imposed a blockade on Germany, and this affected all the Nordic states. In November 1914 Britain closed the North Sea by mining it and the English Channel. Neutral ships, if they wanted to enter, had to accept British pilots. Norway and Sweden immediately protested the closing of such a large area as a violation of their rights, but there was little they could do. Orvik (1953: 42) reports that, by the first six months of 1915, 68% of the ships that came into the North Sea were managed by the British.

As the war went on, Britain tightened the blockade and tried to con-trol more of the trade to Germany. In July 1916, the British affirmed that they considered the 1909 Declaration of London null and void. The Declaration contained an agreed-upon list of contraband during war, which was considered part of the prevailing international law gov-erning neutrality and its rights. Britain looked at the trade of neutrals as trade with the enemy, and sought through a bargaining process to restrict it as much as possible. It made individual agreements with Norwegian firms that by 1916 gave the British administrative control over much of their trade (Orvik 1953: 52–53). The focus on Norway was on fish (a food item) and on copper (a potential ingredient in shells). Britain first attempted to control the trading of Norwegian fish to Germany, by buying it up in large quantities on the open market. This drove up prices so much that it had an impact on the domestic market within Norway. Prices, however, were generally going up due to the war. For instance, the catch of Klipp fish, of which three-fifths was sold to Portugal, declined from 17,660 (thousands of kilograms) in 1913 to 15,880 in 1914, to 7,530 in 1915, and a mere 60 in 1916 (Keilhau 1930: 307–308).

In July 1916 formal negotiations began over the Norwegian fish pro-duce, with Britain demanding that all fish not for domestic consump-tion be sold to it or its representatives (Keilhau 1930: 317). The British could exercise leverage because they stated that they would cease all supplies of "stores, coal, or oil" to the fishermen unless a satisfactory arrangement could be concluded (see Keilhau 1930: 317); they were responsible for approximately 85% of these supplies (Orvik 1953: 53).

After considerable back and forth, Norway agreed to prohibit the export of all kinds of fish (except canned fish), and to sell these to British representatives at a price the latter would control, with the exception of 15% of "the actual catch" which could be freely exported (Keilhau 1930: 319). Orvik (1953: 54) sees the agreement as "definitely a violation of the principles of economic neutrality and as such inconsistent with Norway's duties as a neutral."

Although the agreement was kept secret, when the Germans were refused fish purchases, they retaliated in September with a submarine campaign against Norway's trade in the North going to Archangel, Russia. In a little over a week they sank eleven ships, and by the end of October they had sunk an additional thirty-three.[4] Popular indignation reached a fever pitch, typically associated with the onset of war. The government responded by prohibiting German submarines in any of its territorial waters, to which Germany responded with something close to an ultimatum that the prohibition be withdrawn, since it was not a neutral act in that it applied only to Germany and not the Entente as well (Keilhau 1930: 327). Many both within and outside Norway thought war was likely (Keilhau 1930: 330). The French offered Norway ten submarines and the British twelve airplanes (Orvik 1953: 55) that would have brought Norway into military confrontation with Germany if they had been accepted.

It was during this time that certain elements within the British government, namely Eyre Crowe, considered moving away from the official position of not wanting Norway in the war to trying to bring her in either by giving her assurances or by making threats. The Admiralty and the French favored some forceful action, specifically seizing a base on the coast, most likely Kristiansand. Concerns about overextension by Lloyd George, and the preference of Grey to maintain the current policy, led these suggestions to fall by the wayside, and instead the government pushed for the complete cutting off of coal supplies.[5]

Meanwhile, Sweden and Denmark protested Germany's action, and, according to Orvik (1953: 55), this had some effect on Germany, because it feared that if Norway were brought into the war it would drag in the other two Nordic countries. Simultaneously, Denmark interceded with Britain that Norway should be permitted to make some concessions to Germany regarding fish commerce (Keilhau 1930: 330). Thus, by the end of 1916 Norway came perilously close to being drawn

---

[4] These numbers and events can be confirmed in Orvik (1953: 54–55; see also Keilhau 1930: 325–330).
[5] For documentation of these events and further details see Salmon (1997: 153–154).

into the war. What reversed this was that at the end of November the Germans said they would accept an arrangement on fish if Norway would agree to sell 15% of the average export of the previous five years rather than the current actual catch, which they readily accepted, but it took until the end of January 1917 for everything to be worked out (Keihau 1930: 331–333).

As this crisis was coming to an end in late November, a new one over copper exports arose. In early December the government of David Lloyd George, which came to power committed to a knockout blow, now pressured Norway to stop sending copper ore to Germany and instead to sell it to Britain. At first the meaning of this was unclear, so Norway continued to ship ore that had less than 0.5% copper (Orvik 1953: 56–57). Ultimately, the British threatened to completely stop all coal shipments unless the Norwegians cut off the copper trade. Since the Norwegian government was in delicate negotiations with Germany over the fish and the submarine issues, it did not accede to the British demand, and they cut off coal just before Christmas, resulting in rationing and closings of schools and churches. Once the negotiations over fish had been completed, Norway accepted the British demands on copper, given the embargo on coal. In doing this, along with the earlier agreement on fish, it went from being a neutral to being a "neutral ally."[6] In early February, of course, Germany announced unrestricted submarine warfare throughout the world.

The submarine warfare coupled with British minefields took a heavy toll on Norway's merchant marine. Orvik (1953: 71) reports that Norway suffered a total loss of 2,105 lives on ships and 75 million tons of cargo, with 97 ships lost to mines and 701 to submarines, compared with the U.S. loss of 663 lives on ships and 4 million tons of cargo, with 5 ships lost to mines and 16 to submarines. If one only looks at American lives lost before the U.S. declared war there were 194, of which 50 were enlisted crew on belligerent ships. This disparity in the willingness to enter the First World War shows the difference between minor and major states. The strong do what they can, and the weak suffer what they must. Although they suffered less, Denmark and Sweden still suffered more than the U.S.: 16 million tons, with 38 ships lost to mines and 236 ships lost to submarines for Denmark; and 14 million tons with 76 ships lost to mines and 155 lost to submarines for Sweden.[7] Yet none of the three considered entering the war because of the submarine warfare.

[6] For an analysis of this transformation see Riste (1965: 123–126).
[7] These figures are taken from Orvik (1953: 70–71).

Norway did not enter because its decision-makers knew it would only be worse if they did. Instead, it tolerated Britain gradually taking control of its foreign trade during 1915–1916. As the loss of ships increased with German submarine warfare, it accepted in April 1917 British escorts in convoys, and this reduced the loss. The British pressure made it a neutral ally slowly and against its will. Because of Norway's economic dependence on Britain there was little she could do.

Thus, it is not surprising that in early 1917 the Germans drew up war plans – "Kriegsfall Norwegen" (Haug 2016: 12) – based mostly on a contingency of Norway joining Britain or the latter landing on the coast. Regardless of this contingency, Ludendorff sent three cavalry regiments to Northern Schleswig to counter a British attack on Denmark directly (Salmon 1997: 155). This situation was similar to that in which the U.S. would find itself in early 1917. The main difference was that, unless Britain and France intervened militarily, Norway's actions did comparatively minor harm to Germany, so in the end they did not attack. They had more serious opponents with which to deal. At the same time, Norway was able to remain neutral because the Entente Powers thought that if it entered the war it would be more of a burden (because it would have to be defended) than an asset (Keilhau 1930: 330). Throughout the spring of 1917 the Entente and the Germans went back and forth about the question of taking military action toward Norway, which would for the Germans mean also taking action against Denmark (Salmon 1997: 156). In retrospect, it could have easily gone either way. At issue was a potential security trap where each major state did not want the other to get an advantage. The skilled diplomacy of Norway, led by its foreign minister, Nils Claus Ihlen, certainly played a significant role in avoiding war.

By late 1917 Norway seemed to have escaped the jaws of war, when the British and the Americans decided to mine the area of the North Sea from the Orkneys to the Norwegian coast, which they began in March 1918, and were prepared to go into the three-mile limit with or without Norway's approval (Salmon 1997: 159–161). The Norwegians relented, and informed the Germans as diplomatically as they could after the September 1918 trade agreement with them. The mining was not completed until mid October, shortly before the Armistice, so no consequences resulted.

In summary, although Norway was pushed beyond a benevolent neutrality by Britain, it did not enter the war. Her location on the periphery can account for some of this, but three other factors were also critical. First, she was able to satisfy each side – Britain the most because she was most vulnerable to her, but also Germany. Second, if she entered the war, neither side would get much more than it already had. Third, she was weak; if she entered the war she would become a burden to her defender (i.e. Britain) and her entry would be costly to the challenger (i.e. Germany) because it would expand the war fronts to the Baltic. In the end, while her trade pushed her toward the war, her desire to trade with both sides was a vector that enforced her political, if not her economic, neutrality and kept her out of combat.

Norway was pro-British to begin with and ended up being an economic neutral ally of it, although that was not her preference. Sweden was pro-German and anti-Russian but traded with both and was able to toe a more neutral line. Denmark, because of its relative proximity to Germany and strategic location in the Baltic, had to bend to some of Germany's military demands, although it was not pro-German in sentiment the way Sweden was. In addition, her major trading partners were *both* Britain and Germany.

Denmark

Denmark's strategic location in the middle of the Baltic Sea, blocking the entrance from the North Sea, proved to be critical in undermining her political desire to be strictly neutral. Politically, however, there was much that made her inclined toward neutrality. To the West was Britain and the lucrative trade with it; to the East, Sweden and Russia; to the North, Norway; and to the South, Germany. This location beckoned neutrality, given that Germany and Britain were world powers and Sweden a former one. The economic might of these countries, the contiguity and previous war with Germany over Schleswig-Holstein in 1864, and the English destruction of Denmark's navy in 1807 during the Napoleonic wars all underlined her vulnerability and the cross pressures of her previous history.

After the loss of the Second Schleswig-Holstein War of 1864, Denmark had to come to grips with its inferior position to Prussia and Austria. With Prussia's defeat of Austria in 1866 and then France in 1871, it was clear that Denmark was no match for the new united Germany. It was from this point on that neutrality in any future war became a consensus among the ruling elite. Although the two main groups – conservatives and the liberals/left – disagreed on many things, they agreed on neutrality, albeit they had different approaches to it and disagreements on defense spending (Sørensen 2014: 3).

Like Sweden and Norway, Denmark officially declared her neutrality on August 1. On August 6 she received a request from Germany that she mine the Great Belt; she did that, and also mined the nearby Little

Belt and Drogen Channel. Germany saw this as a defense against British submarines in the Baltic. In 1912 Danish leaders had said they would not do this because this would be hostile to Britain (Sørensen 2014: 5). The German demand threw the government into a crisis, but they decided to comply, with the King involved in the decision (Sørensen 2014: 5). Further requests for more mining were refused, however. These could hardly be seen as neutral acts, but Grey was sympathetic to Danish exposure to invasion (Salmon 1997: 126–127), so nothing came of it.

No other event as drastic as this mining compromised Denmark's neutrality for the rest of the war. The key issue was Denmark's desire, indeed need, to trade with both sides. This was hardly a remarkable stance given that the two were Denmark's major trading partners. In addition, as an agricultural society that exported a great deal, Denmark needed certain imports for its economy to survive, including fuel, raw materials, and animal feed among other things (Sørensen 2014: 5). The British recognition of Denmark's vulnerability to invasion made it more tolerant toward Denmark than it was toward Norway, where it exerted its most pressure, if not outright coercion. Ironically, this gave Denmark more bargaining power, since it was a minor state in between two major states – Britain and Germany. A number of issues arose, but they all basically boiled down to one: as the war wore on, Britain wanted a complete blockade of Germany, including guarantees that imports would not be re-exported to Germany, and Germany wanted as much trade as it could get. In the beginning Britain tried to make deals directly with businesses and other organizations involved in commerce. Initially, the Danish government was willing to look the other way, but eventually it got drawn in.

Trying to navigate the conflicting pressures of its two major trading partners was no mean task, as Cohn (1930) reviews in detail. Nonetheless, this balancing act was fairly successful, in part because of the adroitness of Foreign Minister Erik Scavenius, who was able to convince the belligerents that Denmark's neutrality was in the interest of both sides (Sørensen 2014: 17). The Danish would constantly have to give guarantees to Britain about not exporting imports. They would give in on one issue with Britain and then try to compensate Germany on another. For instance, in 1916 when the British wanted fewer exports to Germany and they complied by keeping more at home and sending them more bacon, the Danes responded to the aggrieved Germans by offering more horses, which they got the British to go along with (Salmon 1997: 137). On the whole, Germany was more cooperative about trade, realizing that Denmark needed imports, if it was to export.

Of course the higher prices the Germans were willing to pay kept them in the game, and a number of merchants profited handsomely, earning the nickname of "Goulash Barons" (Kruizinga 2014: 559). All this worked until 1917, when the U.S. entered the war. With this the U.S. banned all exports in October, and Britain banned everything except coal. Denmark then had to turn to its Nordic neighbors and to Germany to meet minimal needs (Sørensen 2014: 7). While it was able economically to endure the last half of 1917, what it really escaped was the danger that it might be drawn into the war by provocative military action of the major belligerents with the 1918 British and American mining of Norwegian territorial waters (Salmon 1997: 161).

Finally, one thing that irritated the Danish about Germany was the conscription of ethnic Danes from Northern Schleswig. Many in Denmark thought that they were being "forced to fight for a cause that was not their own" (Sørensen 2014: 16). After the war Denmark was able to get the return of Northern Schleswig with a League of Nations plebiscite in 1920.

When looking at the three Nordic neutrals certain differences are noteworthy: Norway was very susceptible to British pressure, Denmark worried about a land invasion, and Sweden was in the best position. At the same time, the underlying commonality of their situation was starkly clear – all were unable to maintain their neutral rights and became subject to intense economic warfare. Orvik (1953: 50) puts it succinctly:

The small neutral countries were not given much of a choice as to the maintenance of their neutrality. Squeezed, battered and beaten from both sides, they were compelled to do what was expedient ... but all neutrals did not submit to the same extent. Their actual bargaining power became the decisive factor in their gradual submission to belligerent pressure. The weaker they were, the greater were their humiliations.

Because of its economic dependence on trade, Norway was the weakest, and it was the only one of the three to become a neutral ally. Sweden was the strongest because of its size and because it was the most self-sufficient economically (Orvik 1953: 50). Its policy was closest to its preferences – a pro-German inclination without becoming a benevolent neutral. It was also in the strongest position because Britain could not alienate it too much and continue its covert transit commerce with Russia across Swedish territory. Denmark, because it was so vulnerable to invasion, got some consideration from Britain, but by 1917 it was under an embargo on everything but coal.

In the end, the three Nordic neutrals managed to stay out of the war even though that was in part due to their astute diplomacy. As Salmon

(1997: 118) points out, the belligerent states had more to gain from Scandinavian neutrality than from their entry into the war, especially given that their contribution to the ongoing war would at best be only marginal. Diplomacy worked within this larger structure, but still it was important because it often made the difference by keeping things cool and by allowing balancing acts. This means theoretically that contingency played some role in maintaining the neutrality of these three countries. The leadership of each of the nation-states – neutral and belligerent – managed to keep the series of crises and economic confrontations from escalating to the use of force. This was no mean feat, and during the Norwegian negotiations over fish and copper things almost collapsed. We know empirically that, as crises repeat, it becomes more difficult to manage them and one often comes along that escalates to war (Leng 1983; Vasquez 1993: Ch. 6). This raises the counterfactual question of whether a continuation of the war would have produced a crisis that ended their neutrality.

The 1918 mining of Norway's coast might have been such a crisis. The British were prepared to do this without Norway's consent, and if the battlefield conditions were more hopeful for Germany on the Western Front, it is not unreasonable that Germany may have attacked Norway to prevent the mining or to counter a British move to establish a base on the Norwegian coast. Such a German decision would have likely also seen them taking some military action against Denmark (Salmon 1997: 155). With these two in the war, Sweden could easily have followed because of some complication with Norway or by making some bargain about the future of the Åland Islands (Salmon 1997: 162–168), which by this time were up for grabs with the collapse of Russia. This is not wild speculation, because the neutrality of the three states was always fragile and dependent on the goodwill of Britain and Germany. Nonetheless, the war did not expand and all the factors outlined above held; that they could have held one more time is not unreasonable. We turn now to the Netherlands, which of all the European neutrals could most easily have been involved in the war.

The Netherlands

If the Netherlands had become drawn into the war, it would have been at the start with the invasion of France. The Netherlands was exempt because Germany decided before the war not to invade it as it did Belgium and Luxembourg. In the original Schlieffen Plan, part of the Netherlands would have been invaded. Moltke revised this and decided as early as 1911 to keep it neutral so it could provide a way of trading;

it would "be the windpipe that enables us to breathe" (quoted in Hull 2014: 28). It was expected that as a neutral the Netherlands could provide transit for imports. In addition, Moltke argued that Germany's acceptance of Dutch neutrality would prove a legal obstacle to Britain violating its neutrality through invasion and thus keep Britain away from its rear (Hull 2014: 28).

Moltke's assessment turned out to be correct. It proved difficult for either side to invade once the Netherlands actually served as a way for Germany to gain imports both from the Netherlands and abroad. This was not easy, however, once the British imposed a blockade and then in 1917 when they tightened it. The Dutch leadership, especially that of John Loudon, its Minister of Foreign Affairs, had to negotiate many obstacles. A key factor in the Netherlands' trading with Germany was that their contiguity permitted them to trade directly without British inspection of the land trade. The Germans also used the market to their advantage since its merchants could simply travel to the Netherlands and buy at higher prices the goods they had bought in peacetime. What proved the sticking point was the naval blockade.

The British had their own ideas about trade, and imposed a blockade on Germany in August 1914 that resulted in neutral ships being held and inspected. This had a tremendous impact on Dutch trade, including the Netherlands' overseas trade with its colonial possessions. Kruizinga (2011: 88) maintains that the blockade brought overseas and colonial trade to "a standstill," resulting in food supplies getting low.

As with other neutrals, Britain wanted to make sure that goods imported into the Netherlands, especially from America, were not then re-exported to Germany. The government, because of its allegiance to principles of international law, felt it could not openly cooperate without violating neutrals' right to trade. Equally important was that this would be a violation of the 1868 Rhine Shipping Treaty with Germany that made all transit trade from the North Sea outside the bounds of government intervention (Kruizinga 2011: 85). The failure of the Dutch government to uphold that treaty could lead to military reprisals. Since only firms and not governments trade, an ingenious solution was implemented. A private organization of businessmen – the Netherlands Overseas Trust – was created, with the organization itself certifying that the goods that were imported would not be exported to Germany, accepting a very punitive fine if it were found out otherwise. The Chairman of the NOT – C. J. K. van Aalst – even managed to get some luxury items from the overseas trade exempted so they could be exported to Germany. He and others connected within the NOT highly profited from these arrangements (Kruizinga 2011: 91).

Because this was done by private citizens, the government could deny that any arrangement had been made with the British, although in fact minister Loudon was involved and insisted on absolute secrecy. The arrangement satisfied the British, and it, along with the blockade itself, was fairly effective. The number of ships entering Dutch ports went down from 16,996 in 1913 to 2,184 in 1917 and 1,779 in 1918 (Kruizinga *et al.* 2014: 12). Nevertheless, it was an infringement of the strict the neutrality the government was so fond of enunciating (Hertog 2011). To balance things, the Dutch had to do things for Germany. They engaged in overland trade quite a bit, and this was very lucrative. More significantly, the Dutch permitted transit trade across their territory to Belgium for non-military purposes. Some of these goods – like sand and grit – could also be dual-use (Abbenhuis 2014b: 5). Additionally, some goods from the Indies, like coffee and tobacco, were exempt, and goods that had 25% German labor or material could count as Dutch exports (Kruizinga 2011: 91). When the Dutch gave the Entente a loan, they followed with one of equal value to the Germans (Kruizinga 2011: 97).

All of this worked out fine until 1917. As the stalemate on the Western Front pushed everyone to desperation, the attempt to win by starving the other side was adopted by both sides – by the Germans obviously with the announcement of unrestricted submarine warfare, but also by the British with the attempt to ban all exports to the Central Powers, a position supported by the Americans. The NOT solution was no longer workable, and the commercial sector split into pro-German trade and those favoring the Entente.

The unwillingness of the Dutch government to adhere to a harsher allied policy led the U.S. and the Entente countries in March 1918 to seize all Dutch ships in their harbors and use them for their own shipping, although financial compensation was set. When this was done, the Germans demanded the right to transport military supplies across the country or they would declare war (Abbenhuis 2014b: 6). A compromise was worked out and the threat dropped, most likely because it was already late in the game and the Germans, like the British and French, could not afford another front. Still, in late spring 1918, the French and British did lay out military plans to counter a German invasion. As discussed at the end of the section on Scandinavia, a continuation of the war could very well have led to further contagion that would have brought in the European neutrals. The strategic idea for all this was laid out at the beginning of the war on July 31, 1914 by Churchill, who advocated taking bases in the Netherlands, Denmark, Norway, and Sweden (Salmon 1997: 124).

The economic power of Britain and its control of the seas permitted it to overcome the contiguous advantage that Germany had. This combined economic and naval power allowed it to override the neutrals' rights to trade. The creation of the NOT as a private organization gave the Dutch government the semblance of legal neutrality, when in fact its merchants were cooperating with the British. Nonetheless, there was extensive trade over land, especially with foodstuffs and at prices that at least in the first two years resulted in prosperity for those involved. Trade with Germany was so lucrative that smuggling became endemic, despite the best efforts of the government to limit it (Abbenhuis 2014b: 7). By 1917 food rationing had increased to the point of provoking rioting in Amsterdam (Kruizinga, Moeyes, and Klinkert 2014: 13), and the government then fell in 1918. Individuals even exported potatoes to both sides while there were severe food shortages at home. With the war coming to an end, the Dutch requested that the Entente release supplies of food, to which the latter complied out of fear of revolution in Amsterdam. With this move toward the Entente, the Dutch government did two things that the Entente did not like: it granted the Kaiser and his family asylum, refusing extradition; and it permitted 70,000 German troops in Belgium to cross the Netherlands and return home, albeit they were disarmed (Kruizinga, Moeyes, and Klinkert 2014: 18).

The Netherlands and the Nordic neutrals all got embroiled in the economic warfare associated with war. This can be seen as a form of contagion in that they were brought into the dynamics and hardships of the war even though they were not drawn into actual combat. What explains this economic contagion is of course the economic dependence model that in fact ended the neutrality of the U.S. Although these countries were on the European periphery, they were geographically much closer to both sides than the U.S. was, and they were subject to more direct action in terms of the enforcement of the Entente blockade and German retaliation through submarine warfare.

The principles of international law that had been worked out and affirmed at the beginning of the century did not help them. The war ended their peace and intruded more and more on their everyday life as the belligerents tried to use trade to bring down the other side. Each neutral, depending on its bargaining power, was able to work out some sort of short-term *modus vivendi* that enabled it to trade with both sides, although clearly in each case one side got more than the other did.

Neutrality proved difficult and a constant struggle. In the end the preference of these states not to join was sustained. The underlying structure laid out at the beginning of the chapter certainly helps explain why, with the two key factors being location on the periphery and absence of grievances. The case analyses filled out this aggregate analysis by looking at decision-making and specific interactions. Here it was found that skillful diplomacy played a major role in keeping them out, as foreign ministers, like Ihlen of Norway, Scavenius of Denmark, and Loudon of the Netherlands were able to walk a tightrope or, as Einar Cohn put it, "balancing on a knife's edge" (quoted in Sørensen 2014: 6). Equally important was that the belligerents, for one reason or another, did not want to attack them. The main reasons responsible for this were that the trade at stake was not enough to break the other side, the ongoing war prevented the opening of another front, and bringing in the neutrals would not add much or could even be a defense burden. These factors applied to all the Northern European neutrals, but not to the Netherlands, which might have been invaded except for Moltke's revision of the Schlieffen Plan.

Switzerland

Switzerland was different in certain respects from all the others in that it had a unique combination of factors that made it less susceptible to the trials and tribulations of the Northern Neutrals. Chief among these was that it was land-locked and thus avoided the naval coercion of Britain and Germany, which was no small matter. Even though it was bordered by major-state belligerents, namely France, Italy, Germany, and Austria-Hungary, it was distant from the naval coercion that was part of the economic warfare carried out in the North Sea and Baltic. This provided a layer of immunity the others lacked.

More obvious was that it was protected by a tradition of neutrality established at the Congress of Vienna in 1815. It was a state created as a permanent neutral, with the Congress declaring that her being free of all foreign influence was in the "true interests of Europe" (Albertini 1952, Vol. III: 685). Although Belgium's neutrality was also established by the great powers in 1839 and that of Luxembourg in 1867, neither of these states was seen as having "golden" neutrality like that of Switzerland, in part because their neutrality had not been established by the last major peace settlement[8] and because Switzerland was more truly a buffer state among the great powers of the time. To this might be added the special role played by Swiss banking for the international system. The extent to which these three factors were critical in distinguishing acceptance of the permanent neutrality of Switzerland from

[8] On the psychological importance of the last major war (and presumably its peace settlement), see Jervis (1976: 281–282).

that of Belgium and Luxembourg, *ex ante*, needs further research. Suffice it to say that Swiss neutrality has stood the test of time, including the onslaught of the Second World War.[9]

In addition to these external factors, there were strong internal factors that preserved Swiss neutrality. This had to do with the diverse nationality and language composition of the state – the Francophone and Swiss German, along with the Italian and Romansh. Their physical concentration in different regions and the strong federal structure of the state made it politically difficult if not impossible for the central government to favor one side over the other. Nonetheless, 75% of the populace were Swiss-German speakers, and some observers, such as a British attaché in 1909, wondered whether this segment of the population would favor Germany in a war (Albertini 1952, Vol. III: 685). Nevertheless, one of the purposes of the federal structure was to make individual cantons that had previously been subject to the influence of neighboring states more insulated from these external pulls. Sometimes these influences could be considerable even after 1815. The most extreme example was Neuchâtel, which was within the federation while simultaneously a principality of the King of Prussia (Abbenhuis 2014a: 48).

The central state was careful not to deviate from a strict neutrality, even though parts of its constituents might have more affinity for one side over the other. This was illustrated by the Oberstenaffäre in 1916, when a Francophone newspaper revealed that two colonels had been removed from their intelligence duties for giving German and Austro-Hungarian military attachés information about French and Russian troop movements (Kruizinga 2014: 569). This confirmed the suspicions of many about the pro-German bias within the military. An uproar occurred among the Francophone speakers, indicating the delicate veneer that covered more deep-seated ethnic affinities that the policy of neutrality kept in control. In the end permanent neutrality was not only part of the Global Governance of the time, but also part of the constitution of the state of Switzerland. Both of these factors prevented others from invading it and helped it avoid temptations to join the war.

Other factors that can account for Switzerland's success in preserving its neutrality according to the Swiss themselves were its system of military defense and its mountainous terrain. Certainly, mountains are more of a barrier than plains, but Geneva could have been occupied by

---

[9] An interesting historical note is that Hitler did consider at one point invading Switzerland and breaking this tradition in the so-called Operation Tannenbaum, but decided to abandon that idea.

the French if they had wanted to devote the resources to it. Other neutrals like the Netherlands and Denmark thought a strong army would deter, but their forces were no stronger than the Belgian forces, so it is unclear how accurate this popular perception is. Instead, the unwillingness of belligerents to devote resources seems key.

The European neutrals that endured the entire war without being dragged in are quite different from the neutrals in Latin America. These are defined as neutral if they did not declare war or sever relations with any of the belligerents.

Latin American Neutrals

The major Latin American neutrals are listed at the bottom of Table 6.1. There are an additional five minor neutrals that are rarely discussed in the literature that will also be briefly analyzed after examining the major neutrals. Among the major Latin American neutrals the main aberrant case is Mexico since it is contiguous with the U.S. and yet did not follow its lead. It is an interesting case because of the role of the Zimmermann Telegram. Some of the Germans thought that Mexico could be "picked off." They thought that, if the U.S. declared war, the ongoing war would provide an opportunity for Mexico to regain lost territory from the Mexican War, if they were to provide the right incentives. The ongoing rivalry with the U.S., its continued infringement of Mexican territory by General Pershing, and the humiliation of the Veracruz attack were all factors Germany hoped would work for intervention. The weakness of the Carranza regime and its land contiguity to the U.S. made an alliance with Germany too risky, to say the least. In addition, Mexico's major European trading partner was Britain. All of this made Carranza hesitant to even consider the offer presented in the Zimmermann Telegram. Nonetheless, the logic behind the offer was consistent with how other states, like Bulgaria, were persuaded to enter on the side of the Central Powers.

When all is said and done, Mexico did not follow the U.S. lead and valence balance. The reason for this had to do with the factors that made Carranza basically anti-Wilson and resistant to U.S. hegemony. The U.S. had acquiesced to recognizing Carranza only because it feared, as Lansing put it, that Germany was seeking to stir up turmoil in Mexico that would prevent any one faction from becoming dominant (Tuchman 1958: 82). Carranza did not like U.S. troops staying in Northern Mexico and demanded their withdrawal, at one point even attacking a scouting party that ignored his warning not to move in any direction except North (Tuchman 1958: 89). All of this instability and the U.S. attempting to interfere and control domestic politics within Mexico led to a rivalry during the years 1911–1920 as Diehl and Goertz (2012: 105) point out. If internal instability and the risk of U.S. invasion kept Carranza from siding with Germany, the bilateral hostility as well as the personal hostility between the two leaders kept Carranza from valence balancing as well. Mexican resistance to hegemony explains why the structure of Imperialism/Hegemony did not make the war diffuse despite the contiguity.[10]

The two major cases of Latin American neutrality are those furthest from the U.S. – on the Southern Cone. Argentina, like most of the other Latin American states, declared its neutrality at the outbreak of the war. When Hipólito Yrigoyen, from the center-left opposition party, took over as President in 1916 from the conservative Victorino de la Plaza, he maintained that policy.

As the U.S. moved away from neutrality with the announcement of unrestricted submarine war in February 1917 and the call for all neutrals to sever relations with Germany, the situation for all Latin American states, including Argentina and Chile, changed. The U.S. declaration of war on April 6, 1917 led a number of states to declare war and/or sever relations. The pressure on Argentina to do the same was greatly increased by two events. The first was the sinking of three Argentine ships and the other was the Luxburg note, which the U.S. deliberately released in September 1917 in an effort to break Argentine neutrality (Tato 2014: 1). In a secret telegram, Luxburg, the German Ambassador in Argentina, referred to the Argentine Foreign Minister as "a notorious ass and anglophile." He then went on to recommend the sinking of Argentinian ships without leaving a trace (Dehne 2011: 70). Despite these pressures, Yrigoyen resisted and maintained neutrality throughout the war.

There were in fact certain factors pushing for involvement. Besides the U.S. desires, Britain had long maintained a propaganda campaign to gain support, and French media were extremely active throughout Latin America. These efforts were countered by German efforts. The attempts by the two sides reinforced the pre-existing domestic leanings of different groups – the *aliadófilos*, who supported the Entente, and the *germanófilos*, who supported the Central Powers (Rinke and Kriegesmann 2014: 7). These leanings were further accentuated by ancestral descent and economic interests due to trade. The British

---

[10] Of course one must be wary that such an explanation is not an ad hoc explanation that simply sees the absence of contagion as "resistance to the structure." In this instance, the turmoil and anti-Americanism in Mexico were real and obvious. Also the Diehl and Goertz measure is an independent indicator.

blacklist of (ethnically) German-owned businesses aggravated these tendencies. However, this blacklist irritated a number of Argentines, including Yrigoyen, who came to power in part on an anti-British platform (Kruizinga 2014: 573). His administration would periodically intervene to get specific companies off the list (see, for example, Dehne 2011: 73–74).

Before the war Argentina had traded with both sides. The British blockade hurt the trade with Germany, and Germany tried to break that blockade in the South Atlantic. Germany's submarine campaign against neutrals affected Argentina, and Germany tried to assuage the Argentinians by providing financial restitution (Dehne 2011: 70). Initially the war disrupted Argentina's economy, and the U.S. even sought to expand its economic influence as belligerent countries had to retrench. As the war went on, however, trade with the Entente, mostly for foodstuffs, became quite lucrative. Argentina even extended credit to the cash-starved British in late 1917 at the U.S.'s urging (Dehne 2011: 78–79). All the while the British and then the U.S. pressured Yrigoyen to end neutrality, while the Germans pushed to maintain neutrality.

In light of domestic and internal pressures to enter, why did Argentina remain neutral? The simple answer is that Hipólito Yrigoyen was a strong leader and would not brook entering the war. The deeper answer has to do with his attitude toward Britain and the U.S. and to the situation in which Argentina found itself in 1917. Yrigoyen was opposed to entering the war on the side of Britain or even valence balancing to satisfy the U.S. because he resented both countries and their attempt to dominate Argentina with their respective hegemonic influences. Cain and Hopkins (2002) have argued that Argentina was economically controlled by Britain prior to the war to such an extent that it was an example of "informal imperialism" (cited in Dehne 2011: 68). Likewise, Yrigoyen resented U.S. attempts at hegemonic control. Whereas the Brazilians had spoken of continental solidarity and Pan-Americanism when they entered the war, Yrigoyen was an advocate of Pan-Hispanism – a movement that emphasized Spanish cultural heritage that was explicitly meant to oppose U.S. "Pan-Americanism" (Tato 2014: 1). This general stance, not unexpected from someone who was supported by the center-left, seems to have been an important factor in Yrigoyen's attitude toward both sides. He saw neutrality as a sign of independence and resistance.

Reinforcing this ideational stance was the material interest of Argentina. It was in a good position – economically growing from trade – and this would not be changed by remaining neutal. In fact, if it were an ally it might be more difficult to engage in the hard bargaining that it was doing. Also, a formal declaration of war would make Germany less restrained in sinking Argentinian ships, and Germany would certainly give up any idea of financial restitution. Domestically, support from the *germanófilos* would also be lost. These conditions pushed Yrigoyen in the same direction and made his ultimate decision unsurprising. Nonetheless, there was considerable pressure, including the economic influence of British trade and considerable investment, for example their ownership of the railroads, working in the other direction. The agency of Yrigoyen as a strong leader thus was crucial. To this must be added the great distance between Argentina and the U.S., not to mention Argentina's distance from the war fronts. Distance, and especially distance across the ocean, had an inoculating effect on the spread of the war. It must be kept in mind that, with the exception of Brazil, Latin American valence balancing did not result in any combat role.

Chile's neutrality was determined by three reinforcing factors – its geographic position, its internal split, and its hostility toward the U.S. Geographically, Chile faced the Pacific and not the Atlantic, so it was further removed from the war than Argentina (Martin 1925: 264). This was especially true after the British pushed the German Navy out of the South Atlantic.

Nonetheless, Chile's role in the First World War was important because it was a main supplier of nitrates, an essential ingredient in explosives for all sides. The German blockade of Chilean trade with Britain was broken at the Battle of the Falkland Islands in December 1914. From 1915 to the end of the war Chile, which had a lively nitrate trade with Germany, saw that trade reduced to zero. The U.S. took up much of the nitrate trade that had gone to Germany (see the table in Bastias Saavedra 2014: 2–3). Germany was able to overcome this by the development of synthetic nitrates. In February 1917, when Germany announced its unrestricted submarine warfare, Chile officially protested, but it did not follow suit with other Latin American states and sever relations. It was little affected by the German campaign.

It also did not valence balance in part because of deep splits within the polity, which were reinforced by propaganda from each of the belligerent sides. The Church and the military leaned toward Germany, while liberals and others supported France and Britain. It should also be noted that it had little to gain from entering the war compared with the domestic costs. Additionally, although Chile had a lower number of European immigrants compared to nearby Latin American states,

German immigrants were organized into a *Volksverband* beginning in 1916, as in Argentina and Paraguay (Rinke 2015). The domestic split was such that at the beginning of the war sentiment favored Germany, but as the war went on it became more pro-Entente.

Also of importance was that a U.S. campaign against German economic influence in Chile backfired and led to a "massive wave of anti-Americanism" (Kruizinga 2014: 572), which kept Chile from valence balancing. Chile had long regarded the U.S. with hostility because it had sided with Bolivia and Peru – its enemies in the War of the Pacific (Martin 1925: 342). This hostility was reinforced when Bolivia and Peru followed the U.S. lead and valence balanced (Kruizinga 2014: 572). The anti-Americanism coupled with the domestic split and distance from the U.S. and the previous War of the Pacific accounts for Chile not severing relations.

Lastly, an important factor that kept Argentina and Chile out of the war from the perspective of the belligerents was the relative weakness of these minor states. They could not add much. Like the European neutrals that were much closer, they were not really needed by each side militarily. The combination of distance and negative affinity toward the U.S. explains their lack of valence balancing. The first factor is most likely associated with less hegemonic control and the second with resistance to that hierarchical relationship.

There were five additional neutrals – the Dominican Republic, Columbia, El Salvador, Venezuela, and Paraguay.[11] The first is the most aberrant case in terms of contiguity, but easily explained. Anti-Americanism played a role in the next two, and the last two had factors associated just with them, but consistent with what one would expect about contagion.

The Dominican Republic is an aberrant case, because it was close to the U.S. and surrounded by states that followed the U.S. lead, yet it did not sever relations. It did not because it had been occupied and administered by the U.S. since May 1916 and in effect had no government. The intervention can be traced back to 1905 with the U.S. takeover of Dominican customs to pay debtors. With the 1912 assassination of its President, the U.S. sent 750 Marines. In 1914 the U.S. forced the resignation of the new president, and the next year the U.S. demanded the disarmament of its military, which it refused. This led to a full takeover in 1916. One of the reasons given was concern over Dominican

---

[11] Rinke and Kriegesmann (2015) is one of the few texts that mentions them, and then only in Table 1, with no discussion.

finances, but there was also a worry that the Germans might try to exploit the situation and use the Dominican Republic as a base.[12]

The Dominican Republic then was not neutral; it was under the complete military and administrative control of the U.S. The Correlates of War project recognizes this, and has it leaving the system on November 29, 1916 and not returning until September 29, 1924.

El Salvador was the only Central American state to remain neutral, and this seems to go against the general pattern of those closest to the U.S. following its lead. Martin (1925: 510) argues that it had "greater immunity" because it faced the Pacific, a point he also made with regard to Chile. Of more importance, however, was that the government had a legal dispute with Nicaragua and the U.S. that it took to the Central American Court of Justice, which decided in favor of El Salvador in March 1917. With the backing of the U.S., Nicaragua ignored the finding. This generated great resentment within El Salvador toward the U.S. (Martin 1925: 511). It is not surprising, then, that El Salvador would resist following the U.S.'s lead. Hegemony involves both subordination and resistance. Here we see resistance due to hostility to the actions taken by the U.S. It was the hierarchy of hegemony that was stultified by El Salvador that can explain its failure to valence balance. Later in the year, though, El Salvador softened this decision by declaring a benevolent neutrality toward the Entente and its allies, including Italy and the U.S. When asked by the U.S. minister what this meant, El Salvador replied that their ships had unrestricted access to El Salvador's harbors and that as "a member of the Pan-American family" it could not regard the U.S. in the same way as it did other belligerents (Martin 1925: 512–513). It did not sever relations, however.

The reaction of Colombia is even more comprehensible, since the U.S. tore part of its territory away to create the new state of Panama in 1903. The U.S. had negotiated a treaty for the construction of a canal across the Panamanian isthmus in return for financial compensation. While the U.S. ratified the treaty, the Colombian Senate refused. At this point Theodore Roosevelt supported a rebellion within Panama to create a new country. The U.S. actively helped the rebels by controlling the railway to prevent Colombian troops from entering. It then sent a warship to solidify the victory and Panama's independence. On November 6, three days after the rebellion began, the U.S. recognized

---

[12] The Department of State Archive is the source for all this information, see https://2001-2009.state.gov/r/pa/ho/time/wwi/108649.htm.

the new Republic of Panama. Later that month the two states signed a treaty giving the U.S. ownership of a new Panama Canal Zone. By 1914 the U.S. had agreed to a treaty providing Colombia with some compensation. At the time of U.S. entry into the First World War this treaty had still not been ratified by the U.S. Congress, and this was a source of resentment that made Colombia unsympathetic to the U.S. (see Martin 1925: 428), even though there was sentiment in favor of France and Britain. Colombia's grievances against the U.S. were much more extensive and greater than those of El Salvador. Its position was closer to that of Mexico. It saw itself as a victim of U.S. hegemony, and when it was in a position to show resistance by not valence balancing it did. Later accusations by the Hearst Press and others (which Colombia vehemently denied) that Colombia had a secret alliance with Germany and was considering providing a submarine base further aggravated the relationship with the U.S. (Martin 1925: 429).

Venezuela's story was different. Its President – General Juan Vicente Gómez, who had his term extended to seven years with no limitation on re-election – was pro-German, even before the outbreak of the war. Although there was widespread pro-French sentiment among the educated elite, the Germans had considerable economic investments – including coffee, railways, and management of commerce in the seaports. General Gómez followed a strict form of neutrality primarily as a way of supporting Germany. This stance, however, was not anti-American as was that of Columbia or El Salvador. Venezuela did not have any grievances against the U.S. (Martin 1925: 462). In fact, the U.S. had often aided Venezuela, most dramatically in its 1895 border dispute with Britain when President Cleveland stepped in, and again in 1902 when Theodore Roosevelt intervened against Germany, which was threatening to bombard the coast (on these disputes see Martin 1925: 463–464). When General Gómez came to power in 1909 this was past history, and his preferences guided foreign policy.

His pro-German sentiments, however, could not take him beyond neutrality. Venezuela was vulnerable to British and even U.S. naval action, so it would have been foolhardy to enter the war. As it was, trade with Germany was cut off by the Entente, and they and the U.S. used their naval superiority periodically in shows of strength to insure that Germany was being kept out.[13] Despite this vulnerability, he would not valence balance, and this was not seen as surprising by those in the know (Martin 1925: 462).

---

[13] See http://histclo.com/essay/war/ww1/cou/r-la/sa/w1c-ven.html.

Paraguay is a land-locked country and that played a role in its neutrality, although other land-locked countries, such as Bolivia, severed relations with Germany. The land-locked nature of these countries would lead to the expectation that they would not enter, and Martin (1925: 480) sees it as a rebuttable assumption that neutrality was what was expected. This is certainly the case, and what needs to be explained is why Bolivia entered despite its location. Here the answer seems to be that it was sympathetic to the U.S., in part because of U.S. support of it against Chile in the War of the Pacific. Ultimately, contingency seems to have played a crucial role. In March 1916 the *Tubantia* was sunk by a German submarine, and a passenger on it was the Bolivian ambassador to Berlin. Bolivia had earlier agreed with the U.S. that such warfare was a violation of neutral rights. It now severed relations with Germany (Martin 1925: 479–480).

Paraguay was not in a similar situation. Its land-locked nature made it much more immune to the war. Nor did it have a history with the U.S., like Bolivia had, that made it particularly obliged to that country. Of great relevance, however, was that Paraguay had suffered great losses in the López War (1864–1870), with most of its male population killed (Sarkees and Wayman 2010: 93). A good deal of its territory was then absorbed by its neighbors. The aftereffects of the war not only made it weak but led to a period of instability that had recently in 1911–1912 resulted in a full-blown civil war (Sarkees and Wayman 2010: 390–391). Given its physical position and its internal problems and weakness, it was too preoccupied with its own affairs to get drawn into the war.

Miscellaneous

Ethiopia

Abyssinia, or Ethiopia as it is known outside of Europe, is rarely listed as a neutral, in part because, like Bhutan, it is in an area where countries were not treated as real members of the international sovereign-state system, but as potential targets of imperial expansion.[14] Until recently Ethiopia was not given much attention. Martin Plaut's work

---

[14] Another miscellaneous neutral was Persia. It declared neutrality on November 1, 1914, but even at that time Russian troops were occupying the northern part of the country. Russian, British, and Ottoman troops violated its sovereignty and fought each other on its territory without Persia formally declaring war, in part because of internal conflict. Since the country, if not the government, played an integral part in the war, it is not treated as a neutral. For more on Persia see https://encyclopedia.1914-1918-online.net/article/persiairan.

has changed that.[15] His work has shown that German agents attempted to get Prince Lij Iyasu, heir to the throne and de facto leader of Ethiopia, to enter the war by making promises for territorial conquest of adjacent areas. Several attempts were made, but they did not come to fruition. The first team was sent in January 1915 and led by Leo Frobenius, a personal friend of Kaiser Wilhelm. He and his team were captured in February in Italian Eritrea. Other attempts followed in June, by which time Italy had entered the war. Eventually word got to the German envoy in Addis Ababa, who raised the proposition directly with Prince Lij Iyasu.

The scheme was to offer the Prince all the territory he could conquer at the expense of the British, French, and Italians as part of a larger effort of an Ottoman attack directly on the Suez Canal. The Ottomans, with German support, had attacked the Suez Canal in February 1915 only to be pushed back; presumably this attack would be followed by others. Under the new scheme the Ethiopians would aid this effort by attacking Eritrea and at the Red Sea – conquering whatever French and Italian territory they could (a proposition to which the Ottomans gave their official endorsement). This attack, coupled with an insurrection in Sudan, would aid a direct attack on the Canal by the Ottomans. The overall German strategy was at minimum to divert British troops from the main front and more grandiosely take the Canal.

Theoretically the approach to Ethiopia was a clear attempt by a belligerent to bring in a neutral party in return for local territorial gain. Germany was providing an opportunity to the Prince to satisfy some of Ethiopia's territorial ambitions. The opportunity–territorial grievance model of contagion clearly applies. What must be kept in mind, however, is that, unlike later attempts to bring in Bulgaria and Romania, here the initiative was primarily with Germany. Actors within Ethiopia were not seeking to take advantage of the war; rather it was the belligerent in the war which was seeking to expand the war to aid its battlefield prospects. In many ways the German attempt to lure Ethiopia into the war was similar, but on a less grand scale, to Zimmermann's telegram to Mexico two years later.

The fact that Ethiopia remained neutral is easily explained in that it fits the pattern delineated in Table 6.1 of other neutrals. It was very

---

[15] My thanks to Steven Holt for bringing Martin Plaut's work to my attention. The discussion of events herein is derived from a BBC news report (www.bbc.com/news/world-37428682) and from Plaut's lecture (https://martinplaut.wordpress.com/2016/10/03/first-world-war-intrigues-in-the-horn-of-africa/), but the theoretical analysis is my own.

much on the periphery. It had no alliances, and no rivalry with any of the belligerents, nor was it contiguous to any of them. Although it was not proximate to the Suez Canal, it was close to the Red Sea and adjacent to British Sudan so that the Germans thought the Ethiopians could have a military impact. In addition, they had several territorial claims against Britain, as can be seen from the table, and an earlier rivalry with Egypt, now under British control. Lastly, Ethiopia had defeated an Italian invasion in 1896 at Adowa. These factors provided a hostility that Germany could exploit. In the end, the Prince explored the possibility by making contact with anticolonial Muslims in Somaliland, including Sayyid, Muhammad Abd Allah al-Hassan, the so-called "Mad Mullah." With this, domestic opposition increased, eventually resulting in his removal (Marcus 1994: 114–115). The domestic opposition, although not directed by the Entente Powers, had their support.

Conclusion

The analysis in Table 6.1 demonstrates that the absence of two or more of the factors that brought about the spread of the war in other countries was most likely at work in keeping these countries neutral. Distance from the battlefield and the absence of rivalry were the two main ingredients. All the neutrals, with the exception of Switzerland and the Netherlands, were on the periphery. Most, with the exception of Spain, did not have alliance ties with any of the belligerents. In addition, most, with the exception of Spain, did not have territorial claims, and if they did, the claims were typically of a colonial nature. In fact, most lacked the kind of territorial rivalries that made the war an opportunity to acquire the new lands, with Argentina's claim to the Falklands and Spain's claim to Gibraltar being the exceptions. With the Latin American states the failure to valence balance also seems to be accounted for by distance from the U.S. coupled with resistance to American hegemony, with the former probably associated with the limit of reach in that two of the three main neutrals were in the Southern Cone, as far from the U.S. as physically possible. All in all, although there were few neutrals, they provide added support for the hypothesis that the presence of contagion factors is associated with the spread of the war and the absence of two or more such factors is associated with neutrality.

The case analyses provide some depth to aggregate analyses. Here it was found that, even though many states were temporarily neutral, typically the opportunity of the ongoing war to satisfy territorial grievances brought them in during the second and third waves. The U.S. was able to stay out the longest, but the economic dependence of the Entente on it and its major-state status brought it in by 1917. The greatest threat of contagion for many European neutrals – the Nordic countries and the Netherlands – was due to economic dependence. All were firmly committed to neutrality and were able to maintain this legal position, but were drawn in by the economic warfare of the major states. Despite their resistance, they kept being drawn in by one demand or another, and had difficulty balancing the conflicting demands. In the end their weakness protected them from being attacked, as it did the main Latin American neutrals, namely Argentina and Chile.

7   How Contagion Actually Worked

This chapter will examine what the dyads that joined the First World War have in common as a way of determining some of the underlying dynamics of war contagion on the basis of how it actually occurred in 1914–1918. The first part of the chapter will begin by delineating the main contagion processes that brought each of the dyads into the war. These will be categorized into those that were primarily responsible for bringing the dyad into the war and those that played a secondary role. If some of these were necessary conditions and others sufficient, that will be indicated. Next, other key factors at work will be delineated, as will any new insights that can be derived from the analysis. Lastly, these new insights provided by the dyad for understanding contagion will be used when warranted to formulate new supplemental hypotheses to the main hypotheses presented in Chapter 1.

The second part of the chapter will present some general conclusions about contagion that can be derived *ex post* from the case research. This section will review what the cases have in common with each other and what separates them from those which remained neutral. This will be done with an eye to separating what is generalizable about contagion in the First World War from what is more idiographic. This section will focus on five general lessons of the First World War that can be derived from this study: the role of alliances, why deterrence failed, the role of opportunity, the underlying causal mechanisms of contagion, and imperialism/hegemony as a diffusion structure.

The last part of the chapter will return to the question of hypotheses on contagion. It will provide an outline of future tasks and research in light of the hypotheses presented in this analysis. It will discuss briefly how the derived hypotheses can be tested deductively on other instances of war contagion that occurred in the past or may occur in the future, including a brief note on the current policy relevance of the First World War for the present.

We can start with the question of contagion – what are its main theoretical aspects that need to be understood so that it can be conceptualized better? An important theoretical assumption about the concept of contagion is that the causes that start a war and bring the initial belligerents into the war are different from the causes that make war spread. Bremer (1995) made that point some time ago. The contagion of war is seen as an identifiable and separate phenomenon from the initial onset of war. Why war spreads is seen as a theoretically different question from that of what causes war. It is assumed that the two questions, although related, will have different answers. The idea of contagion is singular in the study of war in that it maintains that the ongoing war – its dynamics and other characteristics – spreads the war to other parties that initially were not part of the war and typically chose not to be, but were drawn into it after it had started. The processes which drew these parties into the war have been the subject of this book.

War contagion is a fairly rare phenomenon. Richardson (1960: 247–248, 258–259) found that multiparty wars, especially those involving more than three states, are comparatively rare. Sabrosky (1985: 151, 181) showed that during the period 1816–1965 only ten of fifty wars spread beyond their original belligerents. Vasquez and Valeriano (2010: 296) identified twenty-eight of seventy-nine wars during the period 1816–1997 as multiparty wars, and of these only twelve had more than four participants. Contagion is unusual theoretically in that the factors that initially brought the parties to war now bring in new members (joiners) because of something about the ongoing war itself. Something causes war (initially), and now war spreads because of the consequences of its own dynamics. This is not often anticipated.

As war spreads, it wreaks more havoc and has a larger impact. An epidemic is associated with the rapid spread of a disease, and this spread makes it difficult to control. The same is true of war contagion. The contagion of war is a social phenomenon that is complex and is not easily understood, let alone managed from a policy point of view. Part of the reason for this is that the causal mechanisms are not well understood, just as in medieval times the causes of epidemics and the role of infection were not understood. This chapter attempts to make war contagion more understandable by dissecting its various components and how they interact.

What Brought the Dyads into the War?

This section analyzes why each dyad entered the war, utilizing the previous case studies to delineate what role the various contagion processes played and their relative potency with an eye to what can be learned about contagion in general. Where new things have been learned that go beyond the initial hypotheses in Chapter 1, these are presented as supplemental hypotheses. Table 7.1 lists the major factors that brought the first wave of states into the war. These are categorized by indicating the primary contagion process in the case, followed by the secondary process and then other factors. New insights about contagion that can be derived from the case that might be generalizable are listed last.

The First Wave

Austria-Hungary–Serbia The local war between Austria-Hungary and Serbia was produced by the long-term territorial rivalry between the two, and in that way it was a typical war between neighbors over territory. Yet, it had several differences that from the start made it likely to expand. The first difference was that this was now the fourth war that had started in this region, beginning with the Italian war on Tripolitania and Cyrenaica that created an opportunity for the Balkan League (Montenegro, Serbia, Greece, and Bulgaria) to attack the Ottoman Empire while it was busy on another front. This First Balkan War was followed by a Second Balkan War, which resulted directly from the first one. These three wars were not prevented by the major states, although they intervened diplomatically after the wars started to help end or limit them. The Austria-Hungary–Serbia war could have been a Third Balkan War, or at least that was Austria-Hungary's hope. The outcome of the two Balkan Wars in terms of the great increase in Serbia's territory and population made it more of a threat. This, coupled with the assassination of the heir apparent, reflected a new rabid nationalism from the perspective of Austro-Hungarian decision-makers. The previous wars and their outcomes made Austro-Hungarian decision leaders willing to take a harder line and, coupled with the opportunity provided by the assassination, pushed them toward a decision to attack.

Previous wars helped set the stage for the current local war, and in this sense it was a product of contagion, but not from an ongoing war as much as from a repeated use of the practice of war by several parties in a short period of time. During 1911–1914 war was a practice that states resorted to more often. This was in part through emulation or a demonstration effect across wars, but it was also because the outcome of previous wars changed the power distribution of states and made them more vulnerable to attack. Lastly, the reaction of the major states to the previous wars made it clear that the former Concert of Europe and the prevailing political order was limited in what it could do to prevent these territorial wars at the onset. Austria-Hungary, in particular,

Table 7.1. *Categorization of contagion factors by dyad: First wave, 1914*

Dyad	Primary process	Secondary process	Other factors	New insights
The First Wave: 1914				
AUH–SER local war	Territorial rivalry		Third-party support sought to deter war Blank check	
GMY–RUS	Alliances and Failure of coercive game		Contiguity–time pressure	1. Security trap 2. Military–civilian split 3. Competing scripts 4. Previous learning
GMY–FRN	Alliances and Failure of coercive game	Territorial rivalry	Tight alliance Colonial competition	
GMY–BEL	Contiguity			1. Alliance pattern makes Contiguity a factor 2. Anomaly for bargaining theory of war
UKG–GMY	Alliances and Failure of coercive game		Strong leader Government split Colonial competition Moral concerns	
AUH–RUS	Alliances and Failure of coercive game		Third parties	Lack of bargaining
JPN–GMY	Opportunity – necessary condition (Capability and political order) Territorial issue[a] – sufficient condition	Contiguity	Strong leader	
JPN–AUH	Contiguity Opportunity – necessary condition (Capability and political order) Territorial rivalry – sufficient condition	Alliance Alliances		
RUS–OTM			Strong leader Third parties Colonial competition	Major-state intervention

[a] I use the term territorial issue to describe what was going on between Japan and Germany and not rivalry because they did not have a pre-war rivalry in the technical sense of the concept as measured by Thompson (2001) or Diehl and Goertz (2000).

relied on the dastardly patricide to limit the willingness of the major states, especially the Tsar, to aid Serbia, but to no avail. Contagion across wars and the decline of the prevailing political order that restrained minor states from using war as an instrument for change made this local war different from the typical dyadic war between neighbors.

Another difference between the local war and other dyadic wars that helped it spread had to do with the presence of third parties from the very beginning. Both sides appealed to allies to support them, thus setting the table for a possible expansion if the crisis escalated. Both sides also wanted these third parties to play a coercive game of intimidation that would help them get what they sought. The principals differed in their particular goals in playing the coercive game, but all put their hopes for victory in the playing of that game. Berchtold and Franz Josef of Austria-Hungary wanted their ally to be committed to them and to coerce Russia into backing down (the so-called "blank check"). They thus wanted the coercive game to deter a general war, knowing they could win the local one. Serbia, conversely, wanted Russia to prevent Austria-Hungary from attacking in the first place and thus sought to deter the local war. Neither got what it wanted, and deterrence failed on both counts.

Two new supplemental hypotheses can be derived from this dyad about contagion that can be applied and tested on other cases:

S1. Separate wars that cluster in time and space are apt to result from demonstration effects, making the practice of war more likely across states. This in turn weakens any norm within the prevailing political order that constrains the use of war as a unilateral instrument to bring about change, especially territorial change.

S2. Dyadic wars escalating from a multiparty crisis are more apt to spread and enlarge.

Germany–Russia   Germany–Russia was the keystone dyad that spread the local war to a general war. Two contagion processes were essential in this – alliances and playing the coercive game. The playing of the coercive game and its failure had more immediate causal impact. It led both sides to go to war, and they went to war to protect their allies for whom they were playing the game. In the process they brought their other allies in with them. These processes have been explained previously in the analysis and have been well understood. The analysis here does place more weight on the role learning and repeated crises played as a factor for why the July 1914 crisis escalated whereas others, like that of 1908, did not.

Several new insights result from the case study. Of central importance is the introduction of the concept of a "security trap" to explain why the mobilization crisis occurred and led to war when both the Kaiser and the Tsar, it was believed, were sincerely trying to avoid war. The security trap led both the Kaiser and the Tsar, as well as their advisors, to perceive an extreme threat due to the fear of imminent attack. This insecurity overwhelmed any substantive grievances that each side might have had in going to war and was the main factor in their decision-making. The security trap resulted in the power politics script displacing the Concert of Europe script that both were following with the Halt-in-Belgrade plan.[1]

The security trap carried such weight because of the military plans that each side had adopted, especially the Moltke–Schlieffen Plan. Moltke was the most anxious about Russian pre-mobilization, and this was further aggravated by the Kaiser's willingness to abandon the plan in light of Grey's August 1 proposal. Generally, the security trap more affected the military in each side and resulted in a military–civilian split. The security trap worked its way from the military to the civilian leaders, making them abandon the more accommodative script of pursuing a peace plan. One of the things made clearer about such splits in studying this dyad is that they resulted primarily from the role of each actor. The military took the position it did because it is mainly responsible for the defense of the country and for winning the war, if it comes about. It cared less about the diplomatic solutions the Kaiser and the Tsar were trying to negotiate, since these did not directly affect the military's bureaucratic responsibility. This split the decision-making elite, and the cause of the split underlines the limitations of treating either side as a unitary rational actor.

Lastly, a reason for the rise of the security trap and its potency had to do with the time pressure created by the contiguity of the two sides and the proximity of their powerful armies. Mobilization was an important factor because of existing military plans and the preference of offensive doctrines at the time, but the key factor was that contiguity meant that an army with an advantage could overrun the other side and conquer territory.

The security trap helps explain why this dyad went to war in the absence of any explicit territorial claims. There was a rivalry, as Thompson points out, going back to 1740–1807 and again during the period 1890–1945. After the First World War had started, territory was

---

[1] For an exceptional analysis of how the mobilization crisis interacted with and affected the peace proposals see Otte (2014: 406–414, 419, 437–438, 445–446).

a key factor, but during the pre-First World War phase the cause of conflict was the threat that the capability of each posed to the other due to the proximity of their armed forces. This proximity in the context of playing the coercive game made both sides primed for a security trap. Rivalries between major states that are contiguous are, as Colaresi, Rasler, and Thompson (2007: 246ff) show, particularly dangerous.

The German–Russian case, then, suggests some new hypotheses that might be generalizable to other cases of contagion and that deepen our understanding of micro-behavior that results in decisions that spread war. We can begin with three "security-trap" hypotheses:

S3. Crises that result in a security trap increase the likelihood that diplomatic scripts will be abandoned in favor of power politics scripts.
S4. Security traps favor the influence of the military over civilian leaders, and the more imminent the threat of attack the greater that influence and the likelihood that they will prevail.
S5. Contiguity of major states with relatively equal armies are more apt to produce security traps than non-contiguous states or naval competitors.

Germany–France   With the Kaiser's decision to go to war with Russia, the first thing Germany did was to attack France. The failure of the coercive game meant that all the players involved in that game were potential targets. The coercive game was played by four principals consisting of three dyads – Austria-Hungary–Serbia, Russia–Austria-Hungary, and Germany–Russia, with the latter being the key dyad that resulted in the local war spreading to the other parties. France was an important player in this game because it was the staunchest ally of Russia. The Franco-Russian alliance stipulated that, if one or more of the powers of the Triple Alliance should mobilize, then "at first news of this event and without the necessity of any previous concert," the two would mobilize and move their troops to the frontier (Gibler 2009: 198). It was a tight alliance. Of course, German war plans going back to the time of Schlieffen had taken account of this, thereby guaranteeing the spread of the war to France by institutionalizing it within the military and political bureaucracies. The tight alliance was an ancillary factor to the alliance variable and the failure of the coercive game, which were the primary contagion factors. The tight Franco-Russian alliance, however, gave alliances a slightly more potent role because it provided an additional incentive beyond the coercive game for the war to spread.

Unlike most of the dyads that entered in 1914, there was an important secondary contagion process at work here – territorial rivalry. While this rivalry can be traced back quite far (Thompson dates it with Prussia to 1756), its immediate source had to do with the loss of Alsace and Lorraine in 1871 at the conclusion of the Franco-Prussian War. This was the key source of tension and the major grievance on France's side. It was, however, a latent grievance. French political leaders were not actively pursuing it, although they had an official claim. Instead, a colonial competition, where France had had the upper hand, was the source of visible contention, most recently in Morocco (Agadir in 1911). The colonial competition, although irksome for Germany and the Kaiser, in particular, would probably not have resulted in a war between the two, although the Agadir crisis came uncomfortably close despite the accommodationist stance of the Kaiser and Bethmann-Hollweg versus that of State Secretary Kiderlen (see Richardson 1994: 178–179). German leaders were primarily concerned that France not seek the return of Alsace and Lorraine in a revanchist war. French leaders knew this was not possible given their military position. Still, they worried, as in the War in Sight crisis of 1875, that Germany with its relative superiority might attack to keep them down.

The question of Alsace-Lorraine was not a subject of open discussion between the two countries in 1914 or immediately before that. How much of a role it played in France's decision to enter the war is still uncertain. Some things are clear, however. First, it played a key role in French military planning in that a frontal assault on Alsace was the heart of Joffre's offensive strategy. Second, Alsace and Lorraine was a volatile and emotional stake, albeit latent; nationalist sentiments associated with them made them extremely popular issues in the National Assembly and the public. Third, it is fair to assume that Poincaré knew that the only way to get Alsace and Lorraine back was through a war, and this war could not be a bilateral war because France would lose.

Germany–Belgium   This dyad is the exemplar case of contagion through contiguity. Belgium was attacked only because it was in the way. It was in the way, however, because France was an ally of Russia. Although the two had a colonial disagreement in Africa, unlike with Portugal this was not a factor. The idea that it was the spatial factor that brought Belgium in is further confirmed by the fact that Joffre also wanted to go through Belgium. Likewise, the Germans also thought of attacking the Netherlands, but ultimately decided not to do so and keep it as a "windpipe" for trade.

If the bargaining theory of war is valid, the two should have been able to reach a bargain, especially since Germany made reasonable offers. Instead, the case shows the limits of cost–benefit bargaining and the importance of norms and values in decisions to fight. The march through Belgium subsequently made for further contagion as Grey used it as a rationale to bring in the Cabinet, Parliament, and the British people. The anomaly for the bargaining theory of war raises the question of just how many such anomalies there are for this theory, while at the same time providing a theoretical answer as to why they occur. Although this is a sidetrack from the question of contagion, because it arises in a critical case and is likely to occur in other cases of multiparty war, it is worthy of formulating into a supplemental hypothesis:

S6. When weak countries are confronted with an ultimatum demanding surrender or the relinquishing of control of large tracts of territory, they will have a statistically significant likelihood of resisting, typically in the name of honor and freedom, regardless of the power differential.

This hypothesis is a direct contradiction to the bargaining theory of war that maintains that it is primarily lack of information or a commitment problem that increases the likelihood that a bargain cannot be reached and war will break out. Instead, the logic here is that such demands are regarded as a violation of values and a psychological humiliation that touch deep-seated emotions that make for resistance regardless of the likelihood of winning. The Belgian case is consistent with this hypothesis, but so are others like that depicted in the Melian Dialogue. The hypothesis predicts that the likelihood of such outcomes is greater than the null hypothesis, but just how many times such resistance will occur is a fruitful avenue of future research.

Britain–Germany   Britain was the player in the coercive game that was a heavyweight, but did not actively coerce. Nonetheless, her power was such that she was factored in by all the players. The Tsar counted on her as a main deterrent of Germany, thinking all along that it would be crazy for the Kaiser to take on a coalition of Britain, France, and Russia. France depended on Britain, and had – going back to the talks in 1911 – coordinated its defense with the British military. By 1914 she had left her coastal defenses in the hands of the British Navy while she defended British interests in the Mediterranean. Nonetheless, because of the Cabinet, Grey could not draw a line in the sand. This created uncertainty in the French, and lent itself to wishful thinking by Bethmann-Hollweg and the Kaiser.

The governmental split was a key factor in preventing Britain from following the power politics script to the ultimate, the way the other parties did. Whether that would have made deterrence work is a somewhat moot question, because the governmental split prevented a clear commitment from Grey. As a counter-factual question, it is of theoretical interest, but not easily answered unless one accepts realist logic without question. Instead, what seems to be the case is that, once Bethmann-Hollweg and the Kaiser were convinced that Britain would enter, they still went forward and did not back down. They got cold feet and Bethmann-Hollweg pushed the Kaiser's Halt-in-Belgrade plan more vigorously on that fateful weekend, but they did not back down in the face of Russia's threat.

Given the government split, which must be seen as a key inhibiting factor in the spread of the war, Grey did what he could to keep the government intact, and the best way of doing that was to try to avoid the war through diplomatic action. This coincided with the Kaiser's own peace plan and the desire of the Tsar to avoid war. The result was that within the July crisis there were two contradictory scripts being pursued simultaneously – the power politics script of coercion and the Concert of Europe script of accommodation. While these are theoretically distinct scripts (and the Kaiser was most clearly flipped from one to the other), Grey was pursuing a complicated micro-strategy. As the principals were playing a game of coercion, he was simultaneously trying to restrain all the parties while still trying to keep Germany from attacking France.

Grey had every reason to believe that diplomacy would work since all the recent crises between major states had been resolved without a general war (see Afflerbach and Stevenson 2007; Mulligan 2010: 23, 41, 229–231). As the crisis lingered on, the probability of a resolution was seen as higher. The mobilization quickly interrupted this scenario and instead the crisis escalated, despite Grey's extensive efforts.

Grey himself had a plan B that he pursued throughout the crisis in case war were to come about. He was committed to defending France if it were attacked by Germany. His plan B was to find a reason for war that a coalition within the Cabinet would support, and this ended up being the protection of Belgian neutrality. This was a rationale that Grey thought he could peddle, even though it was not the real reason he was willing to go to war. Ultimately, this worked. Grey's insincerity regarding Belgium was evinced by the fact that at a critical moment he decided not to demand German acceptance of Belgium's neutrality because he feared the Germans might accept it, and then he would be left without a rationalization to present to the Cabinet (Williamson and van Wyk 2003: 245). At the same time his preferred strategy was to avoid war. His last-ditch and misleading August 1 proposal to Germany that Britain and perhaps France would remain neutral if Germany attacked only Russia showed the lengths to which he would go to avoid a war, while still protecting France.

A strong leader is the main factor that brought Britain into the war. This was not unlike the situation we will see in Japan and in Italy, later on. Because of the "constitutional" structure of British governance, as Foreign Secretary Grey was able to control foreign policy. Asquith, the Prime Minister, followed this tradition and pretty much agreed with Grey's position. Grey took this position because he believed it was in Britain's interest to defend France and keep it as a part of a balance of Germany. His personal alliance commitment was actually much stronger than anything in the Entente understanding and, of course, anything he would state publicly. This made alliances once again an important contagion process for this dyad, but it worked primarily through Grey as the strong leader who embodied that alliance commitment.

This meant to a certain extent that British entry was very contingent, but does that mean that Britain would not have entered the war if Grey had lost the argument? This is a counter-factual question that puts the role of "a strong leader" as a variable in its proper perspective. Some background factors promoted British intervention. The key background factors were the Anglo-German rivalry that was a product of the rise of German economic strength coupled with colonial competition, both of which were aggravated by the naval race. These factors created hostility, especially on the British side, but also at times, like in the Samoan dispute, on the German side. Nonetheless, Bethmann-Hollweg and the Kaiser wanted to avoid war and hoped throughout the pre-1914 period that Britain would become an ally. Settlements like that on Heligoland in 1890 and agreements like that on the Baghdad railway encouraged such sentiments. In the end, however, the more structural background factors insured that Britain would always favor France over Germany, as was made clear by David Lloyd George's Mansion House speech at the height of the Agadir crisis. The emphasis on decision-making in this study should not lead the reader to underestimate the role of such structures. Indeed, some argue that even if the July crisis had not escalated to war the given structural powder keg would have produced another crisis that would have escalated (see Thompson 2003; cf. Lebow 2007).

The centrality of France to perceived British interest is the key to handling the counter-factual question. Contingency by its very definition can swing both ways. If Grey had lost in August 1914, would he have lost later, as well, or would not a different Foreign Secretary have pursued entry into the war at some later point? The circumstance that would most likely have prompted British entry is if France were threatened with defeat. Assuming that the Battle of the Marne would have had the same outcome as that which did occur, namely, that Paris was defended and a stalemate arose on the Western Front, then we can assume that the very stalemate or some battlefield turn against the French would have created pressure for British entry regardless of the Foreign Secretary. Likewise, some naval action involving the defense of the French coast might have resulted in an intervention. Ultimately, if none occurred early on in 1914, British trade and German submarine warfare would have likely brought in British entry, as it did with the Americans.

In the end, even if Grey had failed to bring in Britain, the battlefield conditions of the ongoing war itself would have jeopardized perceived British national interest in such a way that they would have generated a domestic coalition supporting joining the war on his side of the aisle. These battlefield conditions would themselves work with the background conditions that made Britain hostile to Germany in the first place and friendly to France in the second. More realistic, of course, is the conjecture that if the government fell it would have been replaced by the Conservatives, who would have entered the war.

Interestingly, Grey did succeed in persuading enough of the Cabinet and Parliament to intervene in support of Belgian neutrality. The fact that this was not his real reason meant that moral concerns played a role in bringing about support for war. This provides a very different understanding of the national interest in Britain in 1914, which raises questions about the adequacy of the concept as an explanation of foreign policy decision-making.

Austria–Hungary–Russia   Ironically the last European major-state dyad to declare war was the one that started the coercive game – Austria-Hungary–Russia. The firmness of their key allies – Germany for Austria-Hungary and France for Russia – made them play the coercive game to the hilt. The Tsar, always confident that Russia could beat Austria-Hungary, concentrated his actions on Germany and getting it to stop supporting Austria-Hungary. The idea of a partial mobilization was a signal that Russia was trying not to threaten Germany. Berchtold, for his part, as well as Franz Josef, were bent on overrunning Serbia, and wanted to keep the Kaiser firm so the Tsar would back down as he had in 1908. Third parties were crucial for this dyad, and they spent much of their time on these third parties, rather than directly interacting with each other. This is an important insight for understanding the dynamics of this dyad. In part, this illustrates the limitation of dyadic analysis, while also showing that this limitation can be easily overcome by examining the impact of concerns about third parties.

Nonetheless, the intransigence exhibited by this dyad was critical for the failure of any peace plan. Berchtold and Austria-Hungry had absolutely no interest in the Kaiser's Halt-in-Belgrade plan because the purpose of its ultimatum was not to get Serbia to agree to all the points, but to get it to reject one or more of them so it had an excuse for war. Having Austria-Hungary occupy the capital, so it could conduct its own investigation and satisfy the rejected demand, missed the entire point. For the same reason, Berchtold was not interested in direct negotiations. Nor was Sazonov. Thus both the Kaiser's and Grey's plans fell before the intransigent principals.

To avoid war, what needed to be done was to get a peace plan – most likely the Kaiser's – accepted by both sides. The logic of the situation was that the Kaiser could impose this on Austria-Hungary and that Grey could enlist France to impose it on a willing Tsar. Berchtold foiled the former attempt by trying to pre-empt with the declaration of war and bombardment of Belgrade. Then he ignored Bethmann-Hollweg's belated attempt to blackmail Austria-Hungary with the threat of "withdrawing the blank check" and listened instead to Moltke's back-channel communication. Poincaré did nothing to pressure the Tsar, and Sazonov did nothing to soften the Serbs and Pašić, who was open to anything the Russians would demand.

In the end, the coercive game failed, and Austria-Hungary and Russia came to war each knowing that their allies would be in their corner. Austria-Hungary and Conrad got their local war even if it meant having to fight a general war on the Eastern Front. Russia and the Tsar did not suffer another humiliation, as in 1908, even though mobilizing and going to war went against his better instincts. On August 6 the coercive game had come full circle, and all those that played the game were legally at war. They and their allies had failed to deter, but they had come through by living up to their commitments.

Late Joiners in 1914

The initial joiners, with the exception of Belgium, were all major–major dyads. They all came in because they were in opposing alliances and they were involved in a game of coercion that failed. Some writers conceive of this as the onset of a multiparty war without the need for contagion models (see Levy 2011), whereas this analysis sees it as theoretically informative to think of the local Austria-Hungary–Serbia war as something that could have been a Third Balkan War and not spread to become a general war. It then looks at why it spread to the other major states and then to a host of other states later in the year and thereafter.

The next two dyads that will be analyzed are those that entered in 1914 but after a decent interval. They were the first to join without playing the coercive game that failed. They reflect new contagion processes that made the ongoing war spread further. These more clearly reflect how the ongoing war itself spread and engulfed more actors, although typically through their own volition.

Japan–Germany It is not surprising that the first dyad to enter the war after those which had played the coercive game, and involving the first country outside Europe, was Japan–Germany. It entered for a new reason – the opportunity the ongoing war provided for it to satisfy territorial imperial ambitions, but it used its alliance with Britain as the rationale. The fact that alliance provided a rationalization made it a secondary contagion factor. The use of the alliance by Katō, the foreign minister, made the war diffuse hierarchically, as would be predicted. The real reason, however, was the opportunity the war created for Katō and Japan to do something they could not do in the past – seize nearby German colonies in China and then beyond in the Pacific. This opportunity was a pre-requisite for Japan's actions because the prevailing political order would not otherwise have permitted it. The major states would have opposed this diplomatically, and Japan, knowing that they would, would not have attempted it. Of equal importance is that without Germany being preoccupied with the European war it would have had more than enough capability to fight Japan in a dyadic war. The ongoing war lifted these two obstacles, permitting Japan to seize the opportunity. The removal of the obstacles was only a necessary condition; they were not the reason Japan wanted to go to war. The sufficient condition was Japan's territorial ambitions. Interestingly, unlike some territorial grievances, like Alsace and Lorraine, these were not long-held claims; indeed, Japan had no formal territorial claims against Germany. Rather they became territorially ambitious because the ongoing war made it possible to seize new colonial areas. Instead of reflecting a long-term rivalry, the ongoing war created a territorial grievance.

A secondary contagion factor was contiguity. Part of the reason why Germany had a greatly reduced capability was the great distance between its Asian colonial holdings and Japan's proximity to them. Contiguity played a key role in the mix. These three factors – opportunity, territorial ambitions, and contiguity – were all actualized by a strong leader with a vision of enhancing Japan's territory and power. That leader was Katō. He almost single-handedly shaped this agenda and dealt with the limited opposition that was expressed. More significantly, he navigated through the international shoals to get diplomatic support.

The main new insight from this case has to do with how the opportunity of the ongoing war put a new set of territorial issues on the agenda for Katō and Japan. While Japan had a history of territorial expansion, it had no territorial claims against Germany, nor did it have a rivalry with it. The opportunity to seize Kiaochow changed all that. What was even more remarkable was that Japan's decisive defeat of Germany did not lead the latter to make claims for the return of the lost colonial territory, nor did it seek a revanchist war once it had recovered. This is most likely due to the great distance of Germany from the lands and that this involved colonial territory and not home-land or contiguous territory. Also by this time Germany was seeking Japan as an ally against the Soviet Union and later the West. This suggests two new hypotheses:

S7. Ongoing wars can put new territorial issues on the agenda where there had been no claims before, and these become a basis for intervention.

S8. Decisive victories over far-flung colonial territory where there had been no previous rivalry can lead to the acceptance of loss of terri-tory by the defeated party, as reflected in the absence of any future territorial claim or the seeking of a revanchist war.

Russia–Ottoman Empire   The interesting thing about this dyad is that the Ottoman Empire wanted the war and Russia was forced into declaring it. The Ottoman Empire was similar to Japan in that the ongoing war provided an opportunity for its decision-makers to attain goals that could not be achieved otherwise. The opportunity the war provided, although it involved territory, was fundamentally different. Ottoman decision-makers were concerned that the long-term decline of the Empire, which had taken a recent turn for the worse with internal revolts and wars in the Mediterranean and the Balkans, needed to be stemmed, if not reversed. The war provided this opportunity because it provided the possibility of strong allies. The breakdown of the prevail-ing order also provided the possibility of a rapid change in boundaries. Of course, this was both a risk and an opportunity for the Empire. As with Japan, the Ottoman Empire had a strong leader – Enver Pasha, Minister of War, albeit not as strong as Katō, since he had to serve under Grand Vizier Said Halim, who often opposed him, and he needed allies to help him. The main difference from Japan was that while the latter had only one choice for an ally – the Entente – the Ottoman Empire could join either side to attain its ends. It thus had a problem that would herald the choice of many of the subsequent entries – which side to join.

Unlike these later entries, however, Enver Pasha and his supporters had first to get the outside parties' attention. During the early part of the July crisis neither side was particularly interested in signing an alliance with them. Even Germany, the side they would ultimately join, was reluctant, with Jagow and others not sure of the military value the Ottomans could provide. Likewise, actions like Churchill's canceling the delivery of two battleships alienated them. This reluctance of the third parties had an internal impact on the domestic situation, which made Enver Pasha's leaning toward Germany less attractive to the others than it might have otherwise been.

Once the war had broken out in the first week of August, Germany moved closer to the Ottomans, agreeing to an alliance on August 2. Having gotten their alliance, Enver Pasha and others sought to avoid active combat, while German decision-makers, such as Bethmann-Hollweg and General Falkenhayn, were anxious to open a second front against Russia. This eventually resulted in a provocative naval action in the Black Sea by the German Admiral Souchon, now commanding under the authority of the Ottomans and with the support of Enver Pasha, that produced a Russian declaration of war. The extent to which the Germans were working in collusion with Enver Pasha is still a matter of disagreement, but it is clear that the German officer initiated certain naval actions. By doing so, he aided the efforts of one side of the government, that of Enver Pasha that wanted to go to war. Indeed, after the declaration of war, Cavid Bey and three other ministers resigned (Trumpener 2003: 354). Such intervention by an outside major state is an example of how those at war can actively try to expand the war on their behalf. It reflects a separate conflict process from those that the Ottomans themselves were following. This leads to one new hypothesis based on this case regarding the attempts of major states to get minor states to join them:

S9. Major states will attempt to get minor states to join them when doing so will open another front against their opponent. If they have military or diplomatic personnel on the ground, they will use these to initiate actions that will embroil the minor state in a situation where war becomes highly likely.

The above hypothesis captures precisely what the Germans did in the Black Sea with Enver Pasha's knowledge, if not connivance. Such major-state intervention, as in this case, is often taken to support hardliners in their domestic contention with those opposed to joining the war or a specific side. As such, it is an example of transnational coalition making. This pattern of outside intervention to support one side of the government reached an extreme in the Greek case, where the French and British engaged in armed intervention to bring about a coup d'état against the King. The contagion process outlined in Supplemental Hypothesis S9 is similar to model six on Brute Force, but at a much more minimal and nuanced level.

The late entries in 1914 reflect a distinct set of contagion processes compared with the initial entrants who were playing the coercive game. These processes of opportunity linked with territorial ambitions also dominated the main dyads that were brought in during the second wave of contagion in 1915–1916.

The Second Wave

Table 7.2 lists the dyads that entered in the second and third waves of the spread of the war along with the factors that brought them in.

Italy–Austria-Hungary   By 1914 Italy had fought several wars – three of them with Austria (1848, 1859, 1866) – to unify its *irredenta* into a coherent nation-state. Although it had been over forty years since the last war of unification (1870), revanchist sentiment within Austria-Hungary was still active in some quarters. Conrad, as recently as 1911, had advocated a war against Italy while it was attacking the Ottoman Empire. Italy for its part still had some remaining areas that it sought, even though it had by 1870 most of what we recognize today as modern Italy. No sooner had it won the prize of Venetia in the War of 1866 than it made a new claim to Trentino and Alto Adige. Compared with the previous claims, which were actively pursued by the government as well as non-state nationalist groups, this was relatively dormant.

In part, this was due to Italy entering in 1882 the Triple Alliance with Germany and Austria-Hungary because of its colonial competition with France and its resentment over the French seizing Tunisia close to the tip of Sicily. The Alliance and Germany's role in it helped mute the conflict with Austria-Hungary. The Alliance also had a provision – Article VII – that raised the territorial issue as soon as Austria-Hungary attacked Serbia. This provision provided for Italian compensation if Austria-Hungary increased its territory. The 1914 local war immediately provided a legal opportunity for Italy to gain new territory, and

Table 7.2. *Categorization of contagion factors by dyad: Second and third waves*

Dyad	Primary process	Secondary process	Other factors	New insights
The Second Wave: 1915–1916				
ITA–AUH	Opportunity – necessary (Capability and political order) Territorial rivalry – sufficient		Strong leader	1. Territorial rivalry trumps Alliance 2. Auction
ITA–OTM	Valence balancing Opportunity Territorial rivalry		Compensation norm Diplomatic credit	
BUL–SER	Opportunity – necessary (capability and political order) Territorial issue – sufficient		Government split	1. Auction
GMY–POR	Alliances Imperial hierarchy	Colonial competition Valence balancing		
ROM–AUH	Opportunity – necessary (capability and political order) Territorial issue – sufficient		Government split	1. Territorial rivalry trumps Alliance 2. Auction 3. Contradictory territorial goals
The Third Wave: 1917				
USA–GMY	Economic dependence	Opportunity – breakdown of political order	Strong leader	Strategy of moral ostracism
GRC–AUH/GMY/ BUL	Brute force	Contiguity Territorial rivalry	Government split – necessary condition	Third-party desperation
BRA–GMY	Economic dependence Valence balancing			
NORTHERN EUROPEAN NEUTRALS	Economic dependence			War of attrition
NOR	Economic dependence			Involuntary neutral ally

San Giuliano, the Foreign Minister, and Salandra, the Prime Minister, tried to make good on that opportunity.

At the very start of the war both believed they could obtain territory without actually fighting in the war. Bethmann-Hollweg supported their position because he wanted to avoid Austria-Hungary becoming involved on multiple fronts and thereby reducing its effort on the Eastern Front. These efforts did not bear immediate fruit, so Salandra turned to playing each side off the other, trying to initiate an auction for Italy's entry into the war. The Italian demands were too big for Austria-Hungary to concede, particularly that for the port of Trieste – the main naval base of the Habsburgs. Even when in early 1915 Berchtold was willing to concede Trentino, he was pushed out of office by Conrad and Tisza. The compensation norm then delayed the armed entry of Italy into the war; at the same time, however, it created a structure for the immediate expansion of the war at a legal level in terms of an active diplomatic intervention backed by a latent threat to join the other side if compensation were not forthcoming. This leads to a supplemental hypothesis:

S10. The failure to abide by the norm of compensation increases the probability of war or its expansion, *ceteris paribus*.

All of these negotiations and maneuvering were conducted by two strong leaders – San Giuliano, the Foreign Minister, and Prime Minister Salandra, especially after the former's death. They managed the intricate international situation of dealing with their own allies and those opposing them, especially as the general war broke out and the auction for their allegiance began in earnest. The phenomenon of an auction for enticing neutral minor states – or in this case one of the lesser major states – is fairly rare in world politics, but a hallmark of contagion in the First World War. It is a function of the breakdown of the political order. Whereas the norms of the Concert of Europe had a bias against war and specifically of minor states going off on their own, now the major belligerent states were actively seeking to involve these states in the ongoing war. How this happened becomes clear when we look at opportunity from the perspective of those already at war and why they seek to end the neutrality of non-belligerents. The breakdown of the political order worked at two levels – one in terms of creating an opportunity for those not already involved in the war and one in terms of belligerents, especially major states, trying to bring in new states. Since both sides fighting the war were prone to this behavior, an auction was produced. This worked to the advantage of minor states and weaker major states, and reversed their typical situation of being dependent on the wishes of major states. Nonetheless, once the belligerent had succeeded in bringing in the neutral, the former put demands on the latter to live up to the bargain that its territorial or other goals would be satisfied in return for providing a new front. This process was illustrated in the Italian case when Italy declared war against Austria-Hungary in 1915, but did not declare war against Germany. As the stalemate deepened with Verdun, France put intense pressure on Italy in 1916 to declare war on Germany and cut off trade, so it relented. This valence balancing on Italy's part would come back to hurt it at the battle of Caporetto.

Assuming that Riker's (1962) minimum winning coalition hypothesis has some validity, it would be expected that an auction would take place only in the context of some battlefield stalemate. This in part explains why auctions are fairly rare and why they were not seen in the First World War until 1915 and then became more frequent in 1916. Their effect is to expand the war to more and more neutrals, bringing them in by the combined contagion processes of opportunity and territorial rivalry.

The dynamic at work here is that a belligerent tries to gain an advantage and end the stalemate by opening another front for its enemy. This will split the army of the other side, thereby weakening it, leaving it open to invasion. This makes contiguous states that are neutral prime candidates for auction appeals. Contiguous states that border both sides provide enhanced benefits (or risks) in that if they are brought into one's coalition they not only add a new front to the opponent, but also close off your opponent opening a new front on your border. As a war expands further through such a process, as it did in 1916, there is always some country in the coalition that could benefit or suffer from this enhanced benefit.

The phenomenon of an auction is a new insight that comes to light on examining how contagion worked in the First World War. Since it repeats itself during the war, one would expect that it would be present in other multiparty wars as well. This leads to a new supplemental hypothesis, the Auction Hypothesis:

S11. Wars that drag on due to stalemates will lead belligerents to expand the war by bringing in neutrals; as both sides do this, neutrals will engage in an auction to get the best deal.

This is an example of how the contingency of the battlefield and the agency of individual decision-makers interact to promote war contagion. As noted in the three case studies of Italy, Romania, and Bulgaria, neutrals will not necessarily go with the highest bidder, but will discount an offer according to the prospect of that side winning. Recent battlefield outcomes are also often used to assess that prospect, and in close wars like the First World War, that may lead to errors.

A second insight, and one of the main insights from the Italian case, has to do with the relative potency of alliances and territorial rivalry in determining which side to join. The Italian case is a very useful case for inference in that its alliance pushes it in one direction and its territorial rivalry in another. The fact that other cases, for instance Romania, also go in the same way suggests that this is a pattern. On the basis of these two cases it can be argued that territorial rivalry is a more potent factor in determining which side a state will choose. It should also be noted that Italy's choice in this matter set a precedent for what Romania could do. Switching sides broke an unwritten norm, and this became a matter of internal discussion within Romania. The fact that Italy paved the way eased the Romanian decision. As a precedent, the Italian case promoted contagion through a demonstration effect. It set an example of how this could be done and provided a positive example that switching sides could be beneficial. Of course, while this worked for the Italians, it failed for the Romanians, at least in the short term.

Italy–Ottoman Empire   The key thing to keep in mind about Italy and the Ottoman Empire in the First World War is that Italy entered the Great War to get *irredenta* from Austria-Hungary and not because of any territorial demands against the Ottoman Empire. For Italy, the Ottoman Empire was always a sideshow until the war ended.

Discerning the contagion factors that led Italy to declare war against the Ottoman Empire is complicated because of its recent 1911 war. Italy attacked the Ottoman Empire in 1911 because of its territorial ambitions and a desire to have a colonial empire in North Africa. Although the Great Powers had intervened to get a peace that ended the war near Turkey proper, Italy was still fighting in the hinterland of Tripolitania and Cyrenaica. When it entered the Great War it was only natural that it would take the opportunity of being a formal ally of the Entente to also declare war against the Ottoman Empire as a way of furthering its territorial ambitions against the Ottomans. Thus, in the Treaty of London, where it compiled a number of territorial promises, it also sought and was granted some consideration with regard to the Ottoman Empire. The most secure of these was for the Dodecanese Islands, which it had attacked and occupied during the 1911–1912 war. Much vaguer was a promise that Italy would get a share of the Ottoman Empire if it fell apart (see MacMillan 2013: 283). The problem, of course, was that Italy was stretched thin. It was in no position to actually attack the Ottoman army. Its declaration of war can thus be seen as a way of gaining diplomatic credit – a kind of legal and diplomatic rain check that was being put in the bank to be taken out when Italy was in a better position to cash it or during the peace when the Ottoman Empire was being divided up. Piedmont had done something similar in 1855 when it entered the Crimean War as a way of currying favor with Britain and France for the cause of Italian unification.

Because Italy was not in a position to attack the Ottoman Empire, in this case valence balancing must also be seen as a contagion process at work along with opportunity and territorial rivalry. Italy declared war on the Ottoman Empire to please its allies and live up to its obligation of what a loyal ally was expected to do, even though it knew it could not really participate in any military campaign against the Ottomans. Nonetheless, its territorial ambitions with regard to the Ottoman Empire shaped the kind of valence balancing that went on. In this case it was not so much declaring war on the enemy of my friend as it was declaring war on my enemy because it is also the enemy of my friend. The opportunity was not so much with regard to capability as it was to the changing political order that the ongoing war brought about. Unlike in the 1911 war, Italy could now rely on the Entente Powers to support it over the Ottoman Empire. The vague assurances of the Treaty of London were rectified fairly quickly with the summer 1916 agreement that Italy would receive key areas in Asia Minor during the peace settlement in return for recognizing the Sykes–Picot agreement.

Bulgaria–Serbia   The Bulgars never really liked the Serbs. This went back to 1885 with their first war. After the Balkan Wars they hated them. The source of this sentiment and the key to understanding all Bulgarian–Serbian relations was the mutual desire for Macedonia. Territorial rivalry fueled by nationalist emotions explains most of what went on for decades. Desire is not the same as actual policy, that must be tempered by the ability to attain one's object. The actions of Bulgaria's elite in the Second Balkan War proved to be disastrous – losing to Serbia and Greece in Macedonia, Romania in Dobrudja, and the Ottoman Empire in Thrace. Bulgaria's utter defeat and weakened condition meant it could do nothing about Macedonia, although the desire burnt in the collective heart of its nationalists.

The ongoing war provided an unexpected opportunity to escape from this condition. Given Bulgaria's lack of power, the possibility of acquiring allies and the opportunity to take advantage of Serbia's having to fight on a second front were two factors that encouraged it to enter the war. This was a golden opportunity that made it possible to satisfy the grievance posed by the long-standing territorial rivalry. Together opportunity and territorial rivalry made the war spread. In a sense these two factors infected Bulgarian decision-makers, making them subject to the contagion.

The ongoing war removed the obstacle of Bulgaria's weakness and the territorial rivalry provided its willingness to join, but which side it would join was still somewhat open. This makes this case similar to that of Italy in certain regards. As with Italy, it could try to extract a major concession in return for not fighting or even joining. Bulgaria could have remained aligned with its former patron – Russia – which tried to act as a broker getting Serbia, which was in desperate straits, to make concessions regarding Macedonia.

The split in the government and elite reinforced this dilemma in that affinity for Russia because of its past patronage vis-à-vis the Ottoman Empire was still strong in some quarters. The decision-making group of Prime Minister Vasil Radoslavov and Tsar Ferdinand had moved away from Russia because of its support of Serbia. This group was willing to consider siding with Russia, even though the Dual Alliance could offer a much better territorial division, if they thought the Entente was going to win. Given their experience of the Second Balkan War, Bulgarian decision-makers were cautious and did not want to make another mistake by choosing the wrong side. Battlefield outcomes swayed them in different directions over time. Ultimately, the offer of a joint invasion with Austria-Hungary and Germany, coupled with the latter's success on the battlefield at that time, persuaded them to go with the Dual Alliance.

As with Italy, the desire of major states to get Bulgaria on their side created an auction. Austria-Hungary had long wanted Bulgaria as an ally, and its lack of success at overrunning Serbia in 1914 made it even more anxious to bring this "local war" to a successful conclusion. Russia, already overtaxed on the Eastern and Ottoman fronts, wanted to protect its client from an attack that might very well defeat it. The stalemate in Serbia helped produce the auction as Supplemental Hypothesis S11 would predict, and this case adds evidence to support the hypothesis, as well as a case to illustrate the process by which contagion spreads through auctions.

Germany–Portugal This dyad is one of the few joint nation-state dyads that reflects how the Imperialist System makes for hierarchical diffusion. Almost as soon as the war started, the war diffused through the Imperial hierarchy. Belligerents attacked each other's colonies not only to weaken the strength of their opponent, but more specifically to take over their opponent's colonies. Thus, on August 7, 1914, Britain and France attacked German Togoland in the first week of combat. This also happened in other areas where the belligerents' colonies were contiguous. Contiguous colonial territory provided a way by which the war diffused across the globe. The structure that tied this contiguous territory together was the imperialist structure of the major colonial states.

For Portugal, this colonial diffusion produced by the Imperialist System brought them into hostile combat with Germany in Africa very early in the war in 1914. Portugal permitted British troops to march through Mozambique so they could attack German colonies. Germany attacked Angola several times (Shirkey 2009: 147–148). Such contact was not unusual where the declared belligerents' colonies were contiguous. What was unusual with Portugal was that it was not legally at war with Germany. It had, however, a long-term alliance with Britain. This, in conjunction with colonial disagreements between Portugal and Germany, provided a grievance, or willingness to take advantage of the opportunity of the ongoing war to settle some of these arguments. Britain, as a country that was attacking German colonies in a number of locations, supported its ally. The Imperialist System then made for the hierarchical diffusion of combat, here as in other colonial areas where the belligerents' colonies were contiguous. This, however, did not lead either Germany or Portugal to declare war. It did, however, provide an important background factor for the eventual declaration of war.

This latter outcome was a result of Portugal doing Britain's bidding in impounding the several German and Austro-Hungarian ships in Lisbon harbor. It did this because of its long-term alliance with Britain. As an ally, Portugal early on provided the use of its colonies, such as the Azores, to the British Navy. It also offered to send troops to the Western Front, which in the beginning was shunted aside by Britain and France, but later accepted as the demand for personnel rose after Verdun. Portugal played the role of a loyal ally because the alliance itself was important to Portugal maintaining its far-flung empire, and once the war had started Germany was the main potential challenger to that empire. Alliance, then, was a primary contagion factor in the spread of the war. Alliances, however, worked in conjunction with the Imperialist System. The spread of the war to Portugal because of its alliance can also be seen as a form of valence balancing, but the active way in which Portugal sought to enter that role and its early colonial combat make this much more than just valence balancing.

Romania–Austria-Hungary   Romania–Austria-Hungary was the fifth dyad that joined the war primarily because of the combined effects of opportunity and territorial concerns. All five of these dyads clearly illustrate the impact of the ongoing war in removing obstacles in the international system that prevented them from going to war previously and using war as an instrument to bring about territorial change. For Romania the ongoing war provided an unexpected opportunity to act on one of its long-held but not pursued territorial nationalist goals – the gaining of Transylvania. Given that Austria-Hungary was a major state on its border, there was little Romania could do because of its limited capability. In addition, the constraint of the prevailing political order against war was buttressed by the norm that an ally should not attack an ally, and Romania had been an ally of Austria-Hungary and Germany since 1883. The ongoing war and Italy's violating the Triple Alliance in 1915 helped remove both these obstacles.

Even if Romanian decision-makers did not take this tack, the war also provided an opportunity to pursue another territorial goal – Bessarabia. This was also against another neighboring major state – Russia in this instance – where Romania lacked capability. Here Russia having its hands full on the Eastern Front and also with the Ottomans might permit Romania (with the support of allies) to gain an important territorial objective. Although Bessarabia was not as large as Transylvania and Romanian irredentism toward it was not based on as deep a sentiment, it would be an important addition. Opportunity thus played a critical role in making Romania's leaders think about entering the war.

What complicated the decision was that the territorial concerns pulled it in different directions and toward different sides. Was it better to pursue Transylvania and go to war against Austria-Hungary (and Germany) or Bessarabia and go to war with Russia? In addition, Romanian decision-makers recognized that Romania's entry into the war, could provide an opportunity for Bulgaria to regain Dobrudja, and preventing this was a paramount goal. Hence, although the Romanian case was quite similar to that of other dyads where opportunity and territorial concerns worked for intervention, there were significant differences.

These and additional slight differences from other cases permit us to make some inferences about the relative potency of various contagion processes and the vectors they generated that give us a more nuanced understanding about the role different variables can play, but one must be careful because of the limited number of observations. Rather than drawing conclusions, we can think of these inferences as possible hypothesis to guide future case work.

In the other cases, territorial rivalry worked very much to push the revisionist actor – be it Japan, Italy, or Bulgaria – toward intervention, even though in the latter two cases which side they would ultimately align with was not a foregone conclusion. In Romania's case, there were multiple territorial concerns and they were contradictory, so they created cross pressures not present in the other cases. This made Romania's decision-making more difficult. The territorial vector, rather than reinforcing intervention and making it quicker, actually complicated it and slowed it down. This suggests the hypothesis that, when there are multiple and contradictory territorial goals put on the table by an ongoing war, the opportunity and territory vectors do not interact as smoothly to bring about intervention as they do when the territorial goals are more consistent.

The other major factor that played a role in Romania's decision was its alliance with Austria-Hungary and Germany. This factor interacted with the split in the government between Prime Minister Brătianu, who was anti-Austro-Hungarian and pro-Entente, and King Carol, who was pro-German and in favor of staying within the Triple Alliance. This division between those favoring the Entente and those who were pro-German was mirrored in the domestic parties, which were also split on which side to support. The Kaiser played upon King Carol's connections to Germany's Hohenzollern royal house to make sure that he would live up to his alliance commitments. The King even assured the Austro-Hungarian ambassador during the July crisis that they would remain in the alliance. By August 3 the governing council would not confirm this decision.

The government split, as with Bulgaria, made neutrality the main option in 1914. After the King's death in October 1914, Brătianu was in charge of foreign policy and the pro-Entente forces were more dominant – that did not necessarily mean that a decision was obvious, however. The other factors already mentioned were still there. Of these the adherence to the Triple Alliance as a factor was greatly reduced by Italy's precedent in 1915. Italy's breaking of its commitment did not mean that Romania should do the same; nonetheless, it became easier for her to do so. Italy's decision eventually became contagious, but because of the other larger contagion processes at work. In the end, the larger and more nationalist territorial goal in Transylvania trumped the loyalty to the alliance vector, thus providing a second case in support of the insight that territory is more potent than alliances, a conclusion first reached in the Italian case.

The possibility that Romania could go either way meant, as in the case of Italy and Bulgaria, that the major states engaged in an auction to win Romania over. Here the presence of contradictory territorial goals made the auction more objective and, by implication, more intense. Instead of being reduced to an auction decided by battlefield outcomes and the likelihood of which side would win, the fact that the different sides could provide very different prizes played a role. This nuance suggests that multiple and contradictory territorial objectives affect the dynamics of auctions in the contagion process. Whether such an inference is generalizable to other cases or idiosyncratic to this case will have to await the investigation of other cases. The impact of multiple contradictory territorial goals within contagion is a new insight provided by this case, but the scope of its applicability remains open. Still it is something we did not know about before.

While this is an interesting nuance one must not lose sight of the fact that Romania–Austria-Hungary is another case that supports the auction hypothesis. As in the cases of Italy and Bulgaria, it is not simply the neutral state that plays an active role in the auction; the major states play an equal, if not at times more active, role. Germany as a third party, and explicitly the Kaiser, was very active in trying to keep Romania in the alliance. The Germans promised Romania Bessarabia and even went so far as to say that they were trying to get Bulgaria to join them and that Bulgaria would recognize Romania's control of Dobrudja.

Similarly, early on the Russians said that if Romania remained neutral they would support its claims to Transylvania. Russia for its part was active in the auction, and the Entente as a whole in the end promised Romania all its territorial goals against the Central Powers, not just Transylvania but Bukovina and the Banat, as well as others. Another element in Romania's decision was that joining the Entente meant supporting Serbia, a good ally in the previous war against Bulgaria. The auction got more intense as the war dragged on and, at a critical point during Verdun, Britain and France threatened to walk away if Romania did not decide soon. This incident adds support to the auction hypothesis that stalemate motivates major states to engage in an auction.

It should also be mentioned that domestic politics played a role in that there were different domestic audiences in support of the different territorial goals. Romanians living in Moldavia next to Russia did not support going to war with such a powerful major state on its border, while the large Romanian minority within Transylvania was in active support of attacking Austria-Hungary.

The Romanian case is an important reminder that opportunity does not always work out as calculated. Despite what seemed like reasonable decisions, Romania, after initially being able to invade Transylvania because Austria-Hungary's army could not get back, was quickly overrun – after initial successes – by the Central Powers and Bulgaria, with Bucharest being occupied. In the long run, however, it had chosen the correct side. As the war was ending it was given a second chance to seize Transylvania, which it did. For Romania, the ongoing war and the immediate post-war defeat provided two opportunities to pursue its territorial rivalry, the second time with success. The lesson here is that opportunity is not confined to the main body of the war, but can re-open as the war is ending and one side collapses. Even more obvious, opportunity can produce aftershocks as they did here and later on with the invasion of Turkey by Greece, Italy, Britain, and France in 1918–1919. This suggests another supplemental hypothesis on war endings and aftershocks:

S12. The interaction of opportunity and territorial rivalry re-appears for some parties as the war comes to an end and one or more countries collapse. This gives some actors a second chance to realize their goals.

S13. The aftershocks of a war that occur are typically a function of the combination of opportunity and territorial rivalry created by the drastic change in capability and the breakdown of the pre-war political order.[2]

The Third Wave

Romania entered the war at the end of August, and a few days later there were some more declarations of war due mostly to valence balancing. Then there was an eight-month hiatus until April 6, 1917, when the U.S. declared war, starting a third wave of contagion. This third wave had different contagion processes at work, but these were a function of the stalemate on the Western Front. In the case of the U.S., its trade with the Entente Powers and their economic dependence on it led Germany to attack American shipping. By this time trade with the U.S. had become perhaps the pivotal factor for the Entente's continuation in the war, and Germany knew this. In the case of Greece, the war against Serbia and the attempt of the Entente to save it led France and Britain to resort to brute force through an armed intervention that overthrew

---

[2] For a review of the various aftershocks that followed the First World War, see Mulligan (2014: Ch. 9).

the King to support a government willing to enter the war. Although these are very different contagion processes, the actions of Germany, on the one hand, and France and Britain, on the other, resulted from their desperate attempts to break the stalemate on the Western Front that was draining their manpower by millions.

For Germany, the key to victory was to strangle the Entente to death by cutting off their supplies and resources. The British and French goals in Greece were more limited and regional. They wanted at minimum to save the Serbian army, or what was left of it, and maybe regroup and gain a victory over Bulgaria and eventually in the Balkans, which is ultimately what happened. The stalemate on the Western Front, which prevented victory, led the Entente to hope for something in the Balkans. The larger context in this area was that the Entente Powers were in trouble – they had been stalemated in the Straits and unable to supply Russia through them for most of the war. Now Russia was beginning to crumble on the Eastern Front. Greece was by 1917 the only ally that could help, and it was needed geographically as Bulgaria conquered more territory. A detailed examination of each case will reveal how different they are, but it must be kept in mind that these last key neutrals were brought in not so much by direct actions and decisions of their own as they were by the actions of major-state belligerents which were trying to deal with the stalemate on the Western Front. For Germany, this was a bold attempt to win the entire war. For France and Britain, it was an attempt to keep a region together and not lose it in light of the stalemate on the Western Front.

United States–Germany The main thing to remember about the U.S. entry into the war is that the U.S. joined because it was physically attacked by Germany. Wilson did not want to enter. He delayed more than once while hardliners, such as Theodore Roosevelt and Henry Cabot Lodge, called for war. He was a strong leader, and he alone made the decision, but he was not in favor of war. Only a couple of weeks before he went to Congress to ask for a declaration, he said to an interviewer that, "If there is any alternative, for God's sake let's take it" (quoted in Cooper 2003: 437).

This analysis sees the trade with the Entente as the main factor making for contagion. Other factors, like Wilson's desire to get a seat at the peace conference, are seen as secondary. The success of the British blockade of Germany meant that U.S. trade was biased, even though in the beginning the U.S. wanted the right to trade with any belligerent. American trade with the Entente was tremendous, turning the U.S. from a debtor nation to a creditor nation. The extension of credit provided a huge advantage to the Entente cause. By late 1916 Britain was purchasing £5,500,000 a day (Tuchman 1958: 20). That kind of trade made the Entente dependent on the U.S.; what made them even more dependent was that they had no money to pay for these goods any longer. Members of the British elite knew this, and their hope was for U.S. entry into the war with all its financial resources.

Germany also knew the advantage American trade was providing; it knew that by this time it was a lifeline that if severed would kill the effort on the Western Front and break the stalemate. More than once Germany had bowed to American demands not to engage in unrestricted submarine warfare out of a desire to keep the U.S. out of the war. As the war progressed, however, the importance of the submarine, as opposed to a battleship fleet, became clear. By January 1917 the German Admiralty had built 200 submarines, which they believed was a force sufficient to bring Britain to its knees (see Tuchman 1958: 8). This new information, given the inability to break the stalemate in 1916, provided Germany with a way out, the only way out from a military perspective.

An important theoretical question is why the U.S. entered so late. The answer to this fits the overall analysis in that no other factors promoting contagion were present. The U.S. was not an ally with anyone. It was not contiguous, and was far from the battlefield. It had no territorial ambitions for which the war provided an opportunity. It had a strong leader who was averse to war in general and war in Europe specifically. It had an ideational moralistic culture that found European and especially continental realpolitik repugnant. None of the factors that had brought in all of the other states was present. It brought itself in by insisting on the right to trade. This led the side that was being damaged by that to attack when it thought the severing of trade would strangle the other side.

Wilson was not content to act alone as he pressured Germany to cease unrestricted submarine warfare. He sought to bring others into a moralistic coalition that would ostracize Germany for its criminal acts on the high seas. As soon as Germany started to attack shipping in 1917, Wilson severed diplomatic relations, and the State Department called on all neutrals to do the same, arguing that "it will make for the peace of the world if other neutral Powers can find it possible to take action similar to that taken by the United States" (*Papers of Woodrow Wilson*, Vol. 41: 116). Diplomatic notes were sent to the remaining neutrals in the world, not only in Latin America, but in Asia as well, with notes to China and Siam (Stevenson 2017: 285–286). This effort was meant to morally persuade Germany while simultaneously punishing it by the diplomatic equivalent of "shunning" – an old Puritan practice to punish sinners common among other religions as well. Severing diplomatic relations was often a prelude to declaring war, although Wilson hoped to avoid this step and did so until April. Several of the neutrals that followed his plea to sever relations also subsequently declared war.

This leads to the one new insight provided by this case: the role of the strategy of moral ostracism in promoting contagion. It brought in neutrals that had few grievances and (like the U.S.) none of the main contagion factors that had previously brought in the others. Wilson's plea was an important new factor in bringing them in. It did not work alone, however. It was effective mostly on those nation-states that were in some hierarchical relationship with the U.S., especially those subject to its regional hegemony. The actual declarations of war also reflect valence balancing due to this hierarchical relationship. Nonetheless, the strategy of moral ostracism was fairly unique to the moralistic U.S. and Wilson, and sufficiently theoretically distinct from these two other factors to be separated out. It leads to a new insight and supplemental hypothesis:

S14. The strategy of moral ostracism spreads war on the basis of some violation of a norm.

Unlike other factors that spread the war, this is an ideational factor and an attempt to construct or reinforce a particular normative order. In the attempt to persuade and punish the norm-breaker, the war spreads. It illustrates how norms can spread war, and how ideas can produce contagion. Norms, then, as well as material forces, can spread war. The strategy of ostracism illuminates how neutrals with limited to no material reasons for joining an ongoing war can be "infected" and embroiled in war contagion. Still, it must be remembered that such norms tend to work through a hierarchical system mostly associated with hegemony, which can be seen as a subset or variation of Imperialist Systems. In later years, the U.S. would use moral ostracism as a way of legitimizing its resort to war by attempting to bring in as large a number of neutral states as possible, even if they brought little material resources to the war effort. This is amply illustrated by the Persian Gulf War, but also by the earlier Korean War (police action). Recently, Weitsman (2014) has analyzed alliances as coalitions that make wars spread, focusing on efforts by the U.S. to bring together a large number of states in its wars in the post-Cold War era, a process which she describes as an exercise of hegemony, but one also driven by an attempt to gain legitimation through moral condemnation, a phenomenon not that different from Wilson's strategy of moral ostracism.

When all is said and done, U.S. entry was fairly straightforward theoretically. It involved a single contagion process that came after the war had been going on for three intense years with millions of soldiers on both sides dead and many more wounded. The American entry then promoted further contagion through Wilson's strategy of moral ostracism. The entry of Greece, however, is a more complicated story from a theoretical point of view.

Greece–Austria-Hungary, Germany, Bulgaria Greece had a number of factors that early on could have brought it into the war. These included its territorial rivalry, along with the opportunity the war provided to satisfy them. Its early alliance with Serbia was another factor, albeit a secondary one. More important was its contiguity with Serbia, which was a major battlefield, and it was the ongoing battle there that eventually played a key role in bringing it in. Still, it did not come in until the summer of 1917.

What kept Greece out for the longest time was the severe governmental split. The sharp division between King Constantine and Prime Minister Venizelos and the division of the major parties prevented a decision in favor of war. As the war continued, the split intensified and the government fractured so that neither side was able to impose its will. This fracturing became a pre-requisite for the use of brute force by outside parties to bring in Greece. The government split was a necessary condition in that, without it, there could not be an armed intervention that could impose an outside will on the polity. As the war in Serbia became active on Greece's borders in Salonika and the Bulgarians occupied parts of Macedonia, the close proximity of the battlefields interacted with sharp divisions within the polity so that outside intervention became not only possible, but likely. Contiguity acted as a sufficient condition. France and Britain supported the military coup in Salonika and then actively intervened with troops in Athens, attempting to overthrow the King in order to put Venizelos, who was pro-Entente and willing to enter the war, into power. Brute force occurred in part because of these battlefield contingencies, but more importantly because there was no government in Greece capable of making a definitive decision. Under these conditions the Allies imposed a government to their liking. Territorial rivalry with Bulgaria played a minor and secondary role in the contagion process, mostly by providing domestic support in certain quarters. It is not that anyone disagreed with the territorial goals; it is just that many thought Greece too weak to pursue them. They saw it as imprudent.

That brute force should become a contagion process only late in the war is not surprising. It is a product of the war dragging on and the major states becoming desperate due to the stalemate on the Western Front. There are two ways to increase one's capability in international politics – military buildups and the making of alliances. By 1917 building up one's military was at its height and had no more room for growth. This left only gaining new allies, and Greece was one of the few neutrals left. Although it was not very strong, its strategic position made it an asset, and its neutrality made it a burden. The willingness of an influential and more "democratic" domestic force to support the war was too much of a temptation for the liberal states, which were already occupying parts of the country with their militaries.

Theoretically there were three factors at play. First, the severe government split acted as a pre-requisite or necessary condition for external brute force. Second, the contiguity of the battlefield spilled over into Greece. Third, the desperate situation of the major states made them seek allies even if it was against the will of a sizable portion of the country.

Brazil–Germany   Brazil was the only Latin American state to become actively involved in the war, although it did not meet the Correlates of War threshold. This was because Brazil, like the U.S., was subject to submarine warfare in 1917. It entered because it was attacked. The Germans did not make a specific decision to attack Brazil's shipping, but did so as part of a general sweep. Brazil was caught up in the contagion promulgated by the change in policy affecting the naval war. Thus, economic dependence is seen as one of two primary contagion processes. It must be kept in mind, however, that Brazil's trade was not so important that it would have been singled out without the larger context of the changed policy. Nor is it likely that Brazil would have done anything without a U.S. declaration of war. Still, the sinking of four ships made it do more than just valence balance; it sought to take reprisals.

Without the sinking of its ships, it is unlikely that Brazil would have actively fought in the war. It would, however, have declared war, as did several other Latin American states. *The Brazilian Green Book* (Boyle 1918: 6) says that early on it sought not to be neutral once the U.S. was at war, and it quickly revoked its neutrality out of continental solidarity. Furthermore, it sent a diplomatic circular to neutral South American states encouraging them to follow its lead, and several did. Significantly, Argentina and Chile did not. Valence balancing, then, is also seen as a key contagion process that brought in Brazil. It is likely that this process would have led Brazil to declare war even if there had been no attacks on its shipping.

Although the third wave did not bring many new countries into the war, it pushed the war to the most outward bounds possible – to the furthest and most distant areas in Europe, to the Western Hemisphere and to Asia, with the addition of China and Siam. The third wave made the "Great War" more truly a world war. The causal engine that produced that was the stalemate on the Western Front that promoted a search for allies and led Germany to attack the U.S. Once the U.S. had entered, it acted in such a way as to bring in more states, if only legally. Although many of these states were brought in because of Wilson's strategy of moral ostracism, the war also diffused through the network of American hegemony, including not only the Latin American states, but also Liberia. It is not surprising that most were not actively involved in fighting. Brazil was an important exception, and unsurprisingly it had its own reasons for becoming involved due to the sinking of its ships.

An interesting theoretical question is why the effects of that stalemate did not encompass all the remaining neutrals. One way of investigating this question is to ask what inoculated the neutrals. There are three things. The first, and a key factor the neutrals had in common, was that they were on the periphery – for example Spain and Scandinavia. Yet they had bordering neighbors in the war. Still, their distance from the battlefields made them less able to add much in tipping the stalemate. Second, their relative lack of power made them less useful to either side. On top of that, the side that most likely would have wanted them in did not need them to be in the war. For example, Germany already had what it wanted from Scandinavia – resources that it had acquired from trade. Britain and France did not really want any personnel from Spain – they reluctantly took what Portugal offered. Spain in turn did not need support for what was left of its overseas Empire. Third, they lacked the powerful factors that brought in most of the second wave: they lacked territorial rivalries, and they did not have – with the exception of Spain – alliances with any of the belligerents. In sum, the neutrals lacked key characteristics of those that entered: they were distant and on the periphery; they were not sought after by the belligerents because of their limited value; they lacked territorial rivalries with the belligerents that would have made the war an opportunity for them; and most did not have alliances. The first two characteristics can be considered inoculations and the last two the absence of conditions associated with contagion.

Nonetheless, once the Schlieffen Plan had failed, a stalemate ensued, and the total war became a war of attrition. With the illusion of a short war gone, economic warfare became more intense, and pressures were placed on the Northern neutrals and the Netherlands not to trade with the enemy. The ongoing economic warfare drew them in and infringed on their neutrality and the rights to trade with the enemy more and more as the war continued. The economic dependence model explains what made this happen, even though politically they were able to remain neutral. Although it is obvious why the belligerents would want to do this, the analysis does add some nuance to their actions, and this new insight forms a supplemental hypothesis:

S15. As a multiparty war becomes a war of attrition, belligerents try to starve the other side by blocking its trade. In doing this they place pressure on neutrals to adhere to their policies of economic warfare by using all forms of coercion short of military force.

Norway Among the neutrals, Norway is the most interesting from a theoretical point of view with regard to the above hypothesis, because it crossed the line from benevolent neutrality to being a neutral ally, and did this against its will. Politically, Norway wanted to maintain strict neutrality, according to the principles laid down under international law. Along with its neighbors – Denmark and Sweden – it came together to make a united cause for the neutral position as the war opened. Its need to export to survive economically and, more importantly, its need to import, particularly coal, made it vulnerable to economic coercion. Throughout the war both sides used their economic influence to gain deals and concessions. This put Norway in between two powerful major states – Britain and Germany. Britain had the advantage, and at a critical moment in the war in 1916–1917 it economically coerced Norway to become in effect an *involuntary neutral ally*. By banning all shipping of coal to Norway, it was able to control and manage Norway's trade with Germany. The turning point was the fish deal in 1916. This was later followed up with the deal over copper. This stick was followed up with a carrot when Britain helped Norway with German submarine warfare by providing convoys to protect its trade with Britain and the other Entente Powers.

The use of a complete embargo on an essential item for the population is similar to the logic of economic sanctions. It can be seen as a form of economic compellence, but in this case what was wanted by the stronger side was for the weaker to bandwagon[3] with it – not so much militarily but in terms of economic relations during the war. These

---

[3] On the concept of bandwagoning see Waltz (1979: 126) and Schweller (1994).

events, and Germany's reactions to them, brought Norway perilously close to war. The entire case reminds one of Greece and the use of brute force to bring it into the war while at the same time being an instance of a state being drawn into the war because of economic dependence. In this instance, that did not occur, because of the strength of Norway's government, and because it was not needed by either side militarily. Nonetheless, it was coerced to join a side against its will while maintaining political neutrality diplomatically. In this sense it was fundamentally different from the other European neutrals. The role of stringent economic coercion to make states involuntary neutral allies is a new insight provided by this case on two counts: first in identifying the phenomenon of involuntary neutral ally and second in seeing how economic coercion brought this about. This leads to a supplemental hypothesis that holds when S16 holds:

S17. In the presence of economic dependence, major states economically coerce neutral states to become neutral allies.

In order to be testable and falsifiable, economic dependence would have to be defined as relying on a sufficient supply of a particular good(s) that is necessary for the economic survival of a country – such as food, coal, petroleum. Britain was in this dependent situation with regard to the U.S. in terms of trade on credit in 1917 and Norway was in this position with regard to coal.

The above analysis in Tables 7.1 and 7.2 makes it clear (a) what the different contagion factors were that brought the main dyads into the war, (b) what their temporal ordering was, and (c) what their relative potency was. It also delineates other factors that played a role, and lastly it derives several new insights on how contagion worked that were not known before the empirical analysis began. The latter was used to provide a list of supplemental hypotheses that enhance our knowledge of how wars spread. These are the product of the research design laid out in Chapter 2 and are consistent with the logic of discovery used in qualitative methods. We now turn to more general conclusions that can be derived from the study.

General Conclusions

What are the main conclusions that can be drawn about contagion on examining all the cases as a group rather than individually as done in the previous section? These will be presented as a set of lessons that can be derived not only for understanding war contagion, but for international relations theory in general. The First World War provides significant lessons on alliances, why deterrence fails, how opportunity works, the causal mechanisms of contagion, and how the imperialist system and regional hegemony can provide a structure for the diffusion of war.

Alliances

There are several conclusions that can be drawn about the role of alliances. The most obvious one is that the First World War is the classic example of how alliances can spread war once it has broken out. The underlying alliance structure, which began to be built in 1893 with that fateful alliance between France and Russia that Bismarck had tried so hard to prevent, spread the war rapidly among all but one of the European major states in the system. The alliance system then pulled in a major state outside Europe – Japan. The latter made this a case of hierarchical diffusion and not just contagious diffusion through contiguity. The alliance structure can be compared to a set of ruts down a hillside that make water flow in certain directions. The underlying alliance structure worked similarly and made the war spread in certain directions rather than others. The main lesson from this case is that, *if* war breaks out and spreads, *and* there is a set of alliances that connects states, especially major states, war will spread through this network of alliances. What the First World War case also shows is that a system of alliances can remain in place for a long period of time before a big war occurs. The Dual Alliance of Germany–Austria-Hungary of 1879 and the Franco-Russian alliance of 1893, which were the core of the formal alliances that spread war, were around for about twenty years before the big war erupted. This is why historians like Afflerbach and Stevenson (2007) say that alliances did not cause the First World War.

A key question is whether this network of pre-existing alliances also increases the probability that war *will* spread once it has broken out. This is still an open question. Siverson and King (1979) and Siverson and Starr (1991) provide a useful theoretical frame for thinking about this issue, as well as some statistical evidence. They begin by noting that only a few wars spread, even when allies are present, so the mere presence of alliances does not spread war. What they do find is that allies of belligerents are more apt to intervene in an ongoing war than non-allies, as are neighbors of belligerents. From this finding we can infer that allies are more susceptible to contagion, but is it also the case that the presence of relevant alliances among non-belligerents makes a war more susceptible to spreading? Their aggregate findings suggest this is not the case. Nonetheless, little can be inferred about this question from the study herein. For the 1879–1918 period there were no relevant wars that could have expanded until 1911, so the First World War era (from 1890 on) does not provide much of a test.

What was different in 1914 was that the major states used their allies to play a coercive game, a kind of chicken game that failed.[4] It was the failure of the coercive game to achieve victory through intimidation and resolve that led to the spread of the local Austro-Hungarian–Serbian war to the general war. The alliance system had survived a number of crises without going to war, even when alliances were used to play a nose-to-nose coercive game as in 1908. It was only when the playing of the coercive game failed and no one backed down that the war spread. This was because all but one of the major states lived up to their alliance commitments. When so-called defensive alliances are used in crisis bargaining to intimidate and win, and this fails, then the war that breaks out is highly likely to be a multiparty war. It is the failure of the coercive game linked with alliances that is the key variable. This conclusion moves us beyond Siverson and King (1979) in that it specifies the conditions under which states allied to belligerents are likely to be brought in.

An important lesson from the above is that, if a coercive game fails, then the presence of a system of alliances will increase the likelihood that a war will spread. The probability of this in a multiparty coercive game, as in the July 1914 crisis, is extremely high, because the multiparty nature of that crisis has already brought in third parties. What is not known is whether the presence of alliances increases the probability of multiparty crises and their escalation to war in the first place.

To summarize, the first lesson is that the system of alliances spread the local Austria-Hungary–Serbia war. The main reason for this was not the presence of the alliances, which had been around for some time, but the failure of the coercive game among the aligned major states.

A second lesson is that this analysis has shown how alliances, even when their alleged purposes are defensive, can be dangerous. Alliances often form a network of conflict that encourages war. This is because they do two things. First, they make states take on the issues and grievances of their allies when they are not necessarily their own.

---

[4] July 1914 differs from a classic chicken game in three major ways. First, it was a large multiparty game involving more than three actors and not just a two-party game. This makes empirically determining payoffs difficult. Second, the devastating payoff of mutual defection, as in a nuclear chicken game, was not so clear in 1914 except long after the war had begun. This could be used to argue that July 1914 was not truly a game that would lead to cooperation. Third, this multiparty game was iterative, and few formal models treat such cases.

This expands the scope of conflict, while making it more difficult to resolve issues because they are linked.[5] Second, they aggregate power, making actors think they have advantages that will encourage the other side to back down, or at least this was the case in 1914. Both of these factors helped to make the July crisis escalate to war.

A third lesson regards valence balancing. Alliances in 1914 not only brought the main rivals to war, but also a number of other dyads which would not normally fight a war with each other. They entered the war because they saw the enemy of their ally as their enemy. This happened not only in 1914, but also subsequently in 1915–1917. As more rivals entered the war, like Bulgaria and Serbia, there were further ripple (or knock-on) effects produced by valence balancing, like Russia declaring war on Bulgaria.

Lastly, alliances had two other effects that helped bring about the wider war. First, the support of allies made each side play the coercive game to the hilt. For Austria-Hungary, this was the point of getting the so-called blank check from Germany, and as Berchtold worried that the Kaiser might waffle, he took actions, like the bombardment of Belgrade, to hold Germany near. Similarly, as Moltke worried that the Kaiser and Bethmann-Hollweg would pull back, he telegrammed Conrad to urge actions that would make for no return, namely mobilizing immediately against Russia. In the case of Russia, Poincaré and Ambassador Paléologue were constantly telling the Tsar and his advisors that they had France's full support; indeed, they even were going beyond that and trying to stiffen the Tsar. What they did not do was also important – they did not push Grey's proposal or the Kaiser's Halt-in-Belgrade plan. They also failed to point out the dangers of mobilization, and they provided no support for the Tsar against his hardliners. In addition, although it is difficult to measure, the presence of allies provided a psychological bolstering to playing the coercive game to the hilt.

Second, alliances also played a role in spreading the war by making contiguity more dangerous. This was most evident in the case of Belgium. Belgium was attacked because it was in the way, but it was in the way because the checkerboard nature of the Franco-Russian alliance placed it in the way. Without the firm commitment of France to go to war with Germany if the latter attacked Russia, there would be no need to attack France, and thus no need to go through Belgium.

---

[5] A number of empirical studies find that the more issues and more actors involved in a dispute, the more difficult it is to resolve them and the greater the likelihood of war. For example, James and Wilkenfeld (1984) find that multiparty disputes are more likely to escalate to war (see also Petersen et al. 2004).

Alliances then played several roles in the contagion process, and as a result alliances brought quite a few dyads into the war. In terms of the failure of the coercive game, alliances brought in all the major dyads in 1914: Germany–Russia, Germany–France, Britain–Germany, Austria-Hungary–Russia. Separate from the failure of the coercive game, alliances also played a role in indirectly bringing in Belgium. Alliances also played a role in bringing Portugal into the war. Valence balancing brought in more states, with significant dyads being Serbia–Germany, Britain–Austria-Hungary, France–Austria-Hungary, Britain–Ottoman Empire, France–Ottoman Empire, and Italy–Germany, plus Austria-Hungary–Belgium, Austria-Hungary–Portugal, and U.S.–Austria-Hungary. Also a host of Latin American states and Liberia declared war on Germany, in part, because of valence balancing, the most significant of the latter being Brazil. In the end, alliances formed a network of conflict that brought together a number of factors that promoted deterrence failure in July 1914. With that failure, the latent negative effects of alliances became pernicious and the local war spread rapidly.

The above analysis of alliance does what analysis is supposed to do – it breaks down and dissects and focuses on just one factor. This permits us to see things that we might not, if we did not examine things closely and in isolation. It would be misleading, however, to think that alliances worked alone or in isolation. A key factor working with alliances was rivalry. Territorial grievances in turn helped produce rivalries (Vasquez and Leskiw 2001; Tir and Diehl 2002). Rivalry certainly led states to feel threatened and as a result to seek allies. This was true foremost of France in 1893, which had fought alone in 1870 against Germany and was defeated and now had important allies (Siverson and King 1979: 48).

France saw Germany as its principal enemy and sought security alliances. This was also part of the French hope with the 1904 Entente Cordiale. The first and second Moroccan crises helped transform that colonial understanding into more of a security understanding. Likewise, the French attempt to encourage the 1907 Anglo-Russian Entente had the same motive. On the German side the Dual Alliance, the Three Emperor's League, and the Reinsurance Treaty were all spawned by Bismarck's rivalry with France. He wanted to keep the French isolated, and this succeeded until the Kaiser ascended and pushed him and his alliance structure out. Still, while these are examples, there are plenty of other instances where territorial grievances led to alliances before rivalries were cemented, and still others where alliances formed first and then were followed by rivalry. To get a firm grasp of these possible relationships, Table 7.3 examines three separate hypotheses.

Table 7.3. *Rivalry, territorial claims, and alliance formation: Which come first?*

Country	Country	Rivalry date	Start date; TC before alliance prior to 1914	Date of alliance that went to war	Order	Rivalry/ Alliance	TC/ Alliance	Either
AUH	SER	1903 T	1878, 1904, 1908	1882/none	TC, Alliance, Rivalry	No	Yes	Yes
GMY	RUS	1890 T	None	1882/1893	Alliance, Rivalry	No	No	No
FRN	GMY	1830 K 1756 T	1849, 1870, 1875, 1911	1882/1893	Rivalry TC, Alliance	Yes	Yes	Yes
GMY	BEL	1914 K	1841, 1909	1882/none	TC, Alliance, Rivalry	No	Yes	Yes
UKG	GMY	1887 K 1896 T	1884, 1885, 1887, 1889, 1895	1904/1882	TC, Rivalry, Alliance	Yes	Yes	Yes
AUH	RUS	1768 T	None	1882/1893	Rivalry, Alliance	Yes	No	Yes
GMY	SER	1992 K 1998 S&V	None	1882/none	Alliance, Rivalry	No	No	No
FRN	AUH	1494 T	None	1893/1882	Rivalry, Alliance	Yes	No	Yes
UKG	AUH	None	None	1904/1882	Alliance	No	No	No
JPN	GMY	None	None	1902/1882	Alliance	No	No	No
JPN	AUH	None	None	1902/1882	Alliance	No	No	No
AUH	BEL	None	None	1882/none	Alliance	No	No	No
RUS	OTM	1817 K 1668 T 1827 S&V	1828, 1855, 1856, 1870, 1877, 1878	1893/1914	Rivalry, TC, Alliance	Yes	Yes	Yes
FRN	OTM	1880 K 1881 S&V	1885	1882/1914	Rivalry, Alliance, TC	Yes	No	Yes
UKG	OTM	1827 K 1897 S&V	1857, 1878, 1892, 1901	1904/1914	Rivalry, TC, Alliance	Yes	Yes	Yes

Abbreviations: K, Klein, Diehl, and Goertz; S&V, Senese and Vasquez; T, Thompson; TC, territorial claim.

Table 7.3 lists the 1914 initial belligerents, comparing the dates of the origin of their rivalry according to Thompson, Klein, Diehl, and Goertz, and Senese and Vasquez with the formation of their first alliance that seems relevant to the coercion game that was played. The table also looks at whether there were any territorial claims that preceded alliance formation. Three hypotheses are being probed: (a) rivalry precedes alliance formation, (b) territorial claims precede alliance formation, and (c) alliances precede both rivalry and territorial claims.

Two major conclusions are suggested. First, among the five major-state pairs that went to war as a result of the failure of the coercive game each, except for Germany–Russia, had *either* a territorial claim or a rivalry prior to a relevant alliance. Interestingly, those major states and other dyads that went to war as a result of valence balancing did not have a rivalry before entering the alliance that brought them into the war. This suggests that some grievance precedes the making of an alliance for those that entered the war first. The exceptions are Germany–Russia and Japan–Germany along with the secondary dyads – Germany–Serbia, Britain–Austria-Hungary, and Japan–Austria-Hungary. In these cases, alliances occurred first.

Second, rivalry precedes alliance making in only about half the cases, and the same is true for territorial claims. The dyads that most deviate are the ones that valence balance and the secondary dyad Japan–Austria-Hungary. This is precisely the kind of deviation that would be expected of valence-balancing dyads, however.

Does the temporal precedence of rivalry or territorial claims mean that these are a more likely diffusion mechanism than alliances? This would be a difficult inference to make from our case studies. In fact some evidence suggests the opposite. What is clear is that alliances played a major role in who said they would defend whom. Thus, Franz Josef explicitly asked his ally, Germany, whether the Germans would defend Austria-Hungary if it came to war and the Kaiser and Bethmann-Hollweg gave him this alleged "blank check." They did not assume that Germany would come to their aid because Germany and Russia were rivals. Likewise, the Tsar knew that the Franco-Russian alliance committed France to mobilize and go to war if he did, and he knew this would happen because Poincaré and Ambassador Paléologue constantly informed him of that. He did not think that France would live up to its commitment because it was a rival of Germany – that may have been the reason why France made the alliance, or the reason why Poincaré, in particular, was not averse to war in 1914 (see Vasquez 2014a), but that was not what was said. A related inference that can be made regarding the relative potency of alliances over rivalry in the spread of the First World War is that the Franco-Russian alliance helped bring about the mobilization crisis that actually made the Kaiser turn things over to Moltke because of the time pressure.

Conversely, with Grey and Britain the role of the alliance tie was more uncertain. This in part was because it was unwritten, but also because Grey knew a good deal of the Cabinet would not accept the Entente as a reason for war. He could not give a blank check. Hence, in Grey's mind and private words, it was always a question of "interest" to come to France's defense if it was attacked by Germany. The Entente had been transformed to mean that, but Grey chose to speak of "the interest" rather than the "alliance." This sounds more like a function of the Anglo-German rivalry than of any alliance. This was reinforced by the fact that Grey would not consider going to war to defend Serbia or even Russia. Nonetheless, it does not seem that the Anglo-German rivalry is what made Grey committed to going to war; he went to war because he did not want France to be defeated. That motive was more central than the rivalry. It can be concluded that alliances, even for Grey, were a more potent diffusion mechanism than rivalry, but it must be kept in mind that rivalry or territorial claims often led to the formation of alliances in the first place.

Other analyses, including my own, have postulated and even found evidence for the claim that rivals are more likely to enter an ongoing war than other states (see Vasquez 1993: 240–242, Vasquez *et al.* 2011: 154, 159, 162). This study raises some nuances about that claim that undermine its main point. The analysis has shown that territorial rivalry has been a key factor in expanding the war, but that power politics rivalry among the great powers or major states has played a more circumscribed role. The theoretical implication of the original claim is that rivals are so guided by their hostility (and the actor dimension – see Mansbach and Vasquez 1981: 60, 199) that they will cut off their nose to spite their face. They are therefore prone, *ceteris paribus*, to join an ongoing war when this opportunity arises. This is not the path to war that happened with the great powers in 1914. They were brought into the general war at the end of July not because of this sort of rivalry, but because they were playing a coercive game defending allies and clients. They were not doing this to spite their power politics rivals. Power politics rivalry did not bring them to war, the coercive game did. This sort of rivalry, however, brought them to make alliances and defend them in the coercive game, and perhaps play a coercive game. Nonetheless, one of the lessons of this study is that among late entrants which did not play the coercive game territorial rivalry played a more central and straightforward role than power politics rivalry. This goes against the thrust of the literature and will deserve scrutiny in future cases to see how idiographic this was to the First World War. It nonetheless is a finding of this case.

Why Did Deterrence Fail in July 1914?

An important lesson that can be derived from this analysis is that July 1914 is really a case study in deterrence failure. What can this case tell us theoretically about the factors associated with the failure of conventional deterrence? We begin by looking at *how* deterrence failed and then turn to *why* it failed. Deterrence failed in 1914 because both sides thought if they showed resolve and remained firm the other side would back down. The Kaiser believed this because he and his entourage thought that Russia was not ready for war. The Tsar felt that the Kaiser would be insane to fight a coalition of Russia, France, and Britain. These were not necessarily mutually exclusive assessments, but they do reflect different perceptions that made the leadership overconfident about their military power. Long ago, Ralph White (1970) argued that this is a common phenomenon in crises that escalate to war and found it present in the First World War. So, in terms of how deterrence fails, the first finding is that both sides were committed to showing resolve, and this was coupled with military overconfidence.

While the Kaiser and the Tsar entered the crisis with these perceptions, as events unfolded and Russia began to mobilize, the Kaiser realized that the Russians had engaged in some sort of prior mobilization,[6] then both sides got caught in a *security trap*. Both sides feared imminent attack, so they prepared to go to war. As this threat was perceived, the military on each side frantically pushed for full mobilization. Moltke's adaptation of the Schlieffen Plan was premised on capturing Paris while Moscow slowly mobilized. If the Russians now had a head start of five days or more, this meant the Germans would have to move quickly and mobilize. Meanwhile, in Russia Sukhomlinov and Yanushkevitch (McMeekin 2013: 273, 297) were concerned that if the Germans attacked they would not be able to hold them unless they mobilized as quickly as possible. At a lower salience level fear that Austria-Hungary might pre-empt also aggravated the security trap for the Russian military (see Menning 2015: 236, 246, 267; see also Levy and Mulligan 2017: 759). These demands naturally reflected the role of each military to be concerned primarily with defense and winning the war, concerns

---

[6] See his reaction to the telegram where the Tsar dismisses this concern as measures "taken five days ago for reasons of defense" (Mombauer 2013b: 447, doc 313).

heightened by the ideology of the offensive of the time (Snyder 1984). The end result of this thinking was that the concern about pre-emption derailed the peace attempts that both the Kaiser and the Tsar were trying to cobble together in their telegrams. In particular, the Kaiser's Halt-in-Belgrade plan and the related proposal by Grey were swept aside as the Tsar ordered, rescinded, and then re-ordered mobilization. This, perhaps coupled with the August 1 misunderstanding with Grey, proved too much for the Kaiser, and he literally turned things over to the military and the pre-existing *Kriegsgefahrzustand* plans. This unleashed Moltke and started the trains moving. At a certain point the threat of war and mobilization no longer signaled resolve, but amounted to an attempt to pre-empt and/or win the coming war. With that, the coercive game between Germany and Russia escalated to war, bringing down the house of cards the alliances had built. Deterrence failed because intimidation and resolve gave way to fear and panic. This made the two most authoritarian leaders in the crisis cave in to their militaries, even though both wanted to avoid war. The power politics script took over the Concert of Europe script. The deterrence model gave way to the spiral model.

So, in terms of *how* deterrence fails, the process begins with both sides being committed to showing resolve, which is coupled with military over-confidence. The mutual resolve and military overconfidence produce a security trap, which is often accompanied by a split between the military and civilian leadership. This led each side to move away from a deterrence motive to an attempt to pre-empt and/or win the war if deterrence fails. Deterrence fails because it led to fear, which led to pre-emption.[7]

Alliances played an essential role in each of the above processes, but do defensive alliances generally fail to deter? This cannot be inferred from a single case. We do know, however, that alliances failed to deter in 1939. In this sense the two world wars are the best illustration of not only the failure of defensive alliances to deter war, but also how deterrence failure in multiparty crises results in world wars. Two cases are again hardly a statistical trend, so an answer to this question must await more systematic research across all relevant cases.

Elsewhere, Kenwick, Vasquez, and Powers (2015) review all cases of alliances for 1816–1945 and find that defensive alliances do not significantly reduce the number of wars or the number of MIDs that dyads have had before they formed those alliances. For 1946–2001 the record is different, but these results, which are consistent with Senese and

---

[7] Fear leading to pre-emption is a possible scenario for how deterrence might fail in a nuclear situation.

Vasquez's (2008) finding that after 1945 alliances tend not to promote war escalation, may be a result of nuclear weapons or even the peculiar Cold War alliance structure put in place by the two superpowers (on the latter see Vasquez and Kang 2013). While this research is a start, the difference between the two periods needs to be further investigated before general conclusions can be more firmly inferred. Suffice it to say that for the pre-1946 period defensive alliances do not seem to deter war or MIDs in a statistically significant fashion.

While considerable attention has been devoted to the logic of deterrence, *why* it fails has been less analyzed (see George and Smoke 1974). There are certain key factors that seem associated with the failure of deterrence in 1914 from a causal perspective that may be generalizable to other cases. The first is that this was a repeated game among the players, and this had important effects. Among major states the first or second crises are not likely to escalate to war, and this was the case in the coercive game in 1914 in that more than two crises had occurred previously among the principals (Leng 1983). Actors learn certain lessons from the previous attempts to deter that increase the likelihood that the current coercive game will fail. As Leng (1983) finds, the first thing actors do in the next crisis that occurs between them is to escalate their actions. As the steps-to-war logic maintains, this leads to an increase in the number and/or influence of hardliners on each side committed to escalation and typically to an increase in military spending that can produce an arms race (Vasquez 1993: Ch. 5; Senese and Vasquez 2008: 195–198).

Each of these factors occurred in the span from 1908 to 1914, although not always in a linear pattern.[8] Within Austria-Hungary the number of hardliners increased and they became more influential after the assassination. Conrad was a constant, and had been dismissed in 1911 because of his calls for war against Italy, but he was brought back in December 1912 as a result of the Balkan War crisis. Franz Josef had become increasingly fed up with Serbian nationalism and, like others, felt something needed to be done once and for all. Berchtold was the key decision-maker who shifted, but this was a result of the assassination, which also eliminated the main accommodationist – Franz Ferdinand – as noted earlier. Nonetheless, because the Kaiser did not back up Austria-Hungary during the mobilization crisis in 1912, Franz Josef did not embrace the hard-line option fully until he was assured of support from his German ally. In Russia, 1908 was a turning point for

---

[8] For instance, 1908 was a coercive game where Russia was forced to back down by Germany. In the Balkan Wars Germany did not support Austria-Hungary in this way but worked to defuse the crisis by getting both sides to de-mobilize. In 1914 Germany stood firmly with Austria-Hungary, thinking again that Russia would back down.

the Tsar, with him committed never to back down again and committed to a military buildup. By February 1914, with the dismissal of Kokovstov, which left Krivoshein unimpeded, the balance of hardliners increased. While Krivoshein and some other civilians wanted war because of the straits – a situation aggravated by the Balkan Wars – this was not the case with the Tsar. He was not so much interested in going to war as he was in not backing down to Germany in face of threats, as he had been compelled to do in 1908.

A second important factor in the failure of deterrence in 1914 was that this was a multiparty crisis, which made it more difficult to avoid war. This is a general pattern across crises, because multiple parties make for more difficult negotiations and they bring in additional issues, including hidden agendas that pose barriers. Moreover, the presence of multiple actors can increase the likelihood of misperception.

In summary, on the basis of this case it can be generalized that deterrence fails because, as games *repeat*, decision-makers *escalate* their actions to get the other side to change their position, which increases the influence of *hardliners* on each side and leads to a *hostility spiral* that ends in a crisis that goes to war. These factors are aggravated in a multiparty coercive game that is more difficult to manage.

Interestingly, alliances were used for purposes of coercion primarily in 1914; afterward, they spread war more through valence balancing. The second and third waves of contagion were propelled primarily by other contagion factors, namely opportunity and territorial rivalries.

Opportunity

Reviewing the sequence in which dyads entered the war, it is clear that alliances acted as the initial contagion process bringing in most of the major states. This occurred because they all became entangled in playing a coercive game that centered on Austria-Hungary and Serbia. Once they were in the war, then other dyads were brought in because of the combination of the existence of long-term **territorial rivalries** and the **opportunity** a big ongoing war among major states created for states to act on some of these rivalries. With these dyads the ongoing war was the principal causal factor bringing them into the war in that without the ongoing war they would not have fought each other, at least not at this time. Thus, we see contagion taking place in two distinct temporal steps – (a) the linking of states by alliances to play a coercive game, which when it failed led them to uphold their commitments, and (b) the subsequent ongoing war that brought in other states for which the alliance commitments were non-existent or marginal.

What role did opportunity play in this process? Opportunity was defined in the first chapter as the "removing of an obstacle" that had hitherto prevented states from fighting one another even though they had grievances that might have led them to go to war.[9] Because opportunity lifts an obstacle that prevented war from occurring in the past, it should be seen as a kind of cause that permits war, but is not sufficient for it. Opportunity is seen as necessary for war in a particular case in that it lifts an obstacle that has prevented war. The lifting of an obstacle, however, does not mean that war will take place. There must be some "sufficient cause" that takes advantage of the obstacle being removed. In many of the cases (but not all) that entered after the initial "guns of August" territorial rivalry provided that sufficient cause.

To stipulate that opportunity is the lifting of an obstacle makes the concept less tautological, and to further specify what those obstacles typically are gives the concept some real explanatory power. An ongoing war lifts two key obstacles – the existing distribution of power and the prevailing political order. The former prevents wars because many states are too weak to initiate them and the latter prevents wars because the major states have created a political order that serves their interests, and they have created norms that limit the use of war to change that order. As part of the legacy of the Concert of Europe, the major states saw it as their role to govern the system collectively. This included regulating their own wars and trying to prevent them when possible, putting down revolutions, and making sure that wars waged by minor states in Europe were regulated. This made the system less anarchical (Bull 1977) and more hierarchical (Lake 2009). States, including some major states, cannot just go to war to achieve any goal because the overall material and normative structure may not support that goal.[10] The existence of a bias against wars in which the victor takes all without regard for the collective interests of the major states can be shown in the instances where the major states intervened diplomatically to limit the spoils of the victors. An important example relevant to the First World War was the 1877–1878 Russo-Turkish war, where the Great Powers came together in the Congress of Berlin to limit Russian gains and in particular interfere with the territorial distribution in the Balkans. A second relevant example was the 1895 Sino-Japanese War, where Russia, France, and Germany intervened and made Japan give the Liaotung

---

[9] In Most and Starr's (1989) terms, grievances can be seen as providing a "willingness" to go to war.
[10] For theoretical elaboration see Vasquez (1993: 30–31) commenting on Bull (1977).

Peninsula back to China. Subsequently, Russia got a long-term lease of Port Arthur that greatly irritated Japan.

How does an ongoing war change things? The first thing an ongoing war does is that it forces states to devote most of their forces and resources to a single front. This leaves other possible fronts open. In a large war some states may already have their military divided, and this divides their strength even more. By definition this makes a new challenger relatively stronger and creates an opportunity depending on geography. Since large wars have historically been rare, such an opportunity may come only once in a lifetime, and decision-makers will be tempted to seize it, even if their power is not optimal. This is especially the case if they are being sought as allies by major-state belligerents making promises in terms of aid or joint actions, as was often the case in 1915 and 1916.

While a deleterious change in the existing distribution of capability of a potential opponent occasioned by ongoing fighting amounts to the removal of a very visible obstacle, another powerful obstacle to war is the prevailing political order, even though its force is less material. The prevailing order often determines by its norms when war is permitted, for what purpose it may be fought, and how it may be fought.[11] A prevailing order varies over history, but it is frequently consciously created by the victors after large global wars. The last major order constructed prior to 1914 was the Concert of Europe created at the Congress of Vienna. Even though that system collapsed in 1853 with the Crimean War, its legacy carried on until the last weekend of July 1914 with the Kaiser's and Grey's proposals to avoid war. Nonetheless, the prevailing political order had certain biases against the use of force and war. Minor states or even lesser major states, like Italy, could not just attack even if they thought they could win. They had to be wary of how the major states would react diplomatically, because in the end they could always reduce spoils as they had in the past.

What made the world war so contagious is that it lifted not just one of these obstacles, but typically both. This provided intrinsic opportunities to countries that could not satisfy their territorial ambitions earlier. These intrinsic opportunities were enhanced by the belligerents actively offering bargains and deals that broke previous rules of the

---

[11] Hedley Bull (1977) showed even before Waltz (1979) published that the system is not purely anarchic, like Hobbes's state of nature, where anything can be done so long as one has sufficient force. Rather behavior is regulated by certain informal and formal rules. Thus, as Wendt (1999) argued some time later, anarchy is what states make of it, or more precisely what the major states decide to make of it to institutionalize their interests.

Concert of Europe order. These offers frequently became auctions, as in the case first with Italy and then with Bulgaria and Romania, which made contagion more probable and more intense. The combination of opportunity and territorial rivalry gives us an insight on how states were *infected*.

Decision-makers themselves intuitively understood this. That they did can be seen from the strategy Zimmermann tried to employ in getting Mexico to go to war against the U.S. The primary concern of German decision-makers at this time was that, if the U.S. entered the European war, they wanted it to be as late as possible with something less than its full resources. One strategy to achieve this was to pin it down in Mexico. The U.S. had already deployed many of its soldiers on the Mexican border or in Mexico chasing down Pancho Villa. Zimmermann wanted to entice Carranza with an opportunity the European war provided (with Germany's financial aid and perhaps other support) for Mexico to re-conquer the territory it had lost in the Mexican War. The Germans played upon the old territorial rivalry to bring Mexico into the war. This was the same strategy they had used with Bulgaria and Romania. Carranza was too shrewd to take the bait. Interestingly, however, Mexico was one of the few Latin American states not to follow the U.S. lead and declare war against Germany.

Opportunity, territorial rivalries, alliances, and contiguity encompass four of the seven contagion models presented in this study. Two others – economic dependence and brute force – while important and generalizable, account for fewer entries, and the third – Imperialism/Hegemony – deals with many countries that are not legally sovereign. We now turn to what the cases can tell us about the underlying causal mechanisms at play in war contagion as illustrated in the First World War.

The "Causal" Mechanisms of Contagion

Keeping in mind Hume's caveats that "causes" may not exist in reality, but are something our minds are wont to impose on events to order them, what can be inferred about contagion generally if we think causally? The cases in this book were examined to see how contagion actually works and, if we reflect upon the case in terms of what causal mechanisms might be at work, we can derive some insights.

A starting point is to return to the different assumptions associated with the concept of contagion versus diffusion. The causal mechanism associated with contagion of disease is infection, a complicated process that became understood only relatively recently in human history. The causal mechanism associated with diffusion is less complex, and is seen as an underlying structure that moves a phenomenon, like a ball, in a certain direction once that ball starts moving, without specifying what made the ball move in the first place. Diffusion focuses on spatial characteristics that make things spread.

Assuming that the contagion processes have been correctly identified in this study, what can be said about their underlying causal mechanisms? Why did they make the First World War spread? We can begin with their temporal sequence, since the processes seem to build on one another. The effect of alliances was the first contagion process at work in 1914. The notion of diffusion suggests an underlying structure that would make war spread in certain directions and not others, and this happened from the end of July and the beginning of August. The war encompassed all the major states because of their alliance commitments. These were formal alliances as well as Ententes and the patron–client alignment of Russia and Serbia. With the exception of Italy, wherever there was an alliance commitment among the major states, there was an entry into the war. Contiguity also played a role in this underlying structure, but the entry of Japan, with foreign minister Katō using the rationale of the alliance with Britain and Grey accepting that, makes it clear that what was also at play here was hierarchical diffusion. Hierarchical diffusion tells us why the ball went in the directions it did – the underlying alliance structure directed the war to those with alliance commitments broadly defined. The tight alliances, like the Dual Alliance and the Franco-Russian alliance, started this diffusion among the major states.

Diffusion uncovers the underlying causal structure that makes the ball move in a certain direction, but it provides limited insights about what starts the ball rolling in the first place. True, entangling alliances, which reflect arrangements to deal with grievances with the other side, made major states willing to expand the local war, but there was a more powerful mechanism that activated the well-known alliance structure that moved us from spatial diffusion to contagion. This was the use of alliances to play a coercive game.

The nature of this game is well known and has been discussed several times in this book. Alliances brought the parties to the game in the first place and made them play in a manner that greatly reduced the probability that either side would back down. When the Kaiser and the Tsar went to the brink in the mobilization crisis, deterrence failed. The spiral model took over, with the steps-to-war logic explaining how previous crises and broader factors, such as rivalry and arms races, played a role in making the July 1914 crisis escalate whereas others, for example those in 1908 and 1911–1912, did not.

The spiral model reflects our best understanding to date of the infection process that started the ball rolling. The playing of the coercive game according to the prevailing realist principles of the day and its failure to produce a win as in the 1908 Bosnian crisis was the main cause for the war spreading to a general war out of the local war. It did this because alliances determined the players of the coercive game and, in part, why they did not back down. Of course, crises among major states do not typically escalate to war when they are the first crisis between the parties; there usually have to be repeated crises for this to happen (Vasquez 1993: Ch. 5; Leng 1983). The steps-to-war explanation provides an explanation of the background factors that increase the likelihood of repeated crises among the same parties escalating to war. The success of the Kaiser in the 1908 Bosnian crisis in getting the Tsar to back down by playing the coercion game complemented by Austria-Hungary imposing its will on Serbia emboldened them in 1914. As in 1908, the decision-makers of the Dual Alliance felt, rightly (see Levy and Mulligan 2017), that Russia was not ready for war. At the same time, however, 1908 was a humiliation for the Tsar, and he *learned* lessons from the crisis that would affect how he and other decision-makers in Russia would play a repeat of the coercive game. In the interlude between 1908 and 1914 there was another major crisis between Russia and Austria-Hungary, where the Kaiser played a more "mediating" role and encouraged Austria-Hungary to de-mobilize. This led Emperor Franz Josef in 1914 to secure a commitment from the Kaiser (and Bethmann-Hollweg) that they would stand by Austria-Hungary's side with a so-called blank check. Meanwhile, the Balkan War crises provided Russian decision-makers evidence that Austria-Hungary could be made to back down in the face of mobilization. The lessons derived from the previous crises or play of the coercive game set the table for deterrence failure. This, along with other factors delineated in the steps-to-war explanation (Senese and Vasquez 2008), including rivalry, the rise in influence of hardliners over time, and arms races, increased the probability that deterrence would not work and the crisis would escalate to war. Once deterrence had failed and Austria-Hungary had declared war and bombarded Belgrade, the local war spread because the Kaiser and the Tsar could not limit that war, as in the Halt-in-Belgrade plan. The mobilization crisis and the security trap it created ended the peace efforts while simultaneously producing a deterrence failure. The infection that started the ball rolling – or "a stone" as Bethmann-Hollweg referred to it – was the failure of the coercive game.[12] The causal mechanism of why this game failed in 1914 is pretty much uncovered by the spiral model and the steps-to-war logic.

While alliances and the failure of the coercion game explain the initial expansion of the local war, they do not explain further extensions of the war. Here the role of opportunity as a pre-requisite for contagion is an essential part of the "causal" story. In some ways the subsequent entry of countries into the war after the guns of August is an example of pure contagion in that it was a direct result of the ongoing war and not of bargaining and diplomacy gone awry. The ongoing war produced an opportunity for contagion because it lifted two obstacles that had prevented certain countries, particularly minor states, from fighting wars that their grievances would have otherwise encouraged. In this way the ongoing war was what is sometimes called a permissive cause. It is not sufficient in and of itself to spread war, but it makes it possible. The ongoing war changed not so much the existing overall distribution of power as the distribution of the local military advantage. This, coupled with battlefield stalemates, helped create auctions. By 1917 the belligerents were desperate enough to attack some of the key remaining neutrals in an attempt to reach a tipping point.

What this means is that the war epidemic was brought about in three distinct stages – first the coercive game, then the ongoing war producing an opportunity to resolve territorial issues, then the belligerents attacking key neutrals to gain an advantage in the context of battlefield stalemate. In addition, the seven contagion processes are connected with each other. Each stage or wave builds upon the previous one so that contagion itself becomes contagious. This leads to a new hypothesis.

S18. Contagion occurs in waves with a distinct temporal sequence, each involving different contagion processes and where one wave builds upon the previous one.

Still world wars are rare. Even though the above argument helps account for their rarity by showing how the war built upon itself, world wars are so rare that there are likely to be some systemic conditions that serve as overall necessary conditions that must be in place before a dyadic war could expand to a world war. Elsewhere, I posited three necessary systemic conditions, which are based on the two world wars (Vasquez 1993: 248). This analysis does not refute the earlier one, since the focus here has been on decision-making, but some structural factors no doubt

---

[12] Bethmann-Hollweg said "… but the situation had got out of hand and the stone had started rolling" (Albertini 1952, Vol. III: 15).

helped set up the decision-making that made these dyads prone to a world war at this particular time in history. The three necessary conditions are (1) a multipolar distribution of capability in the system, (2) an alliance system that reduces the multipolarity to two hostile blocs, and (3) neither bloc has a preponderance of power. Each of these conditions was satisfied in the First World War in that the alliance system reduced the multipolar system to two blocs with neither having a preponderance of power. The central role of the alliance structure in these conditions underlines its importance in bringing about world wars. It was, however, not the only systemic structure in place in 1914.

Imperialism/Hegemony and Hierarchical Diffusion

One of the new things that was learned about contagion in this study was the way in which the network of imperialism spread the war throughout the world fairly quickly, at least in terms of the fighting on the ground. Of course, the fact that the main colonial powers, such as Britain and France, took advantage of the personnel their colonies could provide has long been well known, as has, albeit to a lesser extent, the way in which all the major states took advantage of the opportunity of the war to openly attack the colonies of the other side. What has not been understood is how these facts could be explained theoretically in conjunction with the contagion behavior of the legally recognized nation-states.

What is of theoretical interest is that physical fighting spread globally and rapidly as soon as the war broke out. This happened as early as August 1914 in West Africa and East Africa, and by September included Southern Africa, as well as the South Pacific. Britain, the Dominions, France, and Portugal were all involved in fighting Germany and vice versa. Colonial troops were also employed.

These attacks far and separate from, if not tangential to, the main focus of the war can be explained by the combination of opportunity and territorial (colonial) rivalry that the ongoing war provided. Contiguity played an important role here in that it provided the major states with an opportunity to expand their holdings on the basis of the excuse that they were simply attacking the enemy wherever he might be found. However, it also reflects the "ruts in the hill" provided by the structure of the Imperialist System. The global nature of the spread of this fighting suggests that this is clearly an example of hierarchical diffusion. The Imperialist System can be mapped as a network of metropoles and colonies tied together economically and politically. Because the network crossed the entire globe, the diffusion of the war was systemic.

In other words, unlike the spread of the war in Europe, this was not a set of linked dyads where each decided whether and when to join the war, but a systemic contagion, where the imperial states decided for all they could control. Starting in 1914, these acted as ruts in the hill that diffused the war. Those that had higher status in the system, the British Dominions and former colonies, had more of a say in the decision to enter and where they would fight, whereas the colonies themselves saw the fighting brought to them by the major-state armies. Thus, in 1914 the Dominions were automatically brought into the war when Britain went to war, but there was a discussion in Britain as to what choice they had in participation. Canada, for instance, called a special session of its Parliament to pass a war budget and began raising a special expeditionary army. Later, after the Armistice, there was heated discussion of whether they (and India) should have their own delegations at Versailles separate from Britain (see MacMillan 2001: 45).

Events in East Africa provide some understanding of the microfoundations of this diffusion. The governors of both the British and the German colonies hoped to avoid combat by reaching an agreement. Individual commanders, like German Colonel Paul von Lettow-Vorbeck, would have no part of that, and he raised his own force of 2,500 local askaris under the command of 200 white officers.[13] Meanwhile a German cruiser opened fire on a British naval ship. In Nairobi, young colonists bringing their own arms demanded units. These examples suggest that contagion worked in part because the people were patriotic and wanted to take part in the war even though they were on the periphery. However, the larger strategic picture was decided by the central governments.

Further evidence of this sort of diffusion is provided by Entente attacks on the Ottoman Empire, once it had entered the war on November 5, 1914. Britain and France wasted no time in consolidating what they already had and made agreements among themselves and Russia to divide up the rest. Battles were fought throughout the entire war across the Ottoman Empire. The British encouraged and assisted in an Arab revolt, while the Ottomans called for a Jihad by Moslems against them and attacked the Suez canal. Aftershocks, including the invasion and occupation of parts of Turkey, continued until the 1923 Treaty of Lausanne.

The war also spread by bringing colonial and Dominion troops to the fronts in Europe. All the Dominions – Canada, Australia, New Zealand, and the Union of South Africa – saw combat and played

---

[13] This example is taken from Keegan (1998: 210).

central roles over three continents. The British colonies were a vast source of strength. India alone provided about a million and a half troops. The French relied heavily on their colonies for troops in Europe, both from North Africa and from Indo-China. The imperialist system also permitted Britain and France to buy labor from China to work on the Western Front.

Sometimes, colonial powers other than Britain, France, and Germany were involved. Portugal is an interesting case theoretically from this perspective. At first glance, its entry seemed to be a result of its alliance with Britain and valence balancing. The fighting in Mozambique and Angola, however, suggests something else was at work, actually two factors. The first was that Portugal was part of the Imperialist System and could, especially in Africa, be seen as a secondary supporter of Britain (which is what the alliance really indicates). Second, Portugal's colonies were proximate to Germany's, and the ongoing war provided an opportunity for each to expand at the expense of the other. For Portugal, in particular, the war provided an opportunity in terms of the shift in capability and breakdown in the political order to gain support and approval from Britain (and indirectly France). Fighting then spread, and the Portuguese permitted British troops to cross Mozambique to attack Germany's colonies (Shirkey 2009: 147). Interestingly, from a theoretical point of view, no declaration of war was considered by either side because this fighting was within the Imperialist network and outside the state-centric international law of the sovereign states network that required a legal declaration of war. Even though their armies were fighting, their actual governments were not. When eventually Portugal seized Germany's and Austria-Hungary's ships, then the two declared war.

The ruts in the hill created by the structure of global imperialism seem to have included also systems that spread the war by involving states that were not formal colonies but were subservient to a hegemon. The obvious example was how the Latin American states declared war after the U.S. and the order in which they declared war. Those most closely tied to U.S. hegemony declared war sooner, and they declared war on Austria-Hungary as well. This can all be explained by the network of U.S. hegemony. The case of Liberia provides unexpected and compelling evidence for this. Liberia, which had been founded by freed American slaves, declared war within four months of the U.S. Interestingly, while many of these early entries follow a spatial line of diffusion in terms of proximity to the U.S., Liberia does not, indicating that this is hierarchical diffusion based on the level of hegemony and not just spatial diffusion.

What is involved here is much more than valence balancing. David Lake's (2009) notion of hierarchy provides some insight as to why the Latin American states and Liberia declared war and how this is similar to the Imperialist System. Lake (2009) argues that the international relations system is not anarchic as Waltz (1979) argues, but rather has an order to it imposed by various hierarchies linking various states. One example of this that he gives is U.S. hegemony in Latin America. Another example would be the Soviet Union and the Warsaw Pact. Lake's notion of hierarchy is that a powerful state, often in a particular region, provides protection and order to weaker states. They in turn provide benefits to this hegemon, including listening to and often following the directives of the leader. The end result for him is a system of dominant and subordinate states, but one based on the acceptance of authority by the latter (Lake 2009: x, 45, 51). This relationship makes countries primed for contagion if the hegemon becomes involved in a war. For Latin American states this occurred in two phases, with the first on February 1917 when the State Department sent formal notes to all neutrals that asked them to sever relations with Germany if Germany carried out its threat to neutral commerce, and the second after April 6, 1917 when the U.S. declared war on Germany. Wilson's strategy of moral ostracism and the decision to sever relations and/or declare war was adopted by the Latin American states and Liberia that were most subordinate in this U.S. hierarchy.

The states closest to the U.S., including several that had U.S. troops occupying them, declared war early: Panama and Cuba (April 7 – one day after the U.S.), Liberia (August 4), and Brazil (October 26). The same year Bolivia, Peru, Uruguay, and Ecuador severed relations with Germany. In 1918, Guatemala (April 23), Nicaragua (May 8), Costa Rica (May 23), Haiti (July 12), and Honduras (July 19) followed with declarations of war on Germany. Panama and Cuba declared war on Austria-Hungary a few days after the U.S. had declared war, and Nicaragua declared war on it as it declared war on Germany.

One of the important lessons of this study is that the system of Imperialism and of Hegemony that made large numbers of countries and people subordinate to a few strong metropoles created a structure that made for the hierarchical diffusion of war fighting. It also spread the legal condition of war to a large number of states in Latin America. In this way the First World War was truly a global war affecting (infecting) millions of people beyond the industrial world. This leads to the last supplemental hypothesis:

S18. Imperialism and Hegemony in an international system provide a structure of dominant and subordinate countries that makes an ongoing war involving dominant states spread to the subordinate countries through hierarchical diffusion.

The last lure of contagion was the desire to have a seat at the peace conference. As the length of the war and its political importance became better understood, it became clear that the peace ending it would be a major turning point in the history of international relations (IR), like that of the Peace of Westphalia in 1648 or, more aptly, the Congress of Vienna in 1815. In terms of IR theory, a new global order or structure of global governance would be institutionalized, and states – large and small – wanted to participate in the deliberations. Such sentiments clearly affected Wilson, as noted above, although they cannot be seen as the main reason for his decision to enter, but were more of a buttressing factor. Other countries of minor status, such as Siam and China, also sought representation for narrower aims.

Hypotheses on Contagion

This book began with the presumption that Stuart Bremer's (1995) belief that the causes of the onset of war are different from the causes that make wars spread was correct. This study has begun the long search for a way to explain the more complex case of multiparty war by trying to identify the role of contagion in spreading wars. The concept of contagion was chosen over the idea of diffusion because its medical use was seen as giving more attention to explaining how and why contagion occurs, whereas the geographic idea of diffusion tends to be more descriptive. Even its more theoretical idea of hierarchical diffusion never explains where hierarchies, like alliance structures, come from.

To identify the role of contagion, the study took an empirical approach. It selected an exemplary case – the First World War – to empirically examine how contagion actually worked. The strategy was to study a specific case in depth to delineate what factors were at work. No work is ever entirely inductive, and this is particularly true of this one. The study investigated the plausibility of a set of hypotheses, outlined earlier, that were refined into six models – five of which had been delineated before the study and a sixth – brute force – that was identified after beginning the study. The empirical analyses in Part II of this book then refined these hypotheses, added a seventh model – Imperialism/Hegemony – and also uncovered some new hypotheses. The latter included eighteen supplemental hypotheses.

These, together with the eleven hypotheses in Chapter 1, make for a total of twenty-nine hypotheses on contagion. These hypotheses form the main contribution of the study. They have been discussed in the first section of this chapter. Two major tasks for the future remain: to see whether the hypotheses can be confirmed on other cases and to weave these hypotheses into a coherent theory of war contagion. Each of these tasks will be briefly addressed.

Future Research

As stated in Chapter 2, in the research design the philosophical basis of this book is the logic of discovery. Its task is to examine a case in order to delineate hypotheses, *not* to test them by employing the logic of confirmation. This means that the hypotheses in this study cannot be accepted until they have been rigorously and systematically tested on a sufficient number of cases. Testing and confirmation must involve separate cases from the case(s) where patterns were discovered.

The most obvious set of cases on which to test these hypotheses is the previous world wars. These have been identified by Levy (1983: 75, Table 3.2), and were listed in Chapter 2. Beyond these, all other instances of multiparty wars that began as two-party wars and then spread would also be a sample on which to test the hypotheses. Aggregate data analyses could be used to test the hypotheses, but so too could rigorous case studies using structured focus comparison and process tracing. An important start-up cost for the former would be compiling data and collecting it where it did not exist for older cases, although there are some data on alliances, MIDs, and rivalry before 1816. The main problem for qualitative studies will be case selection and comparisons over different historical eras. Still, each approach has advantages and both should be used. Eventually all the cases should be analyzed.

Once conventional comparative historical case studies along the lines of George and Bennett (2005) have been conducted, an interesting set of comparisons would be within large wars, to see how they are related and how one set of wars was connected with another and what contagion processes might be at work. Here the Thirty Years' War, which Levy (1983: 75) separates into four phases, and the French Revolutionary/Napoleonic Wars, which can be separated into several wars, are examples. In this vein it would be interesting to treat the First World War and the Second World War as two phases of one large war. This would be theoretically interesting since many of the factors in the First World War could be investigated to see whether they were reinforced in the Second or absent. This would also be a way of seeing whether factors delineated here, including the supplemental hypotheses, are really generalizable or were random and idiographic. Comparing the two cases would also be of interest in terms of seeing how the First World War affected the Second, in particular whether the Second World War was a result of contagion from the First and the extent to which learning occurred and was applied to decisions taken in the subsequent war. Comparing the two twentieth century wars is a fruitful area of inquiry, as Reiter (1996) has shown with regard to alliance making and neutrality.

Policy Relevance Some have questioned the relevance of a work on the First World War on the basis that interstate wars are on the decline and that nuclear weapons have changed the nature of international relations. The first is an overly optimistic and teleological reading of history that Pinker (2011) has popularized (but see the critical empirical assessment of Braumoeller 2019). Even if this turned out to be the case, which I highly doubt, studying the First World War and the phenomenon of war contagion is of intrinsic interest and always relevant to learning about collective decision-making on matters of life and death.

Nonetheless, I think there are obvious cases of relevance. The first is any case that might spread and get out of control because it might involve a multiparty crisis. Here the seven models of contagion could serve as early warning indicators. As the close of the first quarter of the twenty-first century comes upon us the most relevant case on the horizon is the South China Sea. Hypothesis 6 and others on multiparty crises are all quite relevant. In addition, the contagion models and some of the supplemental hypotheses could be relevant to security threats short of war – specifically the proliferation of nuclear weapons and the temptation to use force to stop such processes. The analysis here would be relevant from a policy perspective in that the hypotheses and models might inform decision-makers of possible pitfalls and dangers that occurred in the past. It could also be used to test the hypotheses and models delineated here by forecasting what might happen if a two-party MID broke out in an arena primed for contagion, like the South China Sea. Likewise, it could be used to inform the dynamics of recent wars, namely the series of wars that have occurred since the

Iran–Iraq war, including the invasion of Kuwait and the Persian Gulf war, the Iraq War, the civil war in Syria, the rise and fall of Islamic State in Syria and Iraq, and Turkey's intervention in Syria. These are a set of interstate and civil wars where one built upon the other and reflect the contagiousness of contagion. These wars could be elucidated by some of the hypotheses delineated here, in particular how one war created the opportunity for subsequent wars and for non-state actors with territorial grievances, like the Kurds.

Lastly, in terms of relevance, there is no reason to believe that nuclear weapons would somehow make war not spread; rather what would happen is that the war would spread instantly. In this regard, if the information could be obtained, nuclear targeting might be a way of testing the accuracy of some of the claims herein. For example, one could assume that alliance ties and contiguity would be key factors in predicting the targets of the U.S. and the U.S.S.R. during the Cold War, as would rivalry. If nuclear states wanted to keep the prospects of recovery low, the economic dependence of the original belligerents on certain states might make them a nuclear target as well. Much would depend on whether the nuclear belligerents saw nuclear war as a way of pulling the house down on them and their enemies. The nuclear target lists should follow a diffusion pattern consistent with the contagion models delineated here, and as such would be a test of the hypotheses herein. In brief, the hypotheses on contagion presented in this book would be relevant for predicting and explaining the rapid spread of all-out nuclear war, as morbid a subject as that is.

Toward a Theory of Contagion   The second major task for the future is to take the seven models and hypotheses delineated here and weave them into a coherent theory. I define theory broadly as "a set of linked propositions that purport to explain behavior" (Mansbach and Vasquez 1981: xiv). This is different from the way theory is defined in the natural sciences, where it is a codified body of knowledge. To construct such a theory it is important to have some underlying logic that will weave the propositions together. Rational choice and cost–benefit analysis are such logics. One can always start with a cost–benefit analysis, but that takes one only so far, then one has to look at how people actually behave and make decisions. This is why behavioral economics has been so informative in that otherwise highly deductive discipline. My approach to theory construction has always insisted on being empirically informed. I would prefer creating a theory that went beyond cost–benefit analysis and used a decision-making "logic" based on empirical cognitive psychology or the biological basis of politics to explain collective decision-making in general. As such a general theory developed, it could be applied to decisions about the use of force and violence. We are still far away from such a theory. Nonetheless, I would encourage interim efforts. The section on causal mechanisms above is intended as a first step in creating such a theory. Such an effort should be made within the larger interdisciplinary sphere of science in general in that knowledge in one field should be informed by advances in others, including the natural sciences. E. O. Wilson's notion of consilience is relevant to this endeavor (see Wayman *et al.* 2014).

This study follows in the footsteps of Lewis F. Richardson and his belief that objective scientific analysis could discern the factors that bring about war. It was his dream that identifying the causes of wars would be a way of controlling and maybe eliminating them so peace could reign and the scourge of war could be eliminated. This was also the dream of J. David Singer, Harold Guetzkow, Walter Isard, and many in the Peace Science Society (International). I hope this study has made a small step in the eventual realization of that dream.

References

Abbenhuis, Maartje (2014a). *An Age of Neutrals: Great Power Politics, 1815–1914*. Cambridge: Cambridge University Press.

Abbenhuis, Maartje (2014b). Foreign policy (the Netherlands). In Ute Daniel, Peter Gatrell, Oliver Janz, Heather Jones, Jennifer Keene, Alan Kramer, and Bill Nasson, eds., *1914–1918-online. International Encyclopedia of the First World War*. Berlin: Freie Universität Berlin, DOI: 10.15463/ie1418.11102.

Achen, Christopher H. (2002). Toward a new political methodology: Microfoundations and ART. *Annual Review of Political Science*, 5, 423–450.

Afflerbach, Holger and Stevenson, David (2007). *An Improbable War? The Outbreak of World War I and European Political Culture before 1914*. Oxford: Oxford University Press.

Aksakal, Mustafa (2008). *The Ottoman Road to War in 1914*. Cambridge: Cambridge University Press.

Aksakal, Mustafa (2011). The limits of diplomacy: The Ottoman Empire and the First World War. *Foreign Policy Analysis*, 7(2), 197–203.

Albertini, Luigi (1952). *The Origins of the War of 1914*, Vols. I–III. Oxford: Oxford University Press.

Barnes, Harry E. (1970 [1926]). *The Genesis of the War: An Introduction to the Problem of War Guilt*. New York: Howard Fertig.

Bastias Saavedra, Manuel (2014). Nitrate. In Ute Daniel, Peter Gatrell, Oliver Janz, Heather Jones, Jennifer Keene, Alan Kramer, and Bill Nasson, eds., *1914–1918-online. International Encyclopedia of the First World War*. Berlin: Freie Universität Berlin, DOI: 10.15463/ie1418.10228.

Bennett, Andrew and Checkel, Jeffrey T. (2015). Process tracing: From philosophical roots to best practices. In Andrew Bennett and Jeffrey T. Checkel, eds., *Process Tracing: From Metaphor to Analytic Tool*. Cambridge: Cambridge University Press, pp. 3–37.

Bobroff, Ronald P. (2006). *Roads to Glory: Late Imperial Russia and the Turkish Straits*. New York: I. B. Tauris.

Bobroff, Ronald P. (2014). War accepted but unsought: Russia's growing militancy and the July crisis, 1914. In Jack S. Levy and John A. Vasquez, eds., *The Outbreak of the First World War: Structure, Politics, and Decision Making*. Cambridge: Cambridge University Press, pp. 227–251.

Boyle, Andrew, ed. (1918). *The Brazilian Green Book, Consisting of Diplomatic Documents Relating to Brazil's Attitude with Regard to the European War,*

1914–1917. Authorized English Version. Rio de Janeiro: Ministério das Relações Exteriores.

Braumoeller, Bear F. (2019). *Only the Dead: The Persistence of War in the Modern Age*. Oxford: Oxford University Press.

Bremer, Stuart A. (1982). The contagiousness of coercion: The spread of serious international disputes, 1900–1976. *International Interactions*, 9(1), 29–55.

Bremer, Stuart A. (1992). Dangerous dyads: Conditions affecting the likelihood of interstate war, 1816–1965. *Journal of Conflict Resolution*, 36(June), 309–341.

Bremer, Stuart A. (1995). Advancing the scientific study of war. In Stuart A. Bremer and Thomas R. Cusak, eds., *The Process of War: Advancing the Scientific Study of War*. Luxembourg: Gordon and Breach, pp. 259–273.

Brocheux, Pierre (2015). Colonial society (Indochina). In Ute Daniel, Peter Gatrell, Oliver Janz, Heather Jones, Jennifer Keene, Alan Kramer, and Bill Nasson, eds., *1914–1918-online. International Encyclopedia of the First World War*. Berlin: Freie Universität Berlin, DOI: 10.15463/ie1418.10613.

Bull, Hedley (1977). *The Anarchical Society*. New York: Columbia University Press.

Cain, Peter and Hopkins, Tony (2002). *British Imperialism, 1688–2002*, 2nd edn, London: Longman.

Campbell, Donald T. and Stanley, Julian C. (1963). *Experimental and Quasi-experimental Designs for Research*. Chicago: Rand McNally & Company.

Carnap, Rudolf (1962). *The Logical Foundations of Probability*. Chicago: University of Chicago Press.

Carr, William (1991). *The Origins of the Wars of German Unification*. London: Longman.

Chi, Sang-Hyun, Flint, Colin, Diehl, Paul F., Vasquez, John A., Scheffran, Jürgen, Rider, Toby, and Radil, Steven M. (2014). The spatial diffusion of war: The case of World War I. *Journal of the Korean Geographical Society*, 49(1), 57–76.

Choucri, Nazli and North, Robert C. (1975). *Nations in Conflict: National Growth and International Violence*. San Francisco: W. H. Freeman.

Christensen, Thomas J. and Snyder, Jack (1990). Chain gangs and passed bucks: Predicting alliance patterns in multipolarity. *International Organization*, 44(2), 137–168.

Clark, Christopher (2012). *The Sleepwalkers: How Europe Went to War in 1914*. New York: HarperCollins.

Cohn, Einar (1930). Denmark. In Eli F. Heckscher, Kurt Bergendal, Wilhelm Keilhau, Einar Cohn, and Thorsteinn Thorsteinsson, eds., *Sweden, Norway, Denmark and Iceland in the World War*. New Haven, Yale University Press, pp. 411–558.

Colaresi, Michael, Rasler, Karen, and Thompson, William R. (2007). *Strategic Rivalries in World Politics: Position, Space and Conflict Escalation*. Cambridge: Cambridge University Press.

Cooper, John Milton (1976). The command of gold reversed: American loans to Britain, 1915–1917. *Pacific Historical Review*, 45(May), 209–230.

Cooper, John Milton, Jr. (2003). The United States. In Richard F. Hamilton and Holder H. Herwig, eds., *The Origins of World War I*. Cambridge: Cambridge University Press, pp. 415–442.

Copeland, Dale C. (2000). *The Origins of Major War*. Ithaca: Cornell University Press.

Copeland, Dale C. (2014a). *Economic Interdependence and War*. Princeton: Princeton University Press.

Copeland, Dale C. (2014b). International relations theory and three great puzzles of the First World War. In Jack W. Levy and John A. Vasquez, eds., *The Outbreak of the First World War: Structure, Politics, and Decision Making*. Cambridge: Cambridge University Press, pp. 167–198.

Crawford, Timothy W. (2003). *Pivotal Deterrence: Third-Party Statecraft and the Pursuit of Peace*. Ithaca: Cornell University Press.

Cronin, Thomas E. (1989). *Inventing the American Presidency*. Lawrence: University Press of Kansas.

Davis, William W., Duncan, George T., and Siverson, Randolph M. (1978). The dynamics of warfare, 1815–1965, *American Journal Political Science*, 22 (November): 772–792.

Declarations of War: Severances of Diplomatic Relations, 1914–1918 (1919). Washington: Government Printing Office.

Dehne, Phillip (2011). Britain's global war and Argentine Neutrality. In Johan den Hertog and Samuël Kruizinga, eds., *Caught in the Middle: Neutrals, Neutrality and the First World War*. Amsterdam: Amsterdam University Press, pp. 67–83.

Dickinson, Frederick R. (2003). Japan. In Richard Hamilton and Holger Herwig, eds., *The Origins of World War I*. Cambridge: Cambridge University Press, pp. 300–336.

Dickinson, Frederick R. (2011). Globalizing ConflictSpace: The view from Asia, *Foreign Policy Analysis*, 7(2), 189–195.

Diehl, Paul F. (1983). Arms races and escalation: A closer look. *Journal of Peace Research*, 20(3), 205–212.

Diehl, Paul F. and Goertz, Gary (2000). *War and Peace in International Rivalry*. Ann Arbor: University of Michigan Press.

Diehl, Paul F. and Goertz, Gary (2012). The rivalry process: How rivalries are sustained and terminated. In John A. Vasquez, ed., *What Do We Know about War?*, 2nd edn, Lanham: Rowman and Littlefield, pp. 83–109.

Diehl, Paul F. and Wright, Thorin (2016). A conditional defense of the dyadic approach. *International Studies Quarterly*, 60(2), 363–368.

Eckstein, Harry (1975). Case studies and theory in political science. In Fred I. Greenstein and Nelson W. Polsby, eds., *Handbook of Political Science*, vol. 7. Reading: Addison-Wesley, pp. 94–137.

Fearon, James D. (1995). Rationalist explanations of war. *International Organization*. 49(3), 379–414.

Ferguson, Niall (1999). *The Pity of War: Explaining World War I*, New York: Basic Books.

Fischer, Fritz (1967). *Germany's Aims in the First World War*. New York: W. W. Norton.

Fischer, Fritz (1975). *War of Illusions: German Policies from 1911 to 1914.* New York: W. W. Norton.

Flint, Colin, Diehl, Paul, Scheffran, Jürgen, Vasquez, John A., and Chi Sang-Hyun (2009). Conceptualizing ConflictSpace: Towards a geography of relational power and embeddedness in the analysis of conflict. *The Annals of the Association of American Geographers*, 99(5), 827–835.

Freyberg-Inan, Annette, Harrison, Ewan, and James, Patrick (2016). Conclusion: Different standards for discovery and confirmation. In Anette Freyberg-Inan, Ewan Harrison, and Patrick James, eds., *Evaluating Progress in International Relations: How Do You Know?* New York: Routledge, pp. 173–184.

Fried, Martin B. (2014). *Austro-Hungarian War Aims in the Balkans during World War I.* New York: Palgrave Macmillan.

Friedberg, Aaron L. (1988). *The Weary Titan: Britain and the Experience of Relative Decline, 1895–1905.* Princeton: Princeton University Press.

Fromkin, David (1989). *A Peace to End All Peace: Creating the Modern Middle East, 1914–1922.* New York: Henry Holt.

Geddes, Barbara (1990). How the cases you choose affect the answers you get: Selection bias in comparative politics. *Political Analysis*, 2, 131–150.

Geller, Daniel S. (1992). Capability concentration, power transition, and war. *International Interactions*, 17(3), 269–284.

George, Alexander L. (1979). Case studies and theory development: The method of structured focused comparison. In Paul Gordon Lauren, ed., *Diplomacy: New Approaches in History.* New York: Free Press, pp. 43–68.

George, Alexander L. and Bennett, Andrew (2005). *Case Studies and Theory.* Cambridge: MIT Press.

George, Alexander L. and Smoke, Richard (1974). *Deterrence in American Foreign Policy.* New York: Columbia University Press.

Gerring, John (2007). *Case Study Research: Principles and Practices.* Cambridge: Cambridge University Press.

Ghosn, Faten, Palmer, Glenn, and Bremer, Stuart A. (2004). The MID3 data set: 1993–2001: Procedures, coding rules, and description. *Conflict Management and Peace Science*, 21(2), 133–154.

Gibler, Douglas M. (2009). *Handbook of International Alliances, 1648–2008,* Washington: CQ Press.

Gibler, Douglas M. (2012). *The Territorial Peace: Borders, State Development and International Conflict.* Cambridge: Cambridge University Press.

Gibler, Douglas M. and Sarkees, Meredith Reid (2004). Measuring alliances: The Correlates of War Formal Interstate Alliance Dataset, 1816–2000. *Journal of Peace Research*, 41(2), 211–222.

Goemans, Hein E. (2000). *War and Punishment: The Causes of War Termination & the First World War.* Princeton: Princeton University Press.

Goertz, Gary (2017). *Multimethod Research, Causal Mechanisms, and Case Studies: An Integrated Approach.* Princeton: Princeton University Press.

Goldstein, Erik (1992). *Wars and Peace Treaties, 1816–1991.* London: Routledge.

Goldstein, Joshua S. and Freeman, John R. (1990). *Three-Way Street: Strategic Reciprocity in World Politics*. Chicago: University of Chicago Press.

Gould, P. R. (1969). *Spatial Diffusion*. Washington: Association of American Geographers.

Haldi, Stacy Bergstrom (2003). *Why Wars Widen: A Theory of Predation and Balancing*. London: Frank Cass.

Hall, Richard C. (2003). Bulgaria, Romania, and Greece. In Richard F. Hamilton and Holger H. Herwig, eds., *The Origins of World War I*. Cambridge: Cambridge University Press, pp. 389–414.

Hamilton, Richard F. and Herwig, Holger H., eds. (2003). *The Origins of World War I*. Cambridge: Cambridge University Press.

Haug, Karl Erik (2016). Norway. In Ute Daniel, Peter Gatrell, Oliver Janz, Heather Jones, Jennifer Keene, Alan Kramer, and Bill Nasson, eds., *1914–1918-online. International Encyclopedia of the First World War*. Berlin: Freie Universität Berlin, DOI: 10.15463/ie1418.10809.

Hawkesworth, Mary (1992). The science of politics and the politics of science. In Mary Hawkesworth and Maurice Kogan, eds., *Encyclopedia of Government and Politics*. London: Routledge, pp. 5–39.

Heaton, John L., ed. (1924). *Cobb of "The World": A Leader in Liberalism*. New York: E. P. Dutton.

Hell, Stefan (2015). Siam. In Ute Daniel, Peter Gatrell, Oliver Janz, Heather Jones, Jennifer Keene, Alan Kramer, and Bill Nasson, eds., *1914–1918-online. International Encyclopedia of the First World War*. Berlin: Freie Universität Berlin, DOI: 10.15463/ie1418.10596.

Hensel, Paul R., Mitchell, Sara McLaughlin, Sowers, Thomas E. II, and Thyne, Clayton L. (2008). Bones of contention: Comparing territorial, maritime, and river issues. *Journal of Conflict Resolution*, 52(February), 117–143.

Hertog, Johan den (2011). Dutch neutrality and the value of legal argumentation. In Johan den Hertog and Samuël Kruizinga, eds., *Caught in the Middle: Neutrals, Neutrality and the First World War*. Amsterdam: Amsterdam University Press, pp. 15–33.

Herwig, H, (2009). *The Marne, 1914: The Opening of World War I and the Battle That Changed the World*. New York: Random House.

Holsti, Ole (1972). *Crisis, Escalation, War*. Montreal: McGill-Queens University Press.

Horn, Michael Dean (1987). *Arms Races and the International System*. Ph.D. dissertation, University of Rochester.

Hull, Isabel V. (2014). *A Scrap of Paper: Breaking and Making International Law during the Great War*. Ithaca: Cornell University Press.

Hunt, David (2017). World War 1 history: Japanese Navy in the Mediterranean. https://owlcation.com/humanities/World-War-1-History-Japanese-Navy-in-the-Mediterranean.

James, Patrick and Wilkenfeld, Jonathan (1984). Structural factors and international crisis behavior. *Conflict Management and Peace Science*, 7(2), 33–53.

Jervis, Robert (1976). *Perception and Misperception in International Politics*. Princeton: Princeton University Press.

Jiménez, Patricia V. (2014). Press (Latin America). In Ute Daniel, Peter Gatrell, Oliver Janz, Heather Jones, Jennifer Keene, Aalan Kramer, and Bill Nasson, eds., *1914–1918-online. International Encyclopedia of the First World War*. Berlin: Freie Universität Berlin, DOI: 10.15463/ie1418.10343.

Joll, James (1984). *The Origins of the First World War*. New York: Longman.

Jones, Daniel, Bremer, Stuart A., and Singer, J. David (1996). Militarized interstate disputes, 1816–1992: Rationale, coding rules, and empirical patterns. *Conflict Management and Peace Science*, 15(2), 163–213.

Kang, Choong-Nam (2012). Alliances: Path to peace or path to war? In John A. Vasquez, ed., *What Do We Know about War?*, 2nd edn. Lanham: Rowman and Littlefield, pp. 27–44.

Keegan, John (1998). *The First World War*. New York: Alfred A. Knopf.

Keiger, John F. V. (1983). *France and the Origins of the First World War*. London: Macmillan.

Keilhau, Wilhelm (1930). Norway. In Eli F. Heckscher, Bergendal, Kurt, Keilhau, Wlhelm, Cohn, Einar, and Thorsteinsson, Thorsteinn, eds., *Sweden, Norway, Denmark and Iceland in the World War*. New Haven: Yale University Press, pp. 281–407.

Kennan, George F. (1984). *The Fateful Alliance: France, Russia, and the Coming of the First World War*. New York: Pantheon.

Kennedy, Paul M. (1980). *The Rise of the Anglo-German Antagonism, 1860–1914*. London: Allen and Unwin.

Kennedy, Paul M. (1984). The First World War and the International Power System. *International Security*, 9(Summer), 7–40.

Kennedy, Ross (2014) Peace initiatives. In Ute Daniel, Peter Gatrell, Oliver Janz, Heather Jones, Jennifer Keene, Alan Kramer, and Bill Nasson, eds., *1914–1918-online. International Encyclopedia of the First World War*. Berlin: Freie Universität Berlin, DOI: 10.15463/ie1418.10405.

Kenwick, Michael, Vasquez, John A., and Powers, Matthew A. (2015). Do alliances *really* deter? *Journal of Politics*, 77(October): 943–954.

Kingdon, John W. (1995). *Agendas, Alternatives and Public Policies*, 2nd edn. Reading: Addison-Wesley.

Klein, James P., Goertz, Gary, and Diehl Paul F. (2006). The new rivalry data set: Procedures and patterns. *Journal of Peace Research*, 43(3), 331–348.

Knock, Thomas J. (1992). *To End All Wars: Woodrow Wilson and the Quest for a New World Order*. Princeton: Princeton University Press.

Koller, Christian (2014). Colonial military participation in Europe (Africa). In Ute Daniel, Peter Gatrell, Oliver Janz, Heather Jones, Jennifer Keene, Alan Kramer, and Bill Nasson, eds., *1914–1918-online. International Encyclopedia of the First World War*. Berlin: Freie Universität Berlin, DOI: 10.15463/ie1418.10193.

Kruizinga, Samuël (2011). NOT neutrality: The Dutch government, the Netherlands overseas trust company and the entente blockade of Germany,

1914–1918. In Johan den Hertog and Samuël Kruizinga, eds., *Caught in the Middle: Neutrals, Neutrality and the First World War.* Amsterdam: Amsterdam University Press, pp. 85–103.

Kruizinga, Samuël (2014). Neutrality. In Jay Winter, ed., *The Cambridge History of the First World War.* Cambridge: Cambridge University Press, pp. 542–575.

Kruizinga, Samuël, Moeyes, Paul, and Klinkert, Wim (2014). The Netherlands. In Ute Daniel, Peter Gatrell, Oliver Janz, Heather Jones, Jennifer Keene, Aalan Kramer, and Bill Nasson, eds., *1914–1918-online. International Encyclopedia of the First World War.* Berlin: Freie Universität Berlin, DOI: 10.15463/id1418.10432

Lake, David (2009). *Hierarchy in International Relations.* Ithaca: Cornell University Press.

Langer, William L. (1967 [1929]). *The Franco-Russian Alliance, 1890–1894.* New York: Octagon Books.

Lebow, Richard Ned (2007). Contingency, catalysts and nonlinear change: The origins of World War I. In Gary Goertz and Jack S. Levy, eds., *Explaining War and Peace: Case Studies and Necessary Condition Counterfactuals.* New York: Routledge, pp. 85–111.

Lebow, Richard Ned (2010) *Forbidden Fruit: Counterfactuals and International Relations.* Princeton: Princeton University Press.

Leeds, Brett Ashley, Ritter, Jeffrey M., Mitchell, Sara McLaughlin, and Long, Andrew G. (2002). Alliance treaty obligations and provisions, 1815–1944. *International Interactions*, 28(3), 237–260.

Leng, Russell J. (1983). When will they ever learn? *Journal of Conflict Resolution*, 27(3), 379–419.

Levy, Jack S. (1982). The contagion of Great Power war behavior, 1495–1975. *American Journal of Political Science*, 26(3), 562–584.

Levy, Jack S. (1983). *War in the Modern Great Power System, 1495–1975.* Lexington: University Press of Kentucky.

Levy, Jack S. (1985). Theories of general war. *World Politics*, 37(3), 344–374.

Levy, Jack S. (1990/1991). Mobilization and inadvertence in the July crisis. *International Security*, 16(1), 189–203.

Levy, Jack S. (1992). Prospect theory and international relations: Theoretical applications and analytical problems. *Political Psychology*, 13(2), 283–310.

Levy, Jack S. (1996). Loss aversion, framing, and bargaining: The implications of prospect theory for international conflict. *International Political Science Review*, 17(2), 177–193.

Levy, Jack S. (2007). The role of necessary conditions in the outbreak of World War I. In Gary Goertz and Jack S. Levy, eds., *Explaining War and Peace: Case Studies and Necessary Condition Counterfactuals.* New York: Routledge, pp. 47–84.

Levy, Jack S. (2011). The initiation and spread of the First World War: Interdependent decisions. *Foreign Policy Analysis*, 7(April), 183–188.

Levy, Jack S. (2014). The sources of preventive logic in German decision-making in 1914. In Jack S. Levy and John A. Vasquez, eds., *The Outbreak of the First World War: Structure, Politics, and Decision Making.* Cambridge: Cambridge University Press, pp. 139–166.

Levy, Jack S. and Mulligan, William (2017). Shifting power, preventive logic, and the response of the target: Germany, Russia, and the First World War. *Journal of Strategic Studies*, 40(5), 731–769.

Lieber, Keir A. (2007). The new history of World War I and what it means for international relations theory. *International Security*, 2(2), 155–191.

Lieven, Dominic (2015). *The End of Tsarist Russia: The March to World War I and Revolution.* New York: Viking.

Link, Arthur S. (1979). *Woodrow Wilson: Revolution, War, and Peace.* Arlington Heights: AHM Publishing.

MacKenzie, David (1994). Serbia as Piedmont and the Yugoslav idea, 1804–1914. *East European Quarterly*, 28(2), 1–98.

MacMillan, Margaret (2001). *Paris 1919: Six Months That Changed the World.* New York: Random House.

MacMillan, Margaret (2013). *The War That Ended Peace: The Road to 1914.* New York: Random House.

Mansbach, Richard W. and Vasquez, John A. (1981). *In Search of Theory: A New Paradigm for Global Politics.* New York: Columbia University Press.

Maoz, Zeev, Terris, Lesley G., Kuperman, Ranan D., and Talmud, Ilan (2007). What is the enemy of my enemy: Causes and consequences of imbalanced international relations, 1816–2001. *Journal of Politics*, 69(1), 100–115.

Marcus, Harold (1994). *A History of Ethiopia.* Berkeley: University of California Press.

Martin, Percy Alvin (1925). *Latin America and the War.* Baltimore: Johns Hopkins University Press.

McMeekin, Sean (2011). *The Russian Origins of the First World War.* Cambridge: Belknap Press.

McMeekin, Sean (2013). *July 1914: Countdown to War.* New York: Basic Books.

Menning, Bruce (2015). Russian military intelligence, July 1914: What St. Petersburg perceived and why it mattered. *The Historian*, 77(Summer), 213–268.

Meyer, G. J. (2016). *The World Remade: America in World War I.* New York: Bantam Books.

Midlarsky, Manus I. (1988). *The Onset of World War.* Boston: Allen and Unwin.

Midlarsky, Manus I. (1990). Big wars, little wars – A single theory? *International Interactions*, 16(3), 171–181.

Mombauer, Annika (2002). *The Origins of the First World War: Controversies and Consensus.* London: Longman.

Mombauer, Annika (2006). Of war plans and war guilt: The debate surrounding the Schlieffen plan. *Journal of Strategic Studies*, 28(5), 857–885.

Mombauer, Annika (2013a). The Fischer controversy, documents and the "truth" about the origins of the First World War. *The Journal of Contemporary History*, 48(2), 290–314.

Mombauer, Annika, ed. (2013b). *The Origins of the First World War: Diplomatic and Military Documents*. Manchester: Manchester University Press.

Morgenthau, Hans J. (1948, 1954, 1973). *Politics among Nations: The Struggle for Power and Peace*, 1st edn, 2nd edn, 5th edn, New York: Alfred A. Knopf.

Morgenthau, Hans J. (1952). Another "great debate": The nationalist interest of the United States. *The American Political Science Review*, 46(4), 961–988.

Most, Benjamin A. and Starr, Harvey (1980). Diffusion, reinforcement, geopolitics, and the spread of war. *American Political Science Review*, 74 (December), 932–946.

Most, Benjamin A. and Starr, Harvey (1989). *Inquiry, Logic, and International Politics*. Columbia: University of South Carolina Press.

Mulligan, William (2010). *The Origins of the First World War*. Cambridge: Cambridge University Press.

Mulligan, William (2014) *The Great War for Peace*. New Haven: Yale University Press.

Nish, Ian (1972). *Alliance in Decline: A Study in Anglo-Japanese Relations, 1909–1923*. London: Athlone Press.

Organski A. F. K. and Kugler, Jacek (1980). *The War Ledger*. Chicago: University of Chicago Press.

Orvik, Nils (1953). *The Decline of Neutrality, 1914–1941*. Oslo: Johan Grundt Tanum Forlag.

Otte, Thomas G. (2014). *July Crisis: The World's Descent into War, Summer 1914*. Cambridge: Cambridge University Press.

Pad Kumlertsakul (2017). Why did Siam join the First World War? http://blog.nationalarchives.gov.uk/blog/siam-enter-first-world-war/.

Paige, Edward (2007). *Tip and Run: The Untold Tragedy of the Great War in Africa*. London: Weidenfeld & Nicolson.

The Papers of Woodrow Wilson, Vol. 41: January 24–April 6, 1917, ed. Arthur S. Link. Princeton: Princeton University Press.

Petersen, Karen K., Vasquez, John A., and Wang, Yijia (2004). Multiparty disputes and the probability of war, 1816–1992. *Conflict Management and Peace Science*, 21(2), 85–100.

Pinker, Steven (2011). *The Better Angels of Our Nature: Why Violence Has Declined*. New York: Viking.

Poast, Paul (2010). (Mis)using dyadic data to analyze multilateral events. *Political Analysis*, 18(4), 403–425.

Poast, Paul (2012). Does issue linkage work? Evidence from European alliance negotiations, 1860 to 1945. *International Organization*, 66(2), 277–310.

Ponce, Javier (2011). Spanish neutrality in the First World War. In Johan den Hertog and Samuël Kruizinga, eds., *Caught in the Middle: Neutrals, Neutrality and the First World War*. Amsterdam: Amsterdam University Press, pp. 53–65.

Ponce, Javier (2014). Spain. In Ute Daniel, Peter Gatrell, Oliver Janz, Heather Jones, Jennifer Keene, Alan Kramer, and Bill Nasson, eds.,

1914–1918-online. International Encyclopedia of the First World War. Berlin: Freie Universität Berlin, DOI: 10.15463/ie1418.10584.

Popper, Karl (1959). *The Logic of Scientific Discovery.* London: Hutchinson.

Qvarnström, Sofi (2014). Sweden. In Ute Daniel, Peter Gatrell, Oliver Janz, Heather Jones, Jennifer Keene, Alan Kramer, and Bill Nasson, eds., *1914–1918-online. International Encyclopedia of the First World War.* Berlin: Freie Universität Berlin, DOI: 10.15463/ie1418.10150.

Radil, Steven M., Flint, Colin, and Chi, Sang-Hyun (2013). A relational geography of war: Actor–context interaction and the spread of World War I. *Annals of the Association of American Geographers,* 103(6), 1468–1484.

Raghavan, Spinath (2016). *India's War: World War II and the Making of Modern South Asia.* New York: Basic Books.

Rasler, Karen and Thompson, William R. (1983). Global wars, public debt and the long cycle. *World Politics,* 35(4), 489–516.

Rasler, Karen and Thompson, William R. (1989). *War and State Making: The Shaping of the Global Powers.* Boston: Unwin Hyman.

Ray, James Lee (2003). Explaining interstate conflict and war: What should be controlled for? *Conflict Management and Peace Science,* 20(2), 1–31.

Reiter, Dan (1996). *Crucible of Beliefs: Learning, Alliances, and World Wars.* Ithaca: Cornell University Press.

Reiter, Dan (2003). Exploring the bargaining model of war. *Perspectives on Politics,* 1(1), 27–43.

Rich, Norman (1985). *Why the Crimean War?: A Cautionary Tale.* Lebanon: University Press of New England.

Richardson, James L. (1994). *Crisis Diplomacy: The Great Powers since the Mid-Nineteenth Century.* Cambridge: Cambridge University Press.

Richardson, Lewis F. (1960). *Statistics of Deadly Quarrels.* Chicago: Quadrangle.

Riker, William H. (1962). *The Theory of Political Coalitions.* New Haven: Yale University Press.

Rinke, Stefan (2015). Propaganda war (Latin America). In Ute Daniel, Peter Gatrell, Oliver Janz, Heather Jones, Jennifer Keene, Alan Kramer, and Bill Nasson, eds., *1914–1918-online. International Encyclopedia of the First World War.* Berlin: Freie Universität Berlin, DOI: 10.15463/ie1418.10537.

Rinke, Stefan, and Kriegesmann, Karina (2015). Latin America. In Ute Daniel, Peter Gatrell, Oliver Janz, Heather Jones, Jennifer Keene, Alan Kramer, and Bill Nasson, eds., *1914–1918-online. International Encyclopedia of the First World War.* Berlin: Freie Universität Berlin, DOI: 10.15463/ie1418.10760.

Riste, Olav (1965). *The Neutral Ally: Norway's Relations with Belligerent Powers in the First World War.* Oslo: Universitetsforlaget.

Röhl, John C. G. (1994) *The Kaiser and His Court: Wilhelm II and the Government of Germany.* Cambridge: Cambridge University Press.

Röhl, John C. G. (2012). The curious case of the Kaiser's disappearing war guilt: Wilhelm II in July 1914. In Holger Afflerbach and David Stevenson, eds., *An Improbable War?: The Outbreak of World War I and European Political Culture before 1914.* New York: Berghahn Books, pp. 75–92.

Röhl, John C. G. (2014). *Kaiser Wilhelm II, 1859–1941: A Concise Life.* Cambridge: Cambridge University Press.

Rollo, Maria Fernanda, Pires, Ana Paula, and Ribeiro de Meneses, Filipe (2017). Portugal. In Ute Daniel, Peter Gatrell, Oliver Janz, Heather Jones, Jennifer Keene, Alan Kramer, and Bill Nasson, eds., *1914–1918-online. International Encyclopedia of the First World War.* Berlin: Freie Universität Berlin, DOI: 10.15463/ie1418.11152.

Rosen, Steven (1972). War power and the willingness to suffer. In Bruce Russett, ed., *Peace, War, and Numbers.* Beverly Hills: Sage, pp. 167–184.

Rosenau, James N. (1966). Pre-theories and theories in foreign policy. In R. B. Farrell, ed., *Approaches to Comparative and International Politics.* Evanston: Northwestern University Press, pp. 27–93.

Rummel, Rudolph J. (1972). U.S. foreign relations: Conflict, cooperation, and attribute distances. In Bruce Russett, ed., *Peace, War, and Numbers.* Beverly Hills: Sage, pp. 71–113.

Sabrosky, Alan Ned (1985). Alliance aggregation, capability distribution, and the expansion of interstate war. In A. N. Sabrosky, ed., *Polarity and War.* Boulder: Westview, pp. 145–189.

Salmon, Patrick (1997). *Scandinavia and the Great Powers 1890–1940.* Cambridge: Cambridge University Press.

Sample, Susan G. (1997). Arms races and dispute escalation: Resolving the debate. *Journal of Peace Research*, 34(1), 7–22.

Sample, Susan G. (2002). The outcomes of military buildups: Minor vs. major powers. *Journal of Peace Research*, 39(6), 669–692.

Sample, Susan G., Valeriano, Brandon, and Kang, Choong-Nam (2013). The societal determinants of impact of military spending patterns. *Political and Military Sociology: An Annual Review*, 41, 109–133.

Sarkees, Meredith Reid and Wayman, Frank W. (2010) *Resort to War 1816–2008.* Washington: CQ Press.

Scheffler, Israel (1967). *Science and Subjectivity.* Indianapolis: Bobbs-Merrill.

Schelling, Thomas C. (1960). *The Strategy of Conflict.* Oxford: Oxford University Press.

Schmidt, Stefan (2007). *Frankreichs Außenpolitik in der Julikrise 1914: Ein Betrag zur Geschichte des Ausbruchs des Ersten Weltkrieges.* Munich: Oldenbourg.

Schroeder, Paul W. (1999). A pointless rivalry: France and the Habsburg monarchy, 1715–1918. In William R. Thompson, ed., *Great Power Rivalries.* Columbia: University of South Carolina, pp. 60–85.

Schroeder, Paul W. (2007). Stealing horses to great applause: Austria-Hungary's decision in 1914 in system perspective. In Holger Afflerbach and David Stevenson, eds., *An Improbable War? The Outbreak of World War I and European Political Culture.* New York: Berghahn Books, pp. 17–42.

Schulze, Frederik (2015). Brazil. In Ute Daniel, Peter Gatrell, Oliver Janz, Heather Jones, Jennifer Keene, Alan Kramer, and Bill Nasson, eds., *1914–1918-online. International Encyclopedia of the First World War.* Berlin: Freie Universität Berlin, DOI: 10.15463/ie1418.10579.

Schweller, Randy (1994). Bandwagoning for profit: Bringing the revisionist state back in. *International Security*, 19(Summer), 72–107.

Scott, James Brown (1918). War between Austria-Hungary and the United States. *The American Journal of International Law*, 12(1), 165–172.

Senese, Paul D. and Vasquez, John A. (2008). *The Steps to War: An Empirical Study*. Princeton: Princeton University Press.

Shirkey, Zachary C. (2009). *Is This a Private Fight or Can Anybody Join?: The Spread of Interstate War*. Burlington: Ashgate.

Singer, J. David (1969). The incomplete theorist: Insight without evidence. In Klauss Knorr and James Rosenau, eds., *Contending Approaches to International Politics*. Princeton: Princeton University Press, pp. 62–86.

Singer, J. David and Small, Melvin (1966). Formal alliances, 1815–1939: A quantitative description. *Journal of Peace Research*, 3(1), 1–32.

Siverson, Randolph M. and King, Joel (1979). Alliances and the expansion of war, 1815–1965. In J. David Singer and Michael Wallace, eds., *To Augur Well*. Beverly Hills: Sage, pp. 37–49.

Siverson, Randolph M. and Starr, Harvey (1991). *The Diffusion of War: A Study of Opportunity and Willingness*. Ann Arbor: University of Michigan Press.

Small, Melvin and Singer, J. David (1969). Formal alliances, 1815–1965: An extension of the basic data. *Journal of Peace Research*, 6(3), 257–282.

Snyder, Glenn H. (1997). *Alliance Politics*. Ithaca: Cornell University Press.

Snyder, Glenn H. and Diesing, Paul (1977). *Conflict among Nations: Bargaining, Decision Making, and System Structure in International Crises*. Princeton: Princeton University Press.

Snyder, Jack (1984). *The Ideology of the Offensive: Military Decision Making and the Disasters of 1914*. Ithaca: Cornell University Press.

Sørensen, Nils Arne (2014). Denmark. In Ute Daniel, Peter Gatrell, Oliver Janz, Heather Jones, Jennifer Keene, Alan Kramer, and Bill Nasson, eds., *1914–1918-online. International Encyclopedia of the First World War*. Berlin: Freie Universität Berlin, DOI: 10.15463/ie1418.10276.

Stapleton, Timothy J. (2016). Union of South Africa. In Ute Daniel, Peter Gatrell, Oliver Janz, Heather Jones, Jennifer Keene, Alan Kramer, and Bill Nasson, eds., *1914–1918-online. International Encyclopedia of the First World War*. Berlin: Freie Universität Berlin, DOI: 15463/ie1418.10848,

Stearns, Peter N. and Langer, William L. (2001). *The Encyclopedia of World History*, 6th edn. Boston: Houghton Mifflin.

Stein, Arthur A. (2015). Respites or resolutions? Recurring crises and the origins of war. In Richard N. Rosecrance and Steven E. Miller eds., *The Next Great War? The Roots of World War I and the Risk of U.S.–China Conflict*. Cambridge: MIT Press, pp. 13–23.

Steinberg, Jonathan (1966). The Copenhagen complex. *Journal of Contemporary History*, 1(3), 23–46.

Steiner, Zara S. and Neilson, Keith (2003). *Britain and the Origins of the First World War*, 2nd edn. New York: Palgrave Macmillan.

Stevenson, David (1996). *Armaments and the Coming of the War: Europe 1904–1914*. Oxford: Oxford University Press.

Stevenson, David (2007). Battlefield or barrier? Rearmament and military planning in Belgium, 1902–1914. *International History Review*, 29(3), 473–507.

Stevenson, David (2011). From Balkan conflict to global conflict: The spread of the First World War, 1914–18. *Foreign Policy Analysis*, 7(2), 169–182.

Stevenson, David (2017). *1917: War, Peace, and Revolution*. Oxford: Oxford University Press.

Sweers, Erik (2016). Neutraal Moresnet: de vergeten ministaat. *Historiën*, www.historien.nl/neutraal-moresnet/.

Tato, Maria Ines (2014). Yrigoyen Hipólito. In Ute Daniel, Peter Gatrell, Oliver Janz, Heather Jones, Jennifer Keene, Alan Kramer, and Bill Nasson, eds., *1914–1918-online. International Encyclopedia of the First World War*. Berlin: Freie Universität Berlin, DOI: 10.15463/ie1418.10091.

Thompson, William R. (1992). Dehio, long cycles and the geohistorical context of structural transition. *World Politics*, 45(1), 127–152.

Thompson, William R. (1995). Principal rivalries. *Journal of Conflict Resolution*, 39(June), 195–223.

Thompson, William R. (2001). Identifying rivalries in world politics. *International Studies Quarterly*, 45(4), 557–586.

Thompson, William R. (2003). A streetcar named Sarajevo: Catalysts, multiple causation chains, and rivalry structures. *International Studies Quarterly*, 47(3), 453–469.

Thompson, William R., and Dreyer, David R. (2012). *Handbook of International Rivalries, 1494–2010*. Washington: CQ Press, Sage.

Tilly, Charles (1975). *The Formation of Nation States in Western Europe*. Princeton: Princeton University Press.

Tir, Jaroslav and Diehl, Paul F. (2002). Geographic dimensions of enduring rivalries. *Political Geography*, 21(February), 263–286.

Tooze, Adam (2014). *The Deluge: The Great War, America and the Remaking of the Global Order, 1916–1931*. New York: Viking.

Trachtenberg, Marc (1990/1991). The meaning of mobilization in 1914. *International Security*, 15(3), 120–150.

Trachtenberg, Marc (2010). French foreign policy in the July crisis, 1914: A review article. *H-Diplo/ISSF*, No. 3.

Trachtenberg, Marc (2017). New light on 1914? Forum in *H-Diplo/ISSF*, ed. Robert Jervis, Frank Gavin, and Diane Labrosse, 16 (September), 10–56 (www.h-net.org/diplo/ISSF1) online.

Trumpener, Ulrich (2003). The Ottoman Empire. In Richard F. Hamilton and Holger H. Herwig, eds., *The Origins of World War I*. Cambridge: Cambridge University Press, pp. 337–355.

Tuchman, Barbara (1958). *The Zimmermann Telegram*. New York: Random House.

Van Evera, Stephen (1984). The cult of the offensive and the origins of the First World War. *International Security*, 9(1), 58–107.

Van Evera, Stephen (1999). *Causes of War: Power and the Roots of Conflict*. Ithaca: Cornell University Press.

Vasquez, John A. (1993). *The War Puzzle*. Cambridge: Cambridge University Press.

Vasquez, John A. (1995). Why do neighbors fight? Proximity, interactions, or territoriality. *Journal of Peace Research*, 32(3), 277–293.

Vasquez, John A. (1996a). The causes of the Second World War in Europe: A new scientific explanation. *International Political Science Review*, 17 (April), 161–178.

Vasquez, John A. (1996b). Distinguishing rivals that go to war from those that do not: A quantitative comparative case study of the two paths to war. *International Studies Quarterly*, 40(4), 531–558.

Vasquez, John A. (2002). The Vienna peace system: Why it worked and why it broke down. In Peter Kruger and Paul Schroeder, eds., *The Transformation of European Politics, 1763–1848: Episode or Model in Modern History?* Münster: LIT Verlag, pp. 235–241.

Vasquez, John A. (2009). *The War Puzzle Revisited*. Cambridge: Cambridge University Press.

Vasquez, John A. (2014a). The First World War and international relations theory: A review of books on the 100th anniversary. *International Studies Review*, 16(4), 623–644.

Vasquez, John A. (2014b). Was the First World War a preventive war? Concepts, criteria, and evidence. In Jack S. Levy and John A. Vasquez, eds., *The Outbreak of the First World War: Structure, Politics, and Decision Making*. Cambridge: Cambridge University Press, pp. 199–225.

Vasquez, John A. and Gibler, Douglas (2001). The steps to war in Asia, 1931–1941. *Security Studies*, 10(Spring), 1–45.

Vasquez, John A. and Henehan, Marie T. (2001). Territorial disputes and the probability of war, 1816–1992. *Journal of Peace Research*, 38(2), 123–138.

Vasquez, John A. and Kang, C. (2013). How and why the Cold War became a long peace: Some statistical insights. *Cooperation and Conflict*, 48(1), 28–50.

Vasquez, John A. and Leskiw, Christopher S. (2001). The origins of interstate rivalry, 1816–1992. *Annual Review of Political Science*, 4(September), 295–316.

Vasquez, John A. and Rundlett, Ashlea (2016). Alliances as a necessary condition of multiparty wars. *Journal of Conflict Resolution*, 60(December), 1395–1418.

Vasquez, John A. and Valeriano, Brandon (2010). Classification of interstate wars. *Journal of Politics*, 72(2), 292–309.

Vasquez, John A., Diehl, Paul F., Flint, Colin, Scheffran, Jürgen, Chi, Sang-Hyun, and Rider, Toby J. (2011). The ConflictSpace of cataclysm: The international system and the spread of war 1914–1917. *Foreign Policy Analysis*, 7(2), 143–168.

Waltz, Kenneth N. (1979). *Theory of International Politics*. Reading: Addison-Wesley.

Wayman, Frank, Williamson, Paul, Polachek, Solomon, and Bueno de Mesquita, Bruce, eds. (2014). *Predicting the Future in Science, Economics, and Politics*. Cheltenham: Edward Elgar.

Weisiger, Alex (2013). *Logics of War: Explanations for Limited and Unlimited Wars*. Ithaca: Cornell University Press.

Weitsman, Patricia A. (2004). *Dangerous Alliances: Proponents of Peace, Weapons of War*. Stanford: Stanford University Press.

Weitsman, Patricia A. (2014). *Waging War: Alliances, Coalitions, and Institutions of Interstate Violence*. Stanford: Stanford University Press.

Wendt, Alexander (1999). *Social Theory of International Politics*. Cambridge: Cambridge University Press.

White, Ralph (1970). *Nobody Wanted War*. Garden City: Doubleday.

Williamson, Samuel R., Jr. (1969). *The Politics of Grand Strategy: Britain and France Prepare for War, 1904–1914*. Cambridge: Harvard University Press.

Williamson, Samuel R., Jr. (1991). *Austria-Hungary and the Origins of the First World War*. New York: Macmillan.

Williamson, Samuel R., Jr. (2014). July 1914 revisited and revised: The erosion of the German paradigm. In Jack S. Levy and John A. Vasquez, eds., *The Outbreak of the First World War: Structure, Politics, and Decision Making*. Cambridge: Cambridge University Press, pp. 30–62.

Williamson, Samuel R., Jr. and Van Wyk, Russel (2003). *July 1914: Soldiers, Statesmen and the Coming of the Great War: A Brief Documentary History*. Boston: Bedford/St. Martin's.

Yamamoto, Yoshinobu and Bremer Stuart A. (1980). Wider wars and restless nights: Major power intervention in ongoing war. In J. D. Singer, ed., *The Correlates of War*, vol. II. New York: Free Press, pp. 199–229.

Zagare, Frank C. (2011). *The Games of July: Explaining the Great War*. Ann Arbor: University of Michigan Press.

Zinn, Howard (1980). *A People's History of the United States*. New York: Harper Colophon.

Zuber, Terrence (2002). *Inventing the Schlieffen Plan*. Oxford: Oxford University Press.

Name Index

Aksakal, Mustafa, 163–169
Albertini, Luigi, 85, 112–114, 148, 151, 209–211, 283

Barnes, Harry E., 103, 104
Bennett, Andrew, 47, 50, 51, 55, 368
Bobroff, Ronald P., 16, 88, 170, 172
Bremer, Stuart A., 11, 56, 59, 246n17, 311

Checkel, Jeffrey T., 50
Chi, Sang-Hyun, 56
Choucri, Nazli, 52n2
Clark, Christopher, 15, 19, 49, 72, 75, 81n14, 89, 91, 100, 103, 110, 112, 124, 125, 130, 143, 165, 194, 195
Cohn, Einar, 297
Colaresi, Michael, 23, 316
Cooper, John Milton, Jr., 38, 225n3, 231n7, 233, 236n13, 241, 338
Copeland, Dale C., 25n14, 36n19, 81n14, 95n30, 100, 100n35

Diehl, Paul F., 27, 54, 56n3, 63, 277

Fearon, James D., 112, 113
Ferguson, Niall, 116n48
Fischer, Fritz, 81n14, 99, 100
Flint, Colin, 55

George, Alexander L., 46, 47, 50, 51, 55, 355
Gibler, Douglas M., 13, 48, 62, 240, 316
Goertz, Gary, 51, 53–55

Haldi, Stacy Bergstrom, 9, 13, 165
Hall, Richard C., 34, 42n24, 85n19, 195–197, 209, 209n11, 210, 212, 247–250

Kang, Choong-Nam, 16n4, 355
Keegan, John, 76n9, 87, 100, 111, 114, 180n88, 212, 232n8, 233, 234, 242, 250n19, 364n12
Keiger, John F. V., 103

Lake, David, 182, 357, 366
Langer, William L., 49, 92n27, 180n88, 181n89
Lebow, Richard Ned, 75n8, 320
Leng, Russell J., 18n7, 79, 129, 293, 355, 361
Levy, Jack S., 11, 208n10, 322
  and world war, 12n1, 48, 368
  British failure to deter
    Germany, 117
  on mobilization, 96n32
  Russia not ready for war, 97

McMeekin, Sean, 170
MacMillan, Margaret, 73n3, 79, 119, 123n56, 129, 200, 214, 257n22, 330
  on crises involving Russia, 129, 130
  on Montenegro, 126, 127
  on Versailles, 364
Mansbach, Richard W., 57, 352, 370
Midlarsky, Manus I., 12, 18n7, 79
Mombauer, Annika, 25, 77, 77n12, 81n15, 81n16, 94n29, 99, 101n36, 103, 111, 353n6

387

Subject Index

Aalst, C.J.K. van, 294
accommodationists, 75, 92, 137, 226
Adbulhamid II, 163
Addams, Jane, 238
Aehrenthal, Alois Lexa von, 85, 128
aftershocks of war, 181, 337
agency, 11, 301, 329
Albania, 81, 130, 163
Albert I of Belgium, 111–114
Alexander I of Serbia, 72
Alexander of Battenberg, 195
Alfonso XIII of Spain, 282
alliances, 13, 40, 346–356, *see also*
    under individual states
    and dyads
  arms races and, 85–92
  checkerboard pattern, 16, 26, 41,
    108, 348
  coercive game failure and, 14–18,
    26–27, 347
  conclusions regarding, 346, 353
  contiguity and, 17, 22–24
  deterrent effect, 354
  hypothesis on, 18, 23
  interaction with other contagion
    processes, 350
  role in contagion process, 349
  Russia, 134–137
  valence balancing, 18–23, 28, 348
Alsace-Lorraine, 105, 148, 317
Angola, 276
ANZAC forces, 182, 275
Argentina
  contagion factors, 278
  neutrality, 300–302
  United States and

Argentine resistance to US
    hegemony, 301–302
arms races, 61, 135–136
  alliances and, 85–92
Asquith, Herbert, 116, 320
auctions, 35–36, 42, 188–189, 193,
    196–197, 273, 328–329,
    329, 336
  hypothesis on, 329
Austria-Hungary. *see also* Central
    Powers; Italy–Austria-
    Hungary dyad; Romania–
    Austria-Hungary dyad; United
    States–Austria-Hungary dyad
  alliance with Germany, 16
Austria-Hungary–Russia dyad,
    127–138, 321–322
  alliances, 134–137
  arms races, 135–136
  coercion game, 361
  contagion factors, 313
  declaration of war, 131–132
  outcome of war, 137
  prior MIDs, 127–131
  reasons for war, 136–137
  role of third parties, 132–134
Austria-Hungary–Serbia dyad,
    71–88, 96, 312–314
  alliances affecting dyad, 85–87
  arms races, 86
  contagion factors, 312–314
  previous MIDs, 79–88, 312–314
  pre-war relations, 72
  pre-war ultimatum to, 77–78
  rivalry measure, 83
  territorial claims, 80